D0163430

THE ENVIRONMENT

THE ENVIRONMENT

From Surplus to Scarcity

ALLAN SCHNAIBERG

New York   Oxford
Oxford University Press
1980

Copyright © 1980 by Oxford University Press, Inc.

Library of Congress Cataloging in Publication Data

Schnaiberg, Allan.
  The environment, from surplus to scarcity.

  Bibliography: p.
  Includes index.
  1. Environmental policy. 2. Environmental
protection. 3. Man—Influence on nature. I. Title.
HC79.E5S29 1980   301.31   79-12439
ISBN 0-19-502610-1
ISBN 0-19-502611-X pbk.

Printed in the United States of America

823823

LIBRARY
ALMA COLLEGE
ALMA, MICHIGAN

To LYNN RENÉE and JILL ANN,
Who Will Inherit the Earth

LIBRARY
ALLAN HANCOCK

839733

PREFACE

This work is the culmination of a long period of reflection, intellectual interaction, and reading and writing on issues of environmental quality and social justice. While the planning and writing of the drafts of the manuscript have preoccupied me over the past five years, my intellectual and collegial indebtedness extend farther back in history.

It was my colleague John Walton who encouraged me in 1972 to pursue analytically some environmental interests I had, and who facilitated the first of my writings. More than any other person, he has provided me with the most sustained constructive criticism and motivation over the years. Judith Greissman persuaded me that I was capable of creating a book, an editorial encouragement that was later to be supplemented by my friends and colleagues Jonathan Latimer and Arlene Daniels. The most crucial period of support came from a research leave granted me by Northwestern University in 1975–76, with the enthusiastic support of Charles C. Moskos, Jr., whose confidence in me and in the project helped to sustain my commitment. With the additional aid of the Board of Sociology and College VIII at the University of California at Santa Cruz, I spent a most productive year in Santa Cruz, writing the first draft of the manuscript. In addition to the friendship, encouragement and bureaucratic aid of John Kitsuse and Dorothy Pearce there, I benefited intellectually from intensive discussions with many faculty at UCSC, including especially Paul Lubeck and Dudley Burton.

Earlier drafts of the manuscript were circulated among a number of people, and I received especially helpful comments from my colleague Remi Clignet, as well as from Dudley Burton, Arlene Daniels, John

Walton, and Nancy DiTomaso. Errol Meidinger contributed many important suggestions, especially for Chapter VII. Within my invisible college of environmental sociologists, Denton Morrison and Riley Dunlap have been most unfailingly generous with their time, criticism, and their own intellectual works. Though many of the people noted above do not share my vision, they have been a crucial resource to me. The preparation of the manuscript has been facilitated in the final year by the bibliographic work and sociological enthusiasm of Vivian Walker at Northwestern University. My efforts have been greatly enhanced by the typing and moral support of Kathy Stone, Susan Vehlow, and Ellen Pool at Northwestern. The long gestation period has been my responsibility, not theirs. Readers will find a much improved text, thanks to the efforts of Nancy Amy at Oxford University Press.

Finally, the long and frustrating period of labor on this manuscript has been possible only through the moral and emotional support I have received from my wife Elayne. She has suffered through my periods of unproductivity and self-doubt, but never failed to provide a supportive working environment for me. And my daughters Lynn and Jill are the continuing spurs for my concern about the future of the environment—for it is their welfare I fear most for, and cherish most. To appreciate and help shape the world that they, along with the rest of the socially vulnerable people of the earth, will inherit—that is the ultimate goal of this work. If it serves to provoke any thought and reaction in this progressive direction, the effort will have been worthwhile.

A. S.

Evanston, Illinois
June 1979

CONTENTS

THE ENVIRONMENT

INTRODUCTION

Almost a decade has passed since Earth Day, the Clean Air Act, and the National Environmental Policy Act in the United States. Scores of books have been written about environmental problems. For many citizens, the problem has been solved, and the issues are no longer important. Academics are less attracted to this area, which lacks both prestige and funding.

So why write this book? It is my view that environmental issues, in various labels and forms, have not only been major social concerns throughout history, but will endure and even intensify in the future. That the mass environmental movement has shrunk in recent years is an interesting phenomenon. But it is not an indicator of a decrease either in our social vulnerability because of our resource base, or in the concerns of many citizens and groups. Indeed, the very decline in the movement raises issues that ought to galvanize social scientists to new research. Some have responded to this challenge, but more have gone on to other problems. There are good reasons for this, too, and they will be addressed later.

This book is necessary today in part because of this decline in visible public concern about our national environment. Scores of books have stimulated and confused. Many of these were polemics from a narrow social perspective, while others were narrow technical reports that lost sight of broader socioenvironmental issues. Such materials have educated Americans to many features of the environment that have been threatened, and to many dimensions of our social structure that are implicated. Yet it is difficult for many readers to gain a socially meaningful perspective of these issues. How has "society" generated these environmental problems? How has "society" responded to such problems in the recent and distant past? What are the long-term social options for responding to future resource problems? Only a handful of social scientists have attempted to deal directly with these questions. And for me, much of this limited work has been either excessively myopic or abstract.

Myopia exists when social scientists concentrate only on the environmental movement, and not the social context from which it arises. Abstractions about our antiecological culture are not much more helpful in addressing the problem. My own approach is to seek an explanation of the social roots of expanded production, through an analysis of social institutions involved in the creation and distribution of social surplus. What social forms induce ever higher levels of industrialization and extraction of resources? How does our social organization obscure the realities of resulting environmental degradation? In what ways do productive and government organizations treat environmental critics and their claims? How does this explain discrepancies between public complacency regarding environmental protection policies, and the growing concerns of many policy analysts? For all these questions, we have inadequate answers in our scientific research to offer each other, our students, and the literate public.

While researching, I have been forced to challenge many of my earlier preconceptions. I hope the result—this book—will do the same for its readers. The organization of the book is straightforward and arbitrary. First the question is raised: How does one think about the diversity of environmental issues in a socially useful way? The reciprocal relationships between social and environmental structure are summarized in Chapter I. Second, the major portion of the book is a critical evaluation of the ways in which society is said to "cause" its environmental problems. Existing explanations in the literature are clustered in four ways: population, technology, consumption, and production are *the* major factors, each often to the exclusion of the others. A more coherent and complex interpretation is offered here (Ch. II–V).

The third part of the book traces our responses to the challenges of the 1960s for our new environmental awareness. It critically analyzes many of the social decision-making techniques used to deal with environmental problems. As well, it traces the shifting patterns of organization and concern of the environmental movement over this century.

Finally, the last chapter attempts to look at our future options. The challenge of adapting advanced industrial societies to the realities of environmental constraints is examined, and some sociologically meaningful directions are suggested.

Throughout these chapters, there is a unifying theme. Social inequalities are viewed as interwoven with each environmental concern. In my perspective, there can be no value-free evaluation of environmental concerns. Our focus on particular environmental concerns, our choice of explanatory models to help us confront these concerns, and our social policies resulting from such explanations—all of these are built around and influence preexisting social inequalities. Thus, this book is not merely about saving the environment: It is about making our social and physical environment a fit place for both the powerless and the powerful to live and work in. From a sociological perspective, it is never sufficient to point to *the* environment as having been protected. The question must always be asked, for whom and from whom has it been protected? Environmental quality and social welfare issues are not socially or politically separable. Physical scientists have greatly increased our understanding of ecological reality. This book is intended to broaden that understanding to encompass social welfare concerns. If it achieves this in any small measure, I will deem my efforts over these past years a success.

Finally, I would like to emphasize the nature of this book as a conceptual effort, one step towards providing some intellectual coherence to the social scientific approach to environmental problems. The framework is strongly grounded in a perspective that sees such problems as inherently derived from a variety of social tensions and conflicts, and that anticipates still further tensions and conflicts. While such an analytic view can explain much of the social base of environmental issues, much remains to be covered by complementary perspectives. For those readers with an open mind, I trust that the arguments in this book will stand on their own, and I have chosen to present them with a minimum of scholarly documentation. For those who see little utility in my perspective, I fear that no amount of documentation will ever suffice to persuade them of the value of my analysis. This volume is, then, an attempt to open a social dialogue, and not to be a definitive work. The arguments here have been refined over six years of my teaching and research in the environmental area. I have no doubt that the future will see further refinement. But the time has come to share a perspective that has profoundly changed my own view of social structures in the modern world, in order to draw more and better minds into this dialogue.

1 THE SOCIAL PROBLEMS OF THE ENVIRONMENT

I THE SOCIAL MEANING OF ENVIRONMENTAL PROBLEMS

A SOCIAL STRUCTURAL VIEW OF THE ENVIRONMENT

What Is the Environment?

In the recent rush of concern about the nature of environmental problems, scientists of all persuasions have seen fit to classify their own work as "environmental." So successful has their quest for fame or notoriety been that it is no longer clear that the term environmental has any unambiguous meaning. It has been used in analyses ranging from the individual psyche to urban structures and finally to world society. In this sense, it has come to take on a formal rather than a substantive meaning: Whatever is outside of the immediate focus of study (the individual, the group, the society) represents its "environment." Should we follow up on this definition, virtually every problem is an "environmental problem." Clearly, this line would empty the term of all its content, an unsatisfactory situation. Therefore, we have two choices: Eliminate the label altogether, or define it more carefully. I have chosen the latter option.

How then shall we define "environment"? The simplest form is the universe of biotic and other physical material, as organized into dynamic systems. These systems are ecological systems or *ecosystems*, which represent the integration of living (biotic) and nonliving elements in the environment. Hence the emphasis is on living and nonliving elements, and their integration.

The area of scientific activity most involved with the environment is *ecology*, which analyzes the structure and function of nature. Ecology, as distinct from other areas of biological interest, examines populations, communities, ecosystems, and the biosphere. This is in contrast with botany and zoology, which cover the levels of organization of living matter ranging from protoplasm and cells to organ systems and organisms. In other words, ecology examines the whole cloth; the other fields of biology, the threads of nature.

The structure and process of the environment, then, is the focus of study of ecology. The elements of this organization are the *populations* of a single plant or animal species: a territorially-based aggregate characterized by birth and death processes. Combinations of populations in a local area represent a *community*. In turn, the interrelation of a community of living species with its nonliving physical elements is an *ecosystem*. The major types of ecosystems are: the seas, estuaries and seashores, fresh water systems, deserts, tundra, grasslands, and forests. Each of these represents a unique form of environmental organization, both qualitative (types of species and physical elements) and quantitative (relative concentration of species). Finally, the entire complex of ecosystems constitutes the *biosphere*, the total life system of the planet earth.[1]

The Societal Meanings of the Environment: Home versus Sustenance

From the preceding definition of the environment, we can begin to construct some societal relevance of the physical environment. At a very abstract level, two views can be seen in recent writings (Dunlap & Catton, 1978:5). The first is environment as a home for mankind. It is this context that undergirds issues of our "fouling the nest" through various forms of pollution. Moreover, as with any home, matters of aesthetics of the physical environment surround such a notion of the environment. People wish to have a pleasant, interesting, diverse, and clean home to live in. Correspondingly, commentators have created a long list of unpleasant visual qualities of the physical environment— littered, despoiled, cluttered, monotonous, ugly—and various social groups have taken as their mission the improvement of our collective home (see Ch. VIII). Without wishing to demean such efforts, we can classify them as "cosmetic" concerns. These affect the physical, psychological, cultural, and some social dimensions of human lives, in ways that we can only dimly understand at present. However, important as these human habitat features are to individuals, groups, and societies, these dimensions will not be the major concern of this book.

Rather, the second notion of environment—that of *sustenance* base for society—will be the primary emphasis here. In this view, environment is seen as the locus of all material support of humankind. While one could properly argue that the first view of environment could be subsumed under this perspective, it will prove more useful to separate the two emphases. We need to understand the productive structure of the biotic-physical environment, and to link it to the productive structure of modern societies. By productive structure, I refer to the living and nonliving elements of the environment that have the potential for human usage, whether or not they are in fact directly or indirectly utilized by present societies. The concept of habitat is appropriate here, too, of course, since the range of an animal's habitat contains the sustenance base for its survival. Yet for humankind, our social and cultural organization permit our dissociating home and sustenance views, especially in modern industrial societies, as we shall see.[2]

During the past decade, there has been a resurgence of interest in the environment in industrial societies. The "environmental movements" (Ch. VIII) created or expanded in the 1960s in most western societies, especially in the United States, focused on various issues of home and/or sustenance. If there has been a trend in this period, it has been toward sustenance issues. This is nowhere better exemplified than in the concern with energy shortages, especially following the 1973–74 energy crisis in consuming nations. As a somewhat lower priority, the beginnings of fears for the near- and far-term resource base for advanced industrial societies was also evidenced publicly. But even the main concerns with industrial pollution abatement often had less to do with survival and sustenance than with reducing the general irritants in man's home: in air, water, and land.

Such a shift in concerns of social reform groups may have little to do with actual environmental changes in the period. Rather, it reflects some reorganization of social intelligence about the issues, along with changing institutional perspectives on environmental problems and their solutions. The emphasis in this book is on the actual relationships between societies and their environments, however, as much as on the shifting character of social concerns. Shifts in specific public environmental concerns often obscure as many socioenvironmental linkages as they elucidate. It may be inconceivable that energy and related environmental sustenance issues will fade from public and political concerns in the decades to come. Yet it would have been no less inconceivable in 1970 that concern with air and water pollution would shrink among publics and politicians alike in such a short time.[3]

In part, such a transitory quality of public attention is a result of a variety of competing social problems (Spector & Kitsuse, 1977). But equally important, it reflects a woeful ignorance on many of our parts of the *systematic* connections between our social and economic structures, and the productive organization of the physical, biotic environment. It is necessary that I first present my own perspective on these systematic connections. Otherwise, the arguments spelling out the social causes and consequences of environmental problems that constitute the major portion of the book may be treated as overly alarmist— or even as overly optimistic.

What the next section specifies is a logical set of production or sustenance relationships between the societies we know, and the environments that sustain them. These are enduring forms of organization and linkages; they must therefore be a large element in both the history of environmental degradation—and in the attempts at environmental reform that characterize especially the last decade. The succeeding sections attempt to provide a general classification of such environmental degradation, and the types of social consequences that flow from it.

While these sections build on a base of technical literature, they are no substitute for it. Rather, they provide a nontechnical working model for socioenvironmental relationships, to serve as a common denominator for readers. In my quest for codification and simplification, there will undoubtedly be errors that offend the more sophisticated reader. I trust they do not undermine the general accuracy of this model, or deter further reading. The attempt is to rise above the particular mix of social perspectives on environmental problems of any recent period, and to appreciate the *enduring* strains between societal and environmental production structures. As with any process of abstraction, information is lost. But these details can be pursued readily elsewhere, while the systematic model is not so directly accessible in the literature I am familiar with.[4]

THE STRUCTURE OF PRODUCTION: ENVIRONMENTAL VERSUS SOCIETAL PERSPECTIVES

Environmental Production: Ecosystems

Ecological systems consist of living actors, existing within a matrix of nonliving nutrients and homes. Insofar as this system has a production function, this consists of the creation of living matter—biomass—by the processes of birth, growth, and decay. Each actor is a species population within some territorial bounds, and each of the actors interacts with others and with the resources of the territory in particular ways. That is, as with societies, we have an organization of actors, with specified rules, roles, and relationships. In this production of living matter, the production medium is *energy*, which *flows* through the ecosystem. All energy in these sytems derives finally from the sun, through solar radiation on earth. This energy flows through various actors, embodied in various forms of living tissue for the life-span of each element of a species in a population. The tissues of life are created from the nutrient in the ecosystem, coupled with the tissues of other life consumed in the process of growth or production.

Unlike the complexities of human societies, ecosystems are subject to only two primary organizational rules, the two laws of thermodynamics. The first, that of Conservation of Matter and Energy, states: Matter and energy cannot be created or destroyed, they can only be transformed. The second law, the Law of Entropy, states: All energy transformations are degradations, changing energy from more to less organized forms.

Regardless of the ecosystem under review, these basic principles hold throughout the biosphere. The environment for every human society is organized around these two simple principles, regardless of the nature of the human society.

The rules also specify the broad outlines for ecosystem structure and functioning. In all ecosystems, energy flows and matter cycles through the biotic system. Life as it appears in ecosystem production may be superficially quite static, in terms of the visible or measureable species and their biomass. Yet the dynamic life function constantly degrades energy from coherent, substantive forms, and ultimately into heat (energy flows). Ecosystems preserve in some form the atoms and molecules of matter, regardless of physical and chemical transformations in the systems (matter cycles).[5]

There are two facets to the ecosystem. From a classical biological perspective, we observe a rich diversity of distinctive species present. The particular production function necessary for each species is a unique mixture of raw materials: other species that are eaten (for nonplant species), macronutrients (water, oxygen, carbon dioxide, nitrogen, phosphorus, potassium), and trace nutrients. The lowest order of production is plants, which use solar radiation directly through photosynthesis. The highest is mammals that are carnivorous. A clear hierarchy of species in a food chain always emerges. The total biomass for orders that consume other species must always be lower than the totals for the orders consumed, because of the second law. In simple ecosystem food chains, where each species eats the one below it, this leads to the familiar triangular diagram. A few large animals are the highest level, and a large biomass of plants is at the base of the triangle, with a more or less regular narrowing from bottom to top.

On the other hand, this rich biological diversity belies the simple dynamic accounting in the system. Energy enters, usually from the sun, and is continuously degraded into smaller volumes of biomass and of heat released. Matter is generally recycled in ecosystems, though often through mechanisms (e.g., water, oxygen cycles) at a level of the biosphere beyond that of the ecosystem itself (Penman, 1970; Delwiche, 1970). The analogue in modern industrial systems is the flow of money that is the common denominator of production accounting. Just as money flows through social systems at different rates, so too does energy flow through ecosystems at different rates. In general, the greater the input of energy (through solar radiation and plant growth by photosynthesis) relative to the decay and turnover of species, the greater the growth of the ecosystem's community (the local semi-autonomous organization of species). So too in human societies: where money flow in is greater than that needed for consumption, the surplus becomes transformed into physical capital investment and residual liquid savings.

For purposes of understanding socioenvironmental production relationships, the discussion above indicates:

1. environmental production takes place under immutable rules;
2. these rules give rise to environmental structures;
3. production is tied closely to limited energy flows;
4. materials circulate within these production systems.

The next section will point to some similarities and differences in production organization in human societies. It will set the stage for consideration of major types of conflicts between societal and environmental production needs and processes.

Societal Production: Economies

In one form or another, every material aspect of human societies derives from the natural environment. This follows from two characteristics of humans. First, as a species population, human consumers are directly dependent on flows of energy and nutrients from their environment: food, water, and oxygen are the principle elements. However, humans are also sociocultural *producers*, apart from any direct contribution to biomass food chains. As with other large mammals at the top of food chains, humans do not generally provide sustenance for other species. Unlike other large predators, however, humans are capable of organized production under principles that apparently differ from the two laws of thermodynamics governing ecosystem organization of production. In fact, since human societies exist within the biosphere, all human production is subject to the same two organizational rules that apply throughout the biosphere (H. Odum, 1971). The apparent evasion of these rules occurs because humans have learned to operate *across* ecosystems, and to view their sociocultural production as nested in a different set of principles— economic, not ecological. The distinctions in the two sets of rules are important in understanding the generation of environmental problems, and the historical development of societal economies.

In the early stages of human societies, the predominant role of man was of biological consumer. During the hunting and gathering stage of human society, the bulk of human activities was oriented to biological survival, as with any species. Gathering involved working close to the base of food chains, with high ecological efficiency in transforming energy: from the sun, to plants, to human biomass. Hunting entailed working somewhat higher in food chains, adding at least an additional stage to energy degradation: the consumption of plants by the animals that man consumed. In terms of direct sustenance, this still involved relatively low energy needs per person, and environmental demands were thus low. While it is true that some hunters have done major damage to environmental organization through over-hunting of certain animals such as mammoths, this appears to be atypical. Individuals and kinship groupings were not highly differentiated in terms of productive activity.

Later developments of plant and animal husbandry into settled agriculture and pastoralism changed some of these societal production features. More differentiation in production was possible and did occur, and groups became more variable in terms of stocks of land, food, and levels of environmental demand. Domestication of plants and animals led to changes in local patterns in species, altered communities and ecosystems, and generally increased the types and degree of environmental input into human production. Concurrent with this was an increase in human populations in a number of pastoral societies, though the evidence for this is not overwhelming. Whether increased societal production led to increased human population, or the latter induced greater productive efforts is not clear. In general, though, the increase was gradual up until the seventeenth century in many areas, and still later in others.[6] While agricultural productivity allowed for greater sustenance and hence the potential for increased kinship and societal size, a variety of climatic and pest variations, along with various diseases, led to considerable shifts in family and community size. Both mortality and fertility appeared to vary according to crop conditions and these environmental pathogens, though our evidence for many of these factors is quite flimsy, even for more modern periods. Recent evidence suggests an instability of food conditions and hence of human mortality as late as the nineteenth century in "industrial" countries like Britain (McKeown et al., 1972; McKeown & Record, 1962). In general, though, the eighteenth and nineteenth centuries saw more rapid increases in human populations, at least in the advanced agricultural and early industrial states of Europe and North America. Conditions were less clear in Asia and Africa, though by the middle of the twentieth century, virtually all these areas had reduced mortality due to food and health improvements, leading to the so-called population explosion decried in the last decade (Wrigley, 1969).

In the language of ecology, humans had increased substantially in their total biomass and in the distribution of this biomass across ecosystems, over the period of human history. This biological expansion may have been far less significant in environmental demands than the sociocultural production increases in this period (Ch. II). Particularly in the industrialization period of the last two centuries, increased production (Ch. V) and the changes in production technology (Ch. III) seem more critical.

From these changes emerged, then, increased population and sociocultural production levels. Part of the production was due to population growth, but most of it was a function of the range of possessions and equipment of the society. Moreover, societies grew in such different ways and with such different speeds that by the modern period the biosphere contained a very diverse range of human societies. What most differentiated these societies, in terms of their environmental demands, was the level and type of production in each of their economies. Such production not only led to quite different levels of environmental demand, but also to rather diverse forms of social and economic organization. For it is the production functions of society that seem to have the greatest impact on societal organization.[7]

In contrast to the general organizational principles of the natural environment, human production seems to have fewer and less clear organizational principles. Early hunting and gathering societies, constituted primarily of biological consumers rather than sociocultural producers, appear to have followed the general rules of ecosystem organization specified in the previous section.[8] As societies developed more sociocultural production, the significance of ecosystem principles diminished for the organization of human populations.

If we were to point to a single factor differentiating human from ecological communities, the nature of *surplus* would be a prime candidate. For in ecosystems, a surplus of energy input leads to growth in species populations higher in the food chain. In human societies, such a surplus of energy is far more likely to be channeled into sociocultural production—a nonbiological model. This is especially so in advanced agricultural and industrial societies. Biomass considerations, which draw upon ecosystem rules, are less and less important to advanced societies, while economic organization grows more so. Such a reality exists despite the fact that all economies depend on environmental inputs for their total material base. As the next section indicates, then, the ecosystem rules operate in rather more subtle ways in social systems, which are dominated by other governing principles. This creates the many contradictions between the two types of systems, and sets the stage for our present (and past) environmental problems.

Ecosystems versus Economies: Complements and Contradictions

Mature ecosystems are those with a large diversity of species. They generally exhibit a diversity of niches, or roles, for the species contained, and a relatively low growth rate in biomass. At a very abstract level, human societies are quite similar in form. Modern industrial economies contain a variety of occupational roles, in an elaborate division of labor. And they tend to be characterized by relatively low rates of fertility and of natural increase—i.e., low rates of human biomass increase.

In past years, both ecological and economic theory also converged on the general stability of advanced, mature systems. Ecosystems with their heterogeneity of species and roles were thought to be immune from severe perturbations of nature, and advanced industrial societies had achieved a level of progress that made them relatively immune from the risks and instabilities of "primitive societies." Research and human experience has called both these models into question, however. For ecosystems, some of the sophisticated modeling has indicated the possibilities of accumulated strains and vulnerabilities in complex ecosystems. Advanced complex industrial societies have experienced major depressions, political upheavals, civil insurrection, and in recent years, resource scarcity—particularly of energy. Simulations of the environmental impacts of industrialization have predicted even more severe environmental constraints on industrial growth in the next century. Neither ecological nor social science research has reached a level of sophistication that permits ready acceptance of either set of models. But elements of uncertainty are now established as part of the future of mature ecosystems and economies, at least in terms of their vulnerability to external threats. For ecosystems, these external threats include those of human economies; and for economies, they include destructive ecosystem conditions.

Beyond these similarities of complexity and perhaps of some stability, the two types of production systems diverge. This divergence starts with the creation and disposition of surplus energy in the system (H.

Odum, 1971), and leads to cumulative divergence as this organizational difference gets reproduced over time. But if the ecosystem changes over time from a simpler, faster-growing one to a more complex, slower-growing entity, almost the reverse is true of human economies. Simpler societies—such as hunters and gatherers and early agriculturalists—had relatively slow growth of production and population. In late agricultural, early industrial, and especially later industrial societies (Ch. III), economic growth proceeds at an unprecedented pace. Both systems react to the creation of a surplus energy (food especially) by initial absorption of this surplus. But whereas the ecosystem reaches a steady-state by permitting the growth of just enough species and populations to offset the surplus, societies tend to use the surplus to *accumulate* still more economic surplus in future periods. Some population growth occurs initially (Ch. II), but much of the surplus is eventually channeled into some form of tools, and later into machines, which act more efficiently on environmental resources to generate higher levels of production (Ch. III, V). Part of this increased production is "consumed" by the population, living at somewhat higher levels then their forebears. A part is accumulated for potential investment and production in the future. This combination of rising consumer expectations (Ch. IV) and greater accumulation or surplus for future production (Ch. V) is a spur to exponentially rising levels of production.[9] Thus societies operate to multiply their surpluses, particularly industrial capitalist societies. In contrast, ecosystems tend to mature by stabilizing numbers of consumers and levels of consumption.

In this discrepancy, the organization of human production changes qualitatively as well as quantitatively. Individual members of society now have a dual role as "consumers": a fundamental ecological-biological sustenance role, and one dictated in part by the economic production system, whose goods they absorb. In addition, the complexities of production systems require specialized roles as "producers," such that individuals have quite varying linkages to direct environmental extraction (Ch. III). The concentration of humans in cities—urbanization—is the most obvious form of differentiation of humans along these lines (Davis, 1971). Urban consumers and producers often have little direct connection to natural resources. Rural producers and consumers may have little control over societal production and the consumer products that emerge. Sedentary occupations, in man-made environments, lead to greater distinctions between biological consumption—the sustenance of the physical body—and sociocultural consumption of various social strata and classes. Indeed, the ultimate expression of this urban liberation from environmental contact is the idea that advanced industrial societies have entered upon a new period of "postindustrialism" (Ch. V), with no resource constraints (Bell, 1973). Such illusions have been partly shattered by the environmental consciousness of the 1960s (Ch. VIII), and especially by the confrontation with rising energy prices and energy shortages of the 1970s. One simplification of this complex process is the view that as economies grow and become more complex, those who allocate surplus are the farthest removed (physically and socially) from the ultimate source of all surplus, the natural environment (Ch. III). In ecosystems, in contrast, all species are intimately involved in the disposition of any surplus energy, either as food or as consumers. Local perturbations tend to influence other community members, until some sort of dynamic balance between input and output is reached.

The key to the contradictory utilization of surplus in the two systems is society's use of tools—of physical technology (Ch. III)—and of organizational forms to mobilize surplus and recreate it in the economy. This is what Mumford (1967, 1970) has called the megamachine or human production system (Ch. V). These are supraindividual changes in the nature of economic systems, though they rest on the intellectual and physical talents of individual humans. Historically connected in some ambiguous ways to this increased organization and technological sophistication is *some* increase in the material consumption of individual societal members (Ch. IV), though in varying degrees, with varying physical, psychological, and social benefits or welfare.

Such a distinction between society and ecosystem growth patterns implies not only contradictory models, but somewhat antagonistic ones as well, for societal production arises from use of environmental resources. As societies increase their production, they "discover" resources and "create" new products. But discovery and creation is merely one component of the natural cycles and flows. Thus, societies do not create energy, they transform one form (e.g., fossil reserves) into another (e.g., electricity). But according to the second law of thermodynamics, some loss of potential energy is involved from one stage to the next. Relative abundance of ecosystem components permits greater societal usage, though with ecosystem disruption as one risk. Human creation of new products and discovery of new resources can only proceed up to limits of particular ecosystems. Beyond this, either new ecosystems must be tapped, or societal production altered.

It is this contradiction between society and ecosystem surplus utilization that leads to a conflict between ecosystem growth and maintenance. How serious and immediate the conflict is, how many ecosystems are affected, are variable in space and time. Recent biospheric limits have been suggested for heating and cooling of the earth itself. Since the contradictions and potential/actual conflicts all revolve around energy and its utilization,[10] we can begin to better appreciate socioenvironmental production relationships, environmental problems, and resultant societal problems by considering briefly the special nature of energy.

Energy: Resource, Mediator, and Indicator

In both ecosystems and economies, energy plays a crucial role, as it also does in the linkages of societies to environments. In ecosystems, biomass can be viewed as potential energy, created from transformations of lower-order biomass from potential to kinetic energy, and/or direct use of solar radiation in photosynthesis (creation of plant potential energy). For each system, energy has three distinct meanings and utilities. *First,* energy is itself a commodity resource to be directly used in production. *Second,* energy is a mediator of system processes, since it is involved in all types of material transformations. For example, eating in ecosystems involves expenditures of potential energy to create movement through the use of kinetic energy: This motion is generally necessary for capture, digestion, and excretion of inputs. Likewise, energy in social production is necessary for resource extraction, resource processing, and distribution of wastes and products. *Third,* energy consumption or production is an index or symptomatic indicator of the total production of a system, because of its diversity of uses just noted. Ecosystems and economies can both be characterized as high- or low-energy systems, though the consequences are different in the two (Cottrell, 1955; H. Odum, 1971). In societies, one of the comparative measures of economic development in widespread use is energy consumption per capita, since it is deemed to be a more sensitive and reliable indicator of level of production than are monetary measures. Indeed, some commentators have even suggested that advanced industrial societies should use energy measures to deal with national accounting or productions, as well as for pricing and other purposes.

But the ubiquitous qualities of energy make it socially elusive as well. The fact that the United States has, in recent years, failed to set an "energy policy" is not surprising. What is surprising is that so many observers are naive enough to believe it possible for such a decentralized capitalist economy to have an overall energy policy without total transformation of the political and economic structure. For, since energy is everywhere intertwined with production, an energy policy that would have tight regulations would be simultaneously a production policy—and that level of production control is still anathema to many Americans (and others).

Interestingly, the recent energy debate following the 1973–74 Organization of Petroleum Exporting Countries' (OPEC) reduction in oil flows to industrial societies has been treated as quite distinct from "environmental policy." It has become a convention to talk of energy issues *and* environmental issues. There are some uses to be served by this distinction, but for purposes of understanding and meliorating society's environmental problems, this distinction could not be more pernicious. For energy is not a commodity, but a lifeblood of both ecosystems and economies, and a major lifeline between the two.[11] Energy and all other socially useful resources are extracted from ecosystems by means of energy. Such material resources can only be processed by various forms of energy. Resultant products must be distributed by energy in transportation, finance, services, and the like. The ways in which energy is used in the societal production system determine, to a considerable extent, the degree and ways in which all environmental resources are extracted from and returned to the biosphere and its ecosystems. Conversely, production processes that directly or indirectly draw upon environmental resources may be transformed in ways that can dramatically alter the energy requirements of a society, as well as the employment structure, the occupational opportunity structure, and the ways of living of societal members (Cottrell, 1955; Mumford, 1963). Thus, for example, different groups in the United States saw the 1973–74 "energy crisis" (a shortfall of 3 percent in oil supplies) in dramatically different ways. Organized labor and capital viewed the problem as one of too little energy, and called for increased domestic energy supplies. Environmentalists, though, saw the situation as a vindication of their attack on the energy and material voracity of the U.S. industrial system, and called for reorganization of national production and consumption. From differing interests and ideologies, each group had a valid perspective. Yet neither saw the full set of implications of energy policies, for environmental *and* economic consequences.

From this perspective, the efforts in this book to relate environmental and societal production issues are efforts to establish an energy perspective and eventually policies linked to energy. To talk of energy divorced from these other realities is to ignore the intimate and socially significant ties between energy, ecosystem structure, and economic structures. Unlike money, which is an economic lifeblood, energy has both a societal and an ecological significance, and any policy for it necessitates a dual accounting of such consequences. Finally, the abstract connections among the three elements afford us a general model for analyzing the "environmental problem." That is our next task.

ENVIRONMENTAL PROBLEMS OF SOCIETAL PRODUCTION

Economic Production Impacts: Withdrawals and Additions

Societal production of all kinds draws upon ecosystems and the biosphere in some broad patterns. First, materials are extracted from ecosystems. Second, these materials are typically transformed through physical and/or chemical production processes. Third, after distribution and use, these material products are disposed of in some way.

These processes of interchange between economies and ecosystems may be viewed at the most abstract level as a series of *additions and withdrawals*. Such additions and withdrawals have the potential to disorganize ecosystems. All the varieties of "environmental problems"—both pollution (addition) and depletion (withdrawal) types of problems—follow from this simple perspective. While much of modern ecological research is capable of specifying the important qualitative and quantitative dimensions of such disorganization, it is nonetheless useful for us to conceptualize the conflict between societal and environmental systems in as simple a way as that above. Societal production entails environmental additions and withdrawals, which in turn may disorganize biospheric systems.

Such societal additions and withdrawals may be further subdivided into those affecting the *living* and *nonliving* components of ecosystems. Modern agriculture, for example:

1. adds pesticides, herbicides, and fertilizer to land and water;
2. adds new animal species and new plant species;
3. adds animal wastes to land and water (through run-off);
4. withdraws existing flora (trees, weeds);
5. withdraws existing predators and rodents (hunting, trapping);
6. withdraws water (by intensive irrigation).

While not all agriculture today has such effects, much of western rationalized agriculture does. In addition to these local ecosystem effects, it draws heavily on energy production to facilitate all of the above, and to distribute and process agricultural products (Pimentel et al., 1973, 1975).

We could readily classify the six environmental impacts of agriculture into *pollution* (1–3) and *depletion* (4–6) effects. Indeed, the recent history of research and social policy has entailed efforts to analyze pollution and control it, to assess depletion rates and slow them down through conservation. Yet this apparently useful division of focus and labor obscures some of the integrated nature of both societal and environmental production.

Consider, for example, a manufacturing industry that produces plastics. The inputs for production include energy sources, oil feedstocks, perhaps some manufactured chemicals (drawn from environmental materials and processed later), manufacturing equipment, and human services (which draw on materials and energy, both in the past for their construction and in the present for their operation). In other words, there is a series of environmental withdrawals associated with the inputs. Many of these withdrawals may have had associated additions to ecosystems: e.g., slag from mining operations, water and air pollution from refining and transporting, air and water pollution from the chemical manufacturing processes. Even production inputs have both withdrawals and additions associated with them. Likewise, the postmanufacturing processes include transportation, packaging, merchandising, use, and disposal. Each of these has a dominant form of environmental impact—e.g., transportation withdraws oil stocks—and a secondary impact—e.g., transportation also adds to water and air pollution (Westman and Gifford, 1973).

For our purposes in this book, it is this integrated dimension of societal production and the complex associated impacts on the ecosystems and biosphere that require emphasis. The central thesis is that a piecemeal attack on environmental problems such as air pollution, water pollution, and energy consumption is ultimately not as effective as a close examination of total production in modern societies. Without such an approach, all types of social contradictions emerge in environmental protection efforts. For example, reduction of auto emissions in the 1960s and 1970s reduced energy efficiency of many automobiles. An approach that examined total environmental impacts of automobiles should have had a dual pollution-depletion concern at the outset. Likewise, air pollution controls in industry both add to energy costs and leave a sludge that, if not "disposed" of somehow, will contribute to water pollution and land degradation. That is, over the long run, a systemic or *synergistic* view of the combined complex effects of societal production makes far more sense for accommodating to ecosystem constraints.

Instead, what we have is a fragmented set of knowledge and a fragmented system of air pollution and similar experts, departments, and agencies (Ch. VI). In part, this is a result of particular legislative directions taken earlier, in part a function of the nature of our scientific personnel, and in part a necessary step for beginning to confront environmental problems. The fact that few societies have solved many of these problems, even in their fragmented form, may be taken as a validation of having wisely chosen to disaggregate a massive problem. For a "wholesale" approach would have been doomed to even greater failure. But an alternate view is that these failures were foreordained by the fragmented approach: without a reorganization of production that takes into account present and imminent ecosystem disorganization, mild reformations of current industrial production systems will merely shift us from one problem to another in the biosphere (Stretton, 1976). Pollution problems will be "solved" at the expense of energy and other resource depletion. Energy problems will likewise be "solved" by exacerbating pollution and other forms of disorganization (Carpenter, 1976).

In principle, what this calls for is an appreciation of the total biospheric impact of all forms of production and consumption, in order to comprehend present and future environmental problems. Such a principle has already been established—though hardly fully implemented—in the logic of the U.S. National Environmental Policy Act (NEPA) of 1969–70. This act specified that all federal government agencies had to specify the total environmental impacts of federally sponsored construction and production projects (Ch. VII). What I am calling for is an extension of this logic to all societal production operations, both private and public (Westman & Gifford, 1973). As with the movements for accountability of both public service agencies and the corporate world to consuming or client populations, this is a quest for a new accountability on environmental dimensions. Moreover, it is not a substitute for social accountability, but an additional requirement, to merge environmental welfare and social welfare considerations (Ch. IX).[12]

What are the kinds of production impacts on the biosphere and its ecosystems? And in what directions might such accounting of production lead us in projecting future environmental problems?[13]

Dimensions of Biospheric Disorganization

Biospheric organization consists of a series of "stocks"—living and nonliving inventories—and change processes, including reproduction and death, accretion, and depletion. The component ecosystems and biospheric cycles exist in a dynamic balance, with the possibility of imbalance ever present. Ecosystems can become more mature and complex, or become less mature and simpler. They can increase or decrease in biomass, depending on energy flows and nutrient shifts. Unlike some simplex views, then, nature is not a harmonious, equilibrated system, but one with certain predicted balances and imbalances, and processes that lead to the rebalancing of ecosystems. Geological and atmospheric shifts can produce great upheavals, with no human intervention. On the other hand, processes of evolutionary change and of system movements to restore temporarily disrupted species and other dimensions of ecosystem communities follow some orderly paths of change, however catastrophic any disruption may be to a set of species, communities, or even ecosystems (as in the Ice Ages).

Human production, in its withdrawals and additions, adds both quantitative and qualitative disruptions to ecosystems and the biosphere. We can classify these demands as to:

1. size of addition/withdrawal;
2. degree of permanence of addition/withdrawal;
3. centrality of the addition/withdrawal for ecosystem organization;
4. range of ecosystems involved in addition/withdrawal.

In a broad sweep, we can state with some confidence that, over human productive history, the *scale* of productive impacts on the biosphere has increased in each of these dimensions. With settled agriculture and developed industrialization, production additions and withdrawals have generally become larger, more permanent, more central, and more diffused across ecosystems. Certainly local ecosystems and particular forms of societal production may prove exceptions, but the total thrust of European, North American, and the "modern" sectors of the rest of the world-system follow this general trend.[14]

Consider the general models of human production. Gatherers collect plant material, and may use fire under some rare circumstances to stimulate plant growth (in the latter cases, this is nomadic agriculture, which falls between gathering and settled agriculture). With small numbers of gatherers (low population densities) especially, the environmental impacts are: small (low biomass removed), temporary (growing cycle), nonvital (only selected plant species are removed), and limited (normally a single ecosystem is involved). Hunters remove limited stocks of animals normally, though they may, on occasion, hunt to virtual depletion of a stock, as with buffalo and mammoths. Their typical impact is somewhat larger (greater biomass removal), temporary (reproductive cycle of animals), nonvital (only selected animal species are removed), and somewhat limited (one or two ecosystems involved). Settled agriculturalists or pastoralists in earlier periods had larger impact (more biomass removal in clearing areas), more permanent effects (reduction of local habitats, elimination of local plants/animals in immediate vicinity), somewhat more vital effects (local communities disrupted, though larger ecosystems less affected), and relatively limited impacts (single ecosystem). Agribusiness and developed industries have impacts that are: far larger (greater biomass removal), more permanent (species extinction, severe depletion by direct removal and habitat removal), more vital (habitat and species removal, reproductive impairment through pollution), and far broader (multiple ecosystems drawn on and disrupted for production needs). The notion of the modern multinational corporation having a "global reach" indicates the extent of ecosystems and biospheric elements involved in large-scale contemporary production (Ch. III).[15]

While some have argued that modern production technology has become more materially efficient per unit production (Ridker, 1972, 1976), even these gains have been offset by increased volumes of production and increased by-products of such new technologies. Modern pollutants tend to have far longer "transition times" in the atmosphere and in the food chain and nutrient systems of the biosphere. At the extreme are radioactive pollutants, which could have persistance and thus risk of biological damage for hundreds of thousands of years.[16] And energy demands have risen exponentially for at least the last century, with a quickening pace in the last fifty years.

Commoner (1972) has eloquently pointed to the fundamental contradiction between societal production as an open system and biospheric organization as a closed system (with the exception of solar radiation input). In earlier forms of localized societal production—as with gatherers or early hunters—societies did in fact approximate closed systems, and appeared little different from other species. With mobility of people and production units, this closure disappeared for any single ecosystem. Societal production, by the rules of the biosphere, was ultimately a closed system within the biosphere. But this ultimate reality had little effect on societal decisions regarding production. Indeed, technological development (Ch. III) led to more far-reaching efforts as local communities and ecosystems became disorganized. Thus economic success (and ecological failure) permitted often still greater economic success (and still greater ecological disorganization).

If this is the case historically, then we must ask: Why do our present "environmental problems" worry us and influence our thoughts about production? What are the risks? Are we overreacting to temporary problems? The next section attempts a broad response to these questions.

Human Threats from Environmental Problems

From the preceding analysis, the range of ecological disorganization seems greater than in prior historical periods. Thus, the modern world-system faces a stock that is subject to greater rates of depletion. Cornucopians argue that the range of stocks is far greater than we estimate, so that we can have more rapid depletion and yet have adequate stock reserves for a considerable period of time. Others seriously question the estimates of stock, and pose more difficult systemic questions about biospheric organization.[17] For example, Goeller and Weinberg (1976) speculate that, should an unlimited supply of energy (e.g., fusion energy) be developed, we would never run out of minerals, since the earth's crust is itself a reserve stock of low concentrations. We could mine the very crust we live on. Leaving aside the metaphor of the man sawing off the limb he's sitting on, we should properly ask what the ecological impacts would be of such mineral withdrawals. The volume of tailings (mineral residues) alone would create enormous pollution and disorganization problems, removing land and water from agricultural and other biological uses for considerable periods of time (or even permanently). Likewise, the minerals thus extracted would themselves be subjected to large-scale transformation in manufacturing processes, with additional volumes of production additions polluting land, water, and air, according to present technologies. And this intrinsic complement to cornucopianism of minerals ignores all the withdrawals and additions associated with the energy extraction and transformation to mass consumption forms.

Debates like these continue and are likely to multiply in forthcoming decades. In part they hinge on important qualitative dimensions—e.g., whether certain chemicals are threats to life or not—and in part on quantitative dimensions, such as the volume of species affected, or the duration of disruption of ecosystems. Given the recency and controversy (Carpenter, 1976) in much of the quantitative research (Ch. VI, VII), I will restrict myself to a brief discussion of the kinds of social risks entailed in ecosystem disorganization such as that occuring in the modern world-system. A starting distinction is between direct biological threats to humans, and threats to the sociocultural production.[18]

DIRECT BIOLOGICAL THREATS   There are three or four major types of biospheric threats of environmental problems that more or less directly affect biological survival of individual humans: (1) carcinogens and environmental toxins, (2) disorganization of food systems currently in production for humans, (3) disorganization of food systems that may be required for human production in the future, and (4) climatic changes that may destroy habitats for man. It is assumed that energy and water shortages in the future will have biological impacts on man primarily through food production, though a combination of a neo-Ice Age and severe shortages may lead to severe hyperthermia (body cooling) for certain populations, according to some models. Energy and water factors are otherwise deemed to operate as constraints on sociocultural production.

Carcinogens and environmental toxins.   While much cancer research in the last decades has focused on virological theories, contemporary researchers are turning increasingly to environmental theories of cancer creation. As much as 85 percent of cancers are now thought to be induced by human contact with environmental carcinogens: in the water, air, food, and some consumer products. Indeed, some apologists have even developed a view of cancer as the price of the comforts of industrialization. Even if this were true, a true social perspective would indicate that some pay the costs, while others reap the benefits (Ch. V). Moreover, acceptance of this risk assumes an immutability of production and carcinogenesis that is immune to re-form or reorganization. This is, at the very least, open to question.[19]

In addition to cancer-causing pollutants and food toxins, there is a variety of other chemical by-products that produce birth defects (Council of Environmental Mutagen Society, 1975) and respiratory and other diseases, which are potentially life-threatening and always debilitating. Such phenomena often occur first in workers in particular industries, and research suggests a later spread to surrounding communities, exposed to lower levels of individual risk. Often the physical properties of these materials are as important as their chemical actions for determining human risk: e.g., particulate size may influence action on lungs or other organs.

At the other extreme, perhaps, is the recent concern with the ozone shield in the atmosphere. Such atmospheric ozone, which screens out harmful, ultraviolet radiation from the sun, has been subject to decomposition by chemical reactions with spray-can propellants released into the atmosphere. In addition, there have been threats to this shield from both the flight and emissions of supersonic aircraft (Hammond & Maugh, 1974). Reduction in the levels of ozone at this level threatens human health—particularly by increasing risks of skin cancer—as well as entailing risks to plant and animal reproduction in food systems and all ecosystems. A number of countries have begun removal of the high-risk fluorocarbon propellants, and the proposed fleets of SST transports have been substantially reduced in scope, in part because of these threats (Hammond, 1975; Maugh, 1976). This has been done despite the uncertainties involved in the research, which has been able to document declines in ozone concentration but not the specific chemical mechanisms involved in this (e.g., Wofsky et al., 1975). However, residual fluorocarbons in the atmosphere, and the remaining stocks available to consumers will both have effects on ozone layers for years to come, with unknown impact on human carcinomas.

Increased research has been done in recent years on such risks. But the obstacles to doing such sustained work are still formidable (Ch. VI), even though countries like the United States have created agencies like the National Institute on Occupational Safety and Health.[20] The problem is that the agency has far too limited resources for the range of tasks assigned.

It is interesting to observe societal responses to a related human health risk: the problems associated with a sedentary life style of industrial occupational and consumption patterns. Rather than questioning the nature of the production system that has generated both environmental threats to life and direct threats to health and life through inactivity, the response has been a personalized and fragmentary one. The medical model of prescribing more individual exercise has partly begun to offset these industrially-related risks, though with interesting social and ecological opportunities foregone in the process. Rather than a thoroughgoing consideration of present production-consumption structures (Ch. IX), experts in industrial countries have encouraged *additional* production and consumption to facilitate individual exercising. The recreational equipment industry has boomed, thereby increasing withdrawals from and additions to the biosphere for this balancing of individual health. A *logical* alternative would have been a restructuring of production to provide occupational exercise, thereby stimulating a production shift that could simultaneously reduce ecological withdrawals and additions, by use of a lower energy and less material technology.

Similarly, there are movements afoot to stifle attempts to reform production to reduce occupational health risks, and instead to compensate workers for additional health risks (Stretton, 1976: footnote 24). This privatization follows in the same medical model as the exercise example above, and indicates the capacity of present productive systems, organizations, and leaders to evade a serious consideration of production reorganization.

Disorganization of Present Food Systems. Until recently, agricultural innovations had been singularly directed at maximizing food production in industrial societies, with little attempt to minimize ecological costs. Modern agribusiness is an energy-intensive activity, which is thereby vulnerable to energy shortfalls at any time. In addition, production of crops has been maximized by utilization of single hybrid species of crops, thereby increasing monocultural pest and climatic vulnerability under extreme environmental shifts. In part, agricultural producers have compensated by means of chemical additions to land to reduce pests and eliminate competing plant species (weeds), and to supplement for inadequate nutrient mixes in the earth. Natural systems of crop protection, involving mixtures of crops, particular cultivation patterns, and use of natural pest predators, fell into disregard. While production was indeed maximized, both the capital and ecological costs of production rose in the modern period, displacing family farmers and disorganizing ecosystems simultaneously. Finally, extensive irrigation has made possible lush agriculture in arid areas such as central California and Israel, but any cut-off of water supplies threatens such systems immediately.[21]

Such agricultural production has removed pest predators, complementary plant life, tree cover (increasing soil erosion), and water from other nearby ecosystems. It has generally reduced the possibility of a sustained agriculture without massive external energy and material inputs (E. Odum, 1969). As such, it maximizes the threat to human survival in the event of sociocultural production difficulties—whether from environmental problems or problems from any other source. Thus, for example, the oil crisis of 1973–74 produced severe difficulties for some agriculture in India, which operated with internal combustion engine pumps for water. This was an economic crisis stemming from OPEC, though, and not yet a genuine world shortage of oil (Stretton, 1976:23–24).

In addition to these shifts in agriculture, and in part because of these and other societal factors, considerable land has been removed from agriculture in industrial societies, for housing, roads, or industrial-commercial purposes (Pimentel et al., 1976). With the usual removal of topsoil and all foliage, such ecosystem communities have been totally destroyed for agricultural production. Since many of these had sufficient soil and water quality to sustain farming with little external factors, societies have lost agricultural potential in the process. In fact, with the potential threats to future chemical and energy inputs into highly mechanized agriculture on marginal land, there will be little reserve of useable ecosystems to fall back upon for food production. This illustrates the general trade-off in ecological systems of production maximization for system protection (E. Odum, 1969).

Water and, secondarily, energy constraints are likely to have the greatest short-term effects on agriculture in countries like the United States. Ironically, these constraints are closely intertwined in the western United States, since future energy supplies will be of coal and will potentially require large amounts of water, thus reducing its availability for ranching and farming. In addition, though, toxins in the air and water may also reduce productivity of soils, by means of interfering with plant growth. These may also affect animal growth and ultimately human health, when humans consume affected meat and plants. DDT and its successors are the most common examples of agricultural toxins, but the range of PCB and PBB (polychlorinated biphenyl and polybrominated biphenyl) pollution of water and land illustrate other distributions of toxins that ultimately affect agricultural production.[22]

Disorganization of Future Food Systems.   To the above list, which catalogues threats to both present and future food systems, must be added a less contemporary view of food production. For decades, experts have predicted future food production from innovations such as hydroculture (farming in water), aquaculture (farming the oceans for plants and seafood), and the manufacture of artificial foods from oil and other substances (H. Brown, 1954). Each of these supposes an adequate stock of materials that is uncontaminated by pollutants. But rapid energy depletion of fossil fuels threatens such production. Likewise, so do pollutants, ranging from wind-borne acid rains (from industrial and transportation air pollution) that affect water quality, to disposal of complex modern chemicals in lakes, rivers, and oceans (such as PCB, DDT, and kepone). Some oil spills are less destructive of oceans and open lakes than previously thought, although this depends on the particular fraction of oil involved, the local ecosystems, and weather conditions.[23]

In addition to these risks for future growth, the simple unavailability of clean water and unrestricted energy supplies may diminish this potential production. Thus, both current and projected additions (e.g., pollutants) and withdrawals (e.g., rapid energy stock consumption) inhibit future degrees of freedom, though to different degrees in different societies.

Climatic Changes.   Two major production impacts on the biosphere have been noted, though both remain controversial in terms of seriousness or quantitative effects. The so-called greenhouse effect involves the combustion of fossil fuels and creation of an increase in atmospheric carbon dioxide and other gases. These gases radiate some of the earth's heat back to the surface of the earth and warm the earth. This could potentially melt polar ice caps, raise ocean levels, and destroy human habitats and production in coastal zones around oceans.

Conversely, the reverse or "ice age" effect operates by increased particulate matter (e.g., dust) released into the atmosphere through industrial and other combustion and physical and chemical transformation operations (milling, refining). These particles reflect sunlight and thus inhibit the volume of solar radiation reaching the earth's surface, decreasing earth temperatures. This could have dramatic effects on agriculture, particularly in the temperate and marginal climate areas of the world system.

Such phenomena are biospheric in scope, though the potential effects they could have on habitat and sustenance would differ across nations and regions. At present, the change in atmosphere itself has been documented, but the degree of change and the future climatic implications are not precisely known. The cornucopian hope is that the two effects will just balance each other, leaving world climate unaffected, certainly the greatest poker game yet played on earth. Unfortunately, though, it is a poker game with a very broad range of participants. For the production of carbon dioxide by man is a result of virtually every form of energy production and use, since combustion of fossil fuels inevitably produces carbon dioxide.[24] Only nuclear energy is free of this by-product (addition). Likewise, most material transformation—including combustion—also produces particulate matter as a potential pollutant, though technologies have been developed to trap more of these particulates and turn them into a sludge whose final disposition in the biosphere is not yet clear. For these reasons, some analysts have argued that the carbon dioxide situation is "the ultimate check" on industrialization and production involving higher energy forms. This remains subject to much dispute.

A more recent risk has emerged through the increase of continental shelf oil exploration and the volume of oil shipments by tankers. This is the increase in oil pollution, particularly of the Arctic ice cap. It is hypothesized that sufficient volumes of such oil could increase the rate of melting the polar ice cap substantially. This would alter ocean volumes and affect habitat and climate of man near the oceans. At present, the estimates of such risks are unclear, in part because recent research has indicated more rapid decomposition of some petroleum products in open seas than had been earlier estimated.[25]

SOCIOCULTURAL PRODUCTION THREATS   Four interrelated types of threats exist, apart from the biological disease and food risks to man: (1) unemployment, (2) income reduction, (3) decreased profitability and capital formation, and (4) decreased availability of public services. Since the level of socioeconomic relations among these four is so intense, it makes little sense to treat each as a separate and distinct phenomenon (Ch. V, IX).

In general, the disorganization of the biosphere tends to create one or both of the following constraints of production in societies: price effects and quantity effects. Withdrawals that have had substantial cumulative effect on stocks mean higher costs of seeking new sources, as in the case of depletion of land sources of U.S. oil and the shift to outer continental shelf exploration. This in turn raises prices of these production commodities, putting strains on profits and on capital formation rising from these profits, on wages (to reduce prices of goods), and on employment (through decreased availability of capital, discretionary income, etc.). Governments are faced with inflation of their costs as well, both through increased costs of goods and services and through the use of public funds (tax credits or subsidies) to reduce high production costs. Similar examples exist in various forms of coal and mineral mining, where decreased resource availability has led to newer technologies. However, some of these have reduced the price for such products, though they have increased the prices of other goods whose production is hindered by such extractive technology. Food production is often inhibited by massive strip mining, say, through elimination of grazing and growing land, and reduction of available clean water. The case of oil production also has such potential impact, since major spills or blowouts on the continental shelf can increase the costs of fish and shellfish production in these or adjacent waters. In some cases, such local oil impacts have eliminated employment, income, and profits from these latter industries, just as strip mining has reduced these from some farming and ranching operations. Moreover, though government revenues may increase from some of the royalties or lease payments in such extractive industries (coal or oil), these may be insufficient to offset increased government costs for cleaning up water in ecosystems more distantly connected to these extractive operations. In recent years, legislation has increased oil and shipping industry responsibility for the costs of local catastrophic impacts and for abatement of some increased pollution.

Quantity effects are often more dramatic and more socially catastrophic for selected groups in the society. These occur when societal production of some type has become virtually impossible to continue because of environmental disorganization. Farmers in areas of extreme soil erosion, fishermen whose catch is inedible because of mercury, PCB, or DDT levels in the species being fished, shell fishermen whose beds have been destroyed by oil fractions of industrial pollutants, and farmers whose soil has been contaminated by long-lived chemicals such as PBB in Michigan or dioxin in Italy are but a few examples of *localized* socioeconomic disruptions that follow severe ecosystem disorganization. Profits, income, and employment can all plummet under such circumstances, though governments are attempting to meliorate such impacts through various insurance models, grants/loans, and facilitation of suits against producers that cause the ecosystem disorganization.[26] Subtler limitations of quantity of production include crop damage from water and air pollution, increased soil erosion from overly intensive forest cutting (which increases silting and irrigation problems, and decreases natural fertilization of other soils), and increased predation of crops and animals by predators displaced from other habitats. Many of these are gradual and less dramatic, and therefore less visible in social considerations of environmental costs (Ch. III).

While some of these quantity effects may seem trivial, it is good to remember that there are substantial precedents for major societal disruption from similar natural disorganization. Whole areas have become uninhabitable and incapable of production because of water limitations, and whole peoples have become dehumanized under conditions of near-starvation. In the post-World War II period, moreover, many of the price and quantity effects of environmental disorganization in industrial societies have been offset in large measure by investment in less-industrial, "Third World" countries. Oil, phosphates, minerals, and natural gas have all flowed to industrial production systems from these societies. Two factors can influence this "escape" in the future: (1) the depletion of stocks in some of these countries (as with tin in Malaysia) and (2) increased resistance of these countries to cheap and high-volume flows of material exports. The latter became less theoretical in the recent OPEC action on oil. However, no other commodities have yet followed this extreme course of short-term quantity and price control. In this arena, too, governments in industrial countries have had pressures to increase funding for such investment ventures by compensating for the nationalization of such industries abroad, and by increasing the tax write-offs in various forms for such capital flights. Both of these strain government budgets and further reduce funds for other public services.[27]

Two things need to be stressed about these effects. First, many of these can be absorbed by and tolerated in a sociocultural production system so long as simultaneous effects are not felt in many sectors of production. When this condition is violated, as it is likely to be in the future under "diminishing returns" models of various sorts, severe recessionary and inflationary impacts can wrench national economies and impose severe hardship on much of the population (Stretton, 1976). Past price and quantity effects have been offset by increased income, profits, and employment in other sectors or regions not affected by environmental disorganization. The more the scale and intensity of such disorganization increases, the less can workers and capital owners alike escape to different places. Some always can and will. But others will be severely pressed by these constraints. Moreover, with such potential reductions in production, profits, and earnings, governments will be decreasingly capable of offsetting these private sector disruptions.

For a glimpse of such models, one can look at economic and ecological disasters in underdeveloped countries, where governments are simply incapable of mobilizing sufficient social and material resources to resolve problems. In some of these situations, the industrial or core societies in the modern world system have provided short-term "humanitarian" aid, which has left situations only marginally better. But in the future, if anticipated ecosystem disruptions materialize, the diffusion of socioeconomic disruption to even the wealthier societies can leave little in the way of a world buffer. And this would be true almost regardless of the political orientations of societies towards "aid." The Rome Food Conference and the events of the 1970s that led up to it are a grim reminder of the social catastrophes that can result from a mixture of mild material scarcity and political conflicts over the disposition of other surpluses (L. Brown, 1974, 1975). If surpluses shrink in the future, this food scene of the 1970s would become a farce, played against the tragedy of future conflicts.

The second feature of these production effects is one that dramatically differentiates them from direct human biological effects. With biological threats, their removal or melioration is a clear gain, since health and life are everywhere preferred to sickness and death. But with production risks, the efforts necessary to meliorate or correct the ecosystem disorganization *themselves* have unwanted price and quantity effects. For, in order to minimize withdrawal effects, we must protect stocks from production, thereby inducing a kind of "managed scarcity" that substitutes for projected depletion (see Ch. IX). In both cases, we end up with quantity checks. Likewise, in pollution abatement, we must pay the costs of changing technology and physical capital. Profits, capital formation, income, and employment are all affected by these reformist efforts. Whether the costs of allowing ecological disorganization to continue are less than those of social melioration of production is not at all clear today, though different groups hold fiercely to differing estimates.[28]

From one perspective, however, either approach reflects the sociocultural costs of ecosystem disorganization. Both reflect the social significance of environmental issues. While environmental protection benefits characterized the late 1960s views (Ch. VIII), current appreciation of their costs prevents easy moralizing and policymaking with regard to production. Indeed, it may be that the prime spur to meliorative action remains those risks noted earlier: biological risks to human life. This would be, perhaps, the greatest irony of the environmental consciousness: to stimulate *sociocultural* action on the basis of *biological* threats to the species population. Such responses were most dramatically represented following the recent nuclear accident in Pennsylvania (Lyons, 1979; Parisi, 1979).

Perspectives from Natural and Social History

Some critics of environmental concern have argued that ecological activists and scientists have an "unnatural" perspective on these problems. Their arguments can be summarized as follows:

1. mankind has always had pollution and depletion problems, both natural and man-made;
2. many of man's most pressing environmental problems have been solved by modern technology—e.g., public works for disease protection through improved sanitation;
3. contemporary environmentalists demand the impossible—a "pristine" environment.

On the first point, it is true that a range of natural phenomena has posed serious threats to specific societies throughout history. These include: volcanic eruptions, earthquakes, droughts, floods, fires, tornadoes, hurricanes, and various environmental disease pathogens (e.g., plagues). In addition, the new geological science of plate tectonics—the movements of large parts of the earth's crust—indicates that major geological upheavals will continue into the far future, with volcanic and earthquake disruptions of major importance. To this must be added an acknowledgement that human societies have always had some impact on their habitat ecosystems (Adler, 1973).

Yet these arguments do not resolve the concerns of contemporary environmental analysts, for social contributions to ecological disorganization merely aggravate the natural disorganization. If volcanic dust circulates in the atmosphere for considerable periods of time and has climatic effects, then the addition of industrial production by-products to this atmospheric stream increases the potential cooling of parts of the earth. Moreover, there is little commensurability of contemporary human effects with the localized, temporary ones cited by these critics as an inherent part of human history. Both qualitative and quantitative shifts have occurred with increases in the intensity and extensity of human production.

Turning to the second point, it is certainly true that some environmental problems that have afflicted humankind have been resolved or meliorated by technological developments of the last two centuries. Most dramatic of these have been the control of environmental diseases through major water and sanitation projects: typhus, typhoid, cholera, dysentery, and related illnesses. In tropical areas lacking such extensive public works, the ravages of these diseases on health and life itself are seen all too clearly. Clean water and its separation from human and industrial sewage have reduced or eliminated these threats in advanced industrial societies. Likewise, many areas periodically threatened by floods and droughts have been protected by public works such as dams and irrigation systems, thereby enabling use of habitat and sustenance production in areas where these were periodically threatened in the past.

Conversely, though, each of these successes has another face. The cost of each of these technological improvements is often not small. For example, water and sewage control has enabled the heavy concentration of people in cities. In turn, this has increased the potential both for massive regional ecosystem damage and for the potential number of victims of any single disease that could evade systems of sanitation (Ch. II). While these risks may be far more acceptable than the known illnesses of the early industrial period, they are risks nonetheless. The same situation exists with other technological "improvements" on natural systems. Flood control dams have severe impact on natural flows of silt and nutrients, reduce agricultural potential in the dam and basin, and may increase the risk of water-borne illnesses, as in the case of the Aswan Dam and schistosomiasis. Drought control through various forms of wells and irrigation may be inadequate in extended periods of drought, and may expose larger numbers of people to risks of starvation and illness. In addition, these water systems often impose handicaps on production in other ecosystems, because of the removal of water and the disorganization of local food chains from the irrigation channels and pipelines.[29]

The last point, referring to a futile search for a "pristine" environment, is largely a diversionary tactic. While it is true (Ch. VIII) that some environmental activists seek something approximating this ideal (Gale, 1972), it is not true of the bulk of activists and scientists working in environmental analysis. There is strong cultural predisposition in western societies to use the environment as a kind of "garden"—predictable, controllable, and aesthetically pleasing (Marx, 1964). But most scientific concerns focus on sustenance issues and on biological hazards to humans and other species. Certainly no ecologist, with any knowledge of ecosystem processes, would even anticipate a return to any stable ecosystem of the natural or social past.

Rather, the efforts that are called for are deemed necessary to reduce *further* disorganization of ecosystems. In addition, for some systems that have been so degraded by past additions and withdrawals, there are efforts toward some reduction in the most destructive cumulative effects. Examples of this include reduction of pollutants in rivers such as the Hudson and the Thames, lakes such as Lake Erie, and smaller seas such as the Mediterranean (e.g., Hellman, 1976). Such reduction includes dredging of solid wastes and the removal of contaminated fish, which absorb toxic pollutants in their fat and organs. In the latter case, the fish accumulate past additions (mercury, PCB, PBB, DDT, etc.) to the ecosystem. By removing and transforming them (by burial and decay, combustion, or chemical decomposition), we effectively "dredge" the waters of these past contaminants. In the absence of future additions, then, the pollution levels of these bodies of water are reduced, though never completely eliminated (Regier & Hartman, 1973).

Thus, while there is some merit in the critics' statements, the contemporary concern with sustenance and habitat disorganization does not seem misplaced. What the critics of environmental concern understate is the qualitative and quantitative impact of modern sociocultural production. For many of the earlier threats to man and production, it sufficed for social groups to move, to flee the localized environmental problems. With the global reach of production withdrawals and additions, though, there are now few refuges for social groups. Indeed, it is perhaps a testimonial to this reality that recent years have brought a spate of proposals for establishing new colonies and workplaces in space—a late industrial version of the flight response of earlier social periods (O'Neill, 1975). The economic and ecological impracticality of space flight leaves the bulk of humankind to confront the varying forms of disorganization of the biosphere outlined here (Ophuls, 1977:122). Systematic attention, reorganization of production, and social reorganization of consumption are proper responses. Denial and flight, while understandable, are not.

Ecological Risks and Uncertainties: Social Responses

While the critics of contemporary environmentalism may be wrong in a number of their charges, they nonetheless point to a critical uncertainty about many ecological disorganization processes, and their sociocultural effects (Ch. VII). Some of these ecological and social linkages are in the realm of risks—calculable, with some sense of the probability of occurrence. Others are genuine uncertainties, in which outcomes are possible, but with no clear sense of how possible, how severe, how widespread. In years to come, if political and economic structures permit, an increased allocation of social resources to research on ecological problems and social consequences may produce greater predictability about ecosystem changes and socioeconomic effects (Ch. VI, VII). Realistically, though, it will not be for many decades before decision-makers will understand precisely what risks are entailed in continuing or altering particular forms of sociocultural production.

This raises a fundamental set of issues. What do we do in the period of uncertainty? How should doubt be socially channeled and controlled? Despite the complexities of this issue, two polar positions may be seen: (1) production processes should be deemed acceptable unless proven otherwise; or (2) production processes have potentially harmful withdrawals and additions, and should therefore always be suspect unless proven otherwise. In one sense, these two positions roughly correspond to "business as usual" versus "stop production," or "cornucopians" versus "jeremiads" (Stretton, 1976). In fact, neither of these quite fit current reality. Some production controls have been accepted, albeit grudgingly, in most societies, for environmental protection. And some forms of production have been accepted as far less injurious, and hence socially and environmentally acceptable. But two facts remain: (1) most production is not subject to such controls, and (2) most production is viewed as having potentially destructive ecological impacts.

There is no simple resolution of this fundamental issue. In theory, the structure of capitalism has encouraged anarchy of production, with no social or ecological constraints. And, in theory again, socialism has maximized social control of production, and hence potentially the ecological impact of production. Thus, in one sense capitalism has encouraged the *society* to take the social and ecological risks of production, while socialism has encouraged the *producer* to take on these risks. In fact, producers in both capitalist and socialist societies have generally ignored many ecological concerns during the past half-century, with important exceptions. Neither has effectively resolved the issue of allocating the burden of proof: is production assumed to be safe or unsafe?

This is a political question, not an economic or an ecological one. Production will be enhanced under greater externalization of risks to society and the environment; it will be virtually eliminated by exclusively ecological criteria. Every society obviously needs some production, but what the optimal level will be is not a technical but a political issue (Carpenter, 1976). How much short-term economic benefits social groups want, or are willing to exchange for enhanced biospheric protection, are also political questions (Stretton, 1976). No amount of economic science can document a technically objective "ideal," based on theories of economic man and assumptions about ecosystem organization. Economic research can, however, elucidate some of the costs and benefits of alternative forms of production (Ch. VII), in conjunction with extensive ecological research.[30]

At the time of this writing, industrial societies have moved from a position of great freedom for producers to a slight reduction in this freedom, based on the legislation and enforcement of environmental protection in the last decade. While this has strengthened the resolve of many committed environmentalists and much of the larger public, it has also led to efforts to remove the fetters on production, on the part of both owners of productive enterprise and many of their workers (e.g., Lindsey, 1978). The hope that better environmental research will lead to some way out of this conflict is frequently voiced. But this seems illusory, since fundamental value questions are involved, as well as economic and ecological facts. The conflict that has emerged is a necessary one, for it means that ecological issues have become politicized. The alternative is not a scientific resolution, but disattention to society's environmental problems. Therefore, the conflict is to be welcomed as a measure of social change towards confronting environmental dilemmas.

THE ORGANIZATION OF THE ARGUMENT

Institutions, Inequality, and Environmental Change

If society is to act on issues of environmental protection, a prerequisite is a fuller understanding of the origins of ecosystem disorganization in society. While I have argued that sociocultural production is the cause of such disorganization, this merely begs the question: Why has production followed this course? At present, there are some basic answers in the analytic literature: industrial production has changed because of (1) population growth, (2) technological imperatives, (3) the desires of increasingly affluent consumers, and (4) the organizational features of producers, particularly capitalistic ones. Chapters II through V take up each of these arguments in turn and assess the logical and empirical basis for many of the common assertions made by analysts. The perspective I offer is an institutional one, focusing on the social organization of modern societies and the world-system. In particular, many of the arguments put forward by others ignore the importance of major differences in income, consumption, and economic and political power that exist within and between societies. When these are taken into account, many of the first three causes of increased societal production and ecological disorganization are not as powerful as they first appear. Moreover, these systematic inequalities raise many issues about both the feasibility and the social justice of ways of solving production and environmental problems that are associated with the first three explanations. Some of the problems of social injustice are removed in considering restructuring of production organization, but this creates other political problems (Ch. V, IX).

To confront both the certainties and uncertainties of environmental issues, it is necessary that society possess an intelligence system attuned to these issues. The argument in Chapters VI and VII is that industrial societies have failed to develop such an adequate system, and that much of this failure results from trends in production organization and the influence of producers. This helps, in part, to explain why mature industrial societies belatedly "discovered" in the 1960s environmental problems that had been growing for decades. More importantly, though, it points to future insensitivity to many environmental issues, despite recent concern, legislation, and regulatory organization.

Such a discussion of societal intelligence would be incomplete without treating the recent and historical movements for environmental protection (Ch. VIII). Pressures exerted on and by such organizations reveal a great deal about both the nature of sociocultural production systems and the difficulty of generating short-term transformations of such systems in the name of environmental protection. The vital monitoring and politicization role of such groups in future conflicts is outlined.

Finally, the outline of a reorganization of sociocultural production, which incorporates concerns with social inequalities in present societies, is in Chapter IX. Rather than being a blueprint, it explores the logic of social policies currently pursued, and presents some alternatives that, from my own bias, appear realistic.

NOTES

1. The definitions of ecosystems and ecology are drawn from E. Odum (1963:3–4). Classifications of ecosystem types are included in Whittaker (1970) and Kormandy (1969), while the concept of the biosphere is explored in Hutchinson (1970).

2. Examples of recent concern with home (including the man-made environment) are Barbara Ward (1976) and Michelson (1977). The term "fouling the nest" is in Luther Carter's (1969) discussion of underdeveloped nations and their development efforts. Some of what I call "cosmetic" concerns are illustrated in Pett (1972) and Lindsay (1970), the former more rural and the latter more urban. On the other hand, serious consideration of production issues has been treated by Childe (1951) and H. Odum (1971).

3. Some early analyses of environmental concerns are in McEvoy (1972) and Morrison et al. (1972), covering the late 1960s. Mitchell (1978) updates results of mass opinion surveys on the environmental problem, and Fischman (1978) does this specifically for energy concerns. Harry (1974) and Dunlap & Catton (1978) gives extensive analyses of the underlying themes covering both public opinion and organized social movements, while Crenson (1971) treats the barriers existing in prior decades to formation of organized opposition to air pollution.

4. Some of the general treatments of environmental problems that are less optimistic than the present book include Ehrlich & Ehrlich (1972), Ehrlich (1970), and de Bell (1970). Technical reviews of resources (NAS/NRC, 1969) and pollution (ACS, 1969) exist in readable form, though assumptions and data are constantly changing in all of these areas. One antialarmist view is that of Adler (1973), and a useful overview of social use of energy is H. Odum (1971).

5. Useful summaries of ecological organization principles include Boughey (1968) on biomass structure, Woodwell (1970a), Oort (1970), and H. Odum (1971) on energy flows, and Hutchinson (1970) on the integration of energy and biomass. Cloud & Gibor (1970) treat the vital oxygen cycle, and Woodwell (1970b) uses the principles of ecosystem organization to discuss potential impacts of pollutants.

6. The general principle of increasing division is elaborated in Emile Durkheim (1964), and Watson & Watson (1969) elaborate on the material and social historical connections. Pages 93–114 of Watson & Watson deal with the transition to agriculture, as does Braidwood (1971). Martin (1973) points to the possibility of mammoth extinction by preagricultural hunters, as an exception to generally low ecological impact of such groups. On the thesis of population and production changes, Harris (1977a,b) views population as growing because of prior sociocultural production, while Boserup (1965, 1976) has proposed the more controversial view that population growth stimulates production technology shifts.

7. While H. Odum (1971) has done a masterful job on treating energy problems and the societal-ecosphere interchanges, earlier work on the changing resource needs of different technological periods includes Forbes (1968), Cottrell (1955), and Mumford (1963). Other than Odum, these authors were optimistic about the future, since these books appeared prior to current pollution and energy concerns.

8. On earlier societies, see the ecosystem effects discussed in Watson & Watson (1969:59–74).

9. The theoretical work on ecosystem instability is discussed in Pielou (1975:127–51) and May (1973). Broader, less technical discussions of biospheric vulnerability include Clark (1973), L. Brown (1970), and Singer (1970). While global and regional models of the Club of Rome are compelling (Meadows et al., 1972; Mesarovic & Pestel, 1974), they have been called into question on a number of grounds (e.g., Gillette, 1972a; Ridker, 1973; Abelson, 1972). The human meaning of these models is most forcefully treated by Stretton (1976), who projects alternative social futures based on declining resources.

10. Shifts in population are treated in Deevey (1971), and the changing agricultural surplus and its impact are in Braidwood (1971), Watson & Watson (1969:93–128), and Mumford (1963), whose treatment of machine technology is still a classic work, despite the passage of over forty years since its first publication in 1934. Cottrell's (1955) work is a much more general treatment of these changes.

11. On energy usage, the best treatments are in H. Odum (1971), Fabricant & Hallman (1971), and the eloquent and controversial recent view of Commoner (1977). Brief treatments of whole-earth heating and cooling are in Plass (1971) and Bryson (1974).

12. A proposal for net energy pricing is in Gilliland (1975), and a counterargument is found in Huettner (1976). Stretton (1976: Ch. 2) treats the consequences of approaching energy and other environmental problems with little comprehensive production reorganization in a rather discomfiting way. Connections between energy, production issues, and ecological disorganization are made forcefully in Cook (1976), Hayes (1976), and in the letter of Woodwell (1974).

13. Stretton (1976) does the best job of considering realistic social welfare outcomes of various production policies. Ophuls (1977) treats the American response to environmental problems and social equity on a more abstract level in his Chapter 6, and has a philosophical overview of the steady-state in Chapter 8.

14. Good overviews of ecological dynamics are in Whittaker (1970), and of natural dislocations in Maugh (1972). H. Brown's (1970) summary of agricultural production shifts is also a good background.

15. The impact of gatherers is described in Watson & Watson (1969:25–74), and the potential impact of hunters in Martin (1973). Braidwood (1971) and Iverson (1971) give a broad and narrow view, respectively, of changing agricultural technology and its effects. Agribusiness, the term used to denote modern corporations engaged in capital and energy-intensive agriculture, is treated in Lappé & Collins (1977) and Barnet & Müller (1974) on the international level. In terms of U.S. agriculture, which follows increasingly the same technological shift of agriculture, good overviews are in Pimentel et al. (1973, 1975).

16. Sagan (1972) describes a broader array of nuclear technology risks than the more conventional view, as in Weinberg's (1972) eloquent treatment of the "Faustian pact." Social alternatives to deal with nuclear energy, despite such risks, are intelligently elaborated in Rochlin (1977).

17. Cornucopian views of minerals are contained in Brooks & Andrews (1974) and a hypothetical model is in Goeller & Weinberg (1976). For more skeptical views

of such solutions, see Cook (1976), Woodwell (1970a), and Meadows et al. (1972).

18. Woodwell (1970b) distinguishes between direct human threats and production problems. Stretton (1976:15–39) posits a socially regressive model of scarcity in which families will be starved for heat, to enable social elites to live well.

19. Carcinogens are chemicals that induce cancers, while mutagens are chemicals that affect genetic structure. While there is not perfect overlap between the two types of effects, there is a high correlation between a chemical's mutagenicity and its carcinogenicity. For discussions of the potential for monitoring chemicals, see Gillette (1974) and the Council of Environmental Mutagen Society (1975). Conflicts around this issue are intense, since industries of various types may be severely curtailed, especially under the new U.S. Toxic Substances Control Act (e.g., Epstein, 1978; Dulbecco, 1976; Wade, 1976a,b).

20. For illustrations of various conflicts around occupational safety and health, I have drawn on the following: Boffey (1976), Wade (1976a,b), Carter (1974), and Maugh (1974).

21. Ecological critiques of agribusiness include Lappé & Collins (1977) and Pimentel et al. (1973, 1975), especially on energy costs, and Miller (1973) and Wade (1972) on reduction of genetic diversity of crops. The Pimentel pieces also include a discussion of dislocation of farmers and a rural labor force.

22. Gillette (1973) treats some of these water issues, and Woodwell (1970b) reviews productivity reduction as a result of pollution. Recent PCB and PBB problems are touched on in Carter (1976), Lyons (1977), and NYT (1978).

23. Uncertainties and changes in assessment of oil spill impacts are discussed in Adler (1973) and Browne (1978).

24. Both types of effects are analyzed in Kellogg & Schneider (1974) and agricultural effects in Damon & Kunen (1976). Hobbs et al. (1974) indicate a possible canceling of the two effects, though Laurmann (1976) emphasizes the carbon dioxide effects.

25. Oil and icebergs have two potential problems: (1) the oil pollution may increase iceberg melting (Ophuls, 1977:108; but see differing views in Adler, 1973, and Browne, 1978); (2) conversely, increased melting of icebergs from polar warming may lead to increased risk of collisions of oil tankers with icebergs (Carter, 1975).

26. Discussion of quantity versus price effects is contained in Schnaiberg (1974) and Stretton (1976). Stretton discusses government cost inflation on pp. 40–71 and catastrophic reductions in material status for groups on pp. 15–71 under the most socially regressive way of resolving resource problems. Fuller (1977) treats the effects of the dioxin pollution in Italy.

27. Barnet & Müller (1974) provide the broadest overview of the extent and mechanisms of control by multinational corporations. Wade (1974a) reviews material dependence by the U.S. on Third World commodities, and potential vulnerability (e.g., Ophuls, 1977:210–18). Some dissenting views of this vulnerability are in Fried (1976). A general overview of government fiscal problems is in O'Connor (1973).

28. The various types of policies that may be followed are examined in Schnaiberg (1975) and Stretton (1976).

29. On the domestic impact of water works, see Morgan (1971), Belt (1975), and Gillette (1972). For implications in the Third World, see Wade (1974b).

30. For capitalist versus socialist solutions, see Anderson (1976) and Stretton (1976). An emphasis on increased economic knowledge is in Ridker (1973) and on values in Krieger (1973).

REFERENCES

ABELSON, PHILLIP H.
1972   "Limits to growth." Science 175 (17 Mar.): 1197.

ADLER, CY A.
1973   Ecological Fantasies: Death From Falling Watermelons. New York: Delta Books.

AMERICAN CHEMICAL SOCIETY (ACS)
1969   Cleaning Our Environment: The Chemical Basis for Action. Washington, D.C.: American Chemical Society.

ANDERSON, CHARLES A.
1976   The Sociology of Survival: Social Problems of Growth. Homewood, Ill: Dorsey Press.

BARNET, RICHARD J. AND R.E. MÜLLER
1974   Global Reach: The Power of the Multinational Companies. New York: Simon and Schuster.

BELL, DANIEL
1973   The Coming of Post-Industrial Society: A Venture in Social Forecasting. New York: Basic Books.

BELT, C.B., JR.
1975   "The 1973 flood and man's constriction of the Mississippi River." Science 189 (29 Aug.):681–684.

BOFFEY, PHILLIP M.
1976   "Cancer from chemicals: DuPont and congressman in numbers slugfest." Science 194 (17 Dec.):1252–1256.
1977   "Academy study finds low-energy growth won't be painful." Science 195 (28 Jan.):380.

BOSERUP, ESTER
1965   The Conditions of Agricultural Growth. Chicago: Aldine.
1976   "Environment, population, and technology in primitive societies." Population and Development Review 21 (1):21–36.

BOUGHEY, ARTHUR S.
1968   Ecology of Populations. New York: Macmillan.

BRAIDWOOD, ROBERT J.
1971   "The agricultural revolution." Pp. 17–25 in P.R. Ehrlich, J.P. Hol-

dren, and R.W. Holm (eds.), Man and the Ecosphere. San Francisco: W.H. Freeman.

BROOKS, DAVID B. AND P.W. ANDREWS
1974   "Mineral resources, economic growth and world population." Science 185 (5 July):13–20.

BROWN, HARRISON
1954   The Challenge of Man's Future. New York: Viking.
1970   "Human materials production as a process in the biosphere." Pp. 115–124 by the editors of Scientific American, The Biosphere. San Francisco: W.H. Freeman.

BROWN, LESTER R.
1970   "Human food production as a process in the biosphere." Pp. 93–104 by the editors of Scientific American, The Biosphere. San Francisco: W.H. Freeman.
1974   By Bread Alone. New York: Praeger.
1975   "The world food prospect." Science 190 (12 Dec.): 1053–1059.

BROWNE, MALCOLM W.
1978   "Science finds some blessings in oil spills." New York Times, April 2.

BRYSON, REID A.
1974   "A perspective on climatic change." Science 184 (17 May):753–760.

CARPENTER, RICHARD A.
1976   "Tensions between materials and environmental quality." Science 191 (20 Feb.):665–668.

CARTER, LUTHER J.
1969   "Development in the poor nations: How to avoid fouling the nest." Science 163 (7 Mar.):1046–1048.
1974   "Cancer and the environment (I): A creaky system grinds on." Science 186 (18 Oct.):239–242.
1975   "Icebergs and oil tankers: USGS glaciologists are concerned." Science 190 (14 Nov.):641–643.
1976   "Michigan's PBB incident: Chemical mix-up leads to disaster." Science 192 (16 April):240–243.

CHILDE, V. GORDON
1951   Man Makes Himself. New York: New American Library.

CLARK, COLIN W.
1973   "The economics of overexploitation." Science 181 (17 Aug.):630–634.

CLOUD, PRESTON AND A. GIBOR
1970   "The oxygen cycle." Pp. 57–68 by the editors of Scientific American, The Biosphere. San Francisco: W.H. Freeman.

COMMONER, BARRY
1972   The Closing Circle: Nature, Man and Technology. New York: Alfred A. Knopf.
1977   The Poverty of Power: Energy and the Economic Crisis. New York: Bantam.

COOK, EARL
  1976 "Limits to exploitation of nonrenewable resources." Science 191 (20 Feb.):677–682.

COTTRELL, FRED
  1955 Energy and Society: The Relation between Energy, Social Change and Economic Development. New York: McGraw-Hill.

COUNCIL OF ENVIRONMENTAL MUTAGEN SOCIETY
  1975 "Environmental mutagenic hazards." Science 187 (14 Feb.):503–514.

CRENSON, MATTHEW A.
  1971 The Un-Politics of Air Pollution: A Study of Non-Decisionmaking in the Cities. Baltimore: Johns Hopkins Press.

DAMON, PAUL E. AND KUNEN, S.M.
  1976 "Global cooling." Science 193 (6 Aug.):447–453.

DAVIS, KINGSLEY
  1971 "The urbanization of the human population." Pp. 267–279 in P.R. Ehrlich, J.P. Holdren, and R.W. Holm (eds.), Man and the Ecosphere. San Francisco: W.H. Freeman.

DE BELL, GARRETT
  1970 The Environmental Handbook. New York: Ballantine.

DEEVEY, EDWARD J., JR.
  1971 "The human population." Pp. 49–55 in P.R. Ehrlich, J.P. Holdren, and R.W. Holm, (eds.), Man and the Ecosphere. San Francisco: W.H. Freeman.

DELWICHE, C.C.
  1970 "The nitrogen cycle." Pp. 69–80 by the editors of Scientific American, The Biosphere. San Francisco: W.H. Freeman.

DILLMAN, DON A. AND J.A. CHRISTENSON
  1972 "The public value for pollution control." Pp. 237–256 in W.R. Burch, Jr., N.H. Cheek, Jr. and L. Taylor (eds.), Social Behavior, Natural Resources, and the Environment. New York: Harper and Row.

DULBECCO, RENATO
  1976 "From the molecular biology of oncogenic DNA viruses to cancer." Science 192 (30 Apr.):437–440.

DUNLAP, RILEY E. AND W.R. CATTON, JR.
  1978 "Environmental sociology: A framework for analysis." Paper presented at meetings of Rural Sociology Society and Society for Study of Social Problems. (Forthcoming, 1979, in T. O'Riodan and R.C. d'Arge (eds.), Progress in Resource Management and Environmental Planning, Vol. 1. Chicester, Eng.: Wiley.)

DURKHEIM, EMILE
  1964 The Division of Labor in Society. Translated by A. Simpson. New York: Free Press.

EHRLICH, PAUL

1970   "Eco-Catastrophe." Pp. 1–14 by the editors of Ramparts, Eco-Catastrophe. San Francisco: Canfield Press.

EHRLICH, PAUL R. AND A.H. EHRLICH

1972   Population, Resources, Environment: Issues in Human Ecology. Second Edition. San Francisco: W.H. Freeman.

EPSTEIN, SAMUEL S.

1978   The Politics of Cancer. San Francisco: Sierra Club.

FABRICANT, NEIL AND R.M. HALLMAN

1971   Toward a Rational Power Policy. New York: Braziller.

FISCHMAN, LEONARD L.

1978   "Public perceptions of the energy problem." Resources 57 (Jan.–Mar.):2ff.

FORBES, R.J.

1968   The Conquest of Nature: Technology and Its Consequences. New York: New American Library.

FRIED, EDWARD R.

1976   "International trade in raw materials: Myths and realities." Science 191 (20 Feb.):641–645.

FULLER, JOHN G.

1977   The Poison that Fell from the Sky. New York: Random House.

GALE, RICHARD P.

1972   "From sit-in to hike-in: A comparison of the civil rights and environmental movements." Pp. 280–305 in W.R. Burch, Jr., N.H. Cheek, Jr., and L. Taylor (eds.), Social Behavior, Natural Resources and the Environment. New York: Harper and Row.

GILLETTE, ROBERT

1972a *The Limits to Growth:* Hard sell for a computer view of doomsday." Science 175 (10 Mar.):1088–1092.

1972b "Stream channelization: Conflict between ditchers, conservationists." Science 176 (26 May):890–894.

1973   "Western coal: Does the debate follow irreversible commitment?" Science 182 (2 Nov.):456–458.

1974   "Cancer and the environment (II): Groping for new remedies." Science 186 (18 Oct.):242–245.

GILLILAND, MARTHA W.

1975   "Energy analysis and public policy." Science 189 (26 Sept.):1051–1056.

GOELLER, H.E. AND A.M. WEINBERG

1976   "The age of substitutability." Science 191 (20 Feb.):683–689.

HAMMOND, ALLEN L.

1975   "Ozone destruction: Problem's scope grows, its urgency recedes." Science 187 (28 Mar.):1181–1183.

HAMMOND, ALLEN L. AND T.H. MAUGH, II
1974   "Stratospheric pollution: Multiple threats to earth's ozone." Science 186 (18 Oct.):335–338.

HARRIS, MARVIN
1977a   Cannibals and Kings: The Origins of Cultures. New York: Random House.
1977b   "Why men dominate women." New York Times Magazine (13 Nov.): 46ff.

HARRY, JOSEPH
1974   "Causes of contemporary environmentalism." Humboldt Journal of Social Relations 2 (1):3–7.

HAYES, EARL T.
1976   "Energy implications of materials processing." Science 191 (20 Feb.):661–665.

HELLMAN, PETER
1976   "For the Hudson, bad news and good." New York Times Magazine (24 Oct.):16–38.

HOBBS, P.V., H. HARRISON, AND E. ROBINSON
1974   "Atmospheric effects of pollutants." Science 183 (8 Mar.):909–915.

HUETTNER, DAVID A.
1976   "Net energy analysis: An economic assessment." Science 192 (9 April):101–104.

HUTCHINSON, G. EVELYN
1970   "The biosphere." Pp. 1–11 by the editors of Scientific American, The Biosphere. San Francisco: W.H. Freeman.

IVERSON, JOHANNES S.
1971   "Forest clearance in the Stone Age." Pp. 26–31 in P.R. Ehrlich, J.W. Holdren, and R.W. Holm (eds.), Man and the Ecosphere. San Francisco: W.H. Freeman.

JOHNSON, WALLACE H.
1976   "Social impact of pollution control legislation." Science 192 (14 May):629–631.

KELLOGG, W.W. AND SCHNEIDER, S.H.
1974   "Climate stabilization: For better or worse?" Science 186 (27 Dec.):1163–1172.

KORMONDY, EDWARD J.
1969   Concepts of Ecology. Englewood Cliffs, N.J.: Prentice Hall.

KRIEGER, MARTIN H.
1973   "What's wrong with plastic trees?" Science 179 (2 Feb.):446–455.

LANDSBERG, HANS H.
1976   "Materials: Some recent trends and issues." Science 191 (20 Feb.):637–641.

LAPPÉ, FRANCIS M. AND J. COLLINS
1977   Food First: Beyond the Myth of Scarcity. Boston: Houghton Mifflin.

LAURMANN, J.A.
1976   "Climate research." Science 191 (12 Mar.):1002–1004.

LINDSAY, JOHN V.
1970   "The plight of the cities." The Progressive (April):29–31. (Issue on: The Crisis of Survival.)

LINDSEY, ROBERT
1978   "Tax-exempt foundations formed to help business fight regulation." New York Times, 12 Feb.

LYONS, RICHARD D.
1977   "Pesticide: Boon and possible bane." New York Times, 1 Dec.
1979   "Middletown keeps count on levels of contamination." New York Times, 8 Apr.

MARTIN, PAUL S.
1973   "The discovery of America." Science 179 (9 Mar.):969–974.

MARX, LEO
1964   The Machine in the Garden: Technology and the Pastoral Ideal in America. New York: Oxford University Press.

MAUGH, THOMAS H., II
1972   "Carbon monoxide: Natural sources dwarf man's output." Science 177 (28 July):338–339.
1974   "Chemical carcinogenesis: A long-neglected field blossoms." Science 183 (8 Mar.):940–944.
1976   "The ozone layer: The threat from aerosol cans is real." Science 194 (8 Oct.):70–72.

MAY, ROBERT M.
1973   Stability and Complexity in Model Ecosystems. Princeton, N.J.: Princeton University Press.

MCEVOY, JAMES, III
1972   "The American concern with environment." Pp. 214–236 in W.R. Burch, Jr., N.H. Cheek, Jr., and L. Taylor (eds.), Social Behavior, Natural Resources, and the Environment. New York: Harper and Row.

MCKEOWN, THOMAS AND R.G. RECORD
1962   "Reasons for the decline of mortality in England and Wales during the nineteenth century." Population Studies 16 (1):94–122.

MCKEOWN, THOMAS, R.G. RECORD, AND R.D. TURNER
1972   "An interpretation of the modern rise of population in Europe." Population Studies 26 (3):345–382.

MEADOWS, DONNELLA H., D.L. MEADOWS, J. RANDERS, AND W.W. BEHRENS III
1972   The Limits to Growth. New York: Universe Books.

MESAROVIC, MIHAJLO AND E. PESTEL
1974   Mankind at the Turning Point: The Second Report of the Club of Rome.
New York: New American Library.

MICHELSON, WILLIAM
1977   Environmental Choice, Human Behavior, and Residential Satisfaction.
New York: Oxford University Press.

MILLER, JUDITH
1973   "Genetic erosion: Crop plants threatened by government neglect." Science
182 (21 Dec.):1231–1233.

MITCHELL, ROBERT C.
1978   "Environment: An enduring concern." Resources 57 (Jan.–Mar.):1 ff.

MORGAN, ARTHUR E.
1971   Dams and Other Disasters: A Century of the Army Corps of Engineers in
Civil Works. Boston: Porter Sargent.

MORRISON, DENTON L., K.E. HORNBACK, AND W.K. WARNER
1972   "The environmental movement: Some preliminary observations and predictions." Pp. 259–279 in W.R. Burch, Jr., N.H. Cheek, Jr., and L.
Taylor (eds.), Social Behavior, Natural Resources, and the Environment.
New York: Harper and Row.

MUMFORD, LEWIS
1963   Technics and Civilization. New York: Harcourt, Brace, and World.
1967   The Myth of the Machine: Technics and Human Development. New
York: Harcourt, Brace, Jovanovich.
1970   The Myth of the Machine: The Pentagon of Power. New York: Harcourt, Brace, Jovanovich.

NATIONAL ACADEMY OF SCIENCES/NATIONAL RESEARCH COUNCIL (NAS/NRC)
1969   Resources and Man: A Study and Recommendations. National Academy
of Sciences/National Research Council. San Francisco: W.H. Freeman.

NEW YORK TIMES (NYT)
1978   "Experts testing 3,500 in Michigan for PBB effects." New York Times,
7 May.

O'CONNOR, JAMES
1973   The Fiscal Crisis of the State. New York: St. Martin's Press.

ODUM, EUGENE P.
1963   Ecology. New York: Holt, Rinehart, and Winston.
1969   "The strategy of ecosystem development." Science 164 (18 Apr.):262–
270.

ODUM, HOWARD T.
1971   Environment, Power, and Society. New York: John Wiley.

O'NEILL, GERARD K.
1975   "Space colonies and energy supply to the earth." Science 190 (5
Dec.):943–947.

OORT, ABRAHAM H.
1970   "The energy cycle of the earth." Pp. 13–23 by the editors of Scientific American, The Biosphere. San Francisco: W.H. Freeman.

OPHULS, WILLIAM
1977   Ecology and the Politics of Scarcity: Prologue to a Political Theory of the Steady State. San Francisco: W.H. Freeman.

PARISI, ANTHONY J.
1979   "Nuclear power: The bottom line gets fuzzier." New York Times, 8 Apr.

PENMAN, H.L.
1970   "The water cycle." Pp. 37–46 by the editors of Scientific American, The Biosphere. San Francisco: W.H. Freeman.

PETT, SAUL
1972   "The quality of life." Pp. 13–22 in R.R. Campbell and J.L. Wade (eds.), Society and Environment: The Coming Collision. Boston: Allyn and Bacon.

PIELOU, E.C.
1975   Ecological Diversity. New York: John Wiley.

PIMENTEL, DAVID, L.E. HURD, A.C. BELLOTTI, M.J. FORSTER, I.N. OKA, O.D. SHOLES, AND R.J. WHITMAN
1973   "Food production and the energy crisis." Science 182 (2 Nov.):443–449.

PIMENTEL, DAVID, W. DRITSCHILO, J. KRUMMEL, AND J. KUTZMAN
1975   "Energy and land constraints in food protein production." Science 190 (21 Nov.):754–761.

PIMENTEL, DAVID, E.C. TERHUNE, R. DYSON-HUDSON, S. ROCHEREAU, R. SAMIS, E.A. SMITH, D. DENMAN, D. REIFSCHNEIDER, AND M. SHEPARD
1976   "Land degradation: Effects on food and energy resources." Science 194 (8 Oct.):149–155.

PLASS, GILBERT N.
1971   "Carbon dioxide and climate." Pp. 173–179 in P.R. Ehrlich, J.W. Holdren, and R.W. Holm (eds.), Man and the Ecosphere. San Francisco: W.H. Freeman.

REGIER, H.A. AND HARTMAN, W.L.
1973   "Lake Erie's fish community: 150 years of cultural stresses." Science 180 (22 June):1248–1255.

RIDKER, RONALD G.
1972   "Population and pollution in the United States." Science 176 (9 June):1085–1090.
1973   "To grow or not to grow: That's not the relevant question." Science 182 (28 Dec.):1315–1318.

ROCHLIN, GENE I.
1977   "Nuclear waste disposal: Two social criteria." Science 195 (7 Jan.):23–31.

SAGAN, L.A.
1972 "Human costs of nuclear power." Science 177 (11 Aug.):487-493.

SCHNAIBERG, ALLAN
1974 "Social conflicts in environmental decisions." Pp. 49-75 in J.E. Quon (ed.), Environmental Impact Assessment. Evanston, Ill.: Technological Institute, Northwestern University.
1975 "Social syntheses of the societal-environmental dialectic: The role of distributional impacts." Social Science Quarterly 56 (June):5-20.

SINGER, S. FRED
1970 "Human energy production as a process in the biosphere." Pp. 93-103 by the editors of Scientific American, The Biosphere. San Francisco: W.H. Freeman.

SPECTOR, MALCOLM AND J.I. KITSUSE
1977 Constructing Social Problems. Menlo Park, Cal.: Cummings Publishing Co.

STEINHART, CAROL E. AND J.S. STEINHART
1974 Energy: Sources, Use and Role in Human Affairs. North Scituate, Mass.: Duxbury Press.

STRETTON, HUGH
1976 Capitalism, Socialism and the Environment. Cambridge: Cambridge University Press.

WADE, NICHOLAS
1972 "A message from the corn blight: The dangers of uniformity." Science 177 (25 Aug.): 678-679.
1974a "Raw materials: U.S. grows more vulnerable to Third World cartels." Science 183 (18 Jan.):185-187.
1974b "Sahelian drought: No victory for western aid." Science 185 (19 July):234-237.
1976a "Control of toxic substances: An idea whose time has nearly come." Science 191 (13 Feb.):541-544.
1976b "Cancer Institute: Expert charges neglect of carcinogenesis studies." Science 192 (7 May):529-531.

WARD, BARBARA
1976 The Home of Man. New York: W.W. Norton.

WATSON, RICHARD A. AND P.J. WATSON
1969 Man and Nature: An Anthropological Essay in Human Ecology. New York: Harcourt, Brace, and World.

WEINBERG, ALVIN M.
1972 "Social institutions and nuclear energy." Science 177 (7 July):27-34.

WESTMAN, WALTER E. AND R.M. GIFFORD
1973 "Environmental impact: Controlling the overall level." Science 181 (31 Aug.):819-825.

WHITTAKER, ROBERT H.
1970 Communities and Ecosystems. New York: Macmillan.

WOFSKY, STEVEN C., M.B. MCELROY, AND N. DAK SZE
1975 "Freon consumption: Implications for atmospheric ozone." Science 187 (14 Feb.):535–538.

WOODWELL, GEORGE M.
1970a "The energy cycle of the biosphere." Pp. 25–36 by the editors of Scientific American, The Biosphere. San Francisco: W.H. Freeman.
1970b "Effects of pollution on the structure and physiology of ecosystems." Science 168 (24 Apr.):429–433.
1974 "Biotic energy flows." Science 183 (1 Feb.):366.

WRIGLEY, E.A.
1969 Population and History. New York: McGraw-Hill.

YERGIN, DANIEL
1978 "The real meaning of the energy crunch." New York Times Magazine, June 4:32ff.

2 THE SEARCH FOR CAUSES AND SOLUTIONS

II POPULATION
Paradoxes of the Hydra Monster

THE LOGIC OF POPULATIONISM

Populationism: Essential Propositions

One of the major theses that has developed in conjunction with the environmental concerns of the last decade is that population control is a key element in protecting the biosphere and its ecosystems. There are diverse forms of this argument. One is: Without population control, any other form of environmental protection is doomed to failure, either immediately or in the longer run. Another is: Population control is an essential accompaniment to any other social program for environmental protection. A third is: Population control is a useful adjunct to other social programs to prevent ecosystem disorganization. These three positions are variants on what I call *populationism*, ranging from the strongest (the first) to the weakest (the third). Populationism is here defined as a social ideology that attributes social ills to the numbers of humans. It is now and has been historically associated with a variety of social movements, many of which have focused on particular categories of humans whose numbers are defined as a problem. This history is important in understanding why many groups oppose the modern version of populationism, and why direct population control efforts, even if desirable to reduce production and biospheric withdrawals and additions, are not likely to be adopted.[1]

As part of the social responses to renewed concern with ecosystem protection, the modern populationist movement—characterized by groups such as Zero Population Growth, Inc.—defines its premises and objectives as follows:

1. Population growth has increased substantially in the last century.
2. This growth has occurred initially in industrial societies, and later in underdeveloped countries.
3. The primary factor in such population growth has been the decline in human mortality.
4. Population growth is greater than food production growth in underdeveloped countries, causing food shortages, hunger, and malnutrition.
5. Population growth in developed industrial countries is causing increases in production, hence biospheric withdrawals and additions, and ecosystem disorganization.
6. Without concerted social efforts, population growth will continue in both developed and underdeveloped countries, increasing both food and other ecosystem resource scarcities.
7. These efforts are required immediately and in the foreseeable future to prevent continuation of population growth and ecosystem disorganization.
8. Such population control efforts must either take priority over any other programs of production and consumption adjustment, *or* be placed on a parity with such programs to protect the biosphere.

The position taken in this chapter concurs fully only with the first three of these propositions. Though there is considerable uncertainty in the literature on population issues, my own responses[2] to the remaining five components of a populationist program are as follows:

4a. Population growth has only occasionally been greater than food production growth; and it has only in part been responsible for hunger and malnutrition in the underdeveloped countries.
5a. Population growth has been responsible for only a modest share of increases in production and biospheric withdrawals and additions.
6a. Population growth has slowed substantially in developed countries, without any overt population control efforts. It has slowed some in underdeveloped countries, in small part because of family planning programs and in larger part because of changed social welfare conditions.
7a. While some family planning efforts are useful at present and in the future to reduce unwanted births, programs of social welfare will be far more important in sustaining and extending reductions of population growth rates in underdeveloped countries. In developed countries, there is little reason to anticipate any sustained significant population growth in the future.

8a. Production and consumption adjustment programs are far more crucial to biospheric protection programs than are population control programs, and may have more impact on population growth reduction in the future as well.

Thus, while I concur that population growth in the modern period is of unprecedented magnitude, my position is at most one of very weak populationism. This chapter will raise questions about our knowledge of how much the increase in population has contributed to sociocultural production growth in the past. This issue will be further pursued in Chapter IV, where several models of a population's consumption growth will be explored. My view is that social factors inducing technological change and increases in production have been more dominant in the modern rise in production, especially in developed industrial societies. Contrary to some antipopulationists, though, I view these social factors as far less directly linked to population growth and growth in consumer demand (Simon, 1977; Neuhaus, 1971).

Two bases for my position are: (1) the relationship between a population's size and its sociocultural production is very weak, except for very extreme cases; and (2) the modern populationism and all its historical precedents have ultimately been socially regressive and reactionary, and often racist as well (Chase, 1971: Ch. XI, 1977: Ch. 16; Neuhaus, 1971). The first assumption raises questions about the environmental control efficacy of any population control program. The second one raises doubts about the social and political efficacy of population control programs, and certainly about the social justice of such programs.

I share Simon's (1977:xxii) position on the economic effects of population growth:

> These facts did not and do not persuade me that population growth is good; the data are too weak for that. But they are strong enough to cause me to distrust Malthusian theorizing which is the basis of almost all academic structures about population growth's ill effects.

Simon points to a number of paradoxes regarding population growth and its effects. I share his concern with the intellectual and moral problems of these paradoxes, though I see somewhat different paradoxes and social responses. The following parable is an illustration.

A Parable

Once upon a time there lived a social scientist who taught in a distinguished American university. During one academic quarter, he taught two courses: one on the "population problem" and one on "environmental problems." In the midst of one of his environmental problems lectures, a strange and embarassing thought crossed his mind. But he dismissed it and finished his lecture. Retreating to the safety of his office, he began to reflect on the awkward thought:

> How strange it is. In my population problems course, I spend much time decrying the rapid growth of population in underdeveloped countries, noting how deleterious it is for development (defined as increased production and consumption per person). The model I use there is: if family size (and hence population growth) were to be reduced, families would have more money to invest and consume, thereby raising their familial welfare and that of the society.
>
> On the other hand, in my environmental problem course, I decry population growth in industrial-developed societies. The model is equally straightforward: with reduced population growth, the society will make fewer demands on scarce resources, since it will produce and consume less.
>
> But these models are logically contradictory. In the first, reduced population growth should lead to *increased* production and consumption per family. In the latter, reduced population growth should lead to *decreased* familial and societal consumption—hence a reduction of future environmental withdrawals and additions.

In the years following, the professor struggled to understand why it had taken him so long to reach this recognition, and what the paradox implied for the role of population growth in both underdevelopment and environmental problems. He is still struggling with these issues in this book.

Reflections on the Parable

Human populations, organized in a society, are abstractions. They are made up of socially more meaningful units called families. In one sense, population is a concept not unlike that of traffic. We define ourselves as somehow *in* it, but do not define ourselves as a component *of* it. Barnett (1970) has demonstrated the discrepancy by his small survey of U.S. parents, who acknowledged the existence of a U.S. population problem, when average size of families exceeded two or three children. They did not see their own families (which exceeded this size) as part of the population problem, however.[3]

Further, parents (or potential parents) make decisions to have additional children. If these additional numbers of children, when aggregated in societies and the world, generate high production and environmental stress, we have to deal with the parents and their decision making. Neither governments nor institutions "have" children: parents do. Neither governments nor institutions directly allocate resources within a family (although they may have substantial influence on this): parents do. Conversely, most parents do not control very many of the factors of production, even their own labor, in much of the modern world.

Let me now return to the parable for a short time. The paradox that emerges can be reformulated first at the familial level. Consider Mr. and Mrs. X, who have two children, aged 4 and 2 years. Their current annual income is $7000, or 7000 rupees (depending on whether you think of them in the U.S. or in India). Let us suppose that an additional child will cost the family about $800 (or rupees) per year, on the average. The development argument would suggest that the parents would be better off by using the $800 saved to (1) invest in some productive activities that the parents are engaged in; (2) invest in better health, nutrition, and education of their two children; (3) some of both; or (4) have the government invest for them in productive infrastructure or equipment.

From an environmental accounting perspective, we have to think very carefully about this expenditure of $800. If the parents had decided to have another child, this would have required some mixture of goods and services to support this additional member of the population/family. But even if this childrearing expenditure is foregone, the parental decision concerning what to do with this extra $800 can greatly influence levels of environmental withdrawals/additions. In only one case—that of social confiscation (or deflation) of this $800—can we be at all certain that environmental withdrawals and additions will be lower than if such parents had opted for the extra child.[4] In every other case, we have to examine closely the allocation of this money to various forms of consumption or savings, both of which result in some form of increased production. Moreover, this is so regardless of whether the parents spend all of the money themselves, or the government taxes away some of this and allocates these funds to various governmental agencies.

How do such behaviors change the biosphere? When families or governments improve familial welfare by conventional expansions of the productive forces of the society, it is likely that the rate of withdrawals/additions is going to increase. As societal freedom to use the additional $800 increases, there is generally a pressure away from traditional sustenance activities of farming and creating shelter for the family (Hall, 1973). Following the historical model (see Ch. III), investments are often made in high-technology enterprises involving higher energy and material extraction. In other cases, these investments can be made in social services, such as education and health services. For these latter types of investments, there may be lower levels of environmental withdrawals and additions than in the child-based expenditure of $800. Insofar as these expenditures are aimed at social activities that are more labor-intensive and less material-intensive than the child-based expenditures, then, we have gained some environmental advantage by foregoing the birth.

How likely are we to realize both familial welfare and environmental stress gains from foregoing births? In theory, parents and society are freer to allocate expenditures when the extra child is not born. But this freedom also permits higher levels of ecosystem disorganization per dollar expended. In underdeveloped countries, there is strong pressure to expand goods production and hence increase withdrawals/additions with additional investments from such savings. But even in developed countries like the United States, it is not clear that the savings from foregoing another child will be channeled into less materially-intensive forms of production.[5] While it is true that families may purchase more services, many of these, including recreational ones, have become far more energy-intensive than traditional forms of services (see Ch. IV). There is no biological necessity for this, of course, but social and economic forces are just as real as biological ones. Moreover, neither banking nor heavy taxation of savings in such families is cause for environmentalist satisfaction. Savings are typically placed in financial institutions, which then allocate these for various forms of production expansion through loans or stock purchases. Taxation of such savings may have mixed blessings as well, as governments enhance the expansion of production (military and civilian), although they can also provide fairly labor-intensive services (O'Connor, 1973) for the tax dollar (see Ch. V).

The paradox of the central parable is transformed, then. We started talking about population increases, but the outcome finally hinges on sociocultural allocation decisions—on the expenditures of families, financial institutions, producers, and governments. With one exception, population issues can be relatively independent of the economic/ allocative ones. The exception is that population growth reduces some societal and familial options. This occurs in both consumption and production organization. In terms of consumption, some additional expenditures are required to support childrearing, though parents and social institutions vary in their allocations per child (Ch. IV).

In terms of production, adults added to the population must find some form of employment, either in the monetized or home production sectors. However, as in the case with consumption, these new labor force entrants can only absorb at any given time the existing capital (both liquid capital and physical plant and equipment) in the society. Therefore, in the short-run (by the child's twentieth birthday), there is little change in the productive capacity of the society. Thereafter, multiple paths are possible, and none determined solely or even primarily by population growth. Labor force additions will use the capital allocated them in sociocultural production that (1) increases the rate of withdrawals/additions per unit capital over the previous average, (2) decreases this rate, or (3) leaves the rate unchanged.

Unless the stock of capital in the society were to go unused in the absence of this growth in labor force (and of consumers)—the problem of capital surplus—these new workers would thereby affect total ecological disorganization in the following ways. For the first case, they would increase total disorganization; for the second, they would decrease it; and for the third, they would leave it unchanged. Other economic and ecological consequences are likewise uncertain, over the long run, because these workers might increase, decrease, or leave unaffected the total pool of capital in the future. In developed societies, the historical pattern has been to increase this pool, though the contributions of labor are not that clear (Ch. III, V). In underdeveloped countries, it is claimed that these new workers absorb scarce capital, thereby reducing the pool of capital in the future—the essence of the underdevelopment problem. Theoretically, this should *reduce* future growth of production and environmental withdrawals and additions.[6]

As with the consumption of this population growth, then, the production implications depend in the short and long run on allocative decisions. Social institutions, such as firms, governments, and (in fewer cases) families will make various of these decisions. In no case is there a necessarily singular direct relationship between growth in consumers or growth in workers and particular forms of sociocultural production and of environmental withdrawals/additions. Even the biological needs of this growth in consumers can be met to varying degrees, and through varying forms of production. People can be more or less nourished and better or worse housed, as in the present differences between and within the developed and underdeveloped blocs. Agricultural production can be more or less labor- or capital-intensive, with varying degrees of ecosystem disorganization. This can be observed historically as well as contemporaneously.[7]

Thus, the paradox of the parable can be resolved in the following way. In the developed world, each additional person has a substantial effect on consumption and production. By channeling this saved consumption and production in less intense use of ecosystem resources, we could meliorate our total withdrawals and additions. In underdeveloped countries, though, each additional person has a smaller effect on consumption and production. If we can avoid adding a number of such persons, it may be possible to increase the intensity of use of ecosystems of the remaining population, without raising the total withdrawals and additions too much. Otherwise, we increase development in the underdeveloped world only at the cost of increasing ecosystem disorganization. The ideal outcome would mean populations in the developed world "undeveloping" or "decoupling" their economies from environmental resources more. Populations in the underdeveloped world would do the reverse—at least as far as energy usage is concerned (Tinbergen, 1975). Whether this is politically feasible is a serious question. But all these options are *demographically* feasible.

A negative response to the above argument would stress that the historical record shows that population increases have caused more environmentally-intense consumption and production, in terms of energy at least. Two problems exist: (1) the supporting data for this are rather weak, and (2) even if this were true in the past, this does not preclude a variety of future options.

The Population Problems Model:
Loopholes, Uncertainties, and Inferential Leaps

The strong populationist argument described earlier is merely the most recent form of a long historical line of population problems models. Poverty, filth, crime, overcrowding, illness, and virtually every social ill can be traced through such a model. Such history is important for understanding the political and social forces (Holden, 1974) surrounding current populationist concerns (see p. 91).[8] My concern here, however, is with the empirical and logical pitfalls in using such models to assess the environmental impact of growing populations in today's biosphere.

Consider any event that society has defined as a problem. Suppose that N number of events occur in a given year, in a society with a population sized P. With no other information, we can immediately construct the following analytic model:

$$N = P \times R$$

where R is the problem rate. From this purely arithmetic operation, devoid of any substantive meaning, we can see the problem as a "population problem." That is, if only we lowered P, then N should be lowered as well. Both the developmental and the environmental problems of our parable have this analytic form. The only difference is that in the former, N represents something like family consumption, while in the latter, it represents extraction of environmental resources.

N can represent the poverty population, criminal acts, or any other social pathology. The equation provides a static decomposition, but suggests the dynamics of a causal system (Ridker, 1972). That is, it is *assumed* that it is P that causes N, at a rate R. In actual fact, many of these models are circular: R is computed by taking the relevant population total and dividing it into N, the total frequency of social ills. If the hidden assumptions are true, then this is a logically and empirically accurate step. These assumptions include: (1) P is the relevant population causing the problem, (2) there are no substantial variations or subdivisions within P, and (3) both P and N are accurately measured. On the other hand, the computations of such a model tell us nothing about the underlying causal processes. If they are inaccurate—that is, if the relationship between P and N is spurious—we can still compute the "impact" of population P according to the algebraic model. In part, the confusion is possible because R

is typically not a rate but a computed ratio between two social accounts: a population account and a social ills account.[9]

This helps to explain the potential for false populationist arguments. Most contemporary societies keep some population accounts—either directly or through the United Nations efforts. And many societies have some records of particular social ills: poverty, illness, pollution, etc. What societies often lack is the detailed record of all the institutional contributions to such problems (see Ch. VI, VII). Thus, it is difficult to see how employers underpay or underemploy workers, how industries may pollute or extract energy, how governments stimulate social welfare or production. We have outcomes, therefore, but lack process data. But we do typically have population data, which is collected for purposes ranging from conscription and taxation to democratic representation in government. Therefore, anyone with a populationist bias can readily draw on the two separate accounts, and make the resulting statement appear to be a processual or causal statement.

If the lack of any causal connection were not enough of a logical problem with such formal models, we have still another confusion that potentially exists. Our construct R can either indicate problems being *caused by P*, or *happening to P*. That is, P can be viewed either as an active causal agent, or the recipient/victim of some social ill (N). For demographers, the concept of a "rate" implies the "risk of an event occuring *in* the population." Demographers speak of fertility rates, in which a population is deciding to have babies. They equally well speak of mortality from cancers, in which the population is attacked by external and internal agents. It is clear that the population is causing babies to be born. But it strains our sense of causation to say that the population is actually causing cancer. It would make more sense to refer to this as a kind of *victimization* rate, as distinct from the causation rate of fertility.

For many underdeveloped countries, then, whatever impact of population growth exists on hunger and malnutrition, it is not environmental degradation that is resulting but population victimization. Such is also the case for some dimensions of overcrowding of the poor, where the effects are visited directly onto these groups and do not affect other ecosystems and the welfare of other parts of the population. Indeed, they often enhance the welfare of the rich by concentrating poverty out of sight. Other aspects of environmental degradation, such as diminution of animal habitat, overgrazing, and deforestation due to firewood needs, are at least in part results of population growth, and thus in part true population problems. But we have little systematic data on *patterns* of environmental usage by a variety of workers and consumers. It is, therefore, very premature to make estimates of any population impact. Households, consumers, workers, governments, owners, and managers: all of these are involved in sociocultural systems of production. To extract from this some simple population, consumer (Ch. IV), or producer (Ch. V) model is premature. We simply cannot yet estimate what the historical environmental "impacts" of population growth have been, and may never be able to partition some of them out (Ch. VII). Second, and more important, the above discussion of the parable indicates that once a sociocultural production system is in operation, it is unclear to what extent these historical impacts will be replicated in the future. It depends on the future allocative decisions made within the social system. On the one hand, as Stretton argues (1976:98–104), such allocative decisions are far freer once societies escape the bedrock of absolute biological scarcity. On the other hand, the political, social, and economic forces established historically are not easy to overcome. This may mean that the environmental impacts will occur with or without population growth in some systems. Other political and social systems may respond differently in productive decisions, depending on future population growth.[10]

Types of Population Problems

Up to now, our discussion of population has been limited to its growth. Unfortunately, the existing literature covers many different aspects of population as contributing to environmental decay. Although all of these are variations on the theme of growth, the differences are important for both analysis and policy evaluation. Each will be critically evaluated in this section.

WORLD POPULATION GROWTH   Perhaps the most intuitive link to the concept of the biosphere or "spaceship Earth" is the concept of world or global population and its growth. This level of concern is most vulnerable to the logical problems enumerated in the previous section. First, it is clear that "the world population" consumes resources at very different rates. Energy consumption rates in the U.S. are perhaps *fifty* times what they are in India. Even food consumption rates per capita in the U.S. appear to be about 2½ times what they are in India, despite the fact that food intake is presumed to reflect universal biological needs. The obverse of this, of course, is the unhappy fact that a substantial portion of India's population is severely malnourished. Second, the actual relationship between a given society's population and its resource usage varies, particularly in contrasting industrial with agricultural societies. That is, the social *causes* are quite different. Contrast the 5 percent of the U.S. population engaged in agriculture with the 60 percent or more of the Indian population so engaged, for example. Conversely, contrast the capital investment per acre in U.S. agriculture with that of India, and a totally different sociocultural structure of man/land relations appears in the two societies (Brown, 1974).

The one logical asset that this concept has is the fact that the world *is* a closed system, as far as human population is concerned. And it is the one level at which large elements of the biosphere, the sinks such as the atmosphere and the oceans, have connections to any social unit. Finally, it is a level at which whole-earth phenomena such as dust or carbon dioxide may have general relevance. Yet most of these analytic assets refer to the effects of environmental disorganization, and not their causes, and thus confuse us still further. These are all models of victimization.

On balance, then, the use of such global models is more detrimental than enlightening. It is partly for these reasons that there has been such extensive criticism of the Club of Rome reports (Ridker, 1973; Gillette, 1972).

REGIONAL POPULATION GROWTH   If global population growth does not form a sound basis for understanding the generation of population-based environmental problems, then what of regional population growth? Two different approaches have been used here. The first is a true regional/continental model, tracing changes in historical population growth (Mesarovic & Pestel, 1974). Asian population growth has been cited as a primary factor in food shortages, malnutrition, and famine. There is a particular irony here, in that many of the areas within Asia are also those in which famines have been endemic over recorded history—well before the more rapid population growth period. Again, the confusion arises between models of victimization and those of causation. Famines appear to be due to climatic features, but the number of victims appears to be related to local population size. The situation is more confused with regard to African history, in part because of the poorer historical records.[11]

The reverse confusion may appear in the case of North American population growth. Although much attention has been focused on the post-World War II growth of U.S. population and subsequent environmental degradation, major elements of environmental decay (from the dustbowls of Kansas to the degradation of Appalachia) occurred in the earlier part of the twentieth century, when U.S. population growth was virtually at its lowest point. Even if we point to the most visible factor in U.S. environmental decay in recent decades—the automobile—it is clear that much of the social structure underlying this was created *before* World War II; and the labeling of population growth as the cause raises serious analytic questions. It is certainly true that more Americans driving their cars more have seriously degraded the environment. But population growth is only the apparent cause of automobile consumption. It explains little of the underlying factors accelerating or decelerating rates of auto usage.

Finally, we have some of the same problems as with global population models. There are substantial variations *within* regions in the population's usage of resources, and sharp changes in these over short historical periods, in which population change is minimal. In his analysis of the post-1945 history of the U.S., Commoner (1972) demonstrates this very clearly over the period of two decades.

NATIONAL POPULATION GROWTH   A narrowing of focus from broad regions to specific nations offers some advantages and some disadvantages. Advantages include a tighter connection between a society and its physical environment. The overall man/land ratio for North America conceals substantial differences among the nations of this region, in terms of industrialization and population density. Thus, examining the U.S. P and its relation to N (the environment within the United States) makes more sense. Likewise, the P/N relationship differs considerably, as between Mexico and Canada; the former has greater population density and lower production per capita.

On the other hand, there are substantial disadvantages. First, national population growth consists of two components: natural increase (the excess of births over deaths) and net immigration (the excess of immigrants over emigrants). Immigration creates certain analytic problems. Its increase in one nation is offset (at the global level) by a decline in another nation's population. For example, the strong concerns expressed in the recent report of the Presidential Commission on Population Growth and the American Future on immigration systematically ignore the fact that such immigration represents a partial solution to other nations' resource pressures (Commission, 1972: Ch. 13).

Second, the national focus obscures important variations in resource consumption by different segments *within* national population, and the shifts in such patterns over time. There is the familiar lack of a clear causal connection between national growth of population and national environmental degradation.

Third, this focus on national population growth often concentrates on *domestic* environmental stress. This has two potential flaws: (1) the "Netherlands fallacy" (Ehrlich & Holdren, 1971)—a domestic population may wreak substantial environmental degradation well beyond its own borders because of patterns of trade, investment, and the like; and (2) conversely, domestic environmental decay may be caused by other nations' populations. Indeed, world-system analyses (Wallerstein, 1974) show this to be the typical pattern of world capitalism with industrial or "core" countries exporting their resource problems to underdeveloped or "peripheral" countries. This leads to an overstatement of the population problem in the latter countries, and an understatement in the former ones.

In summary, then, although national population growth analysis gets us somewhat closer to evaluations of the impact of such growth on environmental stress, we still are far removed from the causal analysis we seek. Although there have been attempts to resolve some of the national/international confusion, the central problem of showing whether and to what extent it is population growth per se that leads to increased environmental disorganization has not been resolved. As in many areas of social analysis, moreover, continued application of the basic model will never resolve the difficulties. Only new types of data and new forms of analysis will do this.

THE PROBLEM OF DENSITY   Up to now, the issue has centered on population growth. In recent years, populationists have increasingly added to the range of causes of environmental decay the factor of population density. Unfortunately, the very definitions of density used are often quite variable. They include: (1) national density, which is merely another form of national population analysis; (2) areal density, which covers units of *territory* ranging from countries to local neighborhoods; and (3) housing unit density, or the level of population per individual housing unit (Day & Day, 1973).

The first and last of these can be treated very quickly. National density analysis suffers from all the problems noted above for national population growth. On the other hand, housing unit density (i.e., persons per room) per se does not clearly cause any significant types of environmental problems. Here again we have the confusion between causation and victimization models. Groups living in high-density quarters may suffer from the lack of space, but the mere fact of this high density doesn't by itself cause *environmental* problems.

What of the density problem? There is certainly some validity to this model. High concentrations of population place excessive demands on local ecosystems (Ehrlich & Holdren, 1971). This would include phenomena as diverse as water pollution (in lakes, rivers, or seashores), air pollution (from transportation or heating), and heat pollution (which can affect local climates through atmospheric changes). Some of these deleterious effects are inevitable consequences of the biological nature of human populations. People eat and generate wastes, they emit body heat, and they occupy some physical space. But many of the effects refer to nonbiological, social activities of these concentrated populations. This raises the question: Is it the population, or is it the set of activities that is the cause? If the density were reduced, would the environmentally deleterious activities be reduced? This is another form of asking whether population density is a necessary condition for such local environmental degradation. Conversely, we can ask: As the density increased in the past, did such activities directly result from such increases, i.e., is density a sufficient condition for environmental degradation? Unfortunately, we do not have clear answers for either of these questions.

Finally, density often permits economies of scale in solution to ecosystem disorganization. Sewage treatment plants, garbage conversion plants, mass transit, and the like may all be more economically feasible in denser areas.

Even more difficult to encompass is that local environmental problems resulting from high density may resolve environmental pressures elsewhere. This is the same problem we encountered in evaluating national population growth effects. Quite different evaluations emerge if we assess the effects of particular density patterns in a society or region, depending on where we drew the boundaries of the environment. The more narrowly we draw them, the more we find destructive effects of density. The more broadly we set them, the less destructive do they appear.

PROBLEMS OF GROWTH VERSUS PROBLEMS OF SIZE   A final issue must be dealt with here: disentangling issues of growth and those of population size. What does growth mean other than increase in size? The problem emerges when populationists focus excessively on population growth *rates*. Frequently (particularly in discussions of national population growth), all growth rates of a particular magnitude are stressed equally as determinants of environmental disorganization. If there is any validity to the population problems model, it is clear that ultimately it is the number of people that consume resources, and not growth rates.

It follows from this that the serious environmentalist concerned with world-system environmental problems must pay most attention to the largest countries, if there is any basis for a general impact of population on environmental decay. Increases or decreases in the major countries of the world are the ones that will have potentially the most global impact. India, China, Pakistan, and Indonesia together constitute over 40 percent of the world's population; the U.S., the U.S.S.R., and Japan together constitute nearly one-sixth of the world total. Yet there are many small countries that have high population growth rates, and these frequently get equal attention. In terms of impact on the flow of resources in the world and the major trends in environmental disorganization, these are not the proper focal points for population policies aimed at substantial improvement in resource availability.

A last comment is needed. The concept of "zero population growth" has gained widespread interest. It has led to important analyses and focused much attention on issues of population growth. But it has also led to another paradox. Even if zero growth were to be obtained instantaneously, national and world populations would stay at their *current* levels. The focus on zero growth often obscures the obverse:

continued levels of resource extraction at current high rates (Wolfers, 1971). If it is true that population is the most important factor, then zero population growth (and indeed, even zero economic growth) merely perpetuates contemporary rates of environmental withdrawals and additions.

The Logical Problems of the Populationist Perspective: Summary and Illustration

Before closing this portion of the chapter, several points need emphasis. First, the difficulties noted above do not necessarily mean that population growth has been irrelevant for environmental degradation. What they indicate is that we cannot yet assess how important a factor population has been. Second, the criticism presented here should demonstrate the fallacy of continuing to rely on the simple-minded arithmetic operations of the population problems model. We need to obtain far better data on what given *groups* of given populations have in fact consumed. The closer we can get to what individuals consume (both directly and indirectly), the more descriptive and useful a model we can construct to evaluate the actual effects of population size and growth. Third, we need to understand the social system factors inducing and/or permitting such consumption, in order to consider alternative forms of consumption. Fourth, even if we reach this stage of research sophistication, we must recognize that this merely gives us a view of socioenvironmental history, and not necessarily any good guide to the future, whether planned or unplanned. What real populations have done in the past is likely to differ from what they do in the future, especially if environmental degradation models are accurate (Stretton, 1976). Thus the population/environment relationship can, at best, give us a partial causation model—but not necessarily a model of solutions to the environmental problems.

To illustrate some of the logical problems noted earlier, consider increases in automobile ownership in the U.S. From 1960 to 1970, population grew by about 23.8 million. In the same period, private automobiles increased by about 21.8 million. Using the population problems model for these two accounts, we can arrive at the following estimates:

Rise in autos from growth of population only: 12.5 million

Rise in autos from population growth, multiplied by growth in per capita ownership: 1.7 million

Rise in autos from growth in per capita ownership only: 7.6 million

21.8 million

Thus, following the logic of Ehrlich and Holdren (1971), population growth accounted for between 12.5 and 14.2 million more cars being on the road in 1970.[12] At a minimum, the population-induced increase would have been 12.5 million. As they note, though, this underestimates the fact that population growth and consumption growth per capita have a joint, multiplicative effect. Therefore, if we wished to classify all of this multiplicative effect as due to population, we would reach the maximum impact of 14.2 (12.5 plus 1.7) million cars increase.

There is, of course, a logical flaw. Virtually all of the population growth must have come from children born in 1960–70. They are all under ten years of age in 1970, and thus could not be direct consumers of automobiles (Chase, 1977:383). Whether the births involved led their families to greater or lesser purchases of cars is an interesting question. But the data available do not allow us to answer. On first principles, we can argue both ways. If there is a population growth factor involved, it would have to relate to growth in the over-16 or over-18 population, and thus changes in the U.S. population going back before 1954, at the most recent. To evaluate this population/auto relationship, we would need information on the pattern of ages of consumers of automobiles in the 1960–70 period, which is not at hand.

But this is a set-up, the skeptical reader will argue. And so it is. Yet it is typical of many (though by no means all) applications of the two-accounts population problems model. Moreover, despite rather different approaches, both Commoner (1972) and Ehrlich (Ehrlich & Holdren, 1971) fall into such traps. Note that the fallacy is brought to our attention by external factors, by facts that lie entirely outside the realm of the formal population problems model.

We can continue to illuminate some of the other logical traps of the model, using a household account instead of a population one. Between 1960 and 1970, the rise in ownership of automobiles was only

0.07 per person, or 0.18 per household. This is a small increase per family. Moreover, the percentage of families with an automobile rose only slightly, from 75.5 percent in 1960 to 79.6 percent in 1970. The greatest significance is the increase in the number of households in this period, following the population growth in the period around World War II. By using age 22 as a rough figure for the formation of independent households, and taking 1965 as the midpoint of the period of consumption, this would center our attention on people born around 1943. With this logic, we would understand that such household formation led to automobile ownership increases.

However, what we find from data on the actual household consumption patterns is that the percentage of households with one car actually declines from 62.1 percent to 50.3 percent. And the percentage with two or more cars rose from 13.9 percent to 29.3 percent, more than doubling the proportion of families with multiple automobile ownership. Whatever the actual growth of households and concomitant increased car ownership, it appears from these figures that what we have is a substantial growth of a multi-car consumption pattern, and not primarily a growth of families who now begin to own a car for the first time. Moreover, the profile of the nonautomobile owning population suggests what a select group they are: under $3,000 in income, aged 65 and over, living in the Northeast, and in cities rather than suburbs. Conversely, those with cars tend to be earning $15,000 and over, middle-aged, living in the West, and suburban or rural.[13] From 1960 to 1970, the poor had the highest population growth rates in the U.S., but the lowest ownership rate. Each of these pieces of information changes our sense of how population growth relates to automobile consumption. Each has very different implications for solutions to automobile-related environmental problems. It is the failure of the general population problems model to take account of these distributional features of consumption that makes it such a weak analytic tool here.

In this simple illustration, our evaluation has changed from an initial estimation that up to two-thirds of the growth in autos is due to very recent population growth, to a decision that absolutely none of it can be so attributed. Equally important, we have moved from considering all households to specifying where the growth in consumption has appeared. None of these theories really explains why such growth occurred. They merely tell us where in social and physical space it took place. But we need to understand the social system basis of such consumption if we are to inhibit it.

This example illustrates some of the pitfalls of thinking in nonsocial ways about social systems of production and consumption, a frequent mistake of discussing populations rather than families. There is a concrete and an abstract principle that may be drawn from our automobile consumption analysis. Concretely, it is entirely likely that increased automobile consumption arises from the increased entry of women into the labor force in the period. Such dual-occupation families often require a second car, except in large cities with good public transportation. Often, the entry of women into the labor force is permitted and stimulated by a choice not to have another child, or not to have any children. In general, increased female labor force participation is associated with decreased childbearing. Thus, we have partly solved a population problem. But the gains are offset by increased consumption, fed in part by the reduced costs of childrearing. Such families follow the developmental model, not the environmental model of the parable. Consumption of remaining family members partly absorbs the savings of foregone childbearing.[14]

At an abstract level, there is an interesting paradox as well. Some theorists have asked how we can mobilize people to be concerned about future environmental and social problems. Why should people defer present consumption for the benefit of future generations? While Heilbroner views this as a need to engage people in identifying with the society, I see it equally as a need to engage them in family systems. In my view, parents often defer their own present consumption for the future benefits of their children. If zero population growth advocates succeed in substantially increasing the proportion of childless couples, one consequence might be a *decreased* concern for the future of societies, for such couples have little kinship-based motivation to defer consumption for the benefit of future generations. Parents, on the other hand, do defer consumption for one or more generations that arise from their own family. They may or may not be identifying with the society; they generally *do* identify with their children and grandchildren. Moreover, as each generation in a family dies off, it is replaced by a moving future, covering another seventy years at least (the life expectancy of children, say). Childless couples neither have this immediate spur to defer gratification, nor do they leave a replacement generation with such a spur. Part of the potential fallacy in the populationist move for zero population growth lies precisely in their assumptions that childlessness arises for socially altruistic reasons. There is far more evidence to suggest that people make childbearing decisions because of their own benefit-cost analysis, not the society's. And childlessness is much more likely to result from women desiring a career, and the consumption that it permits.[15] Such couples have little incentive to defer gratification for the future, when the population consists of generations unconnected to them.

This begins to raise even more questions about the utility of biological models of the population problem, an issue to which I turn next.

POPULATION CONTROL: SOCIAL VERSUS BIOLOGICAL MODELS

The Need for Social Models

Populationism has always been seen from a biological perspective, and the present connection to environmental issues continues this. In part, this results from the fact that the techniques for describing the growth and distribution of human populations are the same as those used for all species—the mathematical tools of formal demography and population biology (Chase, 1971:218–21). If modern biological analysts like Ehrlich and Hardin merely described the growth of populations, this would present no problem.

But the difficulty is that biologists do not concentrate on the features that distinguish humans from other species. In particular, they are not concerned with: (1) the complexities of sociocultural production systems; (2) social, economic, and cultural factors that influence the voluntary aspects of childbearing in families; and (3) the nature of social, political, and economic institutions that impinge on and are affected by family patterns. The first factor creates, as I have shown, many problems in assessing the historical impact of population growth in consumption, as well as likely consumption and ecosystem gains from future reductions of population growth.

The latter two limitations preclude any simple mechanical intervention to alter the course of population growth. From a biological perspective, there are two means of population control: birth decreases or death increases. If humans are like herds of other species, they can be managed by these two means. But humans differ from other species

in their advanced sociocultural production, and because they are participants in political and social systems. Political and social institutions
do not generally permit a straightforward application of biological
controls over fertility, nor of mortality-increasing policies. And the
future gains in productions and consumption reduction from decreased
population growth are quite uncertain, even if such population controls were socially and politically feasible (Ridker, 1972; Espenshade,
1978).

The modern success of biologically oriented populationists has been
unprecedented, though, in two senses. A variety of social and political
analysts accepted for a long time the major premises of the
populationist model. And the world-wide diffusion of family planning
programs over the last two decades is nothing short of remarkable. But
the age of innocence is over. For, although voluntary family planning
programs have achieved some success in reducing birth rates, we have
learned that parents are not yet willing to substantially reduce their
fertility in most underdeveloped countries. Wanted, desired, or acceptable levels of family size indicate a continued relatively high rate of
population growth over the next thirty to fifty years at least, in much
of the Third World. Improved contraception can induce further declines, but the growth rates will remain fairly high.[16]

If knowledge and the availability of contraception does not quickly
bring down growth rates, what does this imply? Social, political, and
economic analysts have in part begun to question the effectiveness of
such approaches. They have tried to (1) understand why parents desire
large families, (2) understand how to reduce parental desires for more
children, (3) question whether the efforts required to change fertility
may exceed the benefits, and (4) probe for other ways of reducing
production and consumption, in the short and long run. The need for
such reappraisals has been partly affirmed by the recent political reaction to the Indian sterilization campaigns of the Indira Gandhi regime,
and the increased political sensitivities of the Third World countries in
the 1974 Bucharest World Population Conference (Finkle & Crane,
1975). Population control is no longer a technical, biological issue. It
is a social, economic, and political issue, and properly so:

> What we seek is human welfare, personal freedom, the quality of
> life, and demographic trends and changes take on meaning only
> insofar as they contribute to such ends. . . . Some costs, in short,
> are too high, for population control is not the final value. (Berel-
> son, 1974:12)

The remainder of this chapter addresses the four reappraisals of the social realities of population change.

Why Have Populations Grown?
The Social Perspective

No two analysts quite agree on answers to this question, but the crude outlines of a synthesis may be found in the extensive literature. First, the greatest spur to growth in the last century has been a reduction in mortality, especially child mortality. After careful review of the evidence, it appears that mortality was reduced primarily by improvements in the quality of nutrition and decreases in public health threats. Increased food production, improved food distribution and storage, and improved quality of drinking water and its reduced contact with raw sewage appear crucial, at least in the developed countries (Wrigley, 1969: Ch. 5-6).

Mortality in underdeveloped countries is less understood, in part because of very poor records up to the present time. In general, mortality rates improved only very slowly through the first half of the twentieth century. Conditions often worsened in periods of war or economic disruption, with subsequent improvement only after World War II. International aid in reducing malaria by spraying and in vaccination for childhood diseases often helped bring about rapid declines in mortality, though rarely to the levels of developed countries. Some improvements in nutrition and public sanitation accompanied these, although they played a lesser role than in the developed countries. Because so little structural change in production occurred in these societies following the lengthy periods of colonial rule and socioeconomic exploitation, these societies remained vulnerable to many of the environmental diseases (malaria, typhoid) and dependent on external public health assistance. In addition, lack of changes in agricultural technology generally increased their vulnerability to food shortages. These were exacerbated by climatic reversals at times, on the one hand, and internal increases in need for food because of population growth. The populationists, then, are certainly correct in their assessment that cutting off all health and food assistance to these countries could increase mortality. They err in their simple assumptions that it is solely indigenous factors that created this vulnerable situation, rather than the historical role of colonialism and the modern version of economic dependency.[17]

The second component of growth has been some small increases in fertility, but more the maintenance of the high fertility of the last century or so. In industrialized societies, fertility rose somewhat in the nineteenth century, and then declined in the later nineteenth and early twentieth centuries—what is called a "demographic transition." Within the Third World of ex-colonial societies, however, fertility may have increased slightly with reductions in mortality of potential parents, but has generally remained fairly high in the twentieth century. In both sets of countries, though, it now seems certain that the largest factors in high fertility levels have been increased marriage rates, decreased age at marriage, and parental actions in controlling (or failing to control) births in families, rather than the indirect effects of decreased mortality (e.g., Wrigley, 1969: Ch. 5–6; Sklar, 1974; Knodel, 1977).

Why have families differed in their family size? Part of the explanation lies in varied access to effective contraception—but the far larger part appears to be in the number of children the couples have more or less consciously chosen to have. Many of us hold that this is a result of changing costs and benefits of children—of their social utility to parents. In middle classes in developed countries, and later in the working classes there, parents found the costs of rearing children increasing and the benefits decreasing. In addition, social alternatives to childbearing appeared to provide for social security and to create opportunities for using time and money in ways that were more satisfying to parents than childrearing. This view is especially germane for women, whose roles expanded beyond the maternal domestic one into patterns of extended consumption (recreation) and nondomestic production (work). Over this past century, we have gone from the large family to the small one, and in both the early and later parts of the twentieth century, to the childless couple. Moreover, unless ecological scarcity or other factors greatly reduce degrees of extrafamilial freedom for women, it is unlikely that any long-term increase in family size in developed countries will be sustained in the future. Where socialist and capitalist countries have, in the twentieth century, attempted to change this path by increasing incentives for families or reducing abortion and contraception availability, couples have quickly adapted, and retained their small families.[18]

While pockets of large family size occur in poverty and minority groups in developed countries, these are slowly disappearing in response to improved social welfare and opportunity conditions as well.

It is likely that they will follow the path above, assuming that social and economic discrimination (race, sex, and class) does not increase to its former high level.

In the underdeveloped countries, there is a small middle-class for whom the model above applies. But the rest of the population operates in a different context. First, mortality control is both more recent and more erratic. Quite high levels of infant mortality frequently occur in many poor rural and urban populations. Coupled with this is an absence of stable supportive social and economic institutions outside the family. While many of the *countries* have increased their levels of production and national income in the twentieth century, relatively little of this national economic growth has gone to improve the quality of life of the working class, both rural and urban. Indeed, income distributions have frequently worsened with development.

These socioeconomic conditions typically involve lower childbearing costs than potential parental benefits. Children provide agricultural labor and the potential for very modest wage supplements to family income. Parents have few clear alternatives for investing their time and money, since both the government and the private sector act in unstable and socially regressive ways. Credit, wages, health care, food distribution, and other amenities do not flow easily to the majority of these populations. Moreover, the need for children as risk-aversion investments, coupled with higher unstable child mortality, makes for higher levels of childbearing. Families are somewhat larger than parents consider desirable, in order to provide a buffer for the possible death of young children. Since child mortality is, on the average, declining for these groups, such families are larger than necessary, on the average, in order to insure each set of parents against these mortality risks.[19]

On the other hand, even within the underdeveloped world, where the conditions of the working classes—and especially conditions of women in these classes—have improved, family size has declined. Educational, employment, recreational, and voluntary communal activities, coupled with more secure forms of social security and public amenities, have led to the declines of family size, as in developed countries. Some of these have, moreover, occurred more quickly because of the presence of governmental family planning programs, to provide contraceptive advice and social reinforcement for smaller families (Mauldin, 1978).

A contemporary summary of these processes is made by Caldwell.

When social conditions change from children helping parents to parents helping children, then family size decreases. How much change is necessary, how it is to be brought about by changes in the productive and governmental institutions, and what the resource costs are of such change are not known precisely. Particular cultural and other conditions may also impede or accelerate this process, but the main features of these familial and societal distributional changes seem reasonably well established after almost two decades of research.[20]

This synthesis provides a variety of inferences for social policies relating to family size and population growth. All of them depend in part on this factual history, and in part on the political and social biases of policymakers and analysts, for population policies ultimately involve intervention in the ongoing lives of families and in the institutions of society, in ways that may be far more disruptive than most other social policies. That is a point that eludes most modern populationists. It is clear that, in theory, population growth be slowed or eliminated by: (1) withholding food supplies and aid, (2) increasing the costs of children to parents by disincentive programs, and/or (3) increasing the benefits to parents from nonchild activities by various social welfare and incentive programs. Each of these will have different mixtures and distributions of economic and ecological costs and benefits. Many of these mixtures and distributions may be amenable to governmental manipulation, under some political circumstances. If we follow Berelson's statement that social welfare is our goal, though, only the third model will work.

In contrast, the populationist program follows the first two models much more frequently, particularly in the last decade. Intellectual, moral, and material roots of this position, and the social consequences of it, are treated next.

Why Have Populations Grown?
The Biological Perspective

By and large, biologically oriented populationists accept the predominance of mortality decreases as the initial cause of modern population growth. However, the notion of a "population bomb" or a "population explosion" implies more fertility increase than has occurred. Mortality decreases are seen as caused by technical western intervention in the recent period to improve health conditions of the Third World. Less attention is paid to indigenous efforts to improve food and public health conditions, or to the eighteenth and nineteenth century intervention of western colonial powers that often disrupted food supplies and introduced new diseases into nonwestern populations. Still less attention is paid to the evidence that precolonial populations often had relatively low child mortality and family-size limitations.[21] From the one-dimensional view of mortality decline, though, "we" created "their" population increase, and therefore "we" have the right and the obligation to "restore" their more "natural" conditions of mortality.

Turning to fertility, many populationists see a rise and perpetuation of high fertility as a consequence of the ignorance of the underdeveloped area populations. People simply do not understand the physiology of reproduction, yet they desire sexual pleasure. They don't appreciate the economic and ecological consequences of increased family size, and therefore take no pains to practice birth control. Or, these cultures have such strong pressures resulting from traditionalism that they can't adapt to the modern need for lower family size, and this collective ignorance obscures individual propensities that might be rational otherwise. In none of these positions is there any analysis of the socioeconomic context of families or its consequences for childbearing strategies or options.

Unlike the Berelson position, there is little concern for familial welfare, but great sensitivity to societal and global welfare: another variation on the familiar theme of loving humanity in general, but hating people in particular. It is population growth, fertility rates, and mortality rates that dominate their attention, rather than family size, childbearing decisions, and the loss of children. In this, though, they are consistent with the ecosystem emphasis on species populations.

There are two great ironies in this view of population growth. First, since such growth occurs in sociopolitical systems, social and related dimensions are relevant for both understanding and altering trajectories of population growth. Second, many of the modern populationists take as their intellectual standard bearer one of the earliest and most distinguished social scientists, Thomas Malthus. Modern "Malthusianism," though, is a tragic and pernicious parody of Malthus's views. Yet the two seemed irrevocably linked in analysis and prescription. They must be separated for a more accurate and balanced view of human population and its dynamics.

Malthusianism: Origin and Degradation

Like many modern populationists, Reverénd Thomas Malthus was both a scientist and a moralist. But the crucial distinction is that he was a *social* scientist. Malthus gets cited by contemporary populationists for the following views:

1. population tends to exceed food supply unless it is checked;
2. this is due to the sexual needs of mankind, and the resultant procreation;
3. checks on population come from either mortality increase (the positive checks of misery), or from avoidance of early marriage and sexual activity (the preventive checks);
4. if preventive checks don't work, then positive checks increase;
5. for the poor, any increase in income goes to increased family size, and eventually this leads to a decline in their food and economic conditions, with increased positive mortality checks and decreased quality of life;
6. wealthier, better-educated people practice later marriage and have smaller families.

From this perspective of 1798, modern "Malthusians" argue that Malthus not only anticipated contemporary population-resource problems, but argued that natural checks on population are painful but inevitable. This provides a rationale for launching campaigns to increase mortality, since this merely speeds up natural mechanisms. It justifies imposition of draconian measures of tax disincentives, compulsory sterilization, or forced contraception, since these merely accelerate preventive checks or substitute for even worse positive (mortality) checks on population growth.

Garrett Hardin is among the most eloquent of these modern Malthusians. His interpretation is:

1. people despoil the environmental commons by reckless breeding, based on narrow self-interest;
2. only social coercion to prevent breeding can overcome this tragedy of the commons;
3. for some underdeveloped societies, such coercion is impossible, and we must then retreat to a mortality control position by withdrawing western food aid and all other assistance, or else these growing populations will soon swamp our western lifeboat that floats on the sea of limited resources;
4. accordingly, we must follow a triage model: decide which underdeveloped countries are hopelessly overpopulated and abandon them; pick others that will solve their population problem without our help and

leave them be; and concentrate all our international food and aid efforts on those countries that are making some population control progress, with our help.[22]

The Malthusian heritage of Hardin seems obvious, in that both theorists were concerned with reproduction checks and mortality alternatives. Hardin's recent work stems from a model of the English commons, where herdsmen overran the resources by incrementally increasing their herds. What was rational for each one in isolation turned out to generate a collective tragedy, with ecosystem disorganization. Accordingly, the commons were enclosed and private interests were then ostensibly linked to ecosystem protection and production. The triage and lifeboat models then follow, in that we would be protecting our environmental resources by enclosing them, and forcing irresponsible populations to sink or swim on their own.

What is ironic about this is that Hardin's example was one of production, not *re*production. Herdsmen were making economic allocative decisions, not familial ones. Moreover, unlike Malthus, Hardin and others fail to appreciate the crucial analytic and policy distinctions between production and reproduction decisions.[23] They ignore the richer analytic heritage of Malthus, whose total contributions to population analysis and policy include the following (Petersen, 1975:154–60):

7. the poor will reproduce at higher rates only if they are kept in a state of ignorance, with little hope for their future;
8. such improvement in welfare is frequently opposed by combinations of the rich—both farmers and urban capitalists—in order to keep wage rates down and parish costs low as well;
9. until such social improvements can be brought about, increased development of agriculture is desirable, to prevent increased misery of the poor, who are powerless to prevent such declines in their quality of life otherwise;
10. the poor can suffer from inflation in the cost of food, as well as from absolute food scarcity; wages should be high enough to offset this inflation, and/or other provisions established to protect them from these nutritional miseries;
11. we have evidence that when these populations do have improved education and opportunities, they avoid large families in the same ways that wealthier families do.

This sample of Malthusian thought is far more rarely cited, for it is inconsistent with both the populationists' use of Malthus, and the popular model of Malthus as a social reactionary. Malthus was, in fact, a keen political economist who understood allocative problems and their relationship to population growth (as both cause and effect). Moreover, his political activism was devoted to increasing the educational and social welfare provisions for the poor and working classes of England. The final irony, perhaps, is that Malthus became more optimistic and more socially sensitive over his lifetime as he continued to examine population and economic trends. It is hard to reconcile the popular and populationist image of Malthus with the following excerpts:

> *1798*   The nominal price of labour... frequently remains the same, while the nominal price of provisions has been gradually increasing. This is... a real fall in the price of labour, and... the condition of the lower orders of the community must gradually grow worse and worse. But the farmers and capitalists are growing rich from the real cheapness of labour.... But the want of freedom in the market of labour... occurs... either from parish laws, or the more general cause of the facility of combination among the rich, and its difficulty among the poor... (1959:12)

> *1798*   Any great interference with the affairs of other people is a species of tyranny, and in the common course of things the exercise of this power may be expected to become grating to those who are driven to ask for support. (1959:32)

> *1798*   Premiums might be given for turning up fresh land, and all possible encouragements held out to agriculture above manufactures, and to tillage above grazing. Every endeavour should be used to weaken and destroy all those institutions relating to corporations, apprenticeships, etc., which cause the labours of agriculture to be worse paid than the labours of trade and manufacture... [This would] furnish the market with an increasing quantity of healthy work, and... raise the comparative price of labour and ameliorate the condition of the labourer. Being now in better circumstances... he would be more able, as well as more inclined, to enter into associations for providing against the sickness of himself or family. (1959:33)

> *1872*   Among the lower classes of people, there appears to be something like a standard of wretchedness, a point below

which they will not continue to marry and propagate their species. . . . The principal circumstances which contribute to raise [this standard] . . . are liberty, security of property, the diffusion of knowledge, and a taste for the comforts of life. Those which contribute principally to lower it are despotism and ignorance. (Petersen, 1975:156)

1872   From a review of the state of society in former periods compared with the present, I should certainly say that the evils resulting from the principal of population have rather diminished than increased. (Petersen, 1975:160)

With proper cautions about the devil being able to cite Scripture, I would claim that the analysis and policy perspectives in this book are far more Malthusian than those of populationists such as Hardin and Ehrlich. Indeed, the cyclical nature of the history of ideas is indicated as much by the fact that Malthus's policy concerns—social justice, allocation of scarcity, investment decisions, and social welfare—are precursors of the most radical contemporary programs for the reformation of sociocultural production systems, including my own.[24] Moreover, if we are to develop a "population policy," these approaches seem far more sane and far more effective than the biological proposals of Hardin and others.

Inequality and Population: An Overview

There is no way to discuss the social and ecological dimensions of population growth without incorporating issues of social inequality: in consumption, production, and power. The following is a partial list of such connections:

1. the poor consume less per capita, and poor countries produce and consume far less in total than do developed societies;
2. in many societies, the total consumption of many resources by the rapidly growing populations of the poor may be less than the consumption by the wealthier minority in the society;
3. populationist models throughout modern history have been advocated by wealthy and dominant social groups as solutions to social ills;
4. the modern populationism has roots in these earlier models, and draws upon some of the same participants;
5. modern populationism was initiated by the wealthier countries, and thrust upon the policy agendas of underdeveloped countries by bilateral and multilateral pressures;

6. such international pressures have often found positive responses within underdeveloped countries from reactionary economic groups and political elites;
7. accompanying international pressures, there has been a continuous threat of withholding aid from underdeveloped countries, and little increase in the volume of aid;
8. such assistance from industrial to underdeveloped countries has frequently served to enhance socioeconomic inequalities in the latter, and not materially improve the condition of the growing population of the poor;
9. reallocations of capital and productive investment, both internationally and internally in societies, is little influenced by the poor and working classes, except under unusual political conditions;
10. in particular, food production and distribution decisions are made by governmental and economic elites, often diverting food from the poorer groups rather than enhancing food availability.[25]

It is certainly true that there are ecosystem problems that have arisen from the growth of even poor populations, with their lower per capita consumption. Deforestation, reduction of animal habitat, species reduction, and water pollution are examples of this (e.g., Eckholm, 1975). But many of these problems are reversible with improved economic conditions in such groups. And most of these affect the localized populations rather more than they do the developed world's populations. That is, the ecosystem problems lead to victimization problems for the very populations that may be said to cause them, in many cases.

Moreover, the sociocultural production of the poorer populations are often influenced by other social agents. Food production is inefficient because of credit barriers, market restraints, and inflated equipment costs imposed by economic and political elites within their societies. Problems are intensified by land and other investments by multinational companies.[26] Because of the external forces, the poor are left without resources to replant forests, to adequately treat sewage, to enhance productivity of agriculture. As a result, they often aggravate local ecological disorganization (Neuhaus, 1971; Chase, 1977: Ch. 16). While improved patterns of production may accelerate ecosystem withdrawals and additions, it is equally possible that system protection can result, given the current poverty levels and lack of control in such underdeveloped area populations. There are examples of such changes, even in "backward" areas such as India (Borders, 1978).

However, populationists have ignored the implications of this external control of the existence of those most accused of population explosions. First, without benign intent on the part of these indigenous and exogenous economic control groups, there is no guarantee that reduced family size will improve either family welfare or the productive system. It is entirely likely that neither social nor ecological welfare will be improved. Second, without clear evidence of changes in the political and economic intent of such groups, the populations of the poor have every reason to suspect the supposedly benign concern of groups asking them to reduce fertility (Schnaiberg & Reed, 1974). And the malign neglect advocated in Hardin's lifeboat model seems hardly designed to improve the confidence of this or any future generation in these countries.

LESSONS AND MODELS FOR POPULATION POLICIES

Lessons: China and India

Within two decades, the two largest underdeveloped societies have moved in different ways to confound earlier populationist models. Massive famines were predicted by analysts of the 1940s and 1950s for both societies in the succeeding decades (Paddock & Paddock, 1967; Ehrlich, 1968). Neither has come to pass, despite climatic and sociopolitical problems in both societies in this period.

China has engaged in a massive, labor-intensive effort at increasing food production through land reclamation, intensification of production and distribution of materials and energy into and out of agriculture. It has improved distribution, nutrition, and the diversity of foodstuffs available to the average family (Sprague, 1975). In addition, it has made sustained efforts to reduce population growth, through social control over early marriage, improved abortion and contraception, and educational efforts at inducing smaller families (Tien, 1973). On the other hand, a variety of social services, ranging from health care to transportation, has improved in the same period, bringing some increases in the quality of life in addition to nutritional benefits.

As a result of these efforts, both mortality and fertility have decreased in China. No accurate statistics exist on the degree of such declines or the specific mechanisms underlying them. Development has occurred, at both the national and the familial level. The ecological costs of such development are unclear. But there is some evidence that with material recycling and human energy, the ecological withdrawals and additions per unit increase in economic and social development are lower here than in many other underdeveloped and industrial societies (Holden, 1974). Problems of air and water pollution exist as well, though.[27]

India's development in this period is somewhat different. Substantial international and domestic funds have been expended on family planning contraceptive and sterilization programs. Some program successes have occurred, though the net reduction in fertility seems fairly small so far. Food production has had both growth and retardation in the period, with some production and productivity increases from imported "green revolution" technology. Lesser advances have come from indigenous efforts at reorganization of agricultural production, since more resources went into industrial development in this period. Nonetheless, India does not have an imminent famine problem, even though malnutrition and hunger are still widespread. India has also exported some surplus grain, which could not be absorbed by the marketplace or government subsidies. Increased green revolution production in the Punjab and elsewhere has clearly improved the economic position of large landowners, though it is unclear how small landowners and agricultural labor have fared.[28] Ecological changes in India as a result of increased production are unclear: some reduction of desertification has occurred, but air and water pollution has increased with industrial production. Little integration of production exists, though many materials are used intensively, with little waste. Energy efficiency in domestic and other production seems not to have increased. Dependency on petroleum imports has increased (Ridker, 1972).

What lessons can we learn from these two cases? The first is that the real world is exceedingly complex, and no mechanical populationist model suffices. Second, the course of population and social welfare is affected by political and social decisions that may be more or less integrated. In China—which lacks the statistics—the integration is nonetheless clear. In India—with reams of statistics—it is clear that there is lesser integration, and lower social payoffs for the poorer groups. Third, it is perfectly clear that with sufficient political commitment, underdeveloped societies like China are capable of choosing their own paths and techniques, with little external pressure. Conversely, India's history indicates that, without this internal political structure, even massive external efforts may produce insubstantial progress—and even social and ecological regression. Fourth, it is unclear what the actual links are between population growth, production growth, and ecological withdrawals and additions, and how mutable they may be. It is certainly possible to have lower ecological costs for increased social welfare under alternative production systems—and China seems superior on this account.

Models: China, India, and Beyond

The most obvious conclusion from the discussion in this chapter is that we know relatively little about how population growth affects the ecosystem, and even less about future possibilities with different growth levels. Caution, not alarmism, is recommended. If it is not certain that we can improve either ecosystem production or its protection with reduced population growth, we should not be advocating immediate and draconian measures. The social and ecological payoffs are simply too small, by my ethical and practical accounting (Callahan, 1972, 1974).

The safest and most humane approach is the Chinese growth and redistribution model, difficult as its implementation may seem for most nonsocialist and nonauthoritarian societies. A dual welfare scheme seems most appropriate, with improvements in social welfare for target groups, *along with* societal efforts at population control. In a broad sense, this fits with incentive models for population growth reduction (Kangas, 1970; Pohlman, 1971). Not only is material welfare enhanced by changes in production, but human services can be improved with lower energy and material costs. Persons whose family size is the target are the recipients of improved goods and services.[29] Ecosystem protection may be improved by growth (collective incentives) of agricultural and other production technologies that (1) increase the efficiency and utilization of human labor and (2) maximize production with concern for sustaining the productive qualities of land. This will typically involve a mixture of traditional agricultural practices, supplemented by improved manufactured fertilizers, some of which can be recycled from human and animal wastes after processing of pathogens. In societies with greater emphasis on private property and production, incentives for family limitation may include tools for agriculture, education for children, and credit for expansion of small-scale enterprises (Chase, 1971: Ch. XI).

A standard objection to such schemes is that poorer countries lack the capital to provide adequate incentives (Teitelbaum, 1975). If this is the case, then in the interim period of 30–50 years, there is a heavy obligation on the developed countries to provide much of this capital. This can be done either bilaterally or through multilateral agencies. The political obstacles to increasing the volume of such aid might be overcome by linking the furor over population growth to such aid programs, in altruistic and/or self-interested ways. If the argument of the populationists is interpreted as *"they* will ruin *our* environment," then the wealthier societies and populations may be mobilized on a self-interested basis. If, on the other hand, the concern with overpopulation is based on genuine concern for the welfare of poorer populations, this same social altruism can be harnessed to incentive aid as well (Myrdal, 1970).

Given the uncertainties of every aspect of the population dilemma—including that of food adequacy—little certainty can exist regarding the usefulness of such incentives. Indeed, social experimentation appears to be the only sound approach. For political and ethical reasons, moreover, such experimentation is far more feasible when incentives rather than populationist disincentives are offered.[30]

To what extent should these incentives be provided before, after, or both before and after family size is reduced over time? Note that China provided incentives *before* fertility reduction, through improvements in nutritional and other areas. Incentive programs that only provide benefits *after* families agree to limit children pose much graver social hazards, because it is so easy politically to shift from this to socially regressive policies, should family size not be reduced. Moreover, the history of internal and external "aid" for many of the world's poor is so unstable and limited that without a good-faith effort at improving standards of living, the poor have little cause to put their faith in uncertain future benefits (Chase, 1971: Ch. XI; 1977: Ch. 16).

Beyond the Chinese and Indian cases, a broader twentieth century perspective requires a cautious optimism regarding such a program. It is ecologically accurate to state that the resource base of the biosphere appears totally inadequate to bring the underdeveloped world up to the material consumption standards of the industrialized world, especially that of the United States. But it is unlikely that such massive increases in material incentives are necessary to reduce fertility. First, we must remember that fertility reduction occurred in the western world in the later part of the nineteenth and early part of the twentieth century. Sociocultural production, both aggregate and per capita, was far lower at that time, and yet it sufficed to induce fertility reductions (Wrigley, 1969: Ch. 5–6). Why should this not be the case in the Third World? Beyond China, there are other instances of recent fertility decline which point in the same direction (Mauldin, 1978).

Second, the level of poverty, hunger, and misery is exceedingly high in those populations that are the primary contributors to the modern "explosion." Contrary to many assumptions, such deprivation did not exist in their precolonial past. It follows, therefore, that the social impact of modest improvements in nutrition, health care, housing, and employment will likely be far greater than an equivalent increment in richer countries or social groups. In economic language, the marginal utility of increases in material welfare is exceedingly high in these populations.

Third, the element of time is crucial. We cannot expect instantaneous success. Populations will continue to grow in the next 30–50 years. It takes time for families to adapt to changing socioeconomic realities, and there are cognitive and cultural lags. The shift from larger families with lower investment per child to smaller ones with higher investment will take at least a generation. It can be accelerated by collective social forces that provide consistent material and social reinforcement for such a shift. But even China, with the socialist capacity to mobilize all institutions, has been unsuccessful in bringing about the shift in less than a generation (1948–78). In the interim, ecosystem disorganization is likely to rise rather than fall because of population growth, and family welfare may fall somewhat before a rise due to new socioeconomic incentives. The alternative to this is a cruel, politically difficult, and unjust increase in misery, which may bring down rates of growth in the interim, only to have these pressures rise again in the future, unless we exceed permanently Malthus's "standard of wretchedness" below which children will not be born.

Finally, there is no purely scientific basis for any population policy. Given the uncertainties of historical environmental impacts of population and of antinatalist policies that have been tried, and given the multiplicity of values concealed in any policy, it follows that:

the welfare judgment one makes about additional people depends on such values as the importance of the short run versus the long run, whose welfare one wishes to take into account in which proportions, and what one believes is the importance to be attached to human life at poorer and richer standards of living . . . the welfare effect . . . is indeterminate in the presence of various widespread differences in value judgments and scientific analyses. (Simon, 1977:12)

This too is in the tradition of Malthus, who understood why poor people resist external controls over their families, and why rich people frequently seek such control. Production, rather than reproduction, is the crucial factor in biospheric disorganization. Its link to population growth is quite problematic. And direct control over many aspects of production will be necessary in the foreseeable future, regardless of any reasonable alternative path of future population growth (Stretton, 1976). These realities are the ones addressed in the remainder of this book. As to population, perhaps the most balanced view is that of the psychologist Edward Pohlman:

The appropriate path, in my view, lies halfway between the too-soft laissez-faire approach of merely helping people to avoid unwanted births, and the too-tough strategy of force. This middle path involves financial rewards for actions that will reduce birthrates . . . to "rig" the economic systems of rewards and penalties heavily toward small families. There are great administrative and political difficulties with incentives, but no successful strategy for population limitation will be easy. Incentives may not work; they have not been tried enough for us to be sure. . . . (1971:10)

NOTES

1. Examples of the three positions include: strongest (Ehrlich, 1968; Hardin, 1968), moderate (Tinbergen, 1975), and weakest (Coale, 1970). Discussions in opposition to populationism include Hall (1973), Raulet (1970), and Chase (1971: Ch. XI; 1977: Ch. 16–17). Few of these, with the exception of Chase, are pure forms of populationism or antipopulationism, though they approach the categories of positions quite closely.

2. While the positions I take here are my own interpretations of historical and recent trends, there are materials supporting many of these. For 4a, see Wade (1976) and Walters (1975); for 5a, see Hawley (1973) and Chase (1977: Ch. 16); for 6a, American illustrations are found in Blake & Das Gupta (1975), western European

in Livi-Bacci (1974), eastern European in Macura (1974), and underdeveloped countries in Mauldin's (1978) review. Arguments in favor of my position in 7a include Hall (1973) and Raulet (1970) with respect to underdeveloped areas, and Ryder (1973) as to the future of U.S. population growth. Ridker (1972) takes a position akin to my 8a one, with respect to the interim term in the U.S. In terms of underdeveloped areas, my position with respect to population programs is partly in agreement with that of McNamara (1977). Poleman (1975) and World Bank (1975) both stress productive reorganization for food production and development, while protecting environmental systems, though neither expressly incorporates population issues.

3. In its extreme form, this illustration would support Hardin's (1968) "tragedy of the commons" thesis, discussed later in this chapter. On the other hand, there is evidence as well that those who perceive aggregate U.S. population problems also have lower ideal family size (Kruegel, 1975), though this has been a matter of some debate (e.g., Blake, 1974). It is not clear whether there is any causal connection between an individual's societal evaluations and his/her own preferences.

4. That is, the total savings would be withdrawn from social circulation, and sociocultural production would be reduced accordingly (Stretton, 1976: Ch. 1, for example).

5. Both Ridker (1972) and Espenshade (1978) indicate that reduced fertility will permit some increased consumption by remaining family members, though they both indicate that up to 85% of the anticipated consumption with higher fertility could be saved. I believe them wrong, in that they assume no future economic adjustment to substantially increase consumption per capita, to prevent future crises of underconsumption relative to production.

6. A typical assumption made in early economic models (e.g., Enke, 1969) has been that in underdeveloped countries the marginal or incremental product of another worker is zero, or close to it. Such workers are unemployed or underemployed, but still derive benefits from production, and thus absorb either private or state capital for such benefits. Unless they are adding to this stock of capital, as is presumably the case for workers in developed countries (e.g., Samuelson, 1978), this leads to a net reduction in capital available for production expansion.

7. Petersen (1976) and Ehrlich & Ehrlich (1976) have both recently expressed pessimism on food production prospects, the first on socioeconomic grounds and the latter on ecological grounds. For less pessimistic views of options, see Poleman (1975) and Vermeer (1976).

8. Both Neuhaus (1971) and Chase (1977: Ch. 16) have rather devastating critiques of the political and social ideology underlying contemporary populationism and, in Neuhaus's case, alarmist environmentalism in general. Chase in particular traces the evolution of contemporary populationism from the class-biased and ethnocentric views of the eugenics movements in the U.S. and Europe. Holden (1974) and Finkle & Crane (1975) both discuss political opposition to populationism.

9. Even very sophisticated econometric models make similar errors. For example, Espenshade (1978) predicts the future reduction in total consumption with a reduction in U.S. fertility by 2020. But he bases his projections on data that do

not contain information on the distribution of expenditures by actual categories of consumers. Rather, he uses materials that contain a population account and a consumption total. The fact that he has a third account, a surrogate consumer income one, does not obviate the fact that the causal connections between them are assumed but not directly measured. For me, this calls all his projections into question.

10. The best discussion of victimization models is in Chase (1971: Ch. XI; 1977: Ch. 16), which is in extreme opposition to the model of causation of Ehrlich & Holdren (1971). Simon (1977) provides an optimistic view of how population growth can stimulate development and equal optimism regarding the availability of resources, based on the Barnett & Morse economic models (1963: Ch. 5). In Stretton (1976), one can find alternative lower-production futures, all of which seem plausible, in which production and consumption have been altered in very different ways, depending on political forces. Interestingly, the most socially progressive models are those in which political movements react strongly against perpetuating victimization.

11. Newman & Pickett (1974) treat climatic and population factors in food supply, as does Wade (1974) in a broader overview of production changes in sub-Saharan Africa.

12. Following data in Wells et al. (1972: tables 1.2, 1.3), we can do the following computations:

$$\left\{ \begin{array}{l} \text{1970 car population} = \text{1970 population} \times \text{1970 ownership rate} \\ \quad 78{,}975{,}000 = 202{,}500{,}000 \times 0.39 \\ \text{1960 car population} = \text{1960 population} \times \text{1960 ownership rate} \\ \quad 57{,}184{,}000 = 178{,}700{,}000 \times 0.32 \end{array} \right.$$

Growth in 1960–70 car population $\cong$ 22 million cars. If there had been no growth in population from 1960 to 1970, we would have had the following growth in car population by 1970:

$= (1960 \text{ population} \times 1970 \text{ ownership rate}) - (1960 \text{ population} \times 1960$
$\quad$ ownership rate)
$= (178{,}700{,}000 \times 0.39) - (178{,}700{,}000 - 0.32)$
$= 12.5 \text{ million}$ (a "pure consumption effect")

If the ownership rate had not changed, but the population had grown, we would have had the following growth in car population:

$= (1970 \text{ population} \times 1960 \text{ ownership rate}) - (1960 \text{ population} \times 1960$
$\quad$ ownership rate)
$= (202{,}500{,}000 \times 0.32) - (178{,}700{,}000 \times 0.32)$
$= 7.6 \text{ million}$ (a "pure population effect")

Since population and ownership rates have both increased, the *additional* stimulus provided by this joint growth is:

$= (1970 \text{ population} - 1960 \text{ population}) \times (1970 \text{ ownership rate} - 1960$
$\quad$ ownership rate)
$= (202{,}500{,}000 - 178{,}700{,}000) \times (0.39 - 0.32)$

$= (23,800,000) \times (0.07)$

$= 1.7$ *million* (a "joint effect of population and consumption growth")

It is rather ironic that the popular writer Chase (1977:383) has similar objections, while the econometrician Espenshade (1978: table 2) relates automobile consumption in year "t" to the proportion of the population *under age 15* in the same year.

13. Increased ownership due to household formation ranges from 40 percent in 1960–65 to 65 percent in 1965–69, while increase in per-family consumption accounts for 50 percent and 35 percent, respectively, in the two periods. Profiles of nonowners are drawn from Wells et al. (1972: table 1.4), and are similar to Jarvis (1972:118–20).

14. Where occupations are convenient, women will work even while rearing children (Darian, 1975). Otherwise, work and childbearing are in various degrees of substitution (Kasarda, 1971; Clifford & Tobin, 1977) in most countries observed. The decline in home consumption and production of meals is likely an outcome in part of the increased work of women: made possible by increased income in the family deriving from the woman's wages, it is also more desirable because of the increased demands on the woman's time. Other consumption changes are also likely, most of which substitute more processing than alternative goods and services for those previously produced at home (Stretton, 1976: Ch. 8). This typically stimulates the economy, but simultaneously increases sociocultural production and hence environmental withdrawals and additions, because many of these goods and services are probably more energy-intensive than the labor-intensive home-produced elements they replace.

15. Heilbroner (1975:169–76) has raised the difficult question of motivating people to defer consumption for future generations, without any clear resolution. Simon (1970) provides some response by noting that natality behavior does not follow market models of discounting the future. Boulding (1973) adds to this the notion that within families there are often exchanges of material goods for love, without direct material equivalence. My own position is that, while identification with the society may be useful (Heilbroner, 1975:114–16) for mobilizing deferring of consumption, there is equal potential for such voluntary behavior by parents concerned about their offspring's futures. Alternatively, of course, coercion by the state can achieve the same goals (Boulding, 1973; Stretton, 1976: Ch. 1). Some discussion of alternative views of incorporating the future—including appreciation as well as discounting—is contained in Krutilla (1973). DeJong & Sell (1977) provide some recent data on profiles of the childless couples in the U.S., indicating their upper-middle-class concentration.

16. A systematic review of family planning programs is in Nortman (1975), and an overview of fertility reduction in Mauldin (1978). Prospects from improved contraception are treated in Jaffe (1971).

17. For discussion of the general mortality decline in the Third World, see Wrigley (1969: Ch. 6) and Petersen (1975:594–607). Some questions about this model have been raised for Ceylon (Sri Lanka), where the mortality effects of DDT spraying have been debated for some time (e.g., Gray, 1975). The extreme populationist position (e.g., Hardin, 1974) of cutting off food aid for these coun-

tries is called into question by both the geopolitics of the modern world (e.g., Finkle & Crane, 1975) and the ethical and practical fact of the historical and continuing extraction of materials and profits from these societies by the industrial countries (e.g., Barnet & Müller, 1974; Frank, 1969; Wallerstein, 1974; Callahan, 1972, 1974).

18. Hawthorn (1970: Ch. IV) treats the social utility model, and Ryder (1973) projects some of its implications. Theoretical contrasts among utility models of children are found in Cochrane (1975), some weak empirical studies in Schultz (1974), and some dissent from the excessively rationalistic model is in Leibenstein (1976, 1977). On the other hand, Dumond (1975) infers that intentional family limitation was practiced in the preindustrial period, and Caldwell (1977) applies the utility of children model to the Third World. Pronatalist policies in western countries are reviewed in Petersen (1975:549–50), and some modern socialist ones in Macura (1974) and Heitlinger (1976).

19. For a general treatment of income inequality, development, and fertility, see Rich (1973). Some peculiar exceptions to this appear in Snyder (1974), though, where short-term increases in income produce higher fertility in an African context, perhaps explained as an interim stage before longer-term changes in family expectation take over (Caldwell, 1977). An extensive discussion of children as risk-aversion investments is in Schnaiberg & Reed (1974) and Schnaiberg & Goldenberg (1975). Some empirical illustrations on returns from children of the Indian subcontinent are in Mamdani (1972) and Cain (1977). The fertility implications of higher child mortality, coupled with a need for children to aid in parent's old age, are treated in Heer & Smith (1968, 1969) and Cochrane (1971), using the Indian example.

20. The restatement of demographic transition theory at the level of the family is in Caldwell (1976, 1977) and its empirical illustration in Nigeria in Okediji et al. (1976). Overviews of the inequality-fertility linkage are in Bhattacharyya (1975), with respect to rural-urban differences. I should note that there is still considerable resistance even among social scientists to accept the relatively simple benefit-cost model of children, because of empirical and theoretical variability. No other model has such explanatory power, though, in my own view of the literature.

21. On the disruptive impact of colonialism, see Geertz (1963) and Peper (1970) on Indonesia, and Ambirajan (1976) on the varying British policies in India. On precolonial societies, see the various interpretations in Spooner (1972) on population leads and lags with respect to agricultural change. The work of Kolata (1974) on the !Kung, and Neel (1970) on South American Indian groups, estimates that these societies had lower mortality than did later colonial societies.

22. The work the populationists generally refer to is Malthus's 1798 *Essay* (Malthus, 1959), the first of seven editions published. Hardin's work includes the "commons" view (1968) and his lifeboat-survival approaches (1972, 1974).

23. The irony may be even more exquisite than Chase's (1977:393–94) critique of Hardin's commons model, though Chase is right in pointing to the economic rather than demographic point of the example. Malthus (1959) decried the effects of the enclosure laws, believing that they *created* dislocation and misery among the poor, through a variety of poor laws and other local controls to handle the resulting

unemployment of herdsmen turned agricultural laborers (e.g., Laslett, 1965:12–15). In one sense, then, the triage model adopted by Hardin from the Paddock & Paddock (1967) proposal is one more example of an economic policy aimed at blaming the poor for a situation not of their own making. My own interpretations are made after a close rereading of Malthus (1959), and discussion of his later development in Petersen (1975:154–60).

24. These include works of Schumacher (1973), Anderson (1976), Stretton (1976), Lovins (1975), and Lovins & Price (1975), all of which are variants on alternative, intermediate, or "soft energy" paths of sociocultural production. See Wade (1975) for a discussion of one group active in developing such technology.

25. This list draws in part upon discussions in Chase (1977: Ch. 16–17), Daly (1971), and Barnet (1978), though it is based on much literature as well in historical and contemporary underdevelopment.

26. See the good overview in Brown (1974) and Barnet (1978). An even more provocative thesis is that of Lappé & Collins (1977), who point to the role of developed countries and their multinational companies in depressing food availability.

27. Sprague (1975) discusses changes in Chinese agriculture, and Tien (1973) and Orleans (1976) the somewhat balanced treatment of Chinese population policies. Approximately 24 percent reduction in recent fertility rates in China is estimated by Mauldin (1978). General developmental policies up to the death of Mao are treated in Anderson (1976:242–51) and Orleans & Suttmeier (1970).

28. For overviews of India's family planning program see Nortman (1975), with an indication of about 16 percent reduction in fertility rates estimated by Mauldin (1978). Changes in rural welfare with the green revolution are treated in detail in Frankel (1971) and somewhat less pessimistically in Cassen (1975). Ehrlich & Ehrlich (1976), however, stress increased petroleum dependency of India as a result of such production gains.

29. Taiwan is treated as a family planning success model, though economic modernization seems far more salient (Coombs & Sun, 1978). Despite societal development, there is still perceived need for children as old age security (e.g., Freedman et al., 1972), suggesting less trickling down of development benefits to workers, and/or lag in perceiving new social security. Some agriculture in Taiwan follows the use of human fertilizer, as in mainland China (Sprague, 1975). But Taiwan's development has followed the path of and has been stimulated by inputs from industrial societies. This is not the model proposed here or in the recent review by the U.S. Bureau of the Census (1977:75–91). Various population incentive schemes have been discussed in Spengler (1969), Wang & Chen (1973) Ridker and Muscat (1973), and treated with approval by Demeny (1977).

30. Critical evaluations of the supposed economic benefits to be derived from population control programs are found in Leibenstein (1969, 1970), Robinson (1973), and the broad review by Robinson & Horlacher (1971). A debate about whether fertility decline leads or lags improved social security can be found in Holm (1975, 1976) and Kelly et al. (1976). An integrated model of risk and uncertainty of benefits is in Schnaiberg & Reed (1974).

REFERENCES

AMBIRAJAN, S.
1976 "Malthusian population theory and Indian famine policy in the 19th century." Population Studies 30 (1):5–14.

ANDERSON, CHARLES H.
1976 The Sociology of Survival: Social Problems of Growth. Homewood, Ill.: Dorsey Press.

BARNET, RICHARD J.
1978 "No room in the lifeboats." New York Times Magazine. 16 April:32–38.

BARNET, RICHARD J. AND R.G. MÜLLER
1974 Global Reach: The Power of the Multinational Corporations. New York: Simon and Schuster.

BARNETT, HAROLD J. AND C. MORSE
1963 Scarcity and Growth: The Economics of Natural Resource Availability. Baltimore: Johns Hopkins University Press.

BARNETT, LARRY
1970 "U.S. population growth as an abstractly perceived problem." Demography 7 (1):53–60.

BERELSON, BERNARD
1974 "An evaluation of the effects of population control programs." Studies in Family Planning 5 (1):2–12.

BHATTACHARAYYA, AMIT K.
1975 "Income inequality and fertility: A comparative view." Population Studies 29 (1):5–19.

BLAKE, JUDITH
1974 "Can we believe recent data on birth expectations in the United States?" Demography 11 (1):25–44.

BLAKE, JUDITH AND P. DAS GUPTA
1975 "Reproductive motivation versus contraceptive technology: Is recent American experience an exception?" Population and Development Review 1 (2):229–249.

BORDERS, WILLIAM
1978 "Indian scientists seek to contain growing desert." New York Times, 14 May.

BOULDING, KENNETH E.
1973 The Economy of Love and Fear: A Preface to Grants Economics. Belmont, Cal.: Wadsworth.

BROWN, LESTER R.
1974 By Bread Alone. New York: Praeger.

CAIN, MEAD T.
1977 "The economic activities of children in a village in Bangladesh." Population and Development Review 3 (3):201–227.

CALDWELL, JOHN C.

1976   "Toward a restatement of demographic transition theory." Population and Development Review 2 (3/4):321–366.

1977   "The economic rationality of high fertility: An investigation illustrated with Nigerian survey data." Population Studies 31 (1):5–27.

CALLAHAN, DANIEL

1972   "Ethics and population limitation." Science 175 (4 Feb.):487–494.

1974   "Doing well by doing good: Garrett Hardin's 'lifeboat ethic.'" The Hastings Center Report 4 (6):1–4.

CASSEN, ROBERT

1975   "Welfare and population: Notes on rural India since 1960." Population and Development Review 1 (1):33–70.

CHASE, ALLAN

1971   The Biological Imperatives: Health, Politics, and Human Survival. New York: Holt, Rinehart, and Winston.

1977   The Legacy of Malthus: The Social Costs of the New Scientific Racism. New York: Alfred A. Knopf.

CLIFFORD, WILLIAM B. AND P.L. TOBIN

1977   "Labor force participation of working mothers and family formation: Some further evidence." Demography 14 (3):273–284.

COALE, ANSLEY J.

1970   "Man and his environment." Science 170 (9 Oct.):132–136.

COCHRANE, SUSAN H.

1971   "Mortality level, desired family size, and population increase: Comment." Demography 8 (4):537–540.

1975   "Children as by-products, investment goods, and consumer goods: A review of some microeconomic models of fertility." Population Studies 29 (3):373–390.

COMMISSION ON POPULATION GROWTH AND THE AMERICAN FUTURE

1972   Population and the American Future. The Report of the Commission on Population Growth and the American Future. Washington, D.C.: Government Printing Office.

COMMONER, BARRY

1972   The Closing Circle: Nature, Man, and Technology. New York: Alfred A. Knopf.

COOMBS, LOLAGENE C. AND T-H. SUN

1978   "Family composition preferences in a developing culture: The case of Taiwan." Population Studies 32 (1):43–64.

DALY, HERMAN E.

1971   "A Marxian-Malthusian view of poverty and development." Population Studies 25 (1):25–37.

DARIAN, JEAN C.

1975   "Convenience of work and the job constraint of children." Demography 12 (2):245–258.

DAY, ALICE T. AND L.H. DAY
1973   "Cross-national comparison of population density." Science 181 (14 Sept.):1016–1023.

DEJONG, GORDON F. AND R.R. SELL
1977   "Changes in childlessness in the United States: A demographic path analysis." Population Studies 31 (1):129–141.

DEMENY, PAUL
1977   "Population policy and the international donor community: A perspective on the next decade." Population and Development Review 3 (1–2):113–122.

DUMOND, DON C.
1975   "The limitation of human population: A natural history." Science 187 (28 Feb.):713–721.

ECKHOLM, ERIK
1975   "The deterioration of mountain environments." Science 189 (5 Sept.):764–770.

EHRLICH, PAUL R.
1968   The Population Bomb. New York: Ballantine.

EHRLICH, PAUL R. AND A.H. EHRLICH
1972   Population, Resources, Environment: Issues in Human Ecology. Second Edition. San Francisco: W.H. Freeman.
1976   "The world food problem: No room for complacency." Social Science Quarterly 57 (2):375–382.

EHRLICH, PAUL R. AND J.P. HOLDREN
1971   "Impact of population growth." Science 171 (26 Mar.):1212–1217.

ENKE, STEPHEN
1969   "Birth control for economic development." Science 164 (16 May):798–802.

ESPENSHADE, THOMAS J.
1978   "How a trend towards stationary population affects consumer demand." Population Studies 32 (1):147–158.

FINKLE, JASON L. AND B.B. CRANE
1975   "The politics of Bucharest: Population, development, and the New International Economic Order." Population and Development Review 1 (1):87–114.

FRANK, ANDRÉ G.
1969   Capitalism and Underdevelopment in Latin America: Historical Studies of Chile and Brazil. Revised edition. New York: Modern Reader Paperbacks.

FRANKEL, FRANCINE R.
1971   India's Green Revolution: Economic Gains and Political Costs. Princeton, N.J.: Princeton University Press.

FREEDMAN, RONALD, A. HERMALIN, AND T-H. SUN
1972 "Fertility trends in Taiwan: 1961–70." Population Index 38 (2):141–166.

GEERTZ, CLIFFORD
1963 Agricultural Involution. Berkeley: University of California Press.

GILLETTE, ROBERT
1972 "*The Limits to Growth:* Hard sell for a computer view of doomsday." Science 175 (10 Mar.):1088–1092.

GRAY, R.H.
1975 "The decline of mortality in Ceylon and the demographic effects of malaria control." Population Studies 29 (2):205–229.

HALL, M.-FRANCOISE
1973 "Population growth: U.S. and Latin American views." Population Studies 27 (3):415–429.

HARDIN, GARRETT
1968 "The tragedy of the commons." Science 162 (13 Dec.):1243–1248.
1972 Exploring New Ethics for Survival. New York: Viking Press.
1974 "Living in a lifeboat." BioScience 24:561–568.

HAWLEY, AMOS H.
1973 "Ecology and population." Science 179 (23 Mar.):1196–1201.

HAWTHORN, GEOFFREY
1970 The Sociology of Fertility. London: Collier-Macmillan.

HEER, DAVID M. AND D.O. SMITH
1968 "Mortality level, desired family size, and population increase." Demography 5:104–121.
1969 "Mortality level, desired family size and population increase: Further variations on a basic model." Demography 6 (2):141–149.

HEILBRONER, ROBERT L.
1975 An Inquiry Into the Human Prospect. New York: W.W. Norton.

HEITLINGER, ALENA
1976 "Pronatalist population policies in Czechoslovakia." Population Studies 30 (1):123–136.

HOHM, CHARLES F.
1975 "Social security and fertility: An international perspective." Demography 12 (4):629–644.
1976 "Reply to Kelly, Cutright, and Hittle." Demography 13 (4):587–589.

HOLDEN, CONSTANCE
1974 "World population: U.N. on the move but grounds for optimism are scarce." Science 183 (1 Mar.):833–836.

JAFFE, FREDERICK S.
1971 "Toward the reduction of unwanted pregnancy." Science 174 (8 Oct.):119–127.

JARVIS, GEORGE K.
   1972   The Diffusion of the Automobile in the United States: 1895–1969. Doctoral dissertation, Dept. of Sociology, University of Michigan.

KANGAS, L. W.
   1970   "Integrated incentives for fertility control." Science 169 (25 Sept.):1278–1283.

KASARDA, JOHN D.
   1971   "Economic structure and fertility: A comparative analysis." Demography 8 (3):307–317.

KELLY, WILLIAM R., P. CUTRIGHT, AND D. HITTLE
   1976   "Comment on Charles F. Hohm's 'Social security and fertility: An international perspective.'" Demography 13 (4):581–586.

KNODEL, JOHN
   1977   "Age patterns of fertility and the fertility transition: Evidence from Europe and Asia." Population Studies 31 (2):219–249.

KOLATA, GINA B.
   1974   "!Kung hunter-gatherers: Feminism, diet, and birth control." Science 185 (13 Sept.):932–934.

KRUEGEL, DAVID L.
   1975   "Comment on Blake." Demography 12 (1):157–158.

KRUTILLA, JOHN V.
   1973   Natural Environments: Studies in Theoretical and Applied Analysis. Baltimore: Johns Hopkins University Press.

LAPPÉ, FRANCIS M. AND J. COLLINS
   1977   Food First: Beyond the Myth of Scarcity. Boston: Houghton Mifflin.

LASLETT, PETER
   1965   The World We Have Lost: England Before the Industrial Age. New York: Charles Scribner's Sons.

LEIBENSTEIN, HARVEY
   1969   "Pitfalls in benefit-cost analysis of birth prevention." Population Studies 23 (2):161–170.
   1970   "More on pitfalls." Population Studies 24 (1):117–119.
   1976   Beyond Economic Man: A New Foundation for Microeconomics. Cambridge, Mass.: Harvard University Press.
   1977   "Beyond economic man: Economics, politics, and the population problem." Population and Development Review 3 (3):183–199.

LIVI-BACCI, MASSIMO
   1974   "Population policy in Western Europe." Population Studies 28 (2):191–204.

LOVINS, AMORY B.
   1975   World Energy Strategies: Facts, Issues and Options. Cambridge, Mass.: Ballinger.

LOVINS, AMORY B. AND J.H. PRICE
1975   Non-Nuclear Futures: The Case for an Ethical Energy Strategy. Cambridge, Mass.: Ballinger.

MACURA, MILOS
1974   "Population policies in socialist countries of Europe." Population Studies 28 (3):369–375.

MALTHUS, THOMAS R.
1959   Population: The First Essay. Ann Arbor, Mich.: University of Michigan Press.

MAMDANI, MAHMOOD
1972   The Myth of Population Control: Family, Caste, and Class in an Indian Village. New York: Monthly Review Press.

MAULDIN, W. PARKER
1978   "Patterns of fertility decline in developing countries, 1950–75." Studies in Family Planning 9 (4):75–83.

MCKEOWN, THOMAS AND R.G. RECORD
1962   "Reasons for the decline of mortality in England and Wales during the nineteenth century." Population Studies 16 (1):94–122.

MCKEOWN, THOMAS, R.G. RECORD, AND R.D. TURNER
1972   "An interpretation of the modern rise of population in Europe." Population Studies 26 (3):345–382.

MCNAMARA, ROBERT S.
1977   "Possible interventions to reduce fertility." Population and Development Review 3 (1–2):163–176.

MESAROVIC, MIHAJLO AND E. PESTEL
1974   Mankind at the Turning Point: The Second Report of the Club of Rome. New York: New American Library.

MYRDAL, GUNNAR
1970   The Challenge of World Poverty: A World Anti-Poverty Program in Outline. New York: Pantheon.

NEEL, JAMES V.
1970   "Lessons from a 'primitive' people." Science 170 (20 Nov.): 815–822.

NEUHAUS, RICHARD
1971   In Defense of People: Ecology and the Seduction of Radicalism. New York: Macmillan.

NEWMAN, JAMES E. AND R.C. PICKETT
1974   "World climates and food supply variations." Science 186 (6 Dec.):877–881.

NORTMAN, DOROTHY
1975   "Population and family planning: A factbook." Seventh edition. Reports on Population/Family Planning (October).

O'CONNOR, JAMES
1973   The Fiscal Crisis of the State. New York: St. Martin's Press.

OKEDIJI, FRANCIS O., J. CALDWELL, P. CALDWELL, AND H. WARE
1976   "The changing African family project: A report with special reference to the Nigerian segment." Studies in Family Planning 7 (5):126–136.

ORLEANS, LEO A.
1976   "China's population figures: Can the contradictions be resolved?" Studies in Family Planning 7 (2):52–57.

ORLEANS, LEO A. AND R.P. SUTTMEIER
1970   "The Mao ethic and environmental quality." Science 170 (1 Dec.):1173–1176.

PADDOCK, WILLIAM AND P. PADDOCK
1967   Famine, 1975! Boston: Little, Brown.

PEPER, BRAM
1970   "Population Growth in Java in the 19th century: A new interpretation." Population Studies 24 (1):71–84.

PETERSEN, WILLIAM
1975   Population. Third edition. New York: Macmillan.
1976   "An 'optimist's' pessimistic view of the food situation." Social Science Quarterly 57 (2):365–374.

POHLMAN, EDWARD
1971   How to Kill Population. Philadelphia: The Westminster Press.

POLEMAN, THOMAS T.
1975   "World food: A perspective." Science 188 (9 May):510–518.

RAULET, HARRY M.
1970   "Family planning and population control in developing countries." Demography 7 (2):211–234.

RICH, WILLIAM
1973   Smaller Families through Social and Economic Progress. Washington, D.C.: Overseas Development Council.

RIDKER, RONALD G.
1972   "Population and pollution in the United States." Science 176 (9 June):1085–1090.
1973   "To grow or not to grow: That's not the relevant question." Science 182 (28 Dec.):1315–1318.

RIDKER, RONALD G. AND R. MUSCAT
1973   "Incentives for family welfare and fertility: An illustration for Malaysia." Studies in Family Planning 4 (1):1–11.

ROBINSON, WARREN C.
1973   "Benefits of fertility reduction." Studies in Family Planning 4 (10):262–266.

ROBINSON, WARREN C. AND D.E. HORLACHER

1971 "Population growth and economic welfare." Reports on Population/ Family Planning, no. 6 (February).

RYDER, NORMAN B.

1973 "Two cheers for ZPG." Pp. 45–62 in M. Olson and H.H. Landsberg (eds.), The No-Growth Society. New York: W. W. Norton.

SAMUELSON, PAUL A.

1978 "Economics of discrimination." Newsweek, 10 July:56.

SCHNAIBERG, ALLAN AND D. REED

1974 "Risk, uncertainty and family formation: The social context of poverty groups." Population Studies 28 (3):513–533.

SCHNAIBERG, ALLAN AND S. GOLDENBERG

1975 "Closing the circle: The impact of children on parental status." Journal of Marriage and the Family (Nov.):937–953.

SCHULTZ, THEODORE W.

1974 Economics of the Family: Marriage, Children and Human Capital. Chicago: University of Chicago Press.

SCHUMACHER, E.F.

1973 Small Is Beautiful: Economics as if People Mattered. New York: Harper and Row.

SIMON, JULIAN L.

1970 "The per-capita income criterion and natality policies in poor countries." Demography 7 (3):369–378.

1977 The Economics of Population Growth. Princeton, N.J.: Princeton University Press.

SKLAR, JUNE L.

1974 "The role of marriage behavior in the demographic transition." Population Studies 28 (2):231–247.

SNYDER, DONALD W.

1974 "Economic determinants of family size in West Africa." Demography 11 (4):613–627.

SPENGLER, JOSEPH J.

1969 "Population problem: In search of a solution." Science 166 (5 Dec.):1234–1238.

SPOONER, BRIAN (ED.)

1972 Population Growth: Anthropological Implications. Cambridge, Mass.: MIT Press.

SPRAGUE, G.F.

1975 "Agriculture in China." Science 188 (9 May):549–555.

STRETTON, HUGH

1976 Capitalism, Socialism and the Environment. Cambridge: Cambridge University Press.

TEITELBAUM, MICHAEL S.
 1975 "Relevance of demographic transition theory for developing countries." Science 188 (2 May):420–425.

TIEN, H. YUAN
 1973 China's Population Struggle: Demographic Decisions of the People's Republic, 1949–1969. Columbus, Ohio: Ohio State University Press.

TINBERGEN, JAN
 1975 "Demographic development and the exhaustion of natural resources." Population and Development Review 1 (1):23–32.

UNITED STATES BUREAU OF THE CENSUS
 1977 Planning for Internal Migration: A Review of Issues and Policies in Developing Countries. ISP-RD-4. Washington, D.C.: Government Printing Office.

VERMEER, DONALD E.
 1976 "Food, farming, and the future: The role of traditional agriculture in the developing areas of the world." Social Science Quarterly 57 (2):383–396.

WADE, NICHOLAS
 1974 "Sahelian drought: No victory for western aid." Science 185 (19 July):234–237.
 1975 "New Alchemy Institute: Search for an alternative agriculture." Science 187 (28 Feb.):727–729.
 1976 "Inequality the main cause of world hunger." Science 194 (10 Dec.):1142.

WALLERSTEIN, IMMANUEL
 1974 The Modern World-System: Capitalist Agriculture and the Origins of the European World Economy in the Sixteenth Century. New York: Academic Press.

WALTERS, HARRY
 1975 "Difficult issues underlying food problems." Science 188 (9 May):524–530.

WANG, C.M. AND S.Y. CHEN
 1973 "Evaluation of the first year of the educational savings program in Taiwan." Studies in Family Planning 4 (7):157–161.

WELLS, JOHN D., N.J. ASHER, M.R. FLOWERS, M.E. KAMRASS, G.R. NELSON, F.F. SELOVER, AND S.A. THOMAS
 1972 Economic Characteristics of the Urban Public Transportation Industry. Arlington, Vir.: Institute for Defense Analyses.

WOLFERS, DAVID
 1971 "The case against zero growth." International Journal of Environmental Studies 1:227–232.

WORLD BANK
 1975 Environment and Development. Washington, D.C.

WRIGLEY, E.A.
 1969 Population and History. New York: McGraw-Hill.

III THE ROLE OF TECHNOLOGY
Deus ex Machina or Social Creation?

TECHNOLOGICAL FACTORS IN ENVIRONMENTAL DEGRADATION

Introduction

The uncertainty expressed in Chapter II regarding the role of population growth in environmental decay will be dealt with in two ways in this chapter. First, there is increasing certainty about the socially risky effects of modern technologies and their environmental withdrawals and especially additions. In the terms of Chapter I, these effects are more voluminous, widespread, long-term, and vital to ecosystem organization than previous sociocultural production effects.

Second, such technological effects can in no way be directly linked to growth in populations. While national increases in population can increase demand for the products of such technologies, marketing for many such goods is global, and located among the slower-growing affluent consumers. More crucially, the decisions to innovate with such technological shifts are not made democratically or demographically, but are located within the firm and the state, not in the population at large.[1]

This chapter, then, addresses several issues. The first is an appreciation of the environmental effects of more modern production technologies. Next, the historical factors that have operated to create such technological restructuring are outlined, particularly with regard to advanced capitalist societies. In the course of this, the altered nature of science and its connection to technological change will be partially explored. Finally, I will note some pressures for technological reform that have arisen in recent decades, and some actual alterations of technology in recent periods.

To set the conditions for this analysis, let me first define my use of *technology:* Borrowing from Freeman (1977:225), technology is here defined as "a utilized method of production." In contrast to definitions that emphasize the pool of potential information, our concern with the consequences of production necessitates this definition (which others have referred to as "technique").[2] For withdrawals and additions to the biosphere depend on more than technological information: "The proper people must possess the information and must be part of an organization which can make effective use of the information" (Freeman, 1977:225).

The emphasis throughout this chapter is on the social bases of technological change. Technological change is seen neither as self-reproducing—a kind of technological imperative—nor as some diffused property of society.[3] Both individuals and, more importantly, organized production and other enterprises *make* technological change. The underlying question is whether:

> those men charged with utilizing these ideas will do so intelligently... not only in the sense of effective exploitation of their productive possibilities but in the larger sense of effective adaption to the material and human environment so as to minimize waste, pollution, social frictions, and other "external costs."
> (Landes, 1969:4)

Our concern is with the environmental "externalities" of contemporary technology: all those costs of sociocultural production which producing organizations externalize outside the firm or government agency to various groups in society.[4]

In evaluating the environmental effects of technology, we must distinguish qualitative from quantitative aspects. Much of the work on technological factors in environmental decay suffers from a confusion between these two issues. Less important than technological invention and innovation—such as the discovery and first use of a product such as DDT—is the subsequent spread of such production. In terms of linking technology to the biospheric organization, this separation is crucial. Any given production element may disrupt on ecosystem.

With rare exceptions, such disruption will be minimal so long as the volume of production remains small. If DDT were spread on only one hundred acres of agricultural land, its persistance as a toxic agent and spread up the food chain would be interesting, but relatively trivial for a concerned environmentalist. As the volume approaches millions of acres, however, the interesting feature becomes transformed into a major biospheric disruption, and eventually into a social problem.

Such considerations lead us back to the axiom of Chapter I: Every technology, if widely enough practiced, will generate environmental problems. Eventually the quantitative environmental effects of technology supercede the qualitative ones. The logic of this follows directly from our biospheric model. Since technology, by definition, always involves some processes of ecosystem withdrawals and additions, unlimited expansion of these processes will generate significant, widespread, and permanent damages. This follows from the first law of thermodynamics. However, there is an optimistic corollary of this axiom. Any technology, no matter how environmentally risky, can always have attendant environmental problems minimized if its applications are limited.[5]

While such extreme statements may be obvious, they lead to an interesting distinction. The quantity of technological applications is clearly closely tied to the volume of production. All questions of technology in this sense become reduced to questions about levels of production, rather than about the nature of the production processes or the goods produced. Conversely, qualitative aspects of technology become especially important where quantity issues are not yet the major problem.[6] Such qualitative dimensions are the focus of this chapter.

Figure 1 presents a logical picture of such differences. Any combination of quantity/quality of technology that falls above the curve DD' generates some level of environmental disruption that we will call an *environmental problem*. Conversely, any combination falling below this does not produce a sufficiently negative impact to merit such a label. For purposes of this chapter, we might call anything to the left of line BB' a *production* problem, and anything to its right a *technological* problem. The line is an arbitrary one, as is the curve. But the essential logic is not arbitrary.

Figure 1 is not a model of sociotechnological history. It is a classification of different kinds of production technologies. Developed industrial societies generally have mixtures of traditional technology

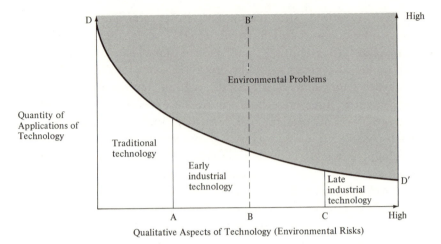

Figure 1   Relationship between environmental problems and the quantitative and qualitative aspects of technology.

(e.g., organic farming), early industrial technology (e.g., subsurface mining), and late industrial technology (e.g., chemical/plastics industries). So do Third World societies. The differences are in the proportions themselves, with industrialized societies like the U.S. having higher concentrations of capital (and labor) in higher-risk early and late industrial technologies. Third World societies are concentrated in traditional and early industrial types.

Moreover, this conceptual model ignores the historical accumulation of some environmental problems: e.g., deforestation because of past usage in traditional technologies (as in India and China), or depletion of mineral reserves because of conventional pit or seam mining (early industrial technology).[7]

Finally, it should be noted that a given production organization may incorporate elements of very different technologies in producing its commodities or services. Consider, for example, the case of generation of electricity. Power plants can include high-risk elements such as nuclear reactors (late industrial technology), along with steam production (early industrial technology). Coal-fired power plants span the range from traditional to early industrial technology of coal mining, coupled with electricity-generating turbines. These cover low- to moderate-risk elements of technology. All power plants produce substantial heat, converted into both electricity and waste heat generation. Heat wastes are low-risk, so long as volumes are not excessive. Recent increases in electricity production have turned many of these low-risk wastes into local, regional, and even global environmental problems, raising water and air temperatures.[8] This is a good illustration of the low-risk, high-volume case represented in the far left side of Figure 1.

Figure 1 can be used to conceptualize certain major categories of environmental problems. As a crude approximation, we can think of technologies on the left hand side as relating more to questions of depletion (ecosystem withdrawals). Those on the right are more related to pollution (ecosystem additions). Both sides thus relate to ecosystem and biospheric disorganization. Nonetheless, it may be helpful to think about low-risk technologies on the left side as relating more to energy and material extraction, and those on the right as relating more to synthetic chemical transformations.

With this conceptual model in mind, the rest of this chapter will relate primarily to the higher-risk technologies that characterize mature industrial societies like the United States—those to the right of BB′. Those to the left of this line relate more to the problem of production, and will be covered in Chapters IV and V.

Technology, Energy, and Matter

To illustrate a complex technology close to line BB′, let us start with a common consumer item: frozen orange juice. The contrast I will make is between this form of production and consumption, and the traditional form of consuming oranges, either as fruit or as domestic, manually produced juice.

Start in the citrus grove, where orange trees are protected by petrochemicals. Pesticides keep insects away from oranges. Herbicides allow full growth of trees. Fertilizer is also added, which may be manufactured from deposits of potash or phosphate rock.[9] All of these factors of production of oranges today are manufactured and then shipped great distances, involving high levels of energy consumption (usually fossil fuels). Moreover, their application in the groves is often energy-intensive as well, being sprayed by ground or aircraft equipment that relies on fossil fuels. Picking of these oranges may be by hand or by machine. The latter involves more energy.

Next, oranges are shipped to a processing plant by truck (energy-intensive). They are cut, squeezed, evaporated by vacuum processes to reduce water content, and packed by machines into containers that are made of paper, plastic, and tin and steel—the latter three being very energy-intensive goods. High energy is involved in machine processing as well. Packaged juice is frozen by energy-intensive refrigeration equipment, shipped by refrigerated truck to a supermarket, where it remains refrigerated until purchased. In the home, it continues to be refrigerated (frozen) until use. The need to keep the juice frozen (a need arising from the deterioration of the taste and vitamin content of orange juice otherwise) requires a continuous expenditure of energy, from the time of packing to the time of consumption. Finally, the consumer thaws the juice, mixes it with water, and drinks it. The container is disposed of. The paper is theoretically biodegradable, but neither the plastic nor tin lids are. Generally, all three would go into local landfills, withdrawing land from other uses. Alternatively, they might be dumped in various bodies of water, disrupting the physical structures and changing the chemical composition of the water, thus leading to alterations in plant and animal species compositions.

Environmentally it is clear that this is a very energy-intensive process, at minimum. On the positive social side, it provides for year-round availability of orange juice anywhere where there are stores with freezers and consumers with freezer units in their refrigerators. On the negative side, it creates substantial biospheric withdrawals: the removal of nonrenewable energy materials such as oil (for energy, agrichemicals, and plastics), and tin and iron (for the lids). In theory, the paper is produced from a renewable resource—trees. Other nonrenewable resources include the fertilizer deposits tapped and mineral resources required for the manufacture of the processing machinery. And the ecosystem additions include the potentially hazardous agrichemicals.

Contrast this with the model of direct consumer use of whole oranges, either cut or hand-squeezed (on a metal, plastic, or ceramic juicer). If we add to this the requirement that the production of oranges be closer to organic farming, the following is an alternative production history. Oranges are fertilized by human labor, using recycled animal, human, or other organic wastes (such as orange peels), supplemented by the minimum additions of manufactured fertilizers (to provide soil balance and continued soil productivity). Weeding and pest removal is done manually, as much as possible. Shipping containers (wood and/or cardboard) are filled with oranges and shipped by train wherever possible (given the heavy regional concentrations of orange groves, rail sidings are entirely feasible). In stores, the oranges do not require much refrigeration, if they are sold quickly. No refrigeration is required by consumers if they consume the oranges within several days of purchase. Shipping containers are reused, requiring transportation by rail back to the groves. Finally, consumers either dispose of peels or use them for compost. (In the previous model, peels may be used to produce orange extract or perfumes, or may simply be disposed of by processing plants, adding to landfills). This second model would produce oranges for some of the year, and more of the period if we permit refrigerated (not frozen) storage of oranges near the groves.

Clearly, this second form of production—a form that predominated until at least after World War II in the United States—is far less environmentally hazardous. It is somewhat less convenient for consumers who desire the taste and nutritional value of oranges through *juice*—but the same qualities exist in the second form. Note that stores today generally carry *both* frozen juice and whole oranges, and consumers frequently purchase both. This is not, as many antienvironmental critics delight in pointing out, a harking back to some future "good old days."[10] Contemporary production/consumption processes include both forms, though the organic growing and rail shipment model of the second form rarely exists.

This single example of consumer goods production demonstrates some environmental effects of a shift from a more traditional low-risk technology to a somewhat higher-risk later industrial one. We can extend it to very high-risk technologies if we add a stipulation that all of the electricity used in the process derives from nuclear power plants—a not unrealistic model, particularly for Florida production of orange juice.

What is true of the unobtrusive shift from fresh oranges to frozen orange juice is typical of most transitions from traditional to late industrial technologies. The majority of these become more energy-intensive: the energy content of all the necessary production processes increases per unit produced. In some, but by no means all of these technical innovations, the matter content of production has also increased. There are many forms of production in which the materials used per unit product have constantly been reduced. But it is rare to find modern technologies operating with smaller total energy inputs than equivalent earlier production processes. The hallmark of modern technology is its typical labor-saving quality—not its energy-saving aspect.[11]

A second aspect of much later industrial technology is the substitution of new synthetic *chemical* forms—often petrochemicals derived from oil—to replace previous natural resources. In our orange juice example, synthetic pesticides and herbicides have replaced some natural agricultural materials. Earlier, the qualities of mixtures of plants themselves were used to repel pests and limit weeds. In like manner, we now replace the natural resource of human labor, as in the substitution of herbicides for weeding labor. Plastics have replaced paper and wood products, as in the orange juice container. Production of plastics involves both chemical and physical processes, generally starting with relatively small amounts of oil products (as contrasted with large amounts of wood pulp, say).

The production of such goods typically involves chemical wastes, nondegradable final products, and potentially harmful wastes in a variety of applications (as in vinyl chloride). Because many of these synthetic chemicals are not similar to natural products, they represent potential environmental hazards in many ways. As they pass among the species in ecosystems, they are not transformed and metabolized (in contrast to human and animal excrement wastes). They are persistent, then, in two ways: (1) they do not readily or predictably decompose and become less toxic, and (2) they do not remain within a single species, but get passed through the food chains in many ecosystems, affecting the structure of many of them. The best-documented example of this is the case of DDT, one of the examples of modern technology that helped initiate strong scientific and political concern and action in the 1960s. The first example of such modern technological activity that aroused substantial scientific activism was the case of nuclear weapons testing and the hazards of nuclear power, emphasizing some continuity of technological concern in environmental movements.[12]

These energy-intensified and synthetic chemical aspects of later industrial technology comprise the basic concern of this chapter. In general, the environmental effects of this technological transformation are subject to much ignorance and increasing dispute, as attempts are made to regulate both energy usage and the production of synthetic chemicals. Petrochemicals have increased chemical transformation of natural resources, and have increased the use of inanimate energy in production. Both have qualitative and quantitative ecosystem impacts that are shared with earlier technologies—such as the impacts that Mumford traces to the fifteenth century:

> The fields are devastated by mining operations . . . the woods and groves are cut down . . . there are exterminated the beasts and birds . . . Further, when the ores are washed, the water which has been used poisons the brooks and streams, and either destroys fish or drives them away. (Mumford, 1963:71)

Qualitatively, this could be a description of modern mining communities, with physical transformation of materials from underground. The discontinuity represented by modern technology is the less visible, often less detectable ways in which ecosystem effects are felt. Oil-based technologies rely on cleaner operations than coal-mining. But they lead to continuous problems of combustion and of oil spillage on land and in the riverways and oceans, with uncertain long-term effects. For "oil" is a term for a highly diverse range of organic materials, each of which has potentially different biological impacts. Nuclear radiation is even less certain in its effects on species, and the dispute continues as to whether there is any "safe level" of exposure, without genetic or cancerous effects. Most synthetic modern chemicals—derived from oil (or earlier, from coal)—fall somewhere between the two extremes of oil and nuclear radiation impacts. Sadly, our level of research is miniscule, relative to the range of such chemicals introduced in this century, particularly following World War II. Both the petroleum and the nuclear-based modern technology, therefore, entail considerable social risks to accompany their internal profitability for industries. They have also brought social improvement as positive social externalities: comfort, freedom from sickness, improved nutrition, and increased material consumption.[13]

THE SOCIAL BASES OF TECHNOLOGICAL CHANGE

Competing Models: Society, Science, Governments, and Firms

Technological changes in the twentieth century are viewed by many analysts in very different frameworks. At a broad level, Mumford notes that in America, "In the act of 'conquering nature' our ancestors too often treated the earth as contemptuously and as brutally as they treated its original inhabitants" (Mumford, 1970:11). While Mumford stresses that harmful technology arises especially from modern social and economic organization, he indicates in numerous ways the pervasive social forces that undergird a careless or "runaway technology" that existed well before the modern period.[14] Following cultural historians, he perceives a dominant ideology of technological extension, since

> either the primeval abundance was inexhaustible, or else . . . losses did not matter, since modern man through science and invention would soon fabricate an artificial world infinitely more wonderful than that nature had provided. . . . (1970:11)

Such an expansionist pressure in western society was eventually coupled, by some views, with an ideology of science, whose "proof of validity was found in its application, to produce 'mastery over the environment'" (Landes, 1969:24). Both Landes and Mumford note the crucial role of technological changes in political developments in early periods. By 3000 B.C., a new social technology, the organization of a state military "megamachine," developed, which was used by kings living off a new agricultural surplus created by prior agricultural technology.[15] Science, the creation of systematic knowledge, is variously seen as ranging from totally unrelated to technological history, to being virtually synonymous with it. Metallurgical science was linked to mineral mining and military armament manufacturing, in one of the earliest ties between science, technology, and the state. This profitable state patronage of science and technology is seen as continuing and expanding over modern history, with the increased involvement of governments in "big science" related to military and aerospace industries.[16]

This theme of government involvement in science and technology ignores the more general autonomy of both science and of technological change agents, at least up to the twentieth century. On the one hand, technological changes prior to and following the first industrial revolution were often based on trial-and-error, organized by individual entrepreneurs, often with little scientific knowledge. Technological development spread slowly, with little conscious organizations of such change. "Little science," although often supported by elite patrons, had relative autonomy. The scientist's work was avocational and not occupational, in many cases. And it frequently was not linked to any major concern with production technology. Exceptions certainly existed for all of these claims. But the general theme of only the loosest association between organized science, organized technological change agents, and the nature of both governments and the private sector businesses seems valid.[17]

Expansions of early industrial technology, based largely on this trial-and-error model of semi-professional or amateur inventors and innovators proceeded through the nineteenth century. Major transformations in materials processing occurred through the increased use of manufactured chemicals (albeit substitutes for preexisting ones) and the increase in the use of coal, wood, and steam. Many of these industries grew to substantial sizes, concentrated by the nature of technology (steam power) and the distribution of resources (coal). And owners of firms accumulated liquid capital from their profitable industries and political power from their increased wealth, displacing old agricultural elites.[18]

In the later periods, beginning towards the end of the nineteenth century and into the first quarter of the twentieth, a number of changes occurred. A variety of technological and scientific educational institutions expanded, based on private and state support. Many of these scientific schools were built around the German research model with focused, narrow research agendas, particularly in the chemical area. And land-grant agricultural and mining schools in the U.S. had practical, technological aims in inducing further technological progress. In the U.S., there were serious attempts to engage in economic planning and research regarding the utilization of public lands and their natural resources, under the rubric of "conservation."[19]

From my limited review of the literature, there is little clear explanation of the timing and form of relationships amongst science, technology, government, and the firm in the following decades. But it seems reasonable that increasing volumes of liquid capital stimulated and responded to new scientific and technological inventions to produce new investment in chemical and electrical industries. In part this appears to reflect the limited growth opportunities in the early technologies of the first industrial revolution (textiles, railroads, heavy chemicals). The linkages between capital owners and technological innovators were still relatively weak, although apparently more support was provided within companies and for outside research. Except for heavy wartime demands, scientists were still relatively autonomous, although those in chemical areas especially found support from industry.[20]

World War II mobilized and concentrated more scientific, technological, and capitalist efforts in military production, and reinforced and extended the notion of social progress through science, technology, and economic growth. The dramatic successes of German chemists in substituting a variety of petrochemical products for the Nazi war machine were a harbinger of later national and international efforts along these lines. Though there are many exceptions to this trend, the shift from a "little science" to "big science" or from "academic science" to "industrialized science" is frequently dated from this period.[21] And the linkages of the atomic weapons and later military and peaceful applications of nuclear fission clearly follows from the wartime integration of scientists and technologists with their national governments and military authorities. While inventions would continue to flow from independent researchers,[22] a new organizational form of routinizing technological development arose—research and development (R and D). This was soon firmly established in virtually every industrial country, and in all large and many smaller firms, which saw "the visible triumph of technology based on applied science. Applied science has now become the basic means of production in a modern economy... [and] industry has been penetrated by science." (Ravetz, 1971:21)

Following the social evils of the Great Depression, and the new economic interventionist theory of Lord Keynes, governments in all industrial countries became more active participants in this new research and development flowering. With some genuine social concerns, a new political reductionism appeared in the postwar period. Economic growth would solve all social problems, and technological development would be the engine for such growth, drawing on the fuel of public support for production sciences.[23] The result was seen as benign technological progress, or malign runaway technology:

> The scientist himself becomes a servant of corporate organizations intent on enlarging the bounds of empire.... Increasingly, the "g.n.p." of industry reflects the gross national product of science. (Mumford, 1970:123)

It has altered the whole man versus environment confrontation in a way which now gives the human agent much more initiative in the adaptive process than he formerly possessed. (Rosenberg, 1972:118)

The engine of innovation and production which we now possess is . . . so pervasive that there is no place to hide from them. . . . In calculating costs and benefits, it ignores . . . in part, the degradation of the natural and human environment. (Ravetz, 1971:53, 55)

There is no assurance that noneconomic exogenous factors—above all, man's incompetence in dealing with his fellow-man—will not reduce the whole magnificent structure to dust. (Landes, 1969:4)

The widely discrepant views of analysts of technology in part reflect both differing political and social views, and different focuses on technological change.[24] Unfortunately, much of the research has accepted rather crude views of the motivations behind modern technological changes, and the resulting distributions of social goods and bads. There has been belated and partial recognition of the ecological externalities of modern technology. Yet the standard economic and political defense is that "we have no right to complain about the consequences" (Rosenberg, 1972:201) because "we" have derived great benefits from modern technology. The "we" and the "why" both require elaboration, though, before this or any other polar position on technological change can be accepted.

The Role of Private Capital in Technological Change

"Like other economic activities, inventive activity is responsive to market forces and the prospects of financial gain . . . a pursuit [directed by] . . . changing perceptions of future profits" (Rosenberg, 1972:6).

This model underlies much of the research on technological change. It states that such change, especially in the U.S., was left in the hands of private enterprise (with the exceptions of military and space research). Moreover, although the relations are complex in this model, the general theme is that new investments stimulate new inventions, which in turn deepen and broaden a technological change.

This is true whether the inventors are private ones or members of research and development teams in the firm, another firm, or a government agency.[25]

Why did the recent technological change take the form it did— synthetic/chemical and energy-intensive? Among other explanations, the most common seem to be (1) the availability of relatively cheap energy; (2) the increase in wages and the organization of industrial labor; (3) the ability to substitute freely for natural resources that were inaccessible, in short supply, or of unpredictable volume or quality; and (4) the ability to lower costs and dominate competitive markets with new products or cheaper processes.[26] Essentially, these all result in technologies that tend to be labor-saving, on balance (though they may also be slightly capital-saving) per unit production.

As I will note later, there are also significant economic changes produced by and stimulating this process, including a concentration of capital into oligopolistic or "monopoly capital" enterprises. These capture economic, technological, and other economies of scales, in that they are buffered by size and production diversity from many of the constraints of the idealized competitive or "free" market. More than just increased short-run profitability, then, the objectives for many technological investments appeared to be protection of an expanded future market for large-scale enterprises. This fulfills the early predictions of Joseph Schumpeter and the later ones of John Kenneth Galbraith:

> Progress becomes "automatized," increasingly impersonal and decreasingly a matter of leadership and individual change. (Schumpeter, 1928:384)

> The modern industry of a few large firms [is] ... an almost perfect instrument for inducing technological change. (Galbraith, 1952:91)

> The empirical data on numbers of innovations and on R and D expenditure on the whole support the view of Galbraith in the concentration of innovative activity in capitalist industries ... enough are [made outside] to facilitate the entry of newcomers into monopolized industries. (Freeman, 1977:255)

While observers vary considerably on the social values they place on this technological change, there is little question of an increasingly concentrated and accelerated stream of innovation in production in large-scale industries. Despite periodic crises of capital shortages, the flow of funds to research and development has continued. Indeed, technological change is the domain in which both domestic and international corporations compete most fully in the modern world-system. Thus national governments not only routinely measure the society's R and D expenditures, but seek to supplement them in areas where private capital is not sufficient and/or where profitability is not high enough for private enterprise to stake the funds. Nuclear and solar development are two recent examples of this.[27]

Contrary to some earlier theories, then, many large-scale industries at least acquiesced in technological change, resisting any challenge to their market positions. But further, they appear to have extended and consolidated their positions precisely through this technological development—which stimulated both the scale of production (see Ch. V) and of profitability substantially. Economists for two decades have been trying to estimate the shares of total economic growth due to technological investment. While there is broad agreement that it is substantial, the lack of detailed institutional studies precludes any socially realistic estimate of such contributions,[28] leaving the citizen with the overview that: "Technological development is the most important source of growth in per capita income, and all nations are interested in increasing their standard of living" (Layton: 1977:197).

This application of private capital to technological research and to its incorporation in production has a number of social consequences, in addition to the ecological ones noted earlier. In general, the historical extraction of both natural resources and human labor in sociocultural production serves to accelerate the risks to both. For profitability in one period frequently becomes transformed later into "new investment in plant and equipment—i.e., . . . it *embodied* technical change" (Freeman, 1977:227). As seen by Marxist theorists, this transformation of human labor in one period into machinery in the next, forces an adaptation by workers to a new set of workplace conditions, and represents an objectification of the control of capital owners over workers:

> The wealth produced by the productive activity of the worker is turned into capital, much of which is subsequently reinvested in technological equipment. This equipment is frequently used simultaneously to harness the worker to a particular type of work, to dictate the rate at which he works, and to achieve the reproduc-

tion and increase of the capital that employs him. (Dickson,
1975:179)

In addition to immediate consequences for some segment of the
labor force, the general process of technological change implies risks
of displacement and disruption for workers. It can, of course, equally
well provide inducements for improved working conditions and wages.
Politically, organized labor may increase its commitments to many
forms of technological change. The recent ability of the large-scale
corporation to innovate technologically at rates fast enough to absorb
existing workers through applications of greater capital per worker
appears, in the U.S. at least, to have been a race in which inducements
have outweighed punishments. It is for this reason that the voice of
organized labor has been conspicuously absent from most complaints
about high-energy industries and from the calls for technologies that
are more benign.[29] Yet there remains in much technological investment a persistent labor threat:

> It was not so much the high level of wages but rather the persistent
> experience of pressures on the labor market, the numerous oppor-
> tunities elsewhere in a resource-abundant environment, and the
> high degree of labor mobility, which conditioned people to expect
> further future increases in the cost of labor relative to other inputs
> (Rosenberg, 1972:55)

That is, the persistent threat needed and/or used to chasten a "free
labor" operating in a "free market" according to competitive theories is
the availability of technologically-altered investments in production,
which are capital- and energy- rather than labor-intensive. In addition
to the general social control of labor, the routinization of technological
change has had important effects on scientific labor as well. The result
has been an "industrialization of science," on the one hand, and an
incorporation of scientists within the firm, on the other:

> Technological communities met their own needs... technology
> became... itself scientific and a generator of the scientific knowl-
> edge most closely associated with practice. (Layton, 1977:209–
> 10)

> Although this new industry of "R. and D." employs many scien-
> tists (indeed, the bulk of graduates in science and technology go
> there rather than into teaching or university research), its working
> ethics are descended from industry, private and state-supported,
> rather than from academic science. (Ravetz, 1971:54)

> The stress placed on the cultural importance of abstract science legitimates the ideology of scientism, yet disguises . . . the very fact that the existence of contemporary science—in terms of support for R and D—results directly from this practical (technological) use. (Dickson, 1975:189)

> The illusion [of] a natural science standing pure . . . is disappearing . . . replaced by the vulgar reduction of science to a branch of commercial or military industry. (Ravetz, 1971:9)

Again, not all scientific labor is so engaged, and not all technological research supports merely the expansion of private sector production and its profitability. Yet the ideology of an industrialized science serves as a model and a competitive opportunity for individuals and organizations that choose to ignore or repudiate such incorporation of "technical progress" views and activities. Consciousness and concern about such trends has shifted in the past decade at least, and the issue is now at least debated, if not resolved: a mark of social progress since the commitment to a uni-directional technological progress of earlier postwar periods.[30]

The Role of the State in Technological Change

Even in the United States, where technological change has been largely in the hands of private enterprise, there have been government supports for such change. In Western Europe, especially following the deprivations of World War II, governments took a far more direct hand. Large-scale public investment in scientific and technological policies was directed toward rebuilding industries and satisfying built-up consumer demand from the Depression and war periods.

In all these societies, though, government involvement took a variety of other supportive roles. Taxation supported science and technology education, the creation of research institutes, grants to researchers in private industry for technological and scientific research, and direct agency research. The last of these was heavily concentrated in military applications, later in atomic weapons and nuclear power research and development, and still later in space exploration.[31] Following Mumford (1963, 1967), the military connection has proven to be an enduring one. In the modern period, the spread effects have been much greater, not only in terms of the social model of the military megamachine. As well, the stimulation of a vast array of "high technology" developments has underwritten private sector extensions of military-derived technology to nonmilitary applications.[32]

While some of these have been ecologically more efficient innovations—such as energy-efficient laser development—many have reinforced continuity of high-energy and synthetic chemical changes. Supersonic passenger aircraft like the Concorde and herbicides like Agent Orange have both represented a reinforcement of these technological paths (with military markets either stimulating the innovations, or enabling an extension of earlier innovations by expanding markets). Nuclear energy has been virtually totally underwritten in its early decades by public-sector investment, and continues to rely heavily on research and development in the public sector. Indeed, with the Atomic Energy Commission, even the agencies charged with "regulating" the private utility industries using nuclear power were simultaneously marketing advocates for this technology.

Beyond these commitments, governments favored a general capital-intensive technology through a variety of tax policies. Lower taxes on capital gains, rapid capital depreciation allowances, local and state tax "holidays," and other subsidies for new capital-intensive industries that would add to property tax rolls: all directed public attention and preference to capital-intensive investments. Conversely, heavier employer-shared employee taxes—such as Social Security and local employment taxes—added a counter-bias against labor-intensity in many cases. While a number of these policies represented a disjointed taxation approach in many countries, especially the United States, they all were congruent with the dominant ideology of (a) economic growth as the solution to all social problems, and (b) technological investment as the most efficient path to growth. By and large, this is still a dominant ideology supporting these patterns of investment, despite a decade of disclaimers noting the ecological and social costs of many of these policies.[33]

Through such policies, governments freed even more private capital for investment in new technologies, which could allow for increasing diversification and power of the "technostructure" of large corporations. Moreover, in matters of public investment in technologically relevant policies—whether in science education or the importance of new energy sources—representatives of the energy and chemical-intensive industries are labelled as experts to be drawn in as consultants to legislatures and executive agencies. While some parallels to American technological politics can be found in the public technocrats in western Europe, at least the latter had potentially greater public accountability for their policies. Private sector technocrats could, with clear legitimacy, argue for public sector commitments with an underlying motive of private sector profitability. In the absence of a public sector debate over "science policy," piecemeal decisions made in the U.S. continuously supported an exponential increase in energy-intensive production and in the expansion of plastics, chemicals, and other industries based on ecologically-risky synthetic and novel chemicals.[34]

If petroleum was the basis of both energy-intensification and the development of petrochemicals, the especially favored status of oil corporations helped undergird the particular directions of technological change. Until the 1973–74 "oil crisis," domestic and international policies stimulated low-cost petroleum production to the greatest possible extent. Governments depended largely on oil corporations for their information on supplies, and on experts from these corporations for taxation and other policies affecting the companies. Regulation of these energy corporations has increased substantially in the last five years. Yet there still remains a heavy dependency on industry expertise for alternative oil policies, despite an increased range of participants brought into the more open "energy policy" disputes in recent years.[35]

All of these policies have varied among western governments, leading to variations in the rate of energy and chemical intensity of production and products in western nations. While the directions have been similar, the considerable variation indicates the importance of political choices that were made. The fact is that "technological development" is a matter of both public and private policy, and not some monolithic *deus ex machina*. It was not inevitable that technology moved so uniformly and rapidly to "forms of energy and materials which are man-made. . . . Technology [was] receptive to offers from science, and natural science, having lost its function of creating world views, itself tends to become merely technical science" (Böhme, 1977:337–38).

SOCIAL RESPONSES TO TECHNOLOGICAL CHANGE
From Invisibility to Visibility

Unlike the earlier wood-based "eotechnics" and later coal-based "paleotechnics" that Mumford (1963) described, the modern "neotechnics" thrive in part because of their social invisibility. In one sense, this seems paradoxical. Capital-intensification of production in this century suggests a more overt and dramatic exploitation of nature, one that ought to raise social visibility or consciousness. Perhaps the most telling indicator of this is the notion of advanced industrial societies like the United States as postindustrial. While such views explicitly incorporate a sense of enormous technological progress, they just as explicitly ignore all the negative social and environmental externalities of such technology, and magnify the positive social externalities to the greatest extent possible. Like Mumford's naive optimism about the social liberation to be derived from neotechnics, these postindustrial theorists systematically ignored the vastly increased industrialization and environmental withdrawals and additions. Rather, the notion was of a liberation *from* nature, a view that technological optimists still hold.

Beyond these lofty observations of social seers, though, lies a foundation of a certain quality of invisibility of modern technological production. A variety of factors explain this: (1) decreased employment in direct production activities, (2) the decentralization of many production functions, (3) especially low employment in environmentally extractive activities, and (4) technological progress viewed as routine, anticipated social change. The first three explain the absence of persistent contact with the interfacing of modern machines and the natural environment.[36] The last explains a lack of desire to probe farther into the workings of technology, and especially into its negative environmental and social externalities.

To illustrate, consider the differences between a subterranean coal mine and a land-based oil well. At first, the latter would appear highly visible to the casual observer, the former highly invisible. If we were to extrapolate from this isolated example, the later technology of oil extraction would appear far more visible than the earlier coal technology. But let us draw the contrasts more carefully. First, how many workers are there in the mine, versus at the well? For most large-scale operations, there are substantially more coal miners and a surrounding community of families. Second, what happens to the products of each operation? Normally, coal is loaded onto long trains of box cars, while oil disappears into a surface pipline or a subsurface one. Third, what residues result from using the two products? Coal produces various grades of ash (particulates), which collect and/or are dispersed into air, water, or land. Oil, in contrast, leaves no ash, and its chemical byproducts (nitrogen oxides, hydrocarbon compounds, sulfur exides) are generally dispersed into the air. Recent emission technologies trap both coal ash and some oil-produced gases in various kinds of filtering devices, ranging from stack-gas electrostatic precipitators to catalytic convertors in automobiles. Yet coal-ash devices produce a much greater volume of sludge than do oil-gas devices.

What do these differences between the two technologies suggest? For society, as opposed to any individual observer, there is in fact a substantially greater visibility, or consciousness, associated with coal production than with oil. Newer and more risky chemical/energy technologies tend, by definition, to have fewer workers associated with direct production. They also generally have less visible packaging and distribution, and less obvious waste products (additions to ecosystems). In part, this is inherent in the nature of these technologies, which are capital-intensive, substitutive of large volumes of raw materials, shipped in the most economical forms of transportation over long distances, and passed quickly through ecosystems into biospheric sinks (atmosphere, oceans). Our earlier contrast of frozen orange juice versus consumption of whole oranges further illustrates this same differentiation: the frozen product is also less socially visible.

In general, the location of many modern, large-scale production activities has been separated from both large segments of corporate employment, and from large population concentrations as well. Electrical machinery power, and even oil-based machinery, are more capable of decentralization than were bulkier steam-based machines. This, coupled with improved costs and speed of transportation, has allowed for the separation of much white-collar work from blue-collar work within the firm. It has, for economic reasons, concentrated financial operations in cities, and manufacturing and extraction in more distant and relatively unpopulated areas (though trends towards suburbanization of populations have altered this in recent years). Man-made environments, then, surround workers and citizens, while the active machines and their environmental withdrawals and additions are socially and physically segregated. Moreover, even many of the rural extractive activities are observed by fewer people, since modern technology has substantially reduced agricultural labor and the rural population.[37]

All of these invisibilities are accentuated when we consider that resource extraction activities have become especially capital-intensified. Mining, lumbering, and agriculture are all in recent decades areas of high machine substitution for human labor. Moreover, even these smaller workforces—as in offshore oil rigs—have less of a community surrounding them, as operations are relatively mobile. Roving oil rigs, shifting mechanical harvesters, movable timber teams and the like afford a portability and impermanence to settlement that intensifies an invisibility or public unconsciousness of such extractive activities.

Finally, what employees and local populations have "seen" when they actually observe technological operations is not the negative social or environmental externalities, but the hallmarks of "progress." The ideological roots of this have been so firmly established that even those with little direct gain from any concrete investment—through jobs, taxes, services—have sensed a social gain from the mere presence of such activities.[38] And proponents of investment patterns have magnified the anticipations of direct economic and social benefits such as jobs and taxes, despite the realities of low employment multipliers and underassessment of many industrial properties.

In the past decade or so, there has been some reversal of this invisibility from a number of sources. One must be careful not to overstate the case, though. Increased consciousness and wariness of technology at the abstract level is not matched by uniformly sustained efforts at serious reform of technological patterns.[39] Nonetheless, technological commitments are at least marginally more socially visible today. The reasons for this are far from clear. Among them we might include (1) increased recreational activity in more remote natural areas; (2) increased dispersion of population into suburban and exurban locations; (3) concentrations of industrial wastes in water, air, and land that accumulated over decades; (4) increased scientific awareness of some ecological impacts; and (5) mobilization of the public by older and newer environmental organizations. Roughly stated, there has been, first, more of a population-at-risk of direct contact with some technology-environment interfaces. Second, there has been more awareness of the extensity and societal risks of these externalities of production. This has produced increased mass awareness, and more importantly, some organized efforts at various types of technology evaluation and reform.

Visibility and Conflicts over Technological Control

To some observers' perspectives, technological development has not only become more socially visible in recent years, but has become threatened to the point of stagnation by "technology harassment."[40] From the view presented above, the only explanation that can be offered to support such a perspective is that, especially in the United States, technological innovation in industry had so little social constraint that any mild reassessment or increment of regulation can only be seen as a dramatic *relative* increase. That there has been increased attention paid to technological issues is unquestionable. But that it has seriously slowed the major tendencies is simply not the case (Nelkin, 1977).

Neither the rate of synthetic, unnatural chemical inventions, nor production, nor the rate of energy consumption has slowed in this period. At most, what we can point to is increased transaction costs of industries using energy and synthetic chemicals—i.e., costs of regulation, public relations, some occupational safety, and pollution abatement equipment that are not routine production costs. Part of these are genuine corporate internalizations of the negative social and environmental externalities of production—i.e., a response to past social claims about such problems. Some, though, are expenses incurred to defuse such claims—to address public interest and governmental claimants in a political fashion without systematically dealing with the claims themselves. Corporate advertising "in the public interest," what in earlier environmental movement days was called "eco-pornography," has increased in a concerted effort by organizations such as the Business Roundtable. These expenses are designed to raise public confidence in large-scale corporations, in technological development, and to attack government regulatory costs and ineffectiveness as "wasteful."[41]

Defenders of existing technologies point to the passage of legislation such as the Clean Air Act, Water Quality Control Act, National Environmental Policy Act, and the recent Toxic Substances Control Act as evidence of increasing social control over production. Likewise, even the development of a Congressional Office of Technology Assessment, designed to provide guidance for federal government investment alternatives, is deemed threatening to the future of "the economy" in the competitive world market. Even the area of clearest change—the diminishing U.S. commitment to nuclear energy—has been vastly overstated by technological advocates. For, though it is true that nuclear energy has become a far less attractive option in the U.S., in part the reason for this is simply the inaccurate benefit-cost ratios assumed by past enthusiasts. While safety concerns have certainly raised the costs somewhat, inflation of virtually every other cost has matched this, and the reliability of modern nuclear power plants has proven less than earlier anticipated.[42]

Moreover, while proponents of high-energy and synthetic chemical technologies have experienced this relative increase in social visibility and social control, they have also followed their traditional responses in attempting to capture the new regulatory agencies. There have been both overt and covert attacks on the new regulatory agencies, enforcement of existing legislation, and the social credibility of public interest groups. Many of these efforts have been successful, though recent public opinion polls still indicate a wariness of technological developments and a commitment to improvement of the environment. Unfortunately, while such public opinion—even if validly measured—is a useful backdrop for political analysis, the area of technology assessment and control is one in which domination by experts still prevails.[43]

Three new developments have altered the potential for future technological changes, beyond tinkering with the present system and internalizing a small share of environmental and social hazards. The first is the increase in oil costs, which has set off conflicting production paths. Conservation (and cost-saving) is pushed, on the one hand, and pressures for increased energy development, on the other. One interesting development, in the United States in particular, has been an increased salience of the socioeconomic processes that transform natural environmental elements into or out of the "resource" category. Petroleum was in the nineteenth century a nonresource, later turned into a major industrial resource for energy and petrochemicals. Coal, in many areas and industries, was turned into a nonresource, accelerated slightly in recent years under the pressures for air pollution control. On the other hand, with the increase in OPEC oil prices, coal has been transformed—at least in government pronouncements—into a more valuable social resource, because it is more domestically available than oil. Uranium, meanwhile, teeters and totters from boom to bust to boom, depending on political decisions regarding the future of nuclear power.[44]

Beyond this change in energy prices and potential unavailability in the next twenty years, there are two other major developments that make for a potentially stronger control over future technological development. The first is the increased political and social concern of scientists and technologists themselves, initiated by the antinuclear weapons campaign of the 1950s and continuing into the environmental concerns of the 1960s and 1970s. Such a "critical science" differs from an earlier academic science, removed from practical concerns, and the more recent industrial science, linked to technological change but without any control over such changes.[45]

The last of the potentially important changes in social responses to the modern technological system is the development of holistic alternatives. Intermediate technology of Schumacher, or alternative technology, or the "soft path" of Lovins, represent models of application of capital and labor that are different from the present industrial system.[46] Importantly, such alternate systems of technology are not piecemeal attacks on the present system, but represent quite different organizational principles, with goals other than simply profit maximization and aggregate national economic growth. Neither are they, like the trenchant analyses of the 1960s, simply critiques of the present system, but proposals for what are seen as practical alternatives. This is, of course, a view from the proponents of such technological reorganization. Defenders of the present industrial system casually dismiss such counterproposals as the "Chinese laundry" system of labor-intensive production.[47]

How seriously do these changes influence the current organization of technology? From the recent vantage point of Galbraith, these are revolutionary ideas and unanticipated dissent:

> The question arises whether the industrial system, in absorbing economic conflict, ends all examination of social goals. Do its techniques of control—its management of market behavior and its identification with and adaptation of social goals—serve also to minimize social introspection? In brief, is the industrial system monolithic by nature? (1971:314)

Yet Galbraith also noted the seeds of dissent a decade ago, without a clear vision of the outcome of such dissent. It is not much easier to envision long-term changes even from our present position of relative hindsight.

Technological Assessment and Change, and the Politics of Externalities

With the recent ferment about the social and ecological costs of technological development, two underlying models may be seen. The first is that many of the negative externalities of high-technology production were unanticipated by private and public sector decision makers at the point of implementation. From this perspective, the needs are for new information for "transferring technical trends into social objectives" (Salomon, 1973:106-7). Such increase in critical science, more involved in technology assessment, will not be easy, though:

> The problem of achieving effective democratic control on the decisions of technological innovation is beset by . . . many difficulties. . . . combinations of contrary purposes, with bureaucratic operations, and the different ideologies. Yet if this problem is not solved, our social lives will come to be ruled to an increasing extent, by blundering bureaucrats and experts. (Ravetz, 1971:362)

At the other extreme, perhaps, is the near-monolithic technostructure. It had prior information about these negative externalities, but a set of profit and power goals that contributes to both ecological and social consequences of technological development:

> Pollution is in large measure the product of deliberate decisions to minimize the direct costs of production on the part of a business firm, public utility, or municipal government. . . . After all, if such destruction were merely wanton, if it could be terminated at no cost whatever, it would presumably be done immediately. (Rosenberg, 1976b:219)

> The enemy . . . is not ideology but the engineer. . . . It is advanced technology and the specialization of men and process that this requires and the resulting commitment of time and capital. . . . It is open to every free-born man to dislike this accomodation. . . . All that is necessary is to undo nearly everything that, at whatever violence to meaning, has been called progress in the last half century. (Galbraith, 1971:49-50; sentence order reversed)

For Galbraith, it is the technological development that has made the large corporation large and powerful—both economically and politically. And it is the calculation and careful coordination of inputs that has made this development and organization so successful in dominating production. While this may be overly simple, it points to an organizational intentionality that has an intelligence and commitment that will not readily be deterred by simple information about environmental or social problems. Enormous political and social conflict—

and perhaps the undoing of "nearly everything"—are the sole mechanisms by which this intentionality can be offset.

The contemporary movements to assess and reform technology struggle between these two models—of unintentionality and intentionality of socioenvironmental risk.[48] Participatory technology, as such movements are termed, vary between mild reformist and dramatic revolutionary approaches to contemporary technology and production organizations embodying it. A middling view is that "assessment itself is a political process involving evaluation of the social desirability or undesirability of specialized technologies" (Nelkin, 1977:429). In one sense, the mildest form of this is a refinement of earlier classical models of consumer sovereignty. Here, though, consumers are more organized, and hence presumably more potent in their counsel to producers. And they occasionally have the force of regulatory and economic powers of the state behind them, with new environmental protection legislation. The production system is seen as readily corrigible, with new inputs of information about harmful effects of technology. A somewhat more politicized view is that better documentation of such effects is necessary, as well as increased public consciousness of these, to effect more political and social pressures on wayward industries.[49]

The latter position has to be the minimum degree of politicization of any technological reformist movement, at least in capitalist societies. The theory of the firm—and one most honored even by the large corporation and its technostructure—is that every firm operates most efficiently when it externalizes all such negative externalities (and attempts to internalize positive ones, wherever possible). Efficiency is the standard of accountability, the ideological basis, for the industrial system and individual corporations. Other goals must be *forced* politically into the calculus of the firm, directly or indirectly, by governments and organized political forces. And long-term efficiency of large-scale, high-technology firms has generally dictated increased control of production and distribution through increased use of energy and synthetic chemicals (Rosenberg, 1971). It has likewise encouraged an evaluation of what were production wastes, to be disposed of in ecosystems as cheaply as possible.

Economic theory dictates that the only exceptions to this are when material recovery from wastes is more profitable, and substitution of lower for higher forms of energy is profitable. One of the great economic ironies is that technological development has made materials relatively cheaper, and hence less worth recovering. In part this is precisely because energy was so cheap and available, and petrochemicals and other materials were substitutable for traditional production inputs, and in smaller quantities per unit production. And petrochemicals were made progressively cheaper, easier to spread widely, and thus uneconomic to recover.[50]

Thus, movements to reform technology will encounter economic and political resistance from producers. They will likewise encounter opposition from those whose investments have enjoyed higher returns because of the particular economic patterns of technological development, ranging from individual to institutional investors. And, within the confines of any reasonable variants on the present industrial system, they will confront opposition from consumers whose *perceived* standard of living has increased because material goods are relatively cheaper due to this technological history.[51] Milder and cheaper reforms are possible, with sufficient political mobilization. But these merely slow the rate of increase of many environmental hazards, and only occasionally reverse these—as in the case of some forms of air and water pollution. And they tend to do so in a somewhat socially regressive way.[52]

On the other hand, more extreme efforts at reorganization of production and its technology address both a wider array of ecological risks, and social equity issues as well. Until recently, such efforts had little credence in industrial societies. In part, this followed from the fact that the basic model of alternative technology initially addressed Third World societies, where there was (1) a paucity of capital, (2) a surplus of labor, and (3) limited natural resources in many cases. Interestingly, even conventional economic growth models pointed towards these directions well before environmental concerns were widespread. These were, then, socioeconomic reforms, not environmental ones.[53]

The transfer of many of these models to the industrial society movements occurred under perceived pollution and especially energy "crisis" pressures, following the 1973–74 OPEC actions. Because of the potential for employment of lower-skilled and unskilled labor in such models, using smaller amounts of capital and energy per worker, there is a greater political potential for mobilization of poverty and some working-class groups to such efforts. Conversely, though, the overt attack on energy-chemical technology in such holistic models mobilizes opposition from investors, owners, managers, and the organized branches of labor employed in high-technology industries. The latter coalition, by any reasonable political analysis, is far more potent than any current combination of alternative technology forces.[54]

Yet there is increased consciousness of socioenvironmental costs of current technology fostered by such movements (including the environmental movement itself). This expands the ranks of potential opponents of such technologies to the point where one could state that fully one-third of California voters voted for a potential nuclear shutdown in that state in the 1976 Proposition 15 referendum. Increased operating and capital costs—public and private—of expanding fossil fuel and nuclear energy sources may potentially change the calculations of investors and managers as well.[55]

Moreover, each increment of change in the present system has similar effects. Banning DDT, controlling PCBs, reducing nuclear power plants and the like can increase both perceived risks of modern technology and the political efficacy of organized opposition to it. Conversely, though, it may lull opponents into complacency and stimulate far more potent forces of reaction from conventional economic interests and their political and public agency supporters:

> In any debate over a proposed innovation, the most loud and consistent voice will be that of the group promoting the new device. At best, they will be honest practitioners, of traditional myopic engineering: their problems are defined in hard, quantitative terms, and their projected solution may well be the only one possible on the assumption that the technological and social context of the problem remains unchanged... [They are now] joined by the apostles of runaway technology, who have the last refuge of "progress":... if an existing device can be made larger, faster and more expensive, then it is violating a law of nature to abstain from doing so. [This]... ideology is given support by the history of technology, both folk-history and scholarly. (Ravetz, 1971:360)

The mobilization of technical expertise and political support has generally been easier for the technostructural system, with its stock of experts and economic supporters. There have been earlier calls for accountability, reform, and reorganization, most of which have been deflected or co-opted by the large corporation. It remains to be seen how soon and how far reformist and reconstructionist movements will compromise with the existing structure, as they are urged to do from every quarter.[56] For Ravetz (1971:428) points to the paradox that, as opposition to current technology increases in effectiveness:

> If one accepts responsibility for the maintenance of a general welfare, including that of one's opponents, one is on the path to corruption and impotence. . . . It is easy [though] to maintain one's integrity when one's words and actions are ineffective. [sentence order reversed]

To understand the "corruption and impotence" that is likely, a fuller understanding of the structure and dynamics of the present economic structure is needed. For it has been unclear to many analysts what the social options are for technological investment and sociocultural production. Indeed, from many theoretical positions, the notion of social options was itself alien until just recently. Alternative consumer, managerial, and political dimensions will be treated in the following two chapters, elaborating and integrating some of the insights broached here. If we are to realistically confront environmental problems, we must appreciate not only the important qualitative technological aspects of these, but the factors that lead to quantitative increases in ecosystem withdrawals and additions. And that requires some overview of the production system as system, with its points of insularity and openness.[57]

NOTES

1. The argument here parallels that of Commoner (1972), which was an early attempt to refute a populationist perspective of Ehrlich especially. Two somewhat more refined versions of his argument are in Commoner (1977a,b).

2. What I term *technology* here is often referred to as *technics* (Mumford, 1963, 1967, 1970) or *technique* (Ellul, 1964; Freeman, 1977). It is consistent with usages in Rosenberg (1972, 1976a,b) and other economists. Defining technology as a pool of knowledge (e.g., Freeman, 1977) is more useful when an analysis is on the scientific and related roots of modern social organization. My focus here is on the environmental effects of and more direct sources of production shifts; and hence I find this term more useful (see similar usage in Ch. VI, VII).

3. In particular, this analysis differs from the global cultural analysis of Lynn White, Jr. (1967). It seeks an institutional elaboration of the roots of technological change beyond the broad brush of Leo Marx (1970), though Marx's view is more consonant with this chapter, as is Moncrief's (1970) refutation of White.

4. Such externalities typically remain outside the purview of neo-classical economists, who deal with the firm and its "internalities": costs of production and the relations of supply and demand. Efficient firms seek to maximize their profits, pricing according to internal costs. In general, in any economy with any degree of competition, it is in a firm's interest to externalize to society at large (realistically, to particular groups and locales in the society) as many costs as possible, to facilitate profit-maximization (e.g., Barkley & Seckler, 1972: Ch. 8). Insofar as government agencies may also be involved in production, the same concepts may apply, though with modification of profit designations, perhaps.

5. This is most clearly indicated in the case of nuclear power. If the world possessed but a few nuclear reactors and a handful of nuclear weapons, even this most hazardous technology would pose little ecological and social risk. Unfortunately, even minor expansions of applications beyond this pose real risks, and such expansion had occurred some two decades ago (Commoner, 1970).

6. For example, Commoner (1977b) notes that petrochemical technology is premised on vastly expanded markets for such products: the economic logic of this and other ecologically hazardous technologies dictates that qualitative risks are joined to quantitative production levels that exacerbate them. Conversely, Waldron et al. (1978) note that recent water pollution abatement procedures seem able to handle a good deal of traditional wastes, products of earlier industrial technology (and human consumption), but cannot deal well with petrochemicals.

7. Mumford's early work (1963; orig. pub. 1934) gives some illustrations of such deforestation and localized depletion (e.g., pp. 72ff).

8. For a discussion of broad climatic influences, see Kellogg and Schneider (1974); such influences include carbon dioxide and pollution effects, as well as heat loss.

9. The fertilizer thus manufactured may not be a petrochemical, and thus not as hazardous; some fertilizers are petrochemicals—i.e., complex, organic compounds that have no natural equivalents in the biosphere. Following Commoner (1977b), the biological hazards arise in part because organisms have no evolutionary mechanisms for dealing with these man-made chemicals.

10. See, for example, NYT (1976) for a typical recent critique. The theme is that both environmental and social hazards were greater in nineteenth century cities.

11. Anne Carter (1970) has shown through input-output analyses that the quantity of materials used for a fixed schedule of American goods has diminished, but the quantity of energy has risen (Schurr & Netschert, 1960), quadrupling from 1850 to 1900, and from 1900 to 1955 (Rosenberg, 1972:157–65). While economists frequently stress some capital-saving aspects of modern technology, the general impact has been more labor-saving (Freeman, 1977:228; Enos, 1962; Samuelson, 1967:720–22).

12. Barry Commoner is the best example of this continuity: his earlier work (1970) emphasized radiation hazards from nuclear weapons testing, drawing on the opposition of atomic scientists in the Federation of Atomic Scientists (now the Federation of American Scientists), exemplified by the writings of Szilard (1961) and *The Bulletin of the Atomic Scientists*. This and Commoner's later work (1972) emphasized increasingly the dangers of petrochemicals (see also his 1977b work).

Another recent effort (1977a) is a critique of nuclear power and energy-intensification in general. The difficulties entailed in sustaining such environmental analyses
are treated in Ch. VI, and the problems in inferring social costs and benefits in
Ch. VII.

13. On the complex effects of oil pollution, see Browne (1978); on radiation
effects, an early attack is in Gofman and Tamplin (1971) and a later one in
Commoner (1977a). See Commoner (1977b) on petrochemical risks and benefits,
and Waldron (1978) on recent political conflicts over assessing and controlling such
chemicals in New Jersey. A typically strong economic case for the benefits of such
technologies is made in Rosenberg (1972) and in many of his essays collected in his
later (1976b) work. Rosenberg (1971), reprinted as Ch. 12 of the latter, makes a
strong case for technological control of additions through pollution abatement, and
of material substitutions as a solution to depletion following high withdrawals. See
also his Ch. 13–14 (1976b), Barnett & Morse (1963) and Hayami & Ruttan (1971)
for similar optimism on solving pollution and depletion problems. None of these
deal very well with ecosystem organization, but focus on single materials and single
problems.

14. The term runaway technology is Jerome Ravetz's (1971, 1977), describing
not only the increase in scale and profitability but the "intoxicating . . . possibility of
the creation of new technical powers" (1971:56).

15. Mumford (1967: Ch. 8) links the development of a collective, power-
seeking state, increased social scale, and increased exactitude to a new organizational
form—the "megamachine"—that was more a social than a mechanical invention.
Landes (1969:31ff) notes mercantilist policies as among the first organized linkages
between science/technology and the state.

16. "Big science" (Price, 1963) is especially notable following World War II,
though Price argues this was a gradual accretion. The linkage of government military policy and technology has been noted by both advocates and critics of modern
technology: e.g., Rosenberg (1971) and Mumford (1963, 1967, 1970).

17. Mumford (1967) stresses the "transcendental aspirations and demonic com-
pulsions" (p. 11) that tended to make for both social influences upon *and* from
science and technology; Dickson (1975:180–89) makes similar observations. Few
other researchers have focused on as broad a cultural and social organizational
interplay as does Mumford, however, and this may account for the notion of
scientific autonomy that pervades most of the other literature in the area. Ravetz
(1971) terms this a period of "academic science." Moscovici (1968) treats this as a
period of transition from artisan to engineering labor, shifting from organic to
mechanical nature. Derek Price (1965) finds little overlap in scientific and
technological work in terms of the written products of each, though his concentration on scientific papers (e.g., Price, 1963) may disguise other links. Rosenberg
(1972:118–20) does indicate some science-basis of technological work in the
nineteenth century, drawing in part on Jewkes et al. (1958). Böhme (1977: 337–
38) also notes some conversion of science into technology in this period; see Hall
(1961) and Koyré (1948) for illustrations.

18. For general trend descriptions, see Mumford (1963), Landes (1969), and
Rosenberg (1972). There are important distinctions between development rates for

various industries, and between capital-goods and consumer-goods industries (e.g., Rosenberg, 1976b: Ch. 1, 2, 8, 10; Rosenberg, 1972:39–54). Landes (1969, 31ff) notes the more rapid development of technology when traditional elites were restrained.

19. For scientific developments, see Ravetz (1971:16–18), Rose & Rose (1969), Derek Price (1963), and Boulding (1965). On the technological views of conservationists in the early part of the twentieth century, see Rosenberg (1976b: Ch. 13) and Hays (1969). Rosenberg sees far more conflicts between conservationists and technological enthusiasts than does Hays.

20. The work of Schmookler (1966) strongly argues that industrial demand for inventions creates its own supply; Rosenberg (1976: Ch. 15) argues that this ignored a variety of obstacles in various industries and countries, though he welcomes Schmookler's syncretic views. Landes (1969:3–4) summarizes the shift from the first to the second and third industrial revolutions, the last of which began in the second quarter of the twentieth century.

21. At an abstract level, Price (1963) follows the development of little science into big science, with its centers and invisible colleges of specialized scientists. Increasing use of scientists in military technology applications is discussed in Layton (1977), Lakoff (1977), and Nelkin (1977:397–401). The resulting industrialized science is critically reviewed by Ravetz (1971, 1977), Greenberg (1967), and Rose & Rose (1969), who note the redirection of academic science to "technical problems," and away from earlier theoretical work and from contemporary social ("practical") concerns.

22. On the importance of independent inventors, see Layton (1977:210–16), Jewkes et al. (1958), Myers & Marquis (1969), and Freeman (1977:250–58). Although this input is an important point in the history of ideas, the fact that most technological innovations require embodiment in capital (Freeman, 1977:225–27; Mansfield, 1968) means that control over technologies rests with private and public capital managers.

23. Galbraith (1971) traces the development of a resulting industrial-governmental "technostructure" following such a commitment. A similar approach is in Baran & Sweezy (1966), though their critique is sharper and more Marxist. Landes (1969) also notes the increase in western European involvement in technology, following the war.

24. For example, Marxists have long sought an industrialized science, serving the interests of society and not simply private capital: see Bernal (1939), Easlea (1973), Ravetz (1977), Rosenberg (1976a), and Dickson (1975: Ch. 2 especially). The efficiency of capitalism in generating productive technological change was noted in *The Communist Manifesto* (Marx, 1954:16–22) as "an immense development to commerce, to navigation, to communication by land. . . . It has been the first to show what man's activity can bring about . . . " (1954:16, 19). Lenin was very favorable to the Taylorist system of labor organization (Braverman, 1974:12–13). This historical commitment to rational scientific expansion of production has led to uneasiness amongst neo-Marxists, though there have been several attempts to provide an environmental and social critique (e.g., Dickson, 1975; Anderson, 1976).

25. See Nelkin (1977) and Rosenberg (1971) on the military connection, and Freeman (1977) on the diversity of sources of innovation.

26. This summarizes some core arguments of Rosenberg (1972), Galbraith (1971), Landes (1969), and Freeman (1977).

27. Freeman (1977) summarizes trends in research and development, and their varied returns. Nelkin (1977) differentiates public and private R and D patterns, while Galbraith (1971) and Baran & Sweezy (1966) integrate the relations of private and public decision-making in R and D.

28. Among the earliest studies were Solow (1957) and Abramovitz (1956), which estimated capital and presumably technological factors in U.S. economic growth. Following and extending this tradition is the detailed empirical work of Machlup (1962) and Denison (1962, 1967, 1974) on the U.S. and other western countries. Denison estimates (1974: Table 8-2) that over ⅓ of the growth in national income from 1929–69 in the U.S. was due to the "advance of knowledge"; i.e., changes in the organization of production. Unfortunately, Denison and his economic colleagues typically measure this technological input as a *residual,* after all other *measured* inputs to production are recorded in statistical records. For this and other reasons of conceptual and theoretical deficiency, there has been much criticism of such types of analyses: e.g., Brown (1966), Lave (1966), Rosenberg (1976b: Ch. 4). Useful discussions are also in Layton (1977) and Freeman (1977).

29. The commitment of high-technology workers especially is noted in Hannon (1975) as one explanation for political opposition to new energy policies. Refinements of earlier Marxist views of class relations point to workers' stakes in the current system. Wolfe (1974) and Giddens (1973) indicate the ways in which post-scarcity conditions have altered such stakes.

30. See Nelkin (1977) and Ravetz (1977) for some overviews of such recent criticism.

31. Layton (1977), Freeman (1977), and Nelkin (1977) summarize some of these trends.

32. Wilford (1978) traces a familiar theme: the civilian benefits from space exploration, the latter itself a first cousin of military rocketry and weaponry. Reciprocal reinforcement occurs when such "economic" benefits are used to rationalize further "national pride" projects (Nelkin, 1977), which in turn stimulates further technological development by having the public sector pick up R and D costs and early innovations.

33. Stretton (1976:44–48) notes the protection of capital gains by most western governments, even under environmental pressures. O'Connor (1973) enumerates the multiplicity of contributions made by the state to private accumulation, a neo-Marxist version of Galbraith's (1971) technostructural model.

34. As a bizarre illustration of the power of multinational petrochemical companies, Borkin (1978) notes that U.S. corporations supplied the Nazi-supporting I.G. Farben industries with crucial information for tetraethyl lead production process in the late 1930s. Moreover, I.G. Farben was left intact after World War II, to engage in multinational technological development with its American "enemies."

35. The single best work on oil companies is John Blair's (1977) work; see also Sampson (1975), whose information was drawn from testimony partly gathered by the Church committee on multinationals (see Barnet & Müller, 1974).

36. Among the postindustrial theorists, the work of Bell (1973) is best known. In the debate between Stearns (1974) and Bell (1974), the latter stresses that workers today "experience a world without dealing with recalcitrant nature (as does a farmer, miner, logger, or fisherman) or in relation to a machine or the making of things" (p. 24).

37. Indeed, one of the measures of improved economic efficiency used in Denison's studies of growth (e.g., 1974) is the *removal* of labor from agriculture.

38. Stretton (1976), for example, consistently stresses the importance of past expectations of lower-income groups that future growth would finally bring them prosperity. He anticipates formidable social opposition to mechanical zero-growth policy. Risks in altering technology are so widely perceived that even organized labor is less unified on matters of occupational safety and health (e.g., Burnham, 1978a; King, 1978).

39. On attitudes to technology, see the California study of Todd LaPorte & D. Methay (1975). Given the conflicting and confusing statements of experts over the years, though, it is hardly surprising that views on energy are far less clear on the need for, say, conservation (e.g., Fischman, 1978).

40. See Leon Green, Jr. (1972) for this view, widely shared by industrialists.

41. Though no universal definition exists, economists see transaction costs as those costs other than production costs necessary to link supply with demand. The model of claimants is drawn from Spector & Kitsuse (1977), that of "ecopornography" from Turner (1970). For general attacks on environmental and other regulations, see Rattner (1978a) and Crittenden (1978).

42. See Hill (1977) for an assessment along these lines, and Burnham (1978b).

43. On technology attitudes, see LaPorte and Methay (1975); on environmental opinions, see Mitchell (1978). Public education, interest, and concern is welcomed by those who see solutions to social problems in more public information-gathering and discussion (e.g., NAS, 1969; Etzioni, 1968, 1969; Heidt & Etzioni, 1969) in an "active society." The question of whether or not such participation gets co-opted is a pressing one, though.

44. See Rosenberg (1976b: Ch. 13–14) for a discussion of how technological development had turned natural resources into social resources, and also how substitution of materials has conversely turned some earlier materials into less socially useful entities. Ironically, Sampson (1975:296–97) notes how OPEC used environmentalist arguments to support their price rise—i.e., as their contribution to "conservation."

45. Ravetz (1971) terms this a critical science movement, while Nelkin (1977) treats it as a participatory one. This more active stance of scientists contrasts with Lakoff's (1977), as well as Schooler's (1971), assessments of the relatively politically impotent role of scientists and technologists up to the present (see also Ch. VI below).

46. Included here would be Schumacher (1973), Lovins (1976), and the "new alchemists" (Greene, 1976). Dickson (1975) and Anderson (1976) review and critique politically many of these alternative production schemes, from a humanistic Marxist perspective, while Stretton (1976) does so from a less doctrinaire social democratic one.

47. This is the term used in Barkley & Seckler (1972:193, footnote 2) for such

increases in labor intensity. Their view arises because, in large part, they take a modified neoclassical economic view that many environmental and related social externalities can be internalized in production, with minimal reorganization. Their position is largely congruent with the economist Rosenberg's (1976b) essays, though his epilogue indicates some increased questioning of the feasibility of such smooth modification of the present technological system (see pp. 280–89).

48. Robert K. Merton (1936) was the first social scientist to deal with such issues of "unanticipated consequences" of social behavior, though it has found widespread usage since. It should also be noted that, even in the 1930s and 1940s, there were social scientists engaged in technology assessment: e.g., see various essays in Ogburn (1964). At this point, it is unclear what effect, if any, they had on the course of social action, politics, or technological development.

49. Such efforts would be needed for "societal guidance," according to Etzioni (1968, 1969), if we were to have a genuinely "active society" devoted to solving and not papering over social problems. On the other hand, Alford & Friedland (1975) question such simple notions of participation in social and political decisions, arguing that with the fragmented political structure in the U.S., much of this participation is noninstitutionalized, co-opted, and repressed (p. 472). Similar concerns, though without such overt political analyses, are in Salomon (1973), Brooks (1976), and Nelkin (1977:422–27).

50. Rosenberg (1976b: Ch. 14) makes some of these observations (e.g., in footnote 2).

51. One major problem is that consumer perception is oriented primarily to overt costs, those of direct consumption. All of negative externalities that operate through increased health, maintenance, and governmental regulation costs are not systematically perceived as connected to such technological development. Indeed, cost-conscious consumers and workers are being encouraged daily by those industries that are regulated to *decrease* regulation (e.g., Crittenden, 1978).

52. See discussions on this in Ch. VII.

53. For an applied focus on this, see Straussman (1968). A general treatment is in Reynolds (1963: Ch. 25, 28) and Rosenberg (1971). Unfortunately, the role of multinational large corporations has undercut much of this logic in practice (Barnet & Müller, 1974).

54. See Hannon (1975) and Schnaiberg (1975) on these distributional issues. Stretton (1976) points to a number of future social options in how to distribute such costs and benefits.

55. Federal science policy is somewhat sensitive to this (Sullivan, 1978), in encouraging less energy-intensive forms of economic growth. European pressures on the U.S., in part a reflection of the declining value of the dollar, act in the same conservation-of-energy direction. But, while there has been some reduction in growth of energy use in recent years, no decline in consumption has yet occurred.

56. The historical and contemporary realities of a biased but superficially objective expertise are treated in a number of places; Benveniste (1972), Meynaud (1968), Eulau (1973), and Myrdal (1969). Nelkin (1977) reviews various biasing factors, ranging from public and private funding (Don Price, 1974) of scientific experts, to the ready retreat to a technocratic solution to more difficult social problems (Ferkiss,

1974; Ravetz, 1971). On the other hand, Smith (1969) gives a more positive view of Rand Corporation expertise in military applications.

57. My perspective here is shared by Alford & Friedland (1975), who stress the importance of appreciating the full political and economic systems, the relationship of the state to capital, and the structure of social class relations. Most discussions of technological development stress the similarity of capitalist and socialist environmental externalities, and I have some sympathy with such observations (e.g., Rosenberg, 1971). But there are important qualitative and quantitative differences. For example, Rosenberg (1971: footnote 15) draws most on the most common illustration—the pollution of Lake Baikal in the U.S.S.R. During the years since Rosenberg wrote, though, remarkable efforts have been introduced to protect the lake (Shipler, 1978). The range of production controls exceeds anything currently in prospect in the U.S. It is likely the case that the U.S.S.R. did this as a showpiece (as similar efforts have been made in Moscow). That they *could* do so much so quickly, though, indicates differences in the political and economic control structure that are potentially important for the future of technological control (see Stretton, 1976, for a discussion of "left" and "right" alternatives).

REFERENCES

ABRAMOVITZ, MOSES
1956   "Resource and output trends in the U.S. since 1870." American Economic Review, Papers and Proceedings 40 (2):1–23.

ALFORD, ROBERT R. AND R. FRIEDLAND
1975   "Political participation and public policy." Pp. 429–479 in A. Inkeles, J. Coleman, and N. Smelser (eds.), Annual Review of Sociology. Volume 1. Palo Alto, Cal.: Annual Reviews Inc.

ANDERSON, CHARLES H.
1976   The Sociology of Survival: Social Problems of Growth. Homewood, Ill.: Dorsey Press.

BARAN, PAUL A. AND P.M. SWEEZY
1966   Monopoly Capital: An Essay on the American Economic and Social Order. New York and London: Modern Reader Paperbacks.

BARKLEY, PAUL W. AND D.W. SECKLER
1972   Economic Growth and Environmental Decay: The Solution Becomes the Problem. New York: Harcourt, Brace, Jovanovich.

BARNET, RICHARD J. AND R.E. MÜLLER
1974   Global Reach: The Power of the Multinational Corporations. New York: Simon and Schuster.

BARNETT, HAROLD J. AND C. MORSE
1963   Scarcity and Growth: The Economics of Natural Resource Availability. Baltimore: Johns Hopkins University Press.

BELL, DANIEL
1973   The Coming of Post-Industrial Society: A Venture in Social Forecasting. New York: Basic Books.
1974   "Reply to Peter N. Stearns." Society 11 (4):10ff.

BENVENISTE, G.
1972   The Politics of Expertise. Berkeley, Cal.: Glendessary Press.

BERNAL, J.D.
1939   The Social Function of Science. London: Routledge.

BLAIR, JOHN M.
1977   The Control of Oil. New York: Pantheon Books.

BÖHME, GERNOT
1977   "Models for the development of science." Pp. 319–351 in I. Spiegel-Rosing and D. de S. Price (eds.), Science, Technology, and Society. London: Sage Publications.

BORKIN, JOSEPH
1978   The Crime and Punishment of I.G. Farben. New York: Free Press.

BOULDING, KENNETH E.
1965   The Meaning of the 20th Century: The Great Transition. New York: Harper Colophon.

BRAVERMAN, HARRY
1974   Labor and Monopoly Capital: The Degradation of Work in the Twentieth Century. New York: Monthly Review Press.

BROOKS, HARVEY
1976   "The federal government and the autonomy of scholarship." Pp. 235–258 in C. Frankel (ed.), Controversies and Decisions. New York: Russell Sage Foundation.

BROWN, MURRAY
1966   On the Theory and Measurement of Technological Change. Cambridge: Cambridge University Press.

BROWNE, MALCOLM W.
1978   "Science finds some blessings in oil spills." New York Times, 2 April.

BURNHAM, DAVID
1978a   "Dispute arises over agency's plan to identify and curb carcinogens." New York Times, 5 March.
1978b   "Atomic energy's allies and foes assail U.S. Nuclear Commission." New York Times, 9 July.

CARTER, ANNE
1970   Structural Change in the American Economy. Cambridge: Harvard University Press.

COMMONER, BARRY
1970   Science and Survival. New York: Ballantine Books.
1972   The Closing Circle: Nature, Man, and Technology. New York: Alfred A. Knopf.

1977a The Poverty of Power: Energy and the Economic Crisis. New York: Bantam Books.

1977b "The promise and perils of petrochemicals." New York Times Magazine, 25 Sept.:38ff.

CRITTENDEN, ANN

1978 "The economic wind's blowing toward the right—for now." New York Times, 16 July.

DENISON, EDWARD F.

1962 The Sources of Economic Growth in the United States and the Alternatives before Us. Washington, D.C.: Committee for Economic Development. Supplementary Paper No. 13.

1967 Why Growth Rates Differ. Washington, D.C.: The Brookings Institution.

1974 Accounting for United States Economic Growth, 1929–1969. Washington, D.C.: The Brookings Institution.

DICKSON, DAVID

1975 The Politics of Alternative Technology. New York: Universe Books.

EASLEA, B.

1973 Liberation and the Aims of Science. London: Chatto and Windus.

ELLUL, JACQUES

1964 The Technological Society. Translated by J. Wilkinson. New York: Vintage Books.

ENOS, JOHN L.

1962 Petroleum Progress and Profits. Cambridge, Mass.: MIT Press.

ETZIONI, AMITAI

1968 The Active Society: A Theory of Societal and Political Processes. New York: Free Press.

1969 "Toward a theory of societal guidance." Pp. 7–31 in S. Heidt and A. Etzioni (eds.), Societal Guidance: A New Approach to Social Problems. New York: Thomas Y. Crowell.

EULAU, HANS

1973 "Social revolution and the consultative commonwealth." American Political Science Review 67 (Mar.):169–191.

FERKISS, V.

1974 The Future of Technological Civilization. New York: Braziller.

FISCHMAN, LEONARD L.

1978 "Public perceptions of the energy problem." Resources 57 (Jan.–Mar.):2ff.

FREEMAN, C.

1977 "Economics of research and development." Pp. 223–275 in I. Spiegel-Rosing and D. de S. Price (eds.), Science, Technology, and Society. London: Sage Publications.

GALBRAITH, JOHN K.

1952 American Capitalism. Boston: Houghton-Mifflin.

1971   The New Industrial State. Revised edition. New York: New American Library.

GIDDENS, ANTHONY
1973   The Class Structure of the Advanced Societies. New York: Barnes and Noble.

GOFMAN, JOHN W. AND A.R. TAMPLIN
1971   Poisoned Power: The Case Against Nuclear Power Plants. Emmaus, Penn.: Rodale Press, Inc.

GREEN, LEON G., JR.
1972   "Technology assessment or technology harassment: The attacks on science and technology." Pp. 195–221 in R.G. Kasper (ed.), Technology Assessment: Understanding the Social Consequences of Technological Applications. New York: Praeger Books.

GREENBERG, DANIEL S.
1967   The Politics of Pure Science. New York: New American Library.

GREENE, WADE
1976   "The new alchemists." New York Times Magazine, 8 Aug.:12ff.

HALL, A.R.
1961   "Engineering and the scientific revolution." Technology and Culture 2 (3):333–341.

HANNON, BRUCE
1975   "Energy conservation and the consumer." Science 189 (11 July):95–102.

HAYAMI, YUJIRO AND V. RUTTAN
1971   Agricultural Development. Baltimore: The Johns Hopkins Press.

HAYS, SAMUEL P.
1969   Conservation and the Gospel of Efficiency: The Progressive Conservation Movement, 1890–1920. New York: Atheneum Books.

HEIDT, SARAJANE AND A. ETZIONI (EDS.)
1969   Societal Guidance: A New Approach to Social Problems. New York: Thomas Y. Crowell.

HILL, GLADWIN
1977   "Nuclear power lags while foes flourish." New York Times, 14 Aug.

JEWKES, JOHN, D. SAWERS AND R. STILLERMAN
1958   The Sources of Invention. New York: St. Martin's Press.

KELLOGG, W.W. AND S.H. SCHNEIDER
1974   "Climate stabilization: For better or worse?" Science 186 (27 Dec.):1163–1172.

KING, WAYNE
1978   "Untangling a textile plague." New York Times, 25 June.

KOYRÉ, A.
1948   "Du monde de l'à peu près à l'univers de la précision." Critique 4 (28):806–823.

LAKOFF, SANFORD A.

1977   "Scientists, technologists and political power." Pp. 355–91 in I. Spiegel-Rosing and D. de S. Price (eds.), Science, Technology, and Society. London: Sage Publications.

LANDES, DAVID S.

1969   The Unbound Prometheus: Technological Change and Industrial Development in Western Europe from 1750 to the Present. Cambridge: Cambridge University Press.

LA PORTE, TODD R. AND D. METHAY

1975   "Technology observed: Attitudes of a wary public." Science 188 (11 Apr.):121–127.

LAVE, LESTER B.

1966   Technological Change: Its Conception and Measurement. Englewood Cliffs, N.J.: Prentice-Hall.

LAYTON, EDWARD T., JR.

1977   "Conditions of technological development." Pp. 197–222 in I. Spiegel-Rosing and D. de S. Price (eds.), Science, Technology, and Society. London: Sage Publications.

LOVINS, AMORY

1976   "Energy strategy: The road not taken?" Foreign Affairs 55(1):65–96.

MACHLUP, FRITZ

1962   The Production and Distribution of Knowledge in the United States. Princeton: Princeton University Press.

MANSFIELD, EDWIN

1968   Economics of Technological Change. New York: W.W. Norton.

MARX, KARL

1954   The Communist Manifesto. Introduction by S.T. Possony. Chicago: Henry Regnery Company.

MARX, LEO

1970   "American institutions and ecological ideals." Science 170 (27 Nov.):945–952.

MERTON, ROBERT K.

1936   "The unanticipated consequences of purposive social action." American Sociological Review 1 (Dec.):894–904.

MEYNAUD, J.

1968   Technocracy. London: Faber and Faber.

MITCHELL, ROBERT C.

1978   "Environment: An enduring concern." Resources 57 (Jan.–Mar.):1ff.

MONCRIEF, LEWIS W.

1970   "The cultural basis for our environmental crisis." Science 170 (30 Oct.):508–512.

MOSCOVICI, SERGE

1968   Essai sur l'Histoire Humaine de la Nature. Paris: Flammarion.

MUMFORD, LEWIS
  1963   Technics and Civilization. New York: Harcourt, Brace and World.
  1967   The Myth of the Machine: Technics and Human Development. New York: Harcourt, Brace, Jovanovich.
  1970   The Myth of the Machine: The Pentagon of Power. New York: Harcourt, Brace, Jovanovich.

MYERS, S. AND D.G. MARQUIS
  1969   Successful Industrial Innovations. Washington, D.C.: National Science Foundation, 69–71.

MYRDAL, GUNNAR
  1969   Objectivity in Social Research. New York: Pantheon.

NATIONAL ACADEMY OF SCIENCE (NAS)
  1969   Technology: Process of Assessment and Choice. Washington, D.C. National Academy of Science.

NELKIN, DOROTHY
  1977   "Technology and public policy." Pp. 393–441 in I. Spiegel-Rosing and D. de S. Price (eds.), Science, Technology, and Society. London: Sage Publications.

NEW YORK TIMES (NYT)
  1976   "Studies find U.S. cities even worse in the past." New York Times, 5 December.

O'CONNOR, JAMES
  1973   The Fiscal Crisis of the State. New York: St. Martin's Press.

OGBURN, WILLIAM F.
  1964   On Culture and Social Change. Edited and introduced by O.D. Duncan. Chicago: University of Chicago Press.

PRICE, DEREK DE SOLLA
  1963   Little Science, Big Science. New York: Columbia University Press.
  1965   "Is technology historically independent of science? A study in statistical historiography." Technology and Culture 6 (4):553–568.

PRICE, DON K.
  1974   "Money and influence: The links of science to public policy." Daedalus (Summer):97–114.

RATTNER, STEVEN
  1978a   "Regulation: Do its costs outweigh its benefits?" New York Times, 18 June.
  1978b   "The cost factor modifies Carter programs." New York Times, 6 Aug.

RAVETZ, JEROME R.
  1971   Scientific Knowledge and Its Social Problems. Oxford: Clarendon Press.
  1977   "Criticisms of science." Pp. 71–89 in I. Spiegel-Rosing and D. de S. Price (eds.), Science, Technology, and Society. London: Sage Publications.

REYNOLDS, LLOYD G.
1963   Economics: A General Introduction. Homewood, Ill.: Richard D. Irwin, Inc.

ROSE, HILARY AND S. ROSE
1969   Science and Society. London: Allen Lane.

ROSENBERG, NATHAN
1971   "Technology and the environment: An economic exploration." Technology and Culture 12 (4):543–561.
1972   Technology and American Economic Growth. New York: Harper Torchbooks.
1976a   "Marx as a student of technology." Monthly Review 28 (July–Aug.):56–77.
1976b   Perspectives on Technology. Cambridge: Cambridge University Press.

SALOMON, JEAN-JACQUES
1973   Science and Politics. Cambridge, Mass.: MIT Press.

SAMPSON, ANTHONY
1975   The Seven Sisters: The Great Oil Companies and the World They Shaped. New York: Viking Books.

SAMUELSON, PAUL A.
1967   Economics: An Introductory Analysis. Seventh edition. New York: McGraw-Hill.

SCHMOOKLER, JACOB
1966   Invention and Economic Growth. Cambridge: Harvard University Press.

SCHNAIBERG, ALLAN
1975   "Social syntheses of the societal-environmental dialectic: The role of distributional impacts." Social Science Quarterly 56 (1):5–20.

SCHOOLER, DEAN, JR.
1971   Science, Scientists, and Public Policy. New York: Free Press.

SCHUMACHER, E.F.
1973   Small Is Beautiful: Economics as if People Mattered. New York: Harper and Row.

SCHUMPETER, JOSEPH A.
1928   "The instability of capitalism." Economic Journal 38:361–386.

SCHURR, SAM AND B.R. NETSCHERT
1960   Energy in the American Economy, 1850–1975. Baltimore: Johns Hopkins Press.

SHIPLER, DAVID K.
1978   "Siberian lake now a model of pollution control." New York Times, 16 April.

SMITH, BRUCE L.R.
1969   "Knowledge—its production, transmission, and consequences." Pp. 35–69 in S. Heidt and A. Etzioni (eds.), Societal Guidance: A New Approach to Social Problems. New York: Thomas Y. Crowell.

SOLOW, ROBERT M.
1957   "Technical change and the aggregate production function." Review of Economics and Statistics 39 (Aug.):312–320.

SPECTOR, MALCOLM AND J.I. KITSUSE
1977   Constructing Social Problems. Menlo Park, Cal.: Cummings Publishing Co.

STEARNS, PETER N.
1974   "Is there a post-industrial society?" Society 11 (4):10–22.

STRAUSSMAN, W. PAUL
1968   Technological Change and Economic Development. Ithaca, N.Y.: Cornell University Press.

STRETTON, HUGH
1976   Capitalism, Socialism and the Environment. Cambridge: Cambridge University Press.

SULLIVAN, WALTER
1978   "A call for industrial research as a key to growth." New York Times, 19 February.

SZILARD, LEO
1961   The Voice of the Dolphin and Other Stories. New York: Simon and Schuster.

TURNER, THOMAS
1970   "Eco-pornography, or how to spot an ecological phony." Pp. 263–267 in G. de Bell (ed.), The Environmental Handbook. New York: Ballantine Books.

WALDRON, MARTIN
1978   "Carcinogens are bad: Are angry voters worse?" New York Times, 30 April.

WALDRON, MARTIN, H. FABER, AND M.L. WALD
1978   "The water's getting better, the hard part lies ahead." New York Times, 6 Aug.

WHITE, LYNN, JR.
1967   "The historical roots of our ecologic crisis." Science 155 (10 Mar.):1203–1207.

WILFORD, JOHN N.
1978   "The spinoff from space." New York Times Magazine, 29 January:10ff.

WOLFE, ALAN
1974   "New directions in the Marxist theory of politics." Politics and Society, Winter:131–159.

IV THE EXPANSION OF CONSUMPTION
Does the Tail Wag the Dog?

FORMS OF PRODUCTION AND CONSUMPTION EXPANSION

Understanding Consumption: Its Determinants and Consequences

In this and the following chapter, the focus on qualitative dimensions of production is complemented by an emphasis on quantitative dimensions. For, as noted in Chapter I, production in industrial economies has changed in volume as well as composition in this century, and such changes have severe environmental consequences. Expansion has occurred in all types of production technologies, primarily but not exclusively in neotechnics, with corresponding patterns of ecosystem withdrawals and additions.

This chapter first documents such quantitative shifts, in order to counter the confusion engendered by recent models of "postindustrialism." Such theories diminish our sense of the expansion of material production and focus attention elsewhere in the social and economic system. Important as this may be for some social concerns, the problem of ecosystem degradation requires a constant attention to the material dimensions of production. In some ways, this emphasis documents the obvious, and yet the pervasiveness of the postindustrial imagery often obscures what lies under our very noses: the enormous expansion of material consumption in recent decades.[1]

Next is an explanation of the expansion of consumption and production. One major thread in environmental analysis and social policy prescriptions is the focus on controlling consumption. The most recent illustration is the coerced or voluntary energy conservation in households. An earlier form was voluntary recycling of newspapers, bottles, and cans in cities. Evidence that consumers have reduced some forms of energy consumption and have voluntarily recycled some of their waste is often held as validation of a thesis that consumer action can be the *primary* stimulus to solving environmental problems. In its simplest form, it confirms the comic strip character, Pogo, in the thesis that "We have seen the enemy, and he is us." A slightly more sophisticated view is that it indicates the power of consumer sovereignty: "We" can now choose between better and worse natural environments, in the patterns of our consumption, on the basis of our needs and wants. Even at this level there is a contradiction, since "voluntary" energy and recycling action has resulted from substantial organized pressures to *change* consumer behavior. In contrast, the neoclassical economist's theory of consumer sovereignty generally assumes consumer wants as givens, not subject to social manipulation.[2] That environmental politics have influenced consumer markets for energy and containers raises important complications in the analysis of consumption as isolated from the texture of social structure.[3]

A second observation regarding these two recent small changes in consumer behavior is that they may affect the sociocultural production system. This is the crucial link between the analysis of this chapter and that of Chapter V. It is important to note that producers lobbying against various provisions of a U. S. energy bill held up the bill for several years, with no clear agreement in sight. Likewise, packaging industries have successfully lobbied against "bottle bills" in a number of states. This prevented changes in production that would substantially reduce solid wastes and energy consumption associated with the beverage industry. How much voluntary consumer action can offset each of these production realities is unclear. What is clear is that the consumer sovereignty model is again weakened. Production systems do not respond to these recent changes in consumer desires, but work against energy and material conservation.[4]

For a social scientist, confronting the confused and contradictory nature of the existing literature on the factors influencing consumption (Zaltman et al., 1973), and the potential role of consumption in altering future levels of production, three positions are possible.

PURE CONSUMER SOVEREIGNTY One can side with neoclassical economists, adhering to a model of *consumer sovereignty* in the marketplace and upholding the theory of revealed preferences, which sees the "consumer's actual behavior as a faithful reflection of his preferences and . . . his preferences as revealed by his behavior" (Scitovsky, 1976:vii). Following this model, we would understand environmental degradation as a result of an historical expansion of production that responded to consumer demands for more goods, and to the growth of population and hence of consumers. The logical form of this model is:

$$
\begin{array}{l}
\text{Ecosystem withdrawals} \\
\text{and additions}
\end{array} =
$$

$$
\begin{bmatrix} \text{Population} \\ \text{size} \end{bmatrix} \times \begin{bmatrix} \text{Consumption} \\ \text{per capita} \end{bmatrix} \times \begin{bmatrix} \text{Withdrawals/additions} \\ \text{per unit consumption} \end{bmatrix}
$$

Such a consumer model of environmental degradation is compelling to many, in its simplicity and clear message for action: control population *and* lower consumption per capita. Neither the data nor the policies for achieving such changes are readily at hand, as noted in Chapter II. Moreover, the neatness of this model ignores the feedback between consumption and production activities.[5]

DISTORTED CONSUMPTION A second position partially incorporates the interplay of consumption and production activities. One variation of this model, the *manipulated consumer*, focuses on advertising and its influence on consumer behavior:

> Although both consumers and producers benefit from the other party's conforming to their wishes, producers have the greater power and influence. American producers spent $20 billion on advertising in 1973—ample evidence of their willingness to use that power. (Scitovsky, 1976:5)

A more depoliticized version of this model is that of the *insatiable consumer*, who responds to changes in production in the manner noted three decades ago by Alfred Marshall: "Each new step upwards is to be regarded as the development of new activities giving rise to new wants, rather than of new wants giving rise to new activities" (1948:89). Following such a model, environmentalists would then focus on reducing advertising, preparing counteradvertising, and on seeking reductions in levels of production, to reduce consumption per capita. The crucial assumption here is that, as between consumers and producers: "We do not know which is more flexible, consumer behavior or producer behavior. Nor do we know which does most of the conforming" (Scitovsky, 1976:6).

STRUCTURED CONSUMPTION   The third model follows from Marxist and neo-Marxist models of capitalist production and its social relationships. We can term this the model of the *worker-consumer*, with emphasis on the social structure:

> If consumer behavior seems odd or perverse, this is due less to any irrationality of individual preferences than to the restricted choice-sets of social activities they face, and to the fact that rational individuals will develop capacities to utilize what is in fact available. (Gintis, 1972:268)

Such a structural view repudiates the second model of changing consumer and producer behavior in any piecemeal fashion, in that it views current patterns as:

> A normal result of the development of capitalism [that] cannot be reduced to the irrationalities of consumer preferences or the autonomous and socially irresponsible exercise of power by controllers of production. (Gintis, 1972:267)

The logic of this model is that altered production and consumption to reduce ecosystem degradation could only come about through "the replacement of capitalism by a set of economic and political relations in day-to-day life which give people power over the determination of social outcomes" (Gintis, 1972:268). This last prescription, though placed in a more intense political context, is congruent with some of the eclectic positions noted earlier among proponents of intermediate or appropriate technology (see Ch. III). However, the neo-Marxist position has vastly stronger concern with social relations than with the organization of productive technology.

Consumer behavior has been analytically treated at levels ranging from psychology to political structure. While the former is important, it will not be emphasized here. I lack the competence and interest to do any adequate synthesis of this area, and Tibor Scitovsky has said it far better already in his book *The Joyless Economy*. What will be emphasized are the societal factors that impinge on consumption patterns, in ways that repudiate model 1 above. These constraints fall somewhere between the remaining two models. As Charles Lindblom (1977) puts it, they fall between Adam Smith's individualism and Karl Marx's structuralism, an interplay between "politics and markets," insofar as consumer autonomy is concerned. This chapter leans more toward Marx, in terms of analysing consumption as a causal factor in environmental degradation. However, consumer variability in cultures and social structures across time and space indicate something more flexible than the neo-Marxist position of Gintis noted above. Even such a technological optimist as Nathan Rosenberg noted such variations: "English observers often noted with no small astonishment that American products were designed to accommodate, not the consumer, but the machine" (1972:44).

The thesis of this chapter, then, is that consumption in industrial societies like the United States cannot be treated as independent of the changing structure of producer power and producer technology. Patterns of consumption growth will be discussed, and some of the shaping influences noted. Finally, limits to a consumption-oriented environmental reform policy will be touched upon. Chapter V will take up the argument from the production side, and treat the often contradictory roles of government in production expansion and environmental protection. The first task, though, is the delineation of expanded consumption.

The Myth of Postindustrialism: Consumption and Production Realities

During the 1960s, it became very fashionable for many social scientists to refer to the emerging era of "postindustrialism" in the United States and some western European societies. Postindustrialism was defined as a new stage in social history, in which consumption was to be increasingly oriented to services rather than to goods. The initial confusion of theorists lay partly in this model of consumption and in the inferences drawn for sociocultural production and its interaction with the biosphere.[6]

This confusion starts at the semantic level. What does *post* imply? Strictly speaking, it refers to a temporal sequence, one stage occuring after a previous one. But the ambiguity of the term is apparent when we refer to consumption. Is postindustrialism to mean *substituting* new forms of service consumption for goods consumption? Or does it mean *adding* new services to older material consumption? A careful reading of some of the postindustrial theorists reveals some lack of specificity on these matters. A common assumption was that consumer "needs" would be easily taken care of by the new productive system. Whether these "needs" were at the standard of affluent, middle-class, or respectable working-class Americans was unclear, yet total and per capita consumption would vary considerably under the three assumptions. In general, a broad middle-class life style seemed assumed by theorists, implying moderate levels of consumption (by American standards). Beyond this, it was assumed that increased income would be used for purchasing services, perhaps of the type that stimulated pleasure, rather than seeking more physical comfort by goods consumption.

While consumption of services has in fact increased, three other realities of consumption are equally important. First, only some of the additional consumer income has gone to services, while the rest has gone to increased goods consumption.[7] Second, the content of the services purchased has differed from the lofty assumptions of nonmaterialism. Many of the consumer services have in fact been complements to goods production and consumption: e.g., automobile repair and financial services to facilitate consumer debt and consumption.[8] Third, for many of the services themselves, energy and material demands have risen sharply—e.g., energy costs for recreational and business travel via airline rather than train.

However fuzzy the consumption assumptions of postindustrialists were, then, the historical reality is clear: material consumption has risen dramatically in recent decades. The notion that consumers were going to move "beyond" goods consumption was wrong. Some nonmaterial services were increasingly consumed, but so were goods, and the energy and material intensification of many services also increased. Recreation, which has grown, has become as much a goods as a services industry, with everything from privately owned sporting goods to private camping vans and trucks as part of this "leisure" activity. Few leisure activities have remained free of this materialization or industrialization. As Landsberg (1976:638) has cogently noted:

> Listening to an opera in the Kennedy Center in Washington is associated with three floors of garage space filled with automobiles that, on the average, may travel 10 to 15 miles . . . each way! . . .

of an estimated $39 billion of consumer expenditures for recreation, fully 17 consisted of durables and 11 of nondurables, while only the remaining 11 . . . were classified as "services" proper.

Why were these consumption predictions of postindustrialism so much in error? To understand this, we need to examine the models of production entailed in these predictions. The postindustrial myth and concomitant speculation about the future of industrial societies stemmed from two sources. First, in the decades following World War II an ever-increasing proportion of the domestic labor force moved out of primary (extractive) and secondary (manufacturing) industries into tertiary (service) industries. In part, some of this reflected multinational corporation activity abroad, especially in the Third World. Domestic agricultural workers were shrinking both in total numbers and as a proportion of the total United States labor force. This was true despite the fact that U. S. domestic agricultural production increased substantially during this period—and that food sector employment, including processing and distribution, also increased. All of this was due to the increased capitalization of agriculture and food processing and distributing industries. This displaced independent farmers and many farm workers, substituting machinery for the production of crops. It simultaneously increased the need for labor in the transportation, warehousing, marketing, and sales sectors. Large-scale agribusiness corporations increasingly consolidated their control of the food industry by vertical integration of all aspects of food production and distribution. A former farm-worker might find employment as a food industry truck-driver, moving from primary industry to tertiary industry in his new "service" role.

Similar changes were occurring in mining, forestry, fishing, and other primary industries. In all of these, increasing volumes of capital served to rationalize production and displace labor.[9] Typically, this was associated with higher production volumes and lower labor input. It also led to increased ecological problems, ranging from the depletion of many stocks of fish (through over-fishing), to the increased need for water, fertilizers, pesticides, and herbicides (to substitute for labor and increase the productivity of land). But for most *social* scientists, the key element was the transformation of the labor force into a service labor force.

From here, it was easy to make the transition to labeling the total economy as a service economy, a postindustrial economy. Since primary and especially secondary industry was the essence of industrialization, it appeared to follow that tertiary employment was the essence of post-industrialization. Analyses of neo-Marxists and institutional economists, though, continued to emphasize the accumulation of industrial capital. Expanded economic control was associated with the perpetuation of an advanced large corporation, "monopoly capital," or the "technostructure," with heavy investments in extraction and manufacturing.[10]

The second major attraction of postindustrialism for social scientists was the expectation that such transformations of the labor force presaged a total shift in the quality of life and labor for the new service economy. The drudgeries of agricultural labor and of the assembly line were to be eliminated. In their place was to emerge the "new service worker": well-educated, physically and emotionally comfortable in his/her new work, and better paid. The problem of production was mysteriously and dramatically solved. A working class would give way to a "new middle class," and blue-collar work to the joys of white-collar work. Knowledge was to be the hallmark of the new worker, mental labor in place of physical labor. Moreover, since the production problem had been solved, the need for all labor was likely to decline, thereby giving rise to more leisure. Dramatic reductions in the hours of work and concomitant increases in free time would result.[11] And of course, poverty at home and in the Third World would be eliminated, as production technology would be extended internationally to produce benefits throughout the world.

Few of these predictions have come to pass. As Harry Braverman (1974) has vividly described, the use of the new service labor force has become increasingly rationalized. Rather than becoming the new middle class, it has merely become an expanded working class, subject to many of the emotional (and even many of the physical) ills of the old working class. Offices have become mechanized, and some tedium and even drudgery of the assembly lines has become extended to white-collar work, especially in the greatly expanded service industries such as finance and marketing. Expanded service occupations both within and outside of tertiary industry have all the dreariness and economic insecurity of the old working class.

Indeed, so striking are many of these changes that some social scientists see an increased proletarianization of the middle class—an expansion of the traditional working class, with fewer class distinctions than existed at the turn of the century. "Knowledge" is viewed as possessed by a relatively narrow stratum of technical and professional workers. Educational exposure of the remaining workers is seen as primarily keeping them out of the labor force, expanding the number of service jobs in education, and making for a more docile working class. The use of knowledge on the job is defined as more constricted, not expanded. Even in the most dramatic growth industry of the service sector—state and local government—job insecurity increases are noted, with increased fiscal crises of all levels of government.[12]

It is clear, then, that technological change and related production changes have not "solved" all the problems of production. Nor have they diminished consumption. In general, patterns of production and consumption have led to accelerated rates of biospheric withdrawals and additions in the post-World War II period, especially in the United States, and in much of western (and, to a lesser degree, eastern) Europe.[13] The reasons for this failure of vision are complex, and will be treated in length in Chapter V. Because of the importance of appreciating some of the social constraints on consumer autonomy, though, a brief analytic overview is covered in the next section. While this analysis does not eliminate the role of consumption shifts in reducing future ecosystem degradation, it points in somewhat different directions. This is an important corrective to the ecological invalidities of the postindustrial thesis.

Advanced Industrialism versus Postindustrialism: Population and Consumption Growth

Although the postindustrialism model is of relatively recent vintage, it has many precursors in intellectual history. Among the most striking is Lewis Mumford's 1934 statement about "neotechnics." Included in the potential outcomes of the technological developments present by the 1930s were: (1) the importance of science, (2) new sources of energy, (3) power and mobility, (4) neotechnic materials, (5) the displacement of the proletariat, (6) a movement from destruction to conservation, and (7) the planning of population.[14] While some elements of the first four of these have come to pass, there has been limited progress on the last three, and on many other of Mumford's predictions. Rather than invalidating Mumford's ideas, though, present realities were anticipated in his work, despite the transcendental quality of his writings:

> Paleotechnic purposes with neotechnic means: that is the most obvious characteristic of the present order. And that is why a good part of the machines and institutions that boast of being "new" or "advanced" or "progressive" are ... in fact ... reactionary. (1963:267)

and

> It would be a gross mistake to seek wholly within the field of technics for an answer to all the problems that have been raised by technics. For the instrument only in part determines the character of the symphony or the response of the audience: the composer and the musicians and the audience have also to be considered. (1963:434)

The thesis of this and the next chapter is that the composer and musicians have not in fact changed—the logic of production expansion has remained. Likewise, the audience has not called for a new symphony—consumption has proceeded at an accelerated pace. This is so despite—indeed, in part because of—changes in technology noted in Chapter III. As a result, the sociocultural production system remains rooted in the "paleotechnic" or nineteenth century models of industrialization, and not oriented towards the liberating social goals of neotechnics.[15]

Essentially, this failure of prediction revolves around the economic logic of technological change, at least in the last decades. Increased capitalization of industry in new higher-energy technologies was premised on increased markets offsetting decreased costs, prices, and profits per unit good. In addition to increases in consumption anticipated from growing populations, decreased relative prices of these new goods permitted intensification of consumption among the existing population of consumers. While not all technological shifts had these qualities, this is the dominant model put forward by economists studying technological change, as well as those studying economic growth.[16] The latter emphasize economies of scale in production, as markets grow, to absorb the high capital costs of monopoly capital or technostructural enterprises. This simultaneously increases profitability by reducing prices and increasing consumption per capita.

There have been many contradictions within this simple model. As capital intensity increased, the use of extractive and manufacturing labor decreased, thereby raising problems of inadequate consumer demand, because of inadequate wages. This problem was partially resolved in four directions: (1) increased wages of technostructural employees, (2) increased employment in nonproduction jobs, (3) increased government transfer payments for the poor and unemployed, and increased government employment, and (4) continued socialization of the consumer into higher per capita consumption of goods. Many of these changes confounded simple Marxian predictions about the collapse of the advanced production system in capitalism: profits would decline as markets failed to grow as rapidly as rationalized production.[17] But the Marxian concern about disjunctures between productive capacity and effective consumer demand for goods presaged a continuing political and economic problem for advanced industrial societies. While Keynesian-based policies followed in the period immediately after Mumford's initial statements, to balance supply and demand, this precarious balancing has led to numerous recessions and other economic problems in the four decades since then. Even Keynes worried about the long-term social costs of such a continuation of an expansionary model,[18] one which Mumford was later to decry:

> First of all, every member of the community must, in duty bound, acquire, use, devour, waste, and finally destroy a sufficient quantity of goods to keep [the] increasingly productive mechanism in operation. . . . Second . . . the majority of the population must forego all modes of activity except those that call for the unremitting use of the "machine" or its products. (Mumford, 1970:329)

A collapse of this demand would threaten the present high-capital and high-energy enterprises, in terms of both profits and employment. While some modest reductions of energy use per unit of capital have proven possible,[19] this is but a minor shift in the trajectory of increased environmental demand for the growing production and consumption.

In terms of this chapter, the key linkage is that consumption in the aggregate must be kept high to maintain the economic structure. While consumers may be relatively free to alter the particular product mix on which they expend their income, this freedom is constrained in a number of ways. First, the consumption package must be heavily weighted towards technostructural products—the "machine" products noted by Mumford. In part, this is assured by favorable price conditions of such products relative to small-scale and more labor-intensive industry, though affluent consumers may choose craft products over machine ones.

Second, wage income must be kept high enough to provide this consumer demand, and/or it must be supplemented by government taxation and transfers of income to keep demand high. Conversely, though, wages need to be kept down if price competition is to succeed. Each firm wants its wages as low as possible, and everyone else's as high as possible. This creates contradictions in corporate and political policies on wages, which have never been fully resolved in advanced industrial societies—particularly in the U. S. That is, no stable "incomes policy" has existed there over any protracted period.

Third, if consumption patterns shift away from conventional products, investment patterns of the technostructure shift so that consumer demand is increased in areas previously untapped. The recreational goods market is a significant example of this, in the U. S., as is the fast-food franchise operation. Both of these increase the material component (goods consumption) of what were previously more labor- or service-oriented economic activities. Increased investment in these areas typically raises the capital per worker, and the level of energy and material consumption per dollar revenue captured. While there are important exceptions to this trend, the trend itself is of major importance to environmental analysis. Much is made of decreased energy and materials decline per unit of production. But, until fairly recently, there was less improvement in energy efficiency per constant dollar of consumption.[20]

We can summarize the underlying theme of these three constraints on consumer autonomy as follows. Consumption cannot be treated as structurally autonomous of production and investment decision making, and the latter has more influence on the former. The organizational coherence of producers and the disorganized state of consumers typically ensure such a disparity. Product choice may be variable, but consumption patterns are far less so. As Scitovsky (1976:176–77) notes, consumers are often faced with the problem of the prisoner's dilemma. Their consumption choices are affected by producer decisions, but they can not or will not expend the effort to alter their consumption, because the relative costs exceed their individual benefits. Moreover, many of the criteria of profit-maximization in production become part of consumer value structures, whether through the consumer's role as worker or through the influence of advertising and other socializing institutions. Thus, for example, the dollar- and labor-saving emphasis in technology is reflected by a similar one in consumption:

> The food processing industry lives by the consumer's desire to save labor, though usually it also profits by using artificial flavors, inferior raw materials and cheap fillers. To avoid them is only a matter of cost . . . proof of the consumer's willingness to sacrifice flavor to save expense. (Scitovsky, 1976:189)

Thus, production expansion increases pressures on consumers towards increased volumes of consumption, subject to income and product constraints. Increased rationalization of production by large-scale, technostructural, or monopoly capital owners and managers typically has increased the volume of environmental withdrawals and additions, because of the nature of production investment. This is true of services and other forms of consumption, and typically involves more producer than consumer influences.[21] Such ecological effects, and producer constraints, will be examined in turn.

Ecological Impacts of the Service Sector

Some environmental writers viewed the development of a service labor force as a form of liberation from ecological constraints. Since service sectors produce only services, their resource demand is minimal when contrasted with primary (extractive) or secondary (manufacturing) sectors.

Two possible fallacies exist in this position, however. First, the growth of the service labor force is itself contingent upon continued expansion of the other two industrial sectors. Sales, marketing organization, advertising, repair services, and a host of white- and blue-collar service occupations relate directly to the types and volumes of *goods* production. The physical separation of these employees from production and the increased social invisibility of production noted in Chapter III merely disguise the dependency.[22] Recent energy crises point to the widespread dependency of even those sectors of employment most socially removed from the production processes in extraction and manufacturing.

Conversely, of course, the expansion of production is contingent upon the activities of the service labor force. Automobile production is dependent upon a network of service agencies, gasoline stations, road-way managers, police services, and the advertising agencies supporting such production. Indeed, the history of this industry (and the well-named highway-automobile complex) is illuminating on this point. Many of the "volunteer" groups and professional agencies stimulating the growth of roads and automobile driving were the products of direct actions by automobile producers. Far from being autonomous services, such employing organizations are an intrinsic part of the production system of the automobile industry—such that it has been estimated that about one-fourth of the U. S. labor force is tied to the automobile system. Every link, from the service station to the franchised repair outlets that provide at least minimal maintenance of automobiles, acts to maintain consumer commitment to the automobile transportation system—and hence to continued production of automobiles.[23] Ser-vices are as dependent upon production as production is upon services.

A second fallacy, as noted earlier, is that services themselves have the low environmental inputs. The prime illustration of this is the transportation sector of the labor force, which absorbs almost one-fourth of the total energy consumption in the United States.[24] That a substantial portion of total consumption is by private automobiles merely poses some intriguing definitional questions. In earlier periods of history, much of this service would have been provided within the marketplace, by public transportation (Mandel, 1975: Ch. 12). That many people drive their own cars merely reflects the ambiguities of our economic classifications, since these people are providing services to themselves, in effect, through driving labor. But even beyond this, the remaining portion of the transportation service labor force, heavily weighted towards trucking and airlines (with a much decreased volume of railroad, barge, and bus transport), is very energy-intensive. In addition to such energy-intensity through the direct operation of vehi-cles, of course, there is the indirect energy and material intensity involved in the construction and maintenance of the vehicles them-selves. Even if we split hairs and claim that the latter activities are not part of "transportation service labor," such labor cannot operate with-out the material and energy inputs from the vehicle production indus-tries.

If we turn to the provision of simple clerical services, the recent energy crisis in the U. S. has increased sensitivity to the energy intensity of such services as well. Lighting, heating, air conditioning, electricity for office machine operations—all of these increase demand for energy substantially.[25] And with the increased rationalization of office labor that Braverman (1974) cites, such demands for energy in fact increase substantially. Moreover, the increased dependency on electrical office machines also stimulates the production and maintenance of such equipment, again pointing to the service/production relationships in the economy. To this must be added the volume of paper production (and related manufacturing—e.g., box construction) that is the concomitant of the modern office. Only the recent recession slowed temporarily the rising demand for paper, an increase that has transformed private and public forest lands from stands of mature trees to standardized fast-growing pulpwoods of reduced ecosystem value (as well as diminished aesthetic-recreational value). Decline of forest fauna through the systematic production of pulp (and timber) woods is a key element in the attrition and elimination of many complex food chains.

Consumption of services, therefore, exists in a variety of relationships to the goods produced by the primary/secondary industrial sectors. First, service industries are consumers of many of the products of these sectors (energy and paper, especially). Second, they stimulate a variety of demands for production goods by other consumers: industrial, government, and private ones. Third, they provide the mechanisms by which consumption of these producer goods can continue—through delivery and repair. In the first category, service industries create a broad panoply of environmental problems: waste production, land removal (for waste disposal), air and water pollution. In the next two roles, they serve as the social institutional structure that maintains and stimulates the growth of production. The file clerk, the computer programmer, the government regulator, and the mechanic—all of these "servicers" form a supportive web for the expansion of production. They do not cause the expansion itself: they do provide for the possibility of expansion, though.

Ecological Impacts of the Nonservice Sectors

The volume of all forms of production has increased exponentially within the twentieth century. This is axiomatic for the late-industrial technological sectors earlier discussed, but it is equally true for the early-industrial technological areas as well. Consider, for example, the case of a fossil fuel such as coal:

> Although coal has been mined for about 800 years, one-half of the coal produced during that period has been mined during the last 31 years. . . . Similarly, for the United States, half the cumulative coal production has occurred during the 38-year period since 1930. (Hubbert, 1969:166)

While there are similar dramatic increases in U. S. domestic oil production through the early 1960s, this later industrial technology has peaked (whether through lack of supply or through more competitive pricing from foreign oil is still not clear). Expansion of production using early industrial technology exists in minerals, foodstuffs, and other renewable and nonrenewable resources in the twentieth century. Although population growth has also increased in the U. S. over this period, its growth has been nowhere near such levels of extraction and production increase (Landsberg, 1976).

Concomitant with such growth in resource usage from early industrial technology is increased usage of such resources as air, water, and land. Air is used in a variety of combustion processes, and as a "sink" for dispersal of a variety of chemical and physical wastes. Water is used as a coolant, a factor in production (as in irrigated agriculture), and as a "sink" for waste discharge. Land is used in a variety of ways: as a factor in production (top-soil in agriculture), a base for locating physical plants (capital equipment), and also as a sink (as in disposal sites for solid and liquid waste). While we lack systematic historical data for the usage of air, the available data documents the substantial exponential increase in water and land usage as part of the extractive and manufacturing processes, as well as for consumer uses.

Despite some substantial economic/accounting economies of scale in this twentieth century extension and modification of technology, then, there appear to be few examples of *ecological* economies of scale—and rather more dominant examples of ecological dis-economies. Volumes of additions/withdrawals per unit production have not decreased enough over this century to offset increased volumes of production. Along with this has come the higher levels of risk and disruption of previously-used ecosystems, and the increased range of ecosystems affected by production. Far more of the extractive/manufacturing activities have produced permanent changes in the living and nonliving components of more and more ecosystems. And finally, as silent testimony to the exponential increase in production and consumption, many of the biospheric cycles (water, oxygen, nitrogen) have themselves been affected: heat balances, air pollution, water pollution—all have been measurably altered by production expansion. Scientific debate may rage over the significance for future social organization, productivity, and human health changes resulting from them. But the fact of the changes has become grudgingly accepted, even by the strongest proponents of industrial expansion and increased consumption (e.g., Rosenberg, 1976: Ch. 12).

CONSUMER DEMAND AND PRODUCTION EXPANSION

Consumer Models and Consumer Sovereignty

Classical economic theory argues that producers in capitalist societies must produce what consumers will purchase. Any excess production over consumer demand will lead to the recessionary accumulation of stock inventories beyond a normal level. For an individual firm, this inventory surplus is an indicator of poor management; for an economy as a whole, it indicates a recessionary state. Private capitalism or "free enterprise" systems are frequently claimed to be far superior to centrally planned socialist or state capitalist systems for just such reasons. In the latter, it is claimed, producers have no feedback from consumers, and thus are encouraged to produce according to bureaucratic inputs. The result is large overstocks and unsatisfied consumer demand.[26]

There is unquestionable truth in some of these comparisons—but a truth that is vastly overstated. In the real world, even that of the nineteenth century, let alone the twentieth, accumulated inequalities between producers and within the consuming population have led to substantial divergence from a simple model of producing because of consumer demand. Indeed, it is questionable whether such an ideal type ever existed in a real economy. While it remains true that producers must sell their products, it does not follow the consumers influence production as significantly as the theory of consumer sovereignty suggests. Indeed, I will argue in Chapter V that a model of producer sovereignty is a much closer approximation to the structure of advanced industrial societies like the United States.

Although the processes influencing consumption have been poorly studied, there is a growing consensus, even among economists who defend the present industrial order, that consumer sovereignty models are inappropriate:

> It is the practice of economists to assume that consumer wants are autonomous and determined independently of the process through which they are satisfied. The consumer is visualized as possessing an ordered structure of preferences and entering into market relationships with the purpose of maximizing his satisfactions subject to a budgetary constraint. . . . For economic growth . . . this assumption is seriously deficient, since a major component of the growth process is a radical transformation of attitudes toward consumption and saving, and toward work and leisure. (Rosenberg, 1976:104)

In more analytic terms, Lindblom (1977) refers to the increasing dominance of authority systems (largely business and government) over markets. Neither these nor other analysts dismiss *some* range of consumer autonomy. The key question has become: How much autonomy, and how much external control over consumption, exists in advanced industrial societies? At the extreme, most analysts acknowledge that consumers can choose from among differing brands of products. Even at this level, though, there are questions about how much this actual brand preference reflects true consumer wishes, and how much the consumer is constrained by misinformation and a variety of other social conditions. Yet we cannot dismiss this limited element of choice, since it is one of the mechanisms that fuels competition even among large corporations with their supposed oligopolistic or monopolistic controls over the market. At the very least, it provides for a culture in which capitalists and managers perceive and use the threat of competition to justify a variety of expansionary policies in goods production.[27]

Beyond this level, debate in the literature has centered upon key unresolved issues. First, how is the consumer's structure of preferences created? To what extent does the consumer respond to his/her intrinsic needs, and to what extent are these needs created by factors external to the individual—by "politics" rather than by "markets"? Second, once such a preference structure is created, can the consumer act upon it freely, or is this behavior constrained by external factors? The first relates to the differences between consumer "wants" and "needs," the latter the differences between consumer "wants" and consumption patterns.[28]

In the following sections, some of the most important constraints on consumer autonomy are listed, though without any assessment of their quantitative impact. No such information exists in the literature.[29] Moreover, whether these constraints imply a model of producer rather than consumer sovereignty is unclear; Chapter V subjects the former to a more detailed review. The final part of this chapter indicates some upper bounds for consumer-based changes in environmental protection, and prepares the way for the production-based considerations in Chapter V.

Some Limitations on Consumer Markets: Nonprivate Consumption

Some crude environmental analyses take total societal production and divide by the population in order to achieve a "consumption per capita" figure. This is the problem of two accounts discussed at length in Chapter II, with one account being population and the other production.

Two important corrections must be made. First, a substantial share of production goes into other forms of production, never reaching the consumer directly. This includes both the traditional producer goods (especially machinery and other capital equipment) and a wide range of commodities that support production and marketing activities. In particular, a good many of these inputs are energy-intensive—including the direct provision of fuels to industries.[30] While these producers may be engaged in goods or service production that eventuates in consumer goods/services, it is crucial to note that production decisions are in the hands of producers, not consumers. For example, the recent shifts in energy patterns of corporate consumers were not caused by shifts in consumer markets. Rather, they were a response to oil prices and other considerations. Unfortunately, when this point is carried to a logical conclusion, it is difficult to draw the line between consumer consumption and corporate consumption, since it is not clear how production alternatives were "chosen" by consumers in their ultimate selection of products. At minimum, the consumption of the industries producing goods and services for businesses must be subtracted from the total production volume, before estimating the direct contribution of consumers to production expansion, through free choice in the marketplace.[31]

A second corrective is the removal of public goods and services production from the operations of the consumer market.[32] As with the limitation noted above, the issue is not whether or not consumers benefit from such goods/services. Rather, it is whether they act *in the marketplace*, exercising their preferences. Following Lindblom's concepts, public goods are provided by politics, not markets. While consumers may enter the process, they do so through other political roles—as citizens, political actors, or the like—and not as consumers. In the United States in particular, the public sector is highly limited in serving private consumer needs. It is limited to:

> (a) cleaning up after the private sector has taken its toll (e.g., . . . minor income transfers, urban renewal, anti-pollution projects), (b) correcting the operation of basic economic institutions . . . (e.g., child labor . . . laws, zoning regulations), and (c) supplying social services outside and not competitive with the private economy. (Gintis, 1972:272–73)

Both of these correctives may be stated as categorical. They refine the concept of "private consumption" at any given point in social history, and make for more realistic assessments of possible consumer influences in production expansion and hence in increases in ecosystem withdrawals and additions. Equally important, though, are the social structural processes reflected in these two correctives, which refine the *theoretical* domain of "consumer influences" on production expansion.

Constraints on Consumer Preference Formation

The first set of critiques of consumer sovereignty models relates to the lack of consumer autonomy in forming a true sense of needs. Three of the most important are discussed in this section: (1) direct manipulation of consumer preferences, (2) contingent preference constraints, and (3) public goods determination. The following section will take up problems in consumer action constraints, following the development of preferences.

DIRECT MANIPULATION OF CONSUMER PREFERENCES The most overt form of product manipulation of consumer preferences is, of course, advertising. Two core functions of advertising are (1) provision of information about goods and service availability, and (2) persuasion of consumers as to product desirability, including biasing of consumers' need perceptions. Unfortunately, there exists little analysis of the relative proportions of each of these components in contemporary and historical advertising, though a substantial share of advertising effort appears to go into the latter task. The distinction is important nonetheless, since the first function does not violate consumer autonomy—indeed, it should provide an "extension of the *effective* range of opportunities facing a person . . . [that] contributes to an increase in his welfare" (Mishan, 1967:109). Critics of capitalist advertising systems are often chided by defenders of the market systems for ignoring this dimension of advertising.

However, direct observation provides us with voluminous evidence that a great deal of advertising is aimed at restructuring consumer perceptions of self and need toward passive consumption of comfort-producing goods and away from stimulating activities.[33] This undermines consumer autonomy of preferences according to many analysts:

> Advertising and salesmanship—the management of consumer demand—are vital for the planning of the industrial system. . . . It is held, of course, that wants are not contrived. They are deeply organic in the human situation. . . . Yet one cannot have it both ways. If wants are inherent, they need not be contrived. (Galbraith, 1971:266–67)

Two extensions of this argument may be important. First, advertising does more than simply skew consumer preferences towards particular products. Following Ewen (1969, 1976) and others, it contributes to a broader "consumer culture" and a consumer social structure. Here private consumption forms a key part of social stratification and social relationships, from family to community. As one illustration, television usage appears to lead to reduced familial interaction, even if family members watch the same programs: Their attention is to the program, not to each other, leading to coaction rather than interaction. While it is true that some material components are a necessary part of much social interaction, the general critique of advertising is that it promotes individual rather than collective consumption. Automobile advertising, for example, shows consumers in an isolated auto, and rarely in normal traffic conditions. Paradoxically, of course, it is the aggregation of just such private usage to massive proportions that leads to environmental degradation and a broad array of urban social problems. Conversely, though, advertising produces its own contradictions through such a process, since individual frustrations rise when the expectations of limitless freedom and mobility are arrested by the reality of traffic congestion:

> Human beings are twisted and turned, urged this way and that, driven towards mutually exclusive ends. . . . The capitalist economy heavily influences the "human needs" of its people, the forms and content of its culture, and the resulting inadequacies of the relation between needs and culture. (Wolff, 1978:54–55)

The second extension is that manipulation of consumers is accomplished in many other ways by producers. Formation of consumer preferences is influenced by the content of schooling, including the "public services" provided by producers in schools. Driver education programs often use free cars provided by major manufacturers as a means of socializing teenagers into automobile usage—all in the name of improving safety, of course. This is just one illustration of the cooperation between government and the private sector in reinforcing the demand for private goods. Corporate public relations provide all consumers with a positive image of the firm, extending to a more positive image of the firm's products. Thus, even the low-profile corporate identification in "public broadcasting" serves to undermine collective goods toward consumer identification with the private sector.

Without touching these two domains, the typical analysis of advertising indicts selective descriptions of products, and persuasion of consumers that such products will provide some utility to consumers. For the persuasive role, such producer activity must operate at two levels: (1) it must raise to a significant level the perception of the consumer as to particular *unmet* needs, and (2) it must argue that just such needs will be fulfilled by the product.[34] In the former role, it destroys the assumption that consumers assess their own hierarchy of needs. In the latter, it often distorts the connection between the act of purchase and actual properties of products (see the next section).

As with any other aspect of consumer sovereignty, moreover, such manipulation has uneven force through the consuming population. Less sophisticated consumers are more susceptible insofar as they lack alternative sources of information. The poor and lower working-class are often assumed to be in such a position, although no clear evidence exists. Often, the major protection for such groups is the lack of income to consume to their limit of wants.[35] In general, though, this is seen by Scitovsky (1976:8) as "mob rule: the crowd's ability to get those things on whose desirability its members agree. One of the main goals of advertising is to promote such agreement." Whether this agreement is independent of the role of more affluent and sophisticated consumers is questionable (see the next section). But it is important to note that the individual consumer is further constrained here by the necessity for some aggregation of wants—the producers provide products only when markets are large enough to meet the economic demands of mass production and mass consumption.

Ironically, these critiques of advertising may only further the claims of the large advertising corporations. What little detailed analysis there is calls into question the actual role of advertising in either brand preferences or commodity preferences, although other producer influences are often seen as producing such specific consumer preferences.[36] Lindbeck (1977) takes the strongest position, in arguing that *some* social forces will always influence consumers, and that "scientific studies of the effects of advertising are weak. . . . [But] why [do] firms spend so much money to study the potential markets for new products?" (pp. 42–43). He properly points to the absence of clear alternative mechanisms of determining and structuring consumer needs,[37] though he acknowledges that in present capitalist societies there is a "disturbing problem, for adherents of a pluralistic society, [in] the strength of various pressure groups, and the uneven distribution of propaganda resources in most societies . . ." (p. 160).

In summary, then, advertising and other consumer manipulability does partially negate a model of consumer autonomy. What is unclear is exactly what system of information and persuasion should or could replace the present one, in order to mediate between producers and consumers. Since consumers are social actors, some social influences will always impinge on their consciousness and preference structure. What is clear is the bias towards consumption expansion inherent in the present advanced capitalist structure.

CONTINGENT PREFERENCE CONSTRAINTS   Consumer sovereignty stresses the freedom of consumers to choose separate items of production, as if each choice was independent. While this may be applicable to some portion of consumer demand, much of the demand is contingent, related to past decisions of producers and consumers as well as decisions of government regulatory and other agencies. Electric heating systems for residences were introduced in a period of relatively low electricity costs. Economies of scale in production, arising from large generator capacity, constrained the resident to "demand" much higher levels of electricity to maintain comfortable temperatures. While consumers may be able to reduce these electricity demands somewhat by such insulation increases as the construction of their homes permit and by lowering temperature settings, there is a relatively little freedom in choosing volumes of electricity supply (and hence of energy resources). The capital equipment—electric heating units—allows for no substitution of fuels or other adjustments. In a similar manner, the past purchase of fuel-inefficient automobiles, refrigerators, ovens, or air conditioners constrains the energy-demand freedom of the individual consumer. Although there are options in each of these areas—most notably in the nonuse of such past purchases—each of these entails constricting effects on consumer comfort, production of goods and services in the home, or time-budgets.

Beyond these fairly direct examples of contingent demand, there are also many others. Perhaps the most notable occurs in transportation, as it relates to housing. American suburbanization is a result of a great many forces, some reflecting true consumer sovereignty and many reflecting the complex forces of producer and governmental actions. Among the latter are subsidies for mortgage payments for single-family and, much later, condominium residences; the lack of mortgage funds for urban construction and the investment by large capital interests in suburban development; and the provision of roadway infrastructure by governments.

Regardless of the complexities of the causes of suburbanization, however, there are many consumer consequences, in terms of contingent demand. Many of these consequences were anticipated by producers, whose planning greatly exceeds the consumer's time horizon. Low density, single-family home construction necessitates automobile consumption for transportation to work, to shopping, to recreation. This, of course, leads to vastly inflated energy demands. In addition, the zoning of such communities constrains commercial development in ways that encourage consumers to consume goods and services privately. Neighborhood laundries or laundromats, for example, that rely on accessibility to substantial middle-class residential density, are replaced by individual home laundries—an enormous production of equipment and resource degradation. Moreover, the whole nature of local commerce shifts to shopping centers, increasing both energy costs for transporting consumers to shopping and the demand for automobiles. This includes second automobiles for families, to provide access for nonworking members. Land area is removed from agriculture and other uses to provide parking spaces and to expand road networks.[38]

Hence the limited concept of "suburbanization" is really a shorthand for a complex shift of consumption patterns, many of which are wholly contingent upon the nature of housing in the area. Virtually all of these are material- and energy-inefficient, in terms of satisfying consumer needs for a variety of family services. To speak of consumer sovereignty, once the choice of a suburban residence has been made, is to negate these institutional realities. Moreover, to think about environmental protection in the face of these massive investments in housing stock is to confront maximal consumer and producer resistance. Rather than thinking about demand for a given type of product, then, we must think of *clusters* of related demands, contingent upon an initial consumer choice or consumer response to extensive supply structures.

PUBLIC GOODS DETERMINATION   The general condition under which consumers make choices is substantially affected by the range of public goods and services offered the consumer.[39] That is, such public commodities not only are a distinctive type of consumption, as noted earlier, but they have a potentially powerful impact on consumer markets. For, under optimal conditions, public goods and services can be effective substitutes for large volumes of consumption and production of private goods/services. Moreover, they help to determine the presence or absence of a consumer culture that helps support production expansion. Conversely, as noted above and in the next chapter, other types of public goods can be powerful stimuli for expanded consumption and production.

Nowhere is this clearer than in the transportation field. A mixture of public and private U.S. enterprises provided urban mass transportation in the first third of this century. Over the next three decades, government policy shifted dramatically towards expanded provision of public highways, stimulating and expanding suburbanization and private automobile usage. Trains, trams, and buses disappeared, only to slowly reemerge following energy problems in the 1970s in U.S. cities and suburban rings. While some parallels existed in other European states, nowhere did the automobile dominate both the journey to work and all other trips as in the U.S. In retrospect, it may be said that no other set of state policies enhanced the large-scale corporation—both inside and outside the automobile-related set of industries—than did these transportation investments. Parallel decisions were made regarding goods transportation, with subsidization of trucking versus more energy-efficient railroads and barges.[40] The decentralization of people and industries that followed these shifts produced higher consumption and production, not lower. And ecological degradation was widely diffused, although some localized problems were thereby reduced.

The political processes underlying the shift to more environmentally costly transportation have been far afield from any model of consumer sovereignty. Although consumers, in some organized groups, have made inputs that relate to contingent demands (e.g., arising from past suburbanization), the decision making for such policies has been heavily weighted in favor of producer groups. Little of this decision making has occurred in open public debate, with informed public representatives present. Organized interest groups have been predominantly (and at times, almost exclusively) auto-truck related industries, the so-called highway-automobile complex. No extension of the consumer demand model can be stretched to cover such decision making.[41] Yet the inevitable consequence has been the shift to totally different patterns of transportation.

Similar patterns of public policies have occurred in the housing area, where taxation and banking regulations have stimulated private residential construction in suburbs, as opposed to ecologically more efficient multiple apartment residences in urban areas. The provisions of the Federal Housing Administration (FHA), tax credits for mortgage payments but not corresponding portions of rental payments, and the localization of social welfare costs have stimulated the suburbanization of much of the middle class in the U.S. Such shifts have involved massive environmental costs, ranging from foregone agricultural production to the substantial energy increases required for such housing. Again, only part of this governmental decision-making, which is an important element in constraining consumer choice of housing, has been subject to any consumer demand. The influence of land development and construction industries, along with the financial industries (banks, savings and loans, life insurance companies), has predominated in such policy formulation.[42]

Despite participation in some of these decisions by consumer and worker representatives, much of this expansionary role of government in the U.S. has been removed from direct political participation of citizens. That is, it frequently involves direct and indirect representation by business interests, because of their supposed expertise. Even without formal participation, such groups exercise power through government expectations of business responses—what has been called "power without participation" (Alford & Friedland, 1975). This not only affects consumers by the type and amount of public goods available, but by the process itself, which has further legitimated a kind of producer sovereignty. It is instructive that much of this expansionary government policy has been termed Keynesian, insofar as it stimulates consumer demand and thereby resolves some perennial capitalist economic crises. But even Keynes was concerned that such policies were at best stop-gap, and in the longrun it was far more important for governments to provide more services and goods and undermine the power of producers (Hymer, 1978).

Though important opposition groups (e.g., Lupo et al., 1971) have existed and been effective on occasion, far more of this public goods determination has been treated as technical, and removed from normal class and interest group politics. Moreover, while U. S. government budgets have risen dramatically in the last decades, more of this increase has gone toward regulating business—an effort that was political and open—than toward supplanting it by providing public goods and services.[43] "Because of the government's constrained choice-set, the welfare payoff of development programs is low. The citizen is therefore impelled to avoid increased taxes and . . . purchase consumption goods that do have some welfare payoff" (Gintis, 1972:272).

Constraints on Consumer Actions

To complement the previous section, this one deals with behavioral limitations imposed on consumers, once the processes of preference structuring occur. It should be stressed that the distinction, while useful analytically, is blurred in social reality. Preferences are shaped in part by expectations of action possibilities, and some potential action never occurs because of the "discouraged consumer" syndrome.[44] Three factors are treated here: (1) the effects of income, (2) the misfitting of demand and products, and (3) the problem of retrospective demand.

THE EFFECTS OF INCOME   It is to the Reverend Thomas Malthus that we are indebted for the distinction between demand and "effective" demand. The latter is simply the demand that can be exercised, given the income constraints on the individual consumer. Malthus introduced this concept to attack the mercantilist theorists of his day. They saw in expansion of population (markets) an unmitigated good for "the society" and of course for major capital interests involved in production and commerce.[45] While classical market theories of supply and demand and perfect competition quickly incorporated this effective demand element, the social ramifications of the concept for the relationship of consumers to producers has never been clarified in such theories.

A number of such ramifications can be determined a priori. The first is that the most affluent consumers, especially those who own at least modest amounts of capital, exercise a disproportionate influence on the patterns of production. This is not the same as simply stating that they consume *more*. Rather it implies that producer decisions are much more influenced by such groups in an inegalitarian society:

> The consumer is sovereign insofar as his choice influences the nature and quantity of the goods and services produced. . . . The more a consumer spends, the greater his voting power. Therefore, consumer sovereignty in a free enterprise economy is a plutocracy, the rule of the rich. (Scitovsky, 1976:8)

While Scitovsky views some consumers as exercising a plutocracy and others a mob rule via mass production, he does not seek to link the two beyond this. Some have argued, though, that the rich influence production and consumption in other ways. They serve as taste setters and product innovators, providing pretesting of market goods prior to genuine mass production. Their higher income permits their absorption of the higher costs of early forms of goods. By adopting these new products, they help form the consensus among the "mob" or "crowd" that provides for a mass market, making mass production economically feasible. Evidence is mixed on the historical accuracy of such models, though it may well be the wealthier consumers who help eliminate from the market about eighty percent of the new products introduced by producers to markets.[46]

Insofar as the bulk of the "mob's" income is wage income, it is determined by social and economic processes far removed from consumer sovereignty: i.e., by social class relationships within capitalism. These processes include, on the one hand, collective bargaining between labor and capital in setting wages, and on the other, the political processes of income and other determination. While the role of the ordinary worker-consumer is not irrelevant to the process, consumer autonomy is of little utility in understanding historical shifts in wage patterns. The latter reflect everything from the economic and political power of organized labor, to labor supply and the changing technological structure. So crucial is this factor in determining consumption that even Marxist critics of neoclassical economics start their criticism by talking of "wants and preferences of consumers . . . apart from the distribution of income . . . and the provision of goods and services that can only be consumed collectively" (Sweezy, 1977:142).

If consumer income has grown, then, it has a twofold relationship to the structure of production. Changing production technologies have permitted higher wage income, on the one hand. On the other hand, they have required higher consumption in order to maintain this productive structure. Both the affluent high-income consumer and the better-paid worker are products of the structure of investment and production, and consumer autonomy has little to do with this. Moreover, governments frequently are intimately connected to this process by means of incomes policies, influencing the entire wage and investment-return structure of economies. The most striking example of this is the recent British attempt to reduce wage demands by reducing income taxes for workers—a direct link between wages and taxes as part of a coherent policy. In the United States, the more typical government behavior is a crude Keynesian policy of tax cuts to stimulate consumption in order to provide employment and increase private investment. Such a de facto incomes policy works in much the same way, to structure the *level* of consumption, although leaving the market to determine what goods will be consumed. Ironically, this market freedom often leads to frustration since employment goals may not be met by such a process, as will be detailed in Chapter V.[47]

The income constraint affects the volume of consumption in a variety of ways. For one thing, it increases cost-control pressures on even the largest technostructural or monopoly-capital firms, who must compete within and between industries for the limited dollars of the consumer's disposable income. This creates a pressure to extend the cost-reduction technological reforms discussed in Chapter III. And it also makes price a very important feature of consumer goods. In the process, the social costs of lower prices are hidden, particularly insofar as the ecological consequences of such forms and volumes of production are concerned. That is, the income constraint, coupled with inadequate public goods, pushes farther into the background ecological dimensions of consumption patterns, making them both less visible to consumers and less important.[48] This is the next reality about consumption I will address.

THE MISFITTING OF DEMAND AND PRODUCTS   The fact that consumers purchase a given product is typically interpreted by economists and managers as reflecting a reasoned choice of this particular product. Particular products have two sets of qualities, which are also thereby assumed to be demanded: (1) the production processes; and (2) the use-values of the product. To this might be contrasted a model in which consumers are demanding some service or utility in their consumption, and in which given products are more or less faithful approximations to this demand for the utility, in terms of product qualities at least.

Critics of consumer autonomy disagree on a number of points. First, consumers may be distracted from evaluations of product utility by trivial product features:

> By creating *apparent* choice in relatively unimportant items such as the texture of car seats or optional cigarette lighters, the *real* choices, such as price, mechanical reliability or ecological impact are obscured and made to appear relatively insignificant. (Dickson, 1975:88–89)

Second, the income constraint often means that the most significant product feature is its price. In the neo-Marxist interpretation, this is a particular example of a more general process by which "exchange values, by influencing the process of [consumer] capacity development, become essential determinants of use values" (Gintis,

1972:275). That is, the market conditions (exchange values) determine consumers' utilities, rather than the reverse process described by consumer sovereignty, in which consumers first seek use-values (individual utilities).

The third critique is that the connection between the production processes underlying the consumer goods and the product features and price is relatively opaque to most consumers. If technological change has meant that even corporate *workers* are removed from the direct participation in actual extraction and manufacturing (see Ch. III), the typical consumer is even farther removed. He or she understands little of the technological structure of product manufacturing, and is not thereby voting on the production process when consumption occurs, but is voting on some other basis. Indeed, even in terms of direct product safety, let alone the ecosystemic costs of a particular product, the following reality holds:

> To the degree of his incompetence, corporate officials make many of his decisions for him. He controls them only imperfectly. If, in addition, corporations deliberately misrepresent their products . . . he is even more crippled. . . . Sellers resolve any doubts . . . about the safety of their products in favor of profit in all those circumstances in which injury to his health cannot be *definitively tied* to use of the product. (Lindblom, 1977:153; my italics)

The emphasis in the passage above refers to legal liabilities as constraints on producers making defective goods. Consumers have recourse to legal action only when such definitive evidence exists. By extension, of course, corporate concern for ecosystem safety would only be evidenced where "definitive" links could be established between specific corporate production processes and specific ecosystem withdrawals and additions (see Ch. VI), *and* where such withdrawals and additions had been expressly prohibited by law (see Ch. VII). Consumer autonomy, then, if it imperfectly deals with individual product safety dimensions, is even farther removed from a model in which consumers "could eliminate much of [our environmental problem] if we decided—or allowed ourselves to be persuaded—that we were prepared to give up some portion of our material output in exchange for a more attractive and livable natural environment" (Rosenberg, 1976:219). The parenthetical phrase—"allowed ourselves to be persuaded"—points to the consumer paradox. Producers have the power and expertise to sway the market on many of these dimensions. Indeed, if the producers are committed to an alternative form of production, consumer acquiescence is likely to follow:

> Increasing specialization inevitably deepens the gulf between the producer's specialist expertise and the consumer's generalist ignorance of the nature and design of manufactured products; it is only natural that producer and consumer alike should have greater faith in the former's judgment of what it takes to give satisfaction. (Scitovsky, 1976:273)

The history of expanded modern production and consumption is one in which producers had every stake in presenting consumers with the positive qualities of production and products. Consumption of such products does not display a "revealed preference" for environmental degradation over material comforts. Only time and conflict will tell how much consumers and producers will be willing to alter consumption and production patterns. Fuller information and persuasion about negative environmental effects of present consumption must enter both the politics and markets of industrial societies.

As one illustration, we should note that the increased "demand" for electricity in American homes is in part a function of post-World War II use of electric space heating in new homes. While consumers sought a comfortable home, producers offered it to them through "electric space heating." They advertised it as "clean" heat (though it was no cleaner than natural gas heating), and the capital cost of such equipment was lower than many alternative furnace systems. In many areas, no alternative fuel systems were feasible, since utilities would only lay gas lines where there was sufficient aggregate demand. Electric space heating thus often implied electric water-heating and electric stoves as well. All of this was ecologically inefficient, because of the energy losses in generating electricity. Even at relatively low postwar electricity prices, it is not clear how much of a bargain such electricity usage was over the lifetime of the home. But consumers were in a position of considerable ignorance in all these areas. Producers, while not anticipating future energy shortages, still possessed a broader knowledge of alternative systems. But the housing market effectively withdrew these because of producer decisions: "When new kinds of goods or new models of goods appear on the market, the older goods or models are not always simultaneously available. They are withdrawn from production *at the discretion of industry*" (Mishan, 1967:110; my italics). To say that consumers "chose" to demand higher electricity is, at the very least, a grossly misleading model. Indeed, even after considerable shifts in U.S. energy supplies and costs, it is not clear how much choice a home-buyer has today (Klein, 1978). That is the final dimension to be treated in this section.

THE PROBLEM OF RETROSPECTIVE DEMAND In a perfect model of consumer sovereignty, producers would withhold production commitments until they had closely questioned consumers as to their preferences. Alternatively, they would be prepared to instantaneously switch production when consumers indicated a lack of enthusiasm for a certain product. In the latter case, too, they would require more information on what consumers wanted in lieu of such products. While a considerable amount of marketing research does go on in advanced industrial societies, much of it either collects or uses consumer information in ways that differ from this model. Only a very small share of marketing budgets goes into such anticipatory and production-guiding activity. The rest of marketing is directed towards increased circulation of goods/services (Firat, 1978). Products are not changed, but advertising is. Consumer reactions to products are used to repackage—both literally and figuratively[49]—goods and services, to increase the consumer's favor toward the product.

In all of this, what role does the consumer have in guiding future production? Can the consumer lead the producer, or can he/she only react to past producer decisions, albeit in the imperfect ways noted above?

> Can even a highly competent informed consumer vote for precisely the product he wants? Only if the corporation has taken the initiative to put the product on the market. Although the consumer wields a power veto, the initiative is largely in corporate hands. (Lindblom, 1977:153)

Leaving aside the realities of actual veto behavior (as constrained by factors noted earlier), this asymmetry is very important. Indeed, there is a great irony in the much touted high consumer rejection rates for new products, which is often used to defend the consumer autonomy argument.[50] For, if anticipatory marketing were performed as the idealization of consumer sovereignty suggests, we would expect to find a *low* rejection rate for new products. After all, with good consumer information, producers would be tailor making products to fit consumer wants. Thus, the high rejection rates for new products may be indictment of the lack of production guidance by consumers, not an affirmation of such guidance. Where consumers are given some autonomy, they exercise it in ways that threaten producer sovereignty. Rather than give them more power, then, corporations often seek to control markets and give consumers less veto power.[51]

In addition to this reality, there is the fact that consumer vetos are further constrained where product alternatives have disappeared. When tramway systems are dismantled, consumers are induced to support private autos or less energy-efficient bus systems. When fuel-efficient autos disappear from the market, consumers must select from among fuel-inefficient vehicles. At this time, it is virtually impossible for a U.S. consumer to purchase a moderately priced family automobile that is low both in emissions and fuel consumption. American producers have not yet fully redesigned their engines, as have some European and Japanese manufacturers. With the declining fortunes of the U.S. dollar, lower-income U.S. consumers must still confront a market dominated by cheaper but fuel-inefficient American cars. Yet the past consumption of efficient, imported cars in the 1960s signaled consumer intentions rather clearly.[52] Producer calculations indicated greater profit in deferring major redesign of engines and bodies, though—once more indicating the limit of consumer influence on supply.

CAN CONSUMERS CONTROL PRODUCTION?

The Consumer versus the Market: The Aggregation Problem

The bulk of this chapter has documented limits of consumer autonomy arising out of the structure of production and government. Both politics and markets, then, serve to confine consumer behavior in important ways. Much of the discussion has revolved around the autonomy of an individual consumer. But the reality of an economic system—in particular a capitalistically organized market system—is that consumption and production are intimately connected.[53] Thus, no matter how much freedom an individual consumer may have, insofar as the economic structure is involved, the aggregation of individual consumer behavior often leads to contrary effects in the production system as a whole.

Two examples immediately come to mind. First, in the enthusiasm over energy conservation in the household, consumer response after 1973–74 was quite noticeable. A variety of household energy demands were reduced, by lowering thermostats and by making other domestic adjustments. One consequence of this was increased energy costs in some areas, as utilities were forced to raise kilowatt-hour rates in order to pay for their fixed capital costs. Such fixed outlays could not be scaled down as electricity demands were lowered, and thus conserving consumers found themselves paying more for less electricity—a form of conservation *dis*incentive. Second, an extension of energy conservation in consumption could substantially decrease the demand for certain technostructural products, and thus lower employment prospects for the skilled blue- and white-collar workers in such industries. These further illustrate the connections noted at the start of this chapter, and point to formidable social problems in seriously altering consumption without anticipating and fighting for changes in the production system.[54]

The schism between discussions of changing consumer behavior and considerations of the restructuring of production stems from a number of sources. The most important may be the social scientist's naive acceptance of economic models that posit *consumer* or *consumption* as distinct and meaningful social categories. Moreover, these are treated as apart from the body of economic research, and hence have not really been treated seriously by economists, other than those connected with marketing research.[55] From a social structural perspective, there is no theoretical basis for treating consumers as distinct from the multiplicity of roles they play in society, for consumption seems to be an outcome of these other roles. That is, consumers are not organized per se, except in the sense of a consumer movement, which has its roots in other political and economic roles of participants quite often. But consumers are typically workers, or dependents of workers, and as such are immediately tied to the production system. They are also citizens, and thereby linked to the political structure. Both producers and the state, then, help shape and are in part shaped by the action of social actors who are engaging in consumption as a component of their lives. It is true that some groups of actors—persons working primarily in the household—have their lives more organized around consumption, and that some institutions such as the family have become increasingly organized around consumption patterns. Yet neither of these relationships are organized primarily around consumption (Gintis, 1972).

In the final analysis, then, consumption cannot be the leading factor in the expansion of production. Increased consumption may permit expanded production, but it does not generally cause it. Wage income shifts typically follow production changes, marketing typically follows production shifts, and consumption follows all three of these factors. Consumer resistance, though, can and does occur, where it is permitted. Some products die because of it. But few are born solely because of consumer wants or needs, independent of the production structure.

Any environmental program that rests solely on altering consumer behavior is unlikely to alter production expansion in the long run, though initial successes may be significant. If production leads, then our efforts must be turned to understanding and altering the production system. Following that, we may want social programs to reeducate consumers. More likely, we may find that in capitalist systems, marketing without serious intervention by nonmarket agents will suffice. In some cases, just removing the political supports for the expansionary system might by itself produce the necessary production and hence consumption changes. In other cases, political efforts equal to those currently supporting expansion will contract production and consumption (Lindbeck, 1977:45–49).

Without this appreciation of the organization of production, and the role of politics, our reform efforts are premature. The next chapter attempts to provide a context for the production system.

NOTES

1. The most noted of the postindustrial theorists is Daniel Bell (1973), positing a model of increased leisure time and the changed nature and volume of work in advanced industrial societies. Some of the issues are clarified in the debate between Stearns (1974) and Bell (1974), and in Bell's later work (1976).

2. In a perceptive review of recent U.S. energy consumption changes, Klein (1978) notes that much of the reduced growth in demand for gasoline results from

more efficient autos and not reduced driving. On the other hand, he notes, increased home insulation has been much more at the homeowner's discretion.

3. The interplay of politics and markets is treated at length in Lindblom (1977) upon which this chapter and the next draws. In sharp disagreement, Lindbeck argues that antibusiness critics ignore the role of nonbusiness "advertising": "It is also possible that a lower volume of 'advertising' by politicians, journalists, and writers for public goods and a good environment would reduce people's preferences for these 'utilities.'" (1977:45)

4. Some of the coalitions and lobbying on recycling bills are reported in Fellows (1977) and Smothers (1977), involving conflicts between business, labor, consumer groups, and state agencies. The political context of energy policy debates is treated by an "insider" in Senator James Abourezk's (1977) report, and the larger context in Smith (1977).

5. One of the early attempts to link the two was made by Hannon (1975), who traces the employment effects of energy conservation in consumption.

6. While Bell (1973) is most associated with the theory of postindustrialism, there were other social scientists positing much the same model: e.g., Fuchs (1968) talked of the "service economy." In many of these approaches, it was never clear whether postindustrialism had arrived or was just developing, and in what temporal framework. Nor was it clear how dominant this change was, or how much of the older industrial societal forms were to remain; see Bell (1974) for a discussion of this, as well as Heilbroner's (1976, 1978) critiques of postindustrialism.

7. For example, the total dollar volume of services rose from $193 billion in 1960 to $693 billion in 1975 (U.S. Bureau of the Census, 1976:393). But goods consumption also rose, from $254 billion to $682 billion in the same period.

8. Pauly et al. (1978) note the recent increase in U.S. consumer debt, which has served to stimulate the recent antirecessionary increase in production by increasing consumer expenditures. In June, 1978, credit for consumer installment purchases totaled $233 billion.

9. While the concept of postindustrialism is most often associated with Bell (1973), much of the criticism offered here is consistent with Bell's detailed analyses, as opposed to the unsophisticated postindustrialism model used by other social observers. Indeed, Bell's 1976 work points even more directly toward the organizational contradictions between the economic-technological sphere—efficiency through an elaborate division of labor—and the sociopolitical spheres, in which workers increasingly demand more material goods. In addition, they view their demands for self-development services as a matter of entitlement.

10. Examples of neo-Marxist works include the influential thesis of Baran and Sweezy (1966) on "monopoly capital" and the later work of O'Connor (1973) linking this structure to the organization of the state. Among institutional economists, the best-known work is that of Galbraith (1958 and especially 1971), who coined the term technostructure to describe the network of large corporations.

11. See, for example, Galbraith (1958), Ch. 24, "Labor, Leisure and the New Class." He essentially referred to the upper-class, white-collar workers, especially the new information-processing workers that form the heart of the technological systems at the core of Bell's (1973) postindustrial society. Unfortunately, although

many of the predictions of both Galbraith and Bell have come to pass, they have done so for only a relatively small proportion of the total service occupations. For many of the service occupations, and others in manufacturing and extraction, it is true that sheer physical labor and hours of work have generally been reduced. Some of this occurred with increased political and economic pressures, including unionization of white-collar workers by older unions. The latter has been especially noted among public employees and has dramatically increased their rates of unionization in recent years (DiTomaso, 1978a; U.S. Bureau of the Census, 1972: vol. 3, no. 3).

12. To be sure, many of these claims are exaggerated, and the apparently imminent "greening of America" (Reich, 1970) envisaged by the 1960s antimaterialists has failed to come about. Work conditions and compensation have improved, generally through organized labor's efforts, with the most dramatic cases involving government employees (DiTomaso, 1978a). On the other hand, the lack of unionization of many service workers outside government may indicate greater worker satisfaction than would be implied by the Braverman (1974) model. Unfortunately, there are few historical data to indicate clearly either (a) the objectively changed conditions of work, or (b) changing worker perceptions of their employment environment. It is likely that the proletarianization thesis is as valid as the postindustrial thesis regarding work: i.e., there have been losses and gains following from the increases in the proportion of employment in service and white-collar occupations.

13. Two pieces of data best summarize this. The first is the substantial increase in energy consumption: a 41% increase during 1945-60, and another 58% during 1960-75 (U.S. Bureau of the Census, 1977:594). The second is an increase, in constant 1972 collars, of 76% in the consumption of consumer durables from 1960-75, and a 24% increase in consumer nondurables. In contrast, consumer purchases of services increased by 54% in the same 1960-75 period (U.S. Bureau of the Census, 1976:634). Thus, while it is true that services are a growing share of consumer expenditures (from 42% to 46% in 1960-75), goods consumption often has grown even faster. And many of the fastest growing durables categories involve equipment with high energy demands—e.g., automobiles and household appliances.

14. Mumford (1963) has an extended discussion of these possible changes in Ch. V through VIII, with the clearest listing of impacts in Ch. V.

15. This is essentially the contradiction of capitalism that Bell (1976) returns to: the technical capacity to satisfy needs, but a cultural system that encourages wants (material and self-developmental) that are difficult to fulfill, requiring increased government involvement (Bell, 1976: Ch. 6) and concomitant inflationary pressures (O'Connor, 1973).

16. For the technological perspective, see Rosenberg (1972). On economic growth, the best empirical work is in Denison (1967, 1974).

17. Government expenditures in the U.S. have grown from $8.5 billion in 1929 to $339 billion in 1975, in terms of purchased goods and services (U.S. Bureau of the Census, 1976:393). Total governmental outlays are far greater than that, because of transfer payments (e.g., the federal government outlay alone in 1975 was $325 billion). Employment growth has paralleled this, especially in state and local governments: during 1950-76, federal employment grew from 2.1 million to 2.8 million workers, state government employment from 1.1 to 3.3 million workers, and local government employment from 3.2 to 8.8 million workers (U.S. Bureau of

the Census, 1977:306). Changes in the private sector employment and compensation are described in Bell (1973, 1976), though he anticipated some of these changes earlier (1962: Ch. 11).

18. Hymer (1978) noted Keynes's concerns about the socially destructive attitudes of capitalism, and his desire to have governments take over some of the productive functions of private capital. But rather than:

> an expansion of the state and public consumption at the expense of the rentier class . . . the alternative preferred by the capitalist was an expansion of the state to promote the growth of private wealth through the stimulation of private investment and private consumption. (Hymer, 1978:26)

Constraints on state expansion of these roles are treated in O'Connor (1973) and Bell (1976: Ch. 6). In both cases, though, these rather ideologically different observers assume a perpetuation of private capital expansion of production, though the more conservative Bell sees rather more stringent limits approaching than does the neo-Marxist O'Connor. Heilbroner (1978) takes a position in which he sees ever greater state expenditures to deal with environmental and economic conflicts, and comes closer to Bell's than O'Connor's expectations.

19. See Klein (1978) for an overview of industrial energy-conservation efforts, and Hollie (1978) for a detailed review of Dow Chemical programs, which have apparently led to little substitution of labor for capital but to more efficient uses of capital equipment.

20. The optimistic view is represented by ratios of energy consumption to absolute dollars of gross national product: they declined from about 216 to 47 trillion BTU's per billion dollars from 1930 to 1975 (U.S. Bureau of the Census, 1977:594; 1976:393). On the other hand, if we look at the energy required for each constant (1972) dollar of U.S. personal consumption, the decline from 1929 to 1950 was only from 110.3 to 100.6. From 1950 to 1960 there was little decline; from 100.6 to 98.4 trillion BTU's per billion dollars (U.S. Bureau of the Census, 1977:429, 594). From 1960 to 1975, there was somewhat more reduction per constant (1972) dollar, from 98.4 to 91.7 trillion BTU's per billion dollars. This may be an overly pessimistic view, since industrial energy conservation typically was just beginning to take place by 1975, although residential conservation was already higher. Landsberg (1976) presents a more optimistic view on materials, indicating little growth in per capita consumption in the last several decades in the U.S.; but he also notes rapid increases in the Third World per capita consumption. In general, then, the technological advances noted in Ch. III have not been especially energy conserving, as noted there, despite the reductions of energy per unit product.

21. The conversion of service industries into more capitalized ones is noted in Mandel "*The logic of late capitalism is therefore necessarily to convert idle capital into service capital and simultaneously to replace service capital with productive capital, in other words, services with commodities:* transport services with private cars, theatre and film services with private television sets" (1975:406). Similar viewpoints are expressed in O'Connor (1973) and Gintis (1972).

22. Indeed, Bell (1973, 1974) stressed that one of the differences in the new services economy was that many of the services were for businesses.

23. On lobbying history of the Interstate Highway system in the U.S., see

Jerome (1972) and Leavitt (1970); Caro (1974) indicates the effects of this in New York policies. Sweezy (1973) discusses the links of the automobile to employment and production components, and gives the labor force estimates cited here.

24. The 1970 figure is 25% and the 1976 is 26% (U.S. Bureau of the Census, 1977:594).

25. See Klein (1978) for some recent changes.

26. For an overview of the different systems, see Lindblom (1977). He notes that in fact there are labor and consumer markets operating in the U.S.S.R. and other planned systems; only the business market has been eliminated (pp. 37–38). Indeed, the western media report that Soviet consumers have rejected some products: the existence of overstocks confirms the existence of a consumer *market*.

27. Lindblom (1977:149–50) argues that even technostructural or monopoly capital firms are more responsive to the aggregate inputs of citizen-consumers than are political or "polyarchal" systems of authority, in terms of direction of response. Even Baran and Sweezy (1966), who coined the term monopoly capital, noted that such capital-intensive industries still faced interindustrial competition of products, a point which Lindblom (1977:151) stresses.

28. Scitovsky (1976) deals extensively with what he sees as the consumer's need for stimulation and the pressures exerted on the consumer to consume goods that produce *comforts*. The former is more service-oriented and related to the domestic rather than market economy that Stretton (1976:185 ff.) seeks as an ecological and social resolution of problems of advanced capitalism. Lindblom (1977), in contrast, deals more with problems of consumer influence in the marketplace, leaving the wants-versus-needs issue aside. One of the few empirical approaches to want creation is in Firat (1978), though the empirical tests are very weak and the results inconclusive.

29. See Firat (1978) for a discussion of the limitations of the marketing literature.

30. For example, in 1976, only 25% of the U.S. energy consumption went directly to residential and commercial applications, and 29% to industrial usage; unfortunately, it is impossible to partition the latter into consumer goods and other uses (U.S. Bureau of the Census, 1977:594). Moreover, in the same year some 19% of energy usage was attributed to losses of conversion of fuels into electricity and other fuel transformations. Again, no consumer or other distinction is possible.

31. Conventional breakdowns of gross national product or national income accounts make it difficult to estimate the corrections we are attempting. One means is to focus on personal consumption expenditures only: in both 1960 and 1975 this stood at only 64% of GNP in the U.S. (U.S. Bureau of the Census, 1976:393). Business expenditures are computed only as "gross private domestic investment," and amounted to 15% of GNP in 1960 and 12% in 1975.

32. Government purchases of goods and services rose from 20% of GNP in 1960 to 22% by 1975, in the United States (U.S. Bureau of the Census, 1976:628). This is only the government role *in the market,* and does not include government services, which account for some 12% of production in 1975, up from 9% in 1960 (ibid.). The role of government includes both such purchases and provision of goods and services, although they cannot be quantified so readily as the separate estimates for each component of the government role.

33. The emphasis on induced consumer passivity in consumption is notable in Scitovsky (1976), Mandel (1975: Ch. 12), and Sweezy (1977). An even more extreme position is that of Gintis (1972:274), who argues that even the active consumer is induced to "use his or her money to gain personal access to those positive social activity-contexts *which exist,* rather than slightly increase their total supply." While his argument is based on a Marxian model of the alienated worker-consumer, Scitovsky's (1976:176–77) model of the individual's benefit-cost analysis not favoring such actions may be more appropriate. They are not incompatible arguments, though. One balance to such arguments is Lindbeck's (1977) position that: (1) no social system exists that does not influence consumer preferences, (2) much of advertising gives essential product information, (3) even where advertising doesn't exist, demand for some products (such as autos in the U.S.S.R.) is still high, and (4) "advertising" includes media and other efforts by politics and environmentalists, who partly offset the passive biases induced by producers (see pp. 32–49, 157–60).

34. The managerial-technological orientation in advertising is exemplified in Sweeney (1972), Spratlen (1972), and Hamburger (1974). Critiques of this include Baran & Sweezy (1966), Galbraith (1971), Chamberlin (1965), and Robinson (1969).

35. This is the focus of the Firat (1978) study, which finds mixed evidence for the adoption of high-income consumption patterns by low-income consumers. As he notes, though, the data to test his model are rather weak, a situation underscored by the epistemological concerns expressed in Zaltman et al. (1973) about marketing studies in general.

36. Scitovsky (1976:205–07) expresses considerable skepticism about the role of advertising beyond brand preference, drawing upon the work of Schmalensee (1972), though he indicates that producer influences operate on consumer tastes through other channels. At the opposite end is the work of Ewen (1976), who sees in advertising the making of a consumer culture; for a critique of his mechanistic approaches, see Wolff (1978). While Lindblom (1977:214–16) expresses some skeptical views of the power of advertising he also indicates that:

> One must entertain a hypothesis that sales promotion may be a powerful, ubiquitous, relentless molder of the culture.... [It] may succeed in pushing the populace toward the pursuit of marketed goods and services... persuading... that buying is the way to popularity, honor, distinction, delight, and security.

37. Berkley (1971:137) notes that approximately 80% of new products introduced into the U.S. market each year fail, a point that Lindblom stresses (1977:214–15), and one that agrees with the preceeding quotation from Lindbeck. Lindbeck's critique of neo-Marxist opposition to current markets is well taken, insofar as there is no clear discussion of effective alternative mechanisms. On the other hand, Lindblom (1977:37) notes that most state socialist societies do have consumer markets, and that is why Lindbeck and other defenders of the capitalist structure have data on the inadequacies of producer decisions in countries like the U.S.S.R. Part of this debate hinges on the confusion between consumer freedom to purchase or reject goods, and true consumer sovereignty: "The consumer is sovereign insofar as his choice *influences* the nature and quantity of the goods and services produced" (Scitovsky, 1976:8). Lindbeck is accurate in his critique of socialist

systems as long as producer decisions are made relatively autonomously of consumer demand. But the differences between socialist and capitalist systems are matters of degree more than of kind, as Lindblom's (1977) comparative analysis indicates.

38. An excellent early discussion of these contingencies of suburbanization is David Riesman's paper, "The Suburban Dislocation" (1964:226–57). The central role of the automobile and of the state provision of highways to stimulate auto and suburban housing demand is lucidly treated in Riesman (1964:258–69, 270–99), Mumford (1963), and Jerome (1972). In contrast, the consumer sovereignty model of the automobile is best expressed in John Rae's (1971) book, which is a call for more and better highways. The fact that the latter was done under a General Motors grant clearly suggests the subtleties of producer influences (Leavitt, 1970).

39. For my purposes, I am defining public goods and services more broadly than the neoclassical economist's definition of indivisible collective goods. Thus, I would include mass transit facilities, which consumers may partly pay for in fares, and which they may choose to use or not use.

40. In postwar U.S., organized lobbying and other efforts in favor of automobile and truck transport have centered around public support of highways (Leavitt, 1970; Lupo et al., 1971; Caro, 1974). I find it difficult to interpret this collective decision making as providing any more control by the poor than does the marketplace, though, in contrast to Okun's (1975:99–100) optimism about such infrastructural decisions.

41. Much of this state investment follows as much a model of participation without power as it does power without participation (Alford & Friedland, 1975), since consumer and other mass interests were ineffectual in altering the process. This is true in analyses as disparate as the personalized description of Robert Moses's influence (Caro, 1974) and the structured lobby efforts for the interstate highway system (Leavitt, 1970). In contrast, the Lupo et al. (1971) book indicates some positive influence of organized consumer and citizen groups, especially in Boston.

42. One of the most detailed description of such influences is in Bradford et al. (1975).

43. Lindbeck (1977:46) notes that some western societies have substantial public goods, Sweden being the most noteworthy with about 30% of total consumption in this category. While Gintis's (1972) position is accurate for the U.S., then, it understates the variability within capitalist economies (Lindblom, 1977).

44. This is an analogue to the "discouraged worker" model in which workers no longer seek jobs because they do not expect to find them. Likewise, consumers do not seek to improve their consumption patterns, as Scitovsky (1976) encourages them to do, because their experience has shown so little prospects for improvement, owing to what Gintis (1972) refers to as constricted activity choice-sets. In fact, both Scitovsky (1976:176–77) and Lindblom (1977:214–17) indicate severe limits on the power of individual consumers to choose wisely, and even Lindbeck (1977:46) argues for more organized forces to counteract producer influences and controls.

45. For a review of the contemporary role of the state in linking social welfare and capitalist interests, see O'Connor (1973), Poulantzas (1973, 1975), and Di-Tomaso (1978b).

46. Firat (1978) presents the strongest model of plutocracy in consumption

patterns, though he finds only partial confirmation in his empirical tests (cf. Tucker, 1964). The estimates of new goods failures is from Berkley (1971:137). It is not clear to what extent wealthier consumers influence such failures, nor whether these goods fail because they are disproportionately introduced by smaller companies who suffer in competition with established technostructural or monopoly-capital firms.

47. Even in the U.S., which lacks a formal "incomes policy" that many social democratic western European societies have had, there have been recent policy shifts (Stelzer, 1977), in part because of high unemployment and high inflation or stagflation (Wicker, 1977).

48. Indeed, the inflationary effects of recent energy price increases in recent years appears to "strain the once-sturdy alliance between consumers and environmentalists that supported the sweeping clean-air and water acts of the late 1960's and early 1970's" (Klein, 1978). This strain is clearest in conflicts over utility rate reforms, where the traditional concern of consumer activists to keep prices as low as possible is in conflict with environmental protection that requires stack gas scrubbers, closed cooling systems, and increased nuclear power safeguards. Utilities have, of course, taken advantage of this wedge (Clymer, 1977).

49. The most interesting case is the substantial increase in packaging in societies like the U.S. Such packaging, which is a major component of solid wastes and increases ecosystem withdrawals as well, is largely for purposes of consumer persuasion, and not product protection. Consumers, of course, pay for this persuasive waste (Lindbeck, 1977:45) as part of the prices of goods and services, and pay again for solid waste treatment—all in the service of manipulating their consumption behavior!

50. See Berkley (1971:137) and Lindblom (1977:214–15) on rejection rates for new products.

51. Market control provides not only profits but predictability, a point stressed by a wide range of social scientists (e.g., Lindblom, 1977; Galbraith, 1971; Baran & Sweezy, 1966; and Rosenberg, 1976).

52. Salpukas (1975) cites a 1925 speech by Charles Kettering noting the finiteness of fuel supplies and the need to reduce fuel consumption if automakers were to have a long-term market. The disparity between this internal knowledge and the producer constructed and/or maintained ignorance of the consuming population is rather great, and indicates not producer ignorance but a different calculus: "Being on opposite sides of the market, producer and consumer may have conflicting interests and the producer's notions of what satisfies the consumer may be influenced by what satisfies him as a producer" (Scitovsky, 1976:273).

53. Hymer & Roosevelt (1977:125–26) note one form of this succinctly: "New needs are created in the same process by which their means of satisfaction are produced." See also Gintis (1972) for a similar position, linking citizen-worker-consumer roles.

54. Hannon (1975) discusses a number of such linkages in the area of energy conservation.

55. In the case of marketing research, the dominant emphasis has been on improved persuasion techniques (Firat, 1978). Indeed, the fact that Zaltman et al. (1973) refer to the "metatheory" of consumption as late as 1973 indicates the lack of

a social scientific base to such research, as does the presumed need for such a book as late as 1973 (the publication of the book indicating a revealed preference for it, by the logic of consumer sovereignty).

REFERENCES

ABOUREZK, JAMES
1977   "Natural gas and the filibuster." New York Times, 9 Oct.

ALFORD, ROBERT R. AND R. FRIEDLAND
1975   "Political participation and public policy." Pp. 429–479 in A. Inkeles, J. Coleman, and N. Smelser (eds.), Annual Review of Sociology. Volume 1. Palo Alto, Cal.: Annual Reviews, Inc.

BARAN, PAUL A. AND P.M. SWEEZY
1966   Monopoly Capital: An Essay on the American Economic and Social Order. New York: Modern Reader Paperbacks.

BELL, DANIEL
1962   The End of Ideology: On the Exhaustion of Political Ideas in the Fifties. Revised edition. New York: Free Press.
1973   The Coming of Post-Industrial Society: A Venture in Social Forecasting. New York: Basic Books.
1974   "Reply to Peter N. Stearns." Society 11 (4):11ff.
1976   The Cultural Contradictions of Capitalism. New York: Basic Books.

BERKLEY, GEORGE E.
1971   The Administrative Revolution. Englewood Cliffs, N. J.: Prentice Hall.

BRADFORD, CALVIN P., D.E. GROTHAUS, AND L.S. RUBINOWITZ
1975   The Role of Mortgage Lending Practices in Older Urban Neighborhoods: Institutional Lenders, Regulatory Agencies and their Community Impacts. Evanston, Ill.: Center for Urban Affairs, Northwestern University.

BRAVERMAN, HARRY
1974   Labor and Monopoly Capital: The Degradation of Work in the Twentieth Century. New York: Monthly Review Press.

CARO, ROBERT A.
1974   The Power Broker: Robert Moses and the Fall of New York. New York: Vintage Books.

CHAMBERLIN, E.
1965   The Theory of Monopolistic Competition. Cambridge, Mass.: Harvard University Press.

CLYMER, ADAM
1977   "Anxious utilities try lobbying directly." New York Times, 13 Nov.

DENISON, EDWARD F.
1967   Why Growth Rates Differ: Postwar Experience in Nine Western Countries. Washington, D.C.: The Brookings Institution.

1974   Accounting for United States Economic Growth, 1929–1969. Washington, D.C.: The Brookings Institution.

DICKSON, DAVID
1975   The Politics of Alternative Technology. New York: Universe Books.

DITOMASO, NANCY
1978a   "Public employee unions and the urban fiscal crisis." Paper presented at meetings of the Society for the Study of Social Problems, San Francisco, September.
1978b   "The organization of authority in the capitalist state." Journal of Political and Military Sociology 6(2):189–204.

EILENSTINE, DONALD AND J.P. CUNNINGHAM
1972   "Projected consumption patterns for a stationary population." Population Studies 26 (2):223–231.

EWEN, STUART
1969   "Advertising as social production." Radical America 3 (May–June):42–56.
1976   Captains of Consciousness: Advertising and the Social Roots of the Consumer Culture. New York: McGraw-Hill.

FELLOWS, LAWRENCE
1977   "The life and death of Connecticut's bottle bill." New York Times, 12 June.

FIRAT, ASIM F.
1978   The Social Construction of Consumption Patterns. Unpublished doctoral dissertation, Graduate School of Management, Northwestern University, June.

FUCHS, VICTOR
1968   The Service Economy. New York: National Bureau of Economic Research.

GALBRAITH, JOHN K.
1958   The Affluent Society. New York: New American Library.
1971   The New Industrial State. Second edition. New York: New American Library.

GINTIS, HERBERT
1972   "Consumer behavior and the concept of sovereignty: Explanations of social decay." The American Economic Review 62 (2):267–278.

HAMBURGER, P.L.
1974   Social Indicators: A Marketing Perspective. Chicago: American Marketing Association.

HANNON, BRUCE
1975   "Energy conservation and the consumer." Science 189 (11 July):95–102.

HEILBRONER, ROBERT L.
1976   Business Civilization in Decline. New York: W.W. Norton.
1978   "Boom and crash." New Yorker, 28 Aug.:52–73.

HOLLIE, PAMELA G.
1978   "The energy strategy of the heaviest energy user." New York Times, 5
Feb.

HOUTHAKKER, H.S. AND L.D. TAYLOR
1966   Consumer Demand in the United States, 1929–70. Cambridge, Mass.:
Harvard University Press.

HUBBERT, M. KING
1969   "Energy resources." Pp. 157–242 in Committee on Resources and Man
(NAS-NRC) (ed.), Resources and Man: A Study and Recommendations.
San Francisco: W.H. Freeman.

HYMER, STEPHEN
1978   "International politics and international economics: A radical approach."
Monthly Review 29 (Mar.):15–35.

HYMER, STEPHEN AND F. ROOSEVELT
1977   "Comment." Pp. 119–137 in A. Lindbeck, The Political Economy of
the New Left: An Outsider's View. New York: Harper and Row.

JEROME, JOHN
1972   The Death of the Automobile: The Fatal Effect of the Golden Era,
1955–1970. New York: W.W. Norton.

KEYNES, JOHN MAYNARD
1933   "National self-sufficiency." The Yale Review 22 (Summer):757–762.
1964   The General Theory of Employment, Interest and Money. London:
Macmillan.

KLEIN, FREDERICK C.
1978   "Embargo aftermath: Patterns of energy use in U.S. are changing five
years after crisis." Wall Street Journal, 7 Sept.

LANDSBERG, HANS H.
1976   "Materials: Some recent trends and issues." Science 191 (20 Feb.):637–
641.

LEAVITT, HELEN
1970   Superhighway—Superhoax. New York: Ballantine Books.

LINDBECK, ASSAR
1977   The Political Economy of the New Left: An Outsider's View. Second
edition. New York: Harper and Row.

LINDBLOM, CHARLES E.
1977   Politics and Markets: The World's Political-Economic Systems. New
York: Basic Books.

LUPO, ALAN, F. COLCORD, AND E.P. FOWLER
1971   Rites of Way: The Politics of Transportation in Boston and the U.S.
City. Boston: Little, Brown.

MANDEL, ERNEST
1975   Late Capitalism. Translated by J. De Bres. London: New Left Books.

MARSHALL, ALFRED
1948   Principles of Economics. Eighth edition. London: Macmillan.

MISHAN, EZRA J.
1967 The Costs of Economic Growth. New York: Frederick A. Praeger.

MUMFORD, LEWIS
1963 "The highway and the city." Pp. 234–246 in L. Mumford, The Highway and the City. First edition. New York: Harcourt Brace and World.
1970 The Myth of the Machine: The Pentagon of Power. New York: Harcourt Brace Jovanovich.

O'CONNOR, JAMES
1973 The Fiscal Crisis of the State. New York: St. Martin's Press.

OKUN, ARTHUR M.
1975 Equality and Efficiency: The Big Trade-off. Washington, D.C.: The Brookings Institution.

PAULY, DAVID, R. THOMAS, AND P.L. ABRAHAM
1978 "When bad news is good." Newsweek, 14 Aug.:45–46.

POULANTZAS, NICOS
1973 Political Power and Social Classes. London: New Left Books.
1975 Classes in Contemporary Capitalism. London: New Left Books.

RAE, JOHN B.
1971 The Road and the Car in American Life. Cambridge, Mass.: MIT Press.

REICH, CHARLES A.
1970 The Greening of America. New York: Random House.

RIESMAN, DAVID
1964 Abundance for What? And Other Essays. First edition. Garden City, N.J.: Doubleday.

ROBINSON, JOAN
1969 The Economics of Imperfect Competition. Second edition. London: Macmillan.

ROSENBERG, NATHAN
1972 Technology and American Economic Growth. New York: Harper Torchbook.
1976 Perspectives on Technology. Cambridge: Cambridge University Press.

SALPUKAS, AGIS
1975 "Detroit has always known smaller cars were coming." New York Times, 2 Feb.

SCHMALENSEE, R.
1972 The Economics of Advertising. Amsterdam: North-Holland.

SCITOVSKY, TIBOR
1976 The Joyless Economy: An Inquiry into Human Satisfaction and Consumer Dissatisfaction. New York: Oxford University Press.

SMITH, HEDRICH
1977 "The big White House error on energy was overconfidence." New York Times, 2 Oct.

SMOTHERS, RONALD
1977 "Dyson opposes plan on recycling plants." New York Times, 9 Oct.

SPRATLEN, THADDEUS H.
1972   "The challenge of a humanist value orientation in marketing." Pp. 403–413 in N. Kangun (ed.), Society and Marketing: An Unconventional View. New York: Harper and Row.

STEARNS, PETER N.
1974   "Is there a post-industrial society?" Society 11 (4):10–22.

STELZER, IRWIN M.
1977   "Portents of an incomes policy." New York Times, 9 Oct.

STRETTON, HUGH
1976   Capitalism, Socialism and the Environment. Cambridge: Cambridge University Press.

SUTTON, FRANCIS X., S.E. HARRIS, C. KAYSEN, AND J. TOBIN
1956   The American Business Creed. Cambridge, Mass.: Harvard University Press.

SWEENEY, D.J.
1972   "Marketing: Management technology or social process?" Journal of Marketing 36 (Oct.):3–10.

SWEEZY, PAUL M.
1973   "Cars and cities." Monthly Review 24 (11):1–18.
1977   "Comment." Pp. 138–147 in A. Lindbeck, The Political Economy of the New Left: An Outsider's View. New York: Harper and Row.

TUCKER, W.T.
1964   The Social Context of Economic Behavior. New York: Holt, Rinehart and Winston.

UNITED STATES BUREAU OF THE CENSUS
1972   Census of Government. Vol. 3. Management-Labor Relations in State and Local Governments. No. 3. Washington, D. C.: Government Printing Office.
1976   Statistical Abstract of the United States: 1976. Washington, D.C.: Government Printing Office.
1977   Statistical Abstract of the United States: 1977. Washington, D.C.: Government Printing Office.

WICKER, TOM
1977   "Fast route to new jobs." New York Times, 6 Feb.

WOLFF, RICH
1978   "Economics, advertising, and consumer culture." Monthly Review 29 (Mar.):49–55.

ZALTMAN, GERALD, C.R.A. PINSON, AND R. ANGELMAR
1973   Metatheory and Consumer Research. New York: Holt, Rinehart and Winston.

V THE EXPANSION OF PRODUCTION
Capital, Labor, and State Roles

TOWARD AN UNDERSTANDING OF ECONOMIC GROWTH COALITIONS
Economic Expansion: Surplus Generation and Distribution

Chapter IV acknowledged that consumers ultimately do support expanded volumes of production by their consumption of goods and services. However, it raised a number of questions regarding the context in which such consumption occurred. In particular, the influence wielded by major business organizations in shaping the consumer context emerged in a variety of dimensions, from advertising to the direction of state investments. At its broadest, the argument has been made that producers shaped a "consumer culture," and this is the basis on which production expansion has been possible in advanced industrial societies.

Such considerations lead to a variety of perspectives about the actual power of producers in such societies. At one extreme, models approaching producer sovereignty have been put forth. These argue that the scale and influence of large-scale capital enterprises is sufficient to dominate markets and governments alike.[1] An intermediate position, and one toward which this chapter leans, is that producers have considerable powers but are subject to market and political constraints.[2] The final position is that producers are merely the servants of society, responding to national needs as expressed by consumers and government decision makers. Only small-scale enterprises approximate this model in contemporary societies.[3]

The three positions may be reinterpreted by a consideration of their assumptions. Expansion of production is a process that builds on and contributes to a sequence of changes in a society. On the one hand, the expansion is dependent upon the mobilization and organization of a surplus produced in a prior period. In general, expanded production requires new inputs, which typically come from an accumulation of capital and availability of labor that was not required for sociocultural or biological needs. This is usually stated in terms of savings and investment potential, which in turn can be used to support new physical capital for expanded production. But the same is true of labor. Growth in population or reduction of labor needs in past production require sufficient surplus from production to support such labor potential—dependents in the broadest sense.[4] And a similar model can be used to think about ecosystem resources as well. Expanded production requires the use of natural resources that are available in part because they have not been used in past production. They can be conceived of as a biospheric "surplus" that was not consumed earlier, a view that is typical of economic growth planners who view ecosystem structure as a series of "stocks" to be tapped in future production.[5]

Conversely, expanded production volumes typically generate their own new levels of sociocultural surplus and leave various biospheric reserves for future production. Both stocks of physical capital and liquid capital savings are generated, as are changes in population and the available labor force. This new wave of capital, labor, and the socially accessible biospheric surplus then becomes accessible for future production changes.

This process is repeated historically. In each period, though, a series of decisions has to be made as to how to mobilize past surplus. This entails a substantial set of issues: e.g., (1) organizational means of gathering this surplus, (2) structuring the organization of such surplus in production, and (3) allocating production gains to various components of the productive system. None of these are givens. All require decisions to be made before determining that a surplus should even be mobilized for production expansion rather than expanded consumption or elimination of surplus.[6] Economic expansion has become so entrenched in our minds that we often forget that some societies have opted for an elimination of surplus at times. The Kwakiutl, for example, engage in such activities during their potlatches, when goods are destroyed in an elaborate social ritual of conspicuous consumption of wealth (Service, 1958:210–11). In like manner, though we decry the "unproductive" use of wealth in underdeveloped countries—where elites often consume rather than invest—this is in fact a decision that is always available in every society (Moore, 1965:28–32). From a purely ecological perspective, we could label such acts of consumption as heroic, since they reduce future possibilities of production expansion. On a social structural basis, of course, we have many sound reasons for thinking otherwise.[7]

Crucial to thinking about production expansion, then, is a series of decisions. In state socialist or state capitalist systems, these are often made by public agencies, ostensibly acting in the name of society. In the capitalist societies that we are focusing on, many of these decisions are made by owners and managers of capital. Insofar as production is largely organized by this group, the responsibility for making the dispositional decisions—for past and future surplus—lies primarily in their hands:[8]

> The businessman . . . has a dimension of choice. He will not risk capital, reputation, or the solvency of an enterprise in order to undertake an entrepreneurial venture unless the conditions are favorable. . . . The particular roles that businessmen are required to play in market-oriented systems they play well only when sufficiently indulged. (Lindblom, 1977:176)

This statement has two dimensions relating to such choice: (1) the fact that the businessman ultimately has some degrees of freedom, and (2) the fact that such freedoms are subject to some potential constraints when the actors are not "indulged," or: "Business simply needs inducements, hence a privileged position in government and politics, if it is to do its job" (Lindblom, 1977:175).

Although Lindblom does not follow the issue of surplus disposition as I do, his work points to some interesting paradoxes in production expansion. First, it is clear that his primary definition of the role of businessmen is as *expanders* of production, as mobilizers of past surplus towards expanded future production. Businessmen, as will be seen later, have the freedom to decide how to allocate past surplus, but not whether to do so. Profits accumulated from a past period will not be destroyed, but they may be held until sufficient inducements arise for some particular allocation. In empirical reality, they are in fact allocated to some productive task—whether by investment in securities or financial institutions for use by other businessmen, or by direct productive investment. "Holding" merely entails use by enterprises other than those generating the surplus. For there is the competition-induced imperative to get some return on past profits through allocation of some type. In terms of our interests in this chapter, it is apparent that businessmen have no a priori interests as businessmen in stopping the expansion of production, and every interest in advancing it. Indeed, their role is defined as directing such expansion, and not merely supervising a steady-state production organization.[9]

But the second part of Lindblom's statement is equally important. For the inducements that he refers to originate in part outside the businessman. This permits some social autonomy within the state and, to some lesser degree, within an organized labor force, to use surplus in ways other than for expansion of production. Social reality is less permissive than this, though. In most capitalist and socialist societies in the modern world, both labor and the state have been committed to production expansion and economic growth, and for quite sound social reasons.[10] They have differed across countries and periods in how the surplus was mobilized, and how the new production surplus was allocated—but not in the desire to mobilize it *for* production expansion. The near universality of this economic growth coalition is a sobering reality that environmentalists have had to confront. While some have sought retreat in utopian schemes that ignore this coalition of social forces, a more appropriate approach is to appreciate the structure of this coalition. For no zero-growth movement can overcome this unanimity in the real world.[11] On the other hand, it may be possible to redirect some of the constituencies within this sociopolitical structure, if we appreciate both the freedoms and constraints of participants.

This chapter addresses these three constituencies of the growth coalition. It first outlines the stakes of each in production expansion. Next, the combination of these in a "treadmill" of production is explored to provide an historical perspective on the dynamics of production growth. The treadmill describes the dominant direction of surplus allocation. But it also permits an examination of the instances where such allocation has been less environmentally pernicious, and/or more socially beneficial. That is, it points to the potential redirection of surplus, in part by examining variations in how such surplus has been allocated across societies and time periods. While the treadmill is a feature of capitalist societies (and many of its features are shared with socialist ones), it is both logically and historically possible to slow as well as accelerate the treadmill of expanded production. The particular roles of labor and the state in such deceleration and acceleration are explored.

Finally, the chapter links these issues to the alternative technology movement, pointing out areas of major conflict as well as opportunities for new coalitions.

Capital, Labor, and the State: Relationships to Production Expansion

There is no simple way to capture the complex relationships between the social constituencies of advanced industrial societies, and their link to production expansion and economic growth.[12] What this section sets out is a schematic representation of some basic connections between each constituency and production expansion. For each sector of the modern society, there are conflicting goals or contradictions in social relationships (the Marxist terminology). This provides for a tension within the socioeconomic system at any given point in time, and thus affords considerable potential for changes in the structure of the system over time. These range from the short-term business cycles to long-term social structural changes in the concentration of capital and the role of the state. Some of the mechanisms of long-term change will be explored in the next section, though they will build upon the connections shown here.

Analytically, it is still important to initially see the major relationships among the three sectors of "postindustrial society."[13] This is true despite the fact that capital, labor, and the state have become more complex, divisible, and heterogeneous in the modern era. Many of the specific predictions of Marxists and neo-Marxists have proven misleading because of the complexity and adaptability of modern capitalist institutions. My own sense of the tensions introduced by the growth/ no growth disputes initiated by environmentalists, though, is that they affirm the utility of the broad institutional perspective of structural analysts such as Marx.[14] This is so regardless of the rise of the "new middle class" of technostructural experts that links capital and labor in modern technological forms of production. It is important to understand the social role of such a class, and its ambiguous relationship to capital and labor as social categories. But even the emergence of such a new category does not negate the usefulness of capital and labor designations for our purposes here.[15]

Initially, we can chart the overarching features of the three institutional entities as follows. Capital and labor are linked in cooperative and competitive relationships in modern capitalist production systems. They are cooperative in their joint contribution to production, with capital supplying the physical technology and labor the human energy for utilizing such technology. To some extent, they are cooperative as well in the consumption relationship. Capital seeks to maximize consumption of produced goods, and labor likewise attempts to maximize physical amenities or comforts. In contrast, they are competitive insofar as capital seeks to extend profits by means of economizing on production costs, including wage income. Labor, on the other hand, seeks to aggrandize both wage income and the security of employment, both of which reduce the flexibility of capital to control costs of production.

With regard to the state, there are close relationships with capital and labor. On the one hand, the state seeks to foster expansion of private capital accumulation through economic growth support. Since private capital is defined as the productive arm of modern society, the state has a substantial interest in economic expansion via capital accumulation and investment. Taxes and political support from capital are both dependent on this relationship. Conversely, though, a democratic state especially must deal with dissatisfaction of labor, since the electoral process provides a means for a political channeling of such discontent. The worker-consumer-citizen model, in the aggregate at least, provides a check on a unidirectional policy of the state, towards simply supporting private capital accumulation. Using Okun's terms, the initial concern with economic efficiency must be balanced with some concern for social equality. State intervention can occur at every level in the socioeconomic system, from involvement in wage negotiations and labor organization to adjustment of tax rates and government transfer payments for income redistribution. Additionally, it may help shape both the form of production and its volumes. The state also aids in management of the externalities of production, as in pollution abatement regulation. This dual role of the state helps, in part, to explain the duality of Lindblom's statement noted earlier. Capital requires inducements from the state, which may or may not be forthcoming, because of the relationship of the state to labor as well as to capital.[16]

In terms of production expansion, the stakes for each of these major social components are somewhat different. For *capital,* two major concerns are: (1) ensuring that expanded production will in fact be consumed by labor; and (2) ensuring that sufficient profits will result to protect the enterprise from competitors and permit future expansion. For *labor,* the concerns include: (1) the increased availability of jobs and wage income; and (2) an improvement in life conditions, including both consumer comforts and qualitative shifts in their social environment (better schools, health services, recreational facilities). For the *state,* production expansion implies: (1) an increased flow or revenues from the private sector (capital and labor taxes); and (2) an increased ability to satisfy the demands of both constituencies for economic and social programs.

Under ideal conditions, production expansion can lead to sufficient economic growth to meet all the expectations. Production will be consumed and profits enhanced to supply more surplus and generate new physical capital investment. Wage income will be high enough to permit this expanded consumption and enhance worker satisfaction somewhat. In turn, the state will have sufficient revenue to supplement this wage income for groups of labor and the unemployed in various ways to defuse any political dissent. Enough will be left over to help support private investment for future demands of both capital and labor. Some of this support is needed for depreciation of public and private capital, and some for increased production to meet the needs of an increased population. But a good portion of this derives from the particular dynamics of large-scale capital enterprise, as I will note later.

However, many of these ideal conditions may not be met in social reality. Income may not rise fast enough to absorb production, or it may rise faster than production. Costs of production may rise too fast and profits may be squeezed because of labor or capital costs. The state may not raise revenue fast enough, because of its taxation policies. Demands from capital and/or labor may outstrip whatever revenue gains occur. Dissent may rise within capital, labor, or both, and the state can find itself in a difficult position, bearing the burden of production internalities *and* their negative externalities. Some of these frictions are short-lived, and can be eased by the infusion of expenditures generated by increased public and private borrowing.[17] These draw on past surplus and the expectations of a future surplus. They are devised to avoid confronting the problems of a socially defined inadequacy of a *present* surplus. Not all sectors can easily increase their borrowing simultaneously, because of limited past surpluses and the threat of overdrawing on future surpluses. Heavier drawing on debt will increase inflation, by increasing the costs of capital and hence of goods and services to all three sectors of society. Such inflation may be short-lived, as recessions reduce the future surplus available to specific groups, to pay for past drawings on these production surpluses. This increases the threat of recession—or of depression, at the extreme.[18]

Thus, the social system is in a tension, depending on the ideal balancing of these diverse interests. Whenever the balance becomes upset, and attempts to redress it are unsuccessful, the possibility of conflict emerges. Such conflict is often reduced to technical disputes about how best to "manage" growth, especially if the imbalance is not too severe. Yet at such points, there is the potential for broader social and political dissent, particularly if social movements exist to stimulate reconsideration of the costs and benefits of a particular growth arrangement of production and distribution.[19]

This model of antagonistic as well as cooperative relationships seems far less obscure now than it may have appeared a decade ago in the United States and other advanced industrial societies, for the historical period following World War II was one in which the dominant relationship among the three social components was one of cooperation. Capital expanded, employment grew, and wages rose. State revenues and employment rose, and a broader array of protective legislation and implementation of New Deal and post–New Deal social equity policies increased. Poverty, unemployment, and environmental problems remained submerged for several decades, relative to a sense of expansionary potential and national well-being. While critics and political dissent were not lacking, even in the United States, the broad coalition supporting and being supported by economic growth held relatively firmly.[20] And, to a considerable extent, this coalition remains quite strong. It is, to my mind, stronger than any other single agglomeration of political or social dissent at this point in U.S. history.

But the cooperative system has suffered a series of "shocks," as economists have phrased it. From an environmental perspective, the initial shock is seen by some as the concern with pollution in the 1960s, and the abatement legislation and enforcement. Far more critical, though, has been the so-called energy crisis, especially after 1973.

Imported oil has become indispensable to the production expansion and the growth coalition. The substantial OPEC price increases, and the immediate- and intermediate-term threats to oil supplies have increased consciousness in all three sectors of the vulnerability of the productive system:[21] "As a commodity, oil is comparable to money—a sophisticated economy cannot run without it; its costs and availability have an impact, direct or indirect, on practically every sphere of economic activity" (Bennett, 1978).

A second series of shocks has been the economic growth slowdown and the emergence of "stagflation" in most advanced industrial societies in the last decade. While not independent of energy and related problems, this is seen as a new problem in the technical and political management of growth. The Keynesian management strategies of the early postwar period have led to a series of conflicting goals: inflation control and economic growth. States are faced with painful dilemmas and considerable uncertainties, now that inflation has occurred in both low- and high-growth periods. Previous economic models had posited an increase in inflation only in high-growth or "overheated" economies, leading to cyclical fluctuations of high inflation–higher employment and low inflation–lower employment.

This boom-and-bust cycle now coexists with a trend towards increasing inflation. Such inflation has led to a new series of interpretations of economic relationships, challenging the Keynesian orthodoxy of economic growth as a solvent for all socioeconomic problems. Moreover, and more importantly, it has provided a basis for new political and social challenges to a simple extrapolation of the economic growth coalition. These challenges arise from diametrically opposed left-wing and right-wing socioeconomic theories and movements. Yet all reaffirm some of the basic conflicts in relationships among capital, labor, and the state.[22]

While cooperative relationships still exist and dominate in many policy approaches, the environmental-economic uncertainties have shattered the peacefulness of this coalition. In some quarters, questions have been raised that undermine the very logic of the postwar production expansion model of state-supported energy-intensive industrialization and postindustrialization.[23] For others, the problems illustrate the previously opaque structure of modern capitalism:

> (1) Competition of capitals generates concentration and centralization. . . . (2) The accumulation process is inherently unstable. . . . Two forms of motion, attributable to related but distinguishable

structural features of the system, characterize the accumulation process: (a) the . . . ups and downs of the business cycle . . . and (b) a long-range and persistent tendency to stagnation manifested in high rates of unemployment and much idle productive capacity. (3) The process of [concentration] . . . exacerbates the tendency to stagnation. (Sweezy & Magdoff, 1975a:1–2)

One of the most direct outcomes of this "stagflation" (the modern version of what Marxists have designated as stagnation tendencies) is the fiscal crisis of the state.[24] Antitax and antiexpenditure movements are but the most visible portion of both the increased role of the state in the postwar period and its unenviable position of being monumentally overextended in commitments relative to tax revenues.[25] It is now commonplace for business proponents to castigate the state for creating the current crisis:

> There is enormous pressure . . . to rein in the agencies before they make an utter hash of the credit markets. There is growing concern that the agencies, however worthy their objectives, are squeezing deserving borrowers out of the market. (*Business Week*, 1974:102)

> Four years into the recovery the Treasury is borrowing as though the economy were still deep into recession. . . . Private borrowers have found room in the credit markets . . . because the Federal Reserve has followed an easier-than-appropriate monetary policy to make sure that borrowers other than the Treasury get money. So a *profligate fiscal policy has bred a profligate monetary policy*, and the two combined have bred high inflation and a weak dollar. (*Business Week*, 1978:82; my italics)

Yet the demands of capital and labor clearly undergird this state policy. The past generation of economic surplus through production expansion has made the state fiscal and monetary programs both possible and necessary. For the postwar growth coalition promised a smooth expansion in production, profits, and consumption. Whenever these have been threatened, the state has come to the rescue of capital and/or labor to varying degrees, in various forms of production or consumption stimulation. Indeed, the historian Gabriel Kolko sees this process as commencing prior to World War I in the U. S.:

> It is business control over politics . . . that is the significant phenomenon of the Progressive Era. Such domination was direct and

indirect, but . . . it provided means for achieving a greater end—political capitalism. *Political capitalism* is the utilization of political outlets to attain conditions of stability, predictability, and security—to attain rationalization—in the economy. . . . *rationalization* [is] . . . the organization of the economy and the larger political and social spheres in a manner that will allow corporations to function in a predictable and secure environment permitting reasonable profits over the long run. (Kolko, 1963:3)

In like manner, the New Deal legislation of the 1930s is seen by some as providing some increased power to organized labor. They, in return, became acquiescent in the rationalization of the economy, and supported the wartime and postwar production expansion as enthusiastically as the capital sector.[25] The success of this coalition can be seen in a variety of indicators. Perhaps the best is the national shock generated by Michael Harrington's (1962) book, *The Other America,* which documented poverty among less organized labor and the unemployed. Though Harrington drew upon readily available sources for his documentation, the dominant view of the 1950s was that poverty was, if not totally eliminated, about to be eliminated in the economic growth of the era. Despite these rumors of the demise of poverty, though, Harrington and others have pointed to continuing inequality problems even in periods of high growth.[26]

To understand the potency of the growth coalition, which exists despite the recent shocks, we need to understand the social logic used to defend growth-via-production expansion, and the actual dynamics of production expansion. The next two sections address these issues.

The Unpolitics of Expansionism: Ideological Bases

Although it is certainly true that there are many objective stakes that major social segments have in production expansion, the social perception of such stakes exceeds even these levels. More importantly, the domination of public policy by conventional models of economic growth inhibits the serious attention to potential choices regarding expanding surplus production and allocation over time and groups. In general, economic efficiency is treated as an unquestioned social good, although many of its externalities are treated piecemeal by various social agencies. This includes environmental as well as socioeconomic inequality problems. Drawing on the work of Crenson (1971), it seems not unreasonable to question the "unpolitics" of economic growth, at least prior to the serious intervention of advocates of intermediate or alternative technology in the 1960s and 1970s. In general, the policy debates in the U.S. and other advanced industrial societies were over the management of maximum growth, not over its desirability. By and large, this is still the dominant form, despite inflation, pollution, energy shortages, unemployment, and other concerns of the last decade, resulting in "continued acceptance of capitalist organization [and its production expansion] as means toward [individuals'] ends" (Gintis, 1972:268).

There are two linked components in this situation. First, there is the matter of ultimate social values being defined in terms of expanded economic growth. Second, within this position there is the variability in how much of this growth is to be generated by expanded material- and energy-intensive high-capital production. Part of the unpolitics of growth resides in the common failure to differentiate the two questions. The theory of economic growth—or more properly, the ideology of economic growth—has been intimately connected with expanded and concentrated capital and production for much of twentieth century America and a good part of the last part of the nineteenth.[27] To use Schumacher's (1973) terms, it has been accepted as a given that "mass production" rather than "production by the masses" is a desirable social form of production. Modern economists, by and large, have defined this as the most "efficient" route to expanded social welfare via economic growth. Even liberal critics such as Okun (1975) share this view, though they wish to add some equalizing policies to the sociocultural production system.

From the nineteenth century views of Adam Smith to the twentieth century economic models of growth, there has been only one dominant shift, and that is in the direction of political capitalism that Kolko (1963, 1976) analysed. For pre- and post-Keynesian capitalist state policies have become less a matter of laissez faire and more a matter of rationalization. As O'Connor (1973) notes, there has been a substantial increase in both social capital (supporting private capital expansion) and in social expenses (maintaining sociopolitical legitimacy of the system).

The central ideological position of economic growth models can be understood as a complex interaction between various factors. First, the theory apparently produced good results, particularly in the post-1945 period, with almost three decades of production expansion at sustained levels. Second, there was enough social expense to keep a social peace during this period, at least until the later 1960s, in the U. S. and other advanced capitalist societies. Third, the economists who defined these growth models were accorded high status in public policy disputes, and their influence was thus disproportionate. Fourth, because they defined economic growth in terms of adjusting techniques, and not in terms of making basic social choices, this view was ever more widely shared in a variety of labor and other circles. The combination of ideology and successful practice led to an increasingly depoliticized view of production expansion as a universal social goal. As economic growth continued under these policies, the model of growth became more accepted. The chief intellectual proponents of the model became more safely ensconced in high decision-making positions in the state. Throughout the last decades, there was little major dispute between these state economists and those representing corporate management. In recent years, the inflationary and recessionary pressures have led to more disputes, though primarily in terms of techniques and not major tenets of growth policies.

The combination of a simple theory and its vindication in everyday life has reinforced this identity of social needs, national economic growth, and production expansion.[28] Expand production and, according to this doctrine, employment, income, savings, revenues, and social services will all increase. Improve the efficiency of this productive expansion, and growth will occur even faster, and social welfare accelerate as well. While this is an oversimplification of growth theory, the essence of the model is captured in this caricature:

> Although growth presents challenges, the subject is really a cheerful one. Without doing much about it specifically, we can expect advanced economies to show a considerable measure of growth in the future as they have in the past . . . in most places the citizenry in their *periodic political decision making* seem to want to step up the rate of growth beyond that implied by their *daily market decisions* on private saving and consuming. (Samuelson, 1967:775–76)

Ironically, what this statement by the dean of liberal American economists suggests belies its initial cheeriness. One interpretation of this contrast between political and private behavior is that it affirms the contradictions of capitalism noted in the earlier neo-Marxist position of Sweezy and Magdoff. The ideology of growth exceeds the political grasp. But the reason for this is the contradictory nature of production organization. It relies heavily on expanded consumption, yet requires sufficient profits and reinvestment from the productive revenues for mobilizing present surplus to grow future ones. Consuming, rather than saving or investing, by labor and the state at least, works in contradictory ways. It supports present growth of production, but may preclude future growth under some circumstances. The crucial difference between the Samuelson (1967) position and that of Sweezy and Magdoff (1975a,b) lies in the relationship between these forces. Samuelson sees a harmony between the two, except under unusual circumstances. In contrast, Sweezy and Magdoff see a continuing tension or contradiction, except under unusual conditions. While the position taken in this chapter leans more toward the latter interpretation, it falls somewhere between the two on the degree of tension and the possibility for reformation.

Perhaps the most important contribution of the recent environmental movement and its intellectual wing in the social and physical sciences lies in the unravelling of many of the dimensions of production expansion and growth. Although empirical efforts to date have been rather primitive, it is reasonably clear that varying levels of ecosystem input can be used to generate equivalent levels of social welfare. In particular, Mazur and Rosa (1974) have done a simple analysis on energy consumption per capita and demonstrated this weak linkage within the block of industrialized nations. What they find is a tight linkage of energy and GNP per capita, but a far looser linkage of energy use and indicators of societal welfare. Weak though their analysis is, it has made problematic both dimensions of the growth model. For if increasing economic growth (GNP per capita) does not produce equivalent increases in social welfare, it makes questionable the degree to which we ought to focus on better and more efficient models of production expansion to enhance economic growth. That is, one implication of their analysis is that *we ought to consider social-welfare maximization as the goal of sociocultural production systems directly, and not pay so much attention to economic growth as the sole means to this welfare.*

For most neoclassical economists, this is a heretical view. It dis-

sociates formal growth models from implied linkages to societal welfare. Some dissident economists have made some of these arguments
before.[29] But they lacked the intellectual, political, and scientific
power of the environmental analysis and movement to buttress their
positions. Indeed, the whole concept of "efficiency" can become
transmuted in such questioning. For the standard concept of economic efficiency *is* economic growth and nothing else. Efficiency-
maximizing mathematical models may still be appropriate in a true
social welfare maximization calculus. But the one-dimensional calculus of "dollars of economic output" will recede and complicate the
life of the analyst. There is some irony here, for economists have
insisted that their "science" is the most appropriate for environmental
analysis. Economists have always dealt with the problem of scarcity,
and the allocation of scarce (fiscal) resources. In fact, in the twentieth
century the bulk of economics has become growth economics, and
scarcity concerns have only operated with production growth as both a
goal and a means to every other goal. A broader environmental agenda
presented in this book is that a no-growth context is more appropriate,
and that welfare maximization with no traditional economic growth is
the new challenge for economists.

One standard response to any new calculus of societal welfare (Crittenden, 1977), and to the redirection of economic policy and structure
towards that end, is that we know so little about mechanisms for such
welfare. The reality, brought home forcefully in the last decade,
though, is that macrostructural economic "science" is equally uncertain in its normal operations. Only the fortuitous combination of
growth-inducing circumstances and policies in the post-1945 period
permitted the smooth growth curve (and its smoothness exists only
when business cycles are ignored). Political action maintained this
growth, when economic science was inadequate. Now that even political actions of the state do not suffice, in the face of stagflation and
resource problems, to guarantee any economic and social welfare
growth, some economic humility seems appropriate.[30] Before the recent advancement of economic growth theorists, moreover, economists did have some of this humility, as in the problems of wartime
to peacetime transition:

> Whether the existing inflationary situation will continue, whether
> it will grow more intense, or whether it will give way to depression

we do not know. . . . How . . . forces [will] combine will determine whether public policy in the transition will have to deal with a major inflation, a major depression, or with one followed by the other. (DeChazeau et al., 1946:8–9)

A major depression would not be impossible even with a considerable increase of civilian expenditure over any previous level. The "how-muchness" is critical and precisely this is uncertain . . . [but this is] not the only source of uncertainty. What will capital expenditures be . . . ? Will we have a wave of technological innovation? . . . Will tax reform enhance the incentive to invest? In the face of these and dozens of similar questions, "forecasting" . . . is a shot in the dark. Yet [the] range may include both serious depression and serious inflation. (DeChazeau et al., 1946:14–15)

While some will argue that improved research and data collection has increased such certainties in the present period, the fact is that there remains as much uncertainty in present growth policies as in any alternatives.[31] And this is due, in part, to the built-in contradictions in goals of the system participants.

THE TREADMILL OF PRODUCTION: ORIGINS, MECHANISMS, AND OPTIONS

The Two Sectors of Production: Controls over Expansion

In a variety of differing analyses, there has emerged in the last decade a distinction between the large, capital-intensive productive segment and the remaining agencies of sociocultural production. Whether the form is called the technostructure, the large corporation, monopoly capital, oligopolistic sector, or the like, analysts of quite different political perspectives have come to emphasize this distinction, as I will.[32] As with these other works, I will concentrate on the large-scale productive sector in later sections. This is where the political, economic, and social power of capital is concentrated, and where major components of production and especially its expansion are located. Ideally, for linking social and environmental concerns, two questions should be answered: (1) what determines the products of this sector; and (2) what determines the absorption of such products in consumer and other markets? Chapter IV addressed the second question somewhat, and we will build on that. In contrast, Chapter III discussed the technological changes, and that too will be a base for a later analysis.

"Monopoly capital" operations were earlier labelled as "the corporation," the "large corporation," or the "Fortune 500" corporation. The defining characteristics of such producer organizations varies from author to author. Most include the following attributes: (1) large scale of production; (2) high levels of fixed capital plant; (3) high usage of "modern technology"; (4) generally high *rates* of profit, or at least large volumes of capital accumulation; (5) bureaucratic management; (6) increased control over all aspects of production and distribution, ranging from raw material controls to marketing and finance; and (7) "public" ownership through issuance of stock in the corporation. In the environmental impact context, we are concerned not only with those corporations engaged in extraction and manufacturing, but in energy-intensive services as well (transportation, marketing).

From the defining characteristics of these corporations, monopoly capital organizations are generally few in number in any area of production. The aggregate of these few in any industrial classification thus constitutes what classical economists refer to as oligopolies.[33] Both from these characteristics and empirical reality, such oligopolies constitute a substantial share of the production in any industry, and have historically increased their share of production or the market for such commodities. Although the dominant emphasis in the social scientific literature is on the domestic character of such organizations, virtually all of these are multinational corporations, operating through various subsidiaries in a number of industrial and nonindustrial societies. This creates problems in distinguishing the causes of environmental degradation within the modern world-system, as well as in the range of producer freedoms.

Competitive capital tends to have the obverse characteristics of monopoly capital, of course. Production volumes are much smaller, there is less capital equipment, lower levels of technology, lower profit rates, more direct entrepreneurial involvement in managing the firm, less control over distribution and sales and raw materials, and more private ownership related to entrepreneurial families. Although many such firms are directly tied to one or more monopoly capital corporations as suppliers of material/equipment/parts, or as distributors, the operating condition of such firms is quite different than that of the large corporate producer. These producers are much more subject to the whims of consumers—both private consumers and other producers. Resulting from this are higher levels of risk in the marketplace, far higher rates of stagnation and bankruptcy (typically involving the loss of capital accumulated over previous years of production), and substantial variability in annual production levels. In many ways, they approximate the ideal type of the producer in classical economic theory, subject to the forces of competition. However, they differ substantially by virtue of having to compete not only among themselves, but with the monopoly capital producers. They differ also in the cooperative relationships they sometimes have with the latter group, and the cooperative relationships among themselves. Various associations of producers, of more or less specificity, exist today: from the Society of Plastic Industries to local, state, and national Chambers of Commerce.

All of the defining differences between these two major categories of producers either stem from or contribute to one essential difference. Monopoly capital corporations have far more effective control over all factors that determine profit levels (capital accumulation) than do competitive capital producers. This applies to production inputs as well as production outputs. From this perspective, they come far closer to the theoretical ideal of producer sovereignty than do competitive capital producers. But there is no perfect sovereignty. In historical change perspective, what is most notable about monopoly capital producers is the degree to which they do approximate producer sovereignty, compared to their nineteenth centure precursors. To understand their role in production expansion, though, we need to understand the practice and perception of competition.

Theorists such as Giddens (1973) take exception to the label of "monopoly" capitalism: competition still exists within this level, albeit a kind of managed competition (Tanzer, 1971). As Galbraith (1971) has so eloquently put it, the risks of competition are avoided by enterprises that have the power to do so—while they maintain a public ideology as to the virtues of the "competitive free enterprise system." The reality of the 1960s, as both liberals such as Galbraith (1971) and neo-Marxists such as Baran and Sweezy (1966) saw it, was that monopoly capitalism transformed the central economic problem from one of confronting *scarcity of capital* to one of confronting *surplus capital disposal*. This does not mean that every monopoly capital corporation confronts too large a surplus of profit every year. Rather, over the last decades, such surplus became more typical. Moreover, the problem is tied to production *oversupply*. Because of the capacity of the monopoly capital sector to administer and collude on prices, higher profit levels have been achieved at lower levels of production, leaving such industries with excess productive capacity. Excess capacity persists partly because of the lack of low-risk outlets for investment of the profits derived from current levels of production. One result is economic stagnation, with periodic and sustained levels of fairly high unemployment.[34] These coexist with environmental costs, arising from the still-high levels of production.

On the other hand, in the last decade the bloom is partly off the monopoly-capital rose. Far from confronting excess capital, the corporate sector trumpets about the "capital crisis," which all agree is at least a liquidity crisis: too little liquid capital around to pay the bills and reinvest. While interpretations differ greatly as to the degree of crisis and the future of the U. S. economy, the shift from over- to under-liquidity in less than a decade underscores the persistent vulnerability of even oligopolistic producers. The problems of a Lockheed, American Motors, or of major stock brokerage houses like DuPont create a culture of vulnerability that undergirds capitalist and managerial behavior. How much actual vulnerability exists is unclear. But the decline in stock values and the competition for capital and reasonable prices indicates real potential for variability in profits, even if corporate survival is not a general problem for monopoly capital.[35]

Even in relatively good periods of growth and profits, though, the large corporations must exercise some forms of controls, in response to external constraints. Consumption or effective demand is monitored and manipulated in part by distributional employees. The technological wing of the corporation seeks to maintain a relatively modest cost of production, altering production technology to reduce costs and keep profits at a stable level. But neither of these are such pressing restraints as those associated with early capital enterprises. Costs are not necessarily minimized, but kept above some minimum. And the search for consumers is not nearly as desperate as in competitive capitalist models. Production and distribution technologies allow fair profits to be made even when production is well below capacity, because of somewhat reduced consumer sensitivity to price increases.

Two additional factors also reduce the pressures on such corporations for extreme demand-inducing measures and cost-cutting. First, many of these firms have achieved greater control over suppliers of raw materials (often holding joint ownership in such primary or secondary industries). This allows for relatively stable and modest price levels for industrial input, permitting greater control over production costs. In recent years, though, some changes have occurred, particularly where Third World raw materials suppliers have nationalized sources. The OPEC situation in petroleum is the most striking example, of course.[36]

Second, more of the financing of production is done internally in these corporations, or through the stock market, reducing external pressures from financial institutions for true profit maximization. Historically unprecedented profit volumes permitted more self-financing in the 1950s and 1960s. When the issuance of stock provides additional capital, moreover, capital thus raised appears to be generated less by maximum profit volumes than by the reputation of these firms for stability and orderly growth. Indeed, as Brooks (1973) has recently noted, even the ratio of stock prices to corporate capital is not a useful predictor of the attractiveness of such stocks to various buyers. In part, this was due to the increased institutional investment in the stock market, and the concomitant demand for steady profits rather than maximum profits. Unlike the situation in which the stock market speculator provides venture or risk capital, the social and economic transformation of the stock market for large monopoly capital organizations now means less risk not only for the investors, but less risk for the producer corporations as well.

However, the ability of corporations to raise equity capital itself varies. In the last five years especially, there has been a decline in stock prices, and individual and institutional investment outside the stock market. This arose, in part, because of the higher rates of return on other investments: government bonds and private bonds, in particular. Demonstrating once more the contradictory nature of the system of production, these higher rates of return both further stimulated and were dependent upon the increasing corporate reliance on debt (especially short term) for financing production expansion. The corporate costs of such debt also increased because of government borrowing, which in part was a response to needs of capital for social capital. And they increased because of consumer debt, which increased corporate revenues as well. But large borrowers have readier access to such debt capital, and pay lower prime rates of interest. Competitive capital enterprises, in contrast, have to compete with monopoly capitalists as well as other borrowers, and are in a tighter economic position.[37]

Nowhere is the contradictory position of the corporation clearer than with respect to government expenditures. While stimulative expenditures help increase effective demand, they also provide pressures for increased taxation or larger public debt. Increased taxation is resisted, whether it be corporate or individual: the former reduces profits directly, and the latter reduces effective demand of consumers. Government support of technological change—e.g., in the nuclear and now the solar energy field—is vital for sustained profitability (Kolko, 1976: Ch. 9). But it demands either new revenues, greater borrowing, or the political risks of reduced services to labor. Freedom and constraint coexist.

Finally, the drive to protect enterprises stems from a genuine risk of corporate takeover, corporate failure, or a declining market position and reduced flow of future profits. If the capitalist class fit the caricature put forth by some neo-Marxists, every major capitalist would essentially agree on some permanent division of markets. A stationary or slowly expanding corporation would be feasible. But domestic and international competitors cannot be readily summoned to such a conclave. The threat always exists of a powerful newcomer absorbing firms and/or markets (Tanzer, 1971). Indeed, although the formation of conglomerates (Brooks, 1973) has protected monopoly-capital interests in some ways, the diversification increases the number of potential competitors for capital, markets, and new firms to acquire (Tanzer, 1971:14–24).

In sharp contrast to this is the competitive capital sector, which does come far closer to the risk-capital constraints of early capitalism. These firms usually require external funding, which is closely tied to short-run profitability in many cases, whether in the stock market or in loan criteria from lending institutions. Performance criteria are much more sharply applied, and unstable profit rates and bankruptcy rates are testimony to the risks involved. Cost control is essential, demand is more unstable, and profits are thus more variable from year to year. That many of these firms may be suppliers to monopoly-capital firms does not necessarily enhance their stability. The latter may choose to pass along their residual risks to these suppliers, by changing suppliers to gain cost advantages or arbitrarily lowering prices.

From a theoretical perspective, the rise of monopoly-capital controls is more of a challenge to neoclassical economic theory than it is to Marxian theory. Marx did in fact anticipate the potential for large capital interests to produce a fairly stable middle class with effective demand providing stability for production. He also anticipated the freedom arising from the stock-market financing of major corporations as well. Managers could then engage in market administration and planning, rather than respond to the vagaries of an ever-changing market for production and the supply of capital. In addition, he foresaw the negative impact of such developments on what we have called competitive capitalists, driving many of them back into the noncapitalist group. Indeed, he also foresaw the need of monopoly capitalism to draw in the powers of the state to maintain stability and producer control.[38]

The model presented above, then, indicates both the powers of and constraints on monopoly-capital producers. It acknowledges that competitive-capital enterprises operate under much more severe constraints. The former sector occasionally approaches the ideal type of the sovereign producer, while the latter reinforces a model of consumer sovereignty. Increased dominance of production in this century by monopoly capitalism indicates that the consumer sovereignty model is increasingly inappropriate for advanced capitalist societies such as the U.S. While there remains a substantial number of competitive capital firms, many consumer goods are increasingly subject to the control of monopoly capital firms. This is true in two senses: (1) increased range of goods subject to such control: e.g., the whole spectrum of food processing has increasingly become dominated by the agribusiness complex; and (2) increased dominance by monopoly capital within a given sphere of consumption: e.g., increase in concentration of production in transportation goods (autos, trucks, buses, and railroad equipment).[39] Mechanisms under which monopoly capital operate thus become of increasing importance in understanding trends in production and production's environmental and social effects.

With these discussions, we have seen the potency of and the constraints upon monopoly capitalism. But, as yet, we lack a clear understanding of (1) how this aggrandisement of the monopoly capitalism sector has occurred historically, and (2) why it has such an intimate association with the spread of late industrial technology in production. Since both these quantitative and qualitative dimensions directly create twentieth century environmental degradation, such an analysis is vital to our understanding of the origins of our problem.

Monopoly Capitalism, Profits, and Employment: The Treadmill of Production

Monopoly capitalism is embedded in the structure of advanced industrial societies, but how did it come to be so vital a portion of these
societies? What were the institutional arrangements which permitted
and channeled production along these lines? At one level, Galbraith
has a succinct analysis of how this sector perpetuates itself:

> Production only fills the void it has created . . . the individual who
> urges the importance of production is precisely in the position of
> the onlooker who applauds the efforts of the squirrel to keep
> abreast of the wheel that is propelled by his own efforts.
> (1958:125)

> It would, prima facie, be plausible to set a limit on the national
> product that a nation requires. . . . The device for insuring that
> there is no terminal objective as regards income is advertising and
> the related arts of salesmanship. Here we have another of the
> interlocking developments which so admirably serve the industrial
> system.
>   Management of consumer demand [is] vital for planning in the
> industrial system. At the same time, the wants so created insure
> the services of the worker. Ideally, his wants are kept slightly in
> excess of his income. Compelling inducements are then provided
> for him to go into debt. The pressure of the resulting debt adds to
> his reliability as a worker . . . few producers of consumer goods
> would care to leave the purchases of their products to the spontane-
> ous and hence unmanaged responses of the public. Nor, on reflec-
> tion, would they have much confidence in the reliability of their
> labor force in the absence of pressure to purchase the next car or to
> meet the payments on the last. (1971:266–67)

Galbraith has eloquently linked employment, income, and the expansion of production in these passages. Paralleling his concept of the
squirrel cage, we can trace out a "treadmill" of production, in Table
5.1 below. This schematic device helps explain why production expands, why monopoly capitalism expands its share of production over
time, and why production becomes increasingly capital-intensive. I
will note both in the table and in the text below that there are many
theoretical and historical options within the treadmill structure. A
number of these have been operational in different societies at differing times. Some have been increasingly advocated by environmentalists favoring "appropriate" technology or "soft" energy paths.

Table 5.1   The Treadmill of Production

Main Propositions	*Theoretical Options*
1. In order to satisfy consumption needs, most of the labor force in advanced capitalist societies must sell their labor to generate wage income.	Small-scale entrepreneurialism can yield self-employment. This is often driven out by competition with large-scale enterprises, though, without state protection.[40]
2. Consumption needs are inversely related to public goods and services.	These needs may be variably inflated by advertising. They may be reduced by direct public provision of some goods and services, outside the market.[41]
3. Private producers' needs are related to production levels that generate profit.	Profit needs themselves vary, in part depending on competition for capital.[42]
4. Production expansion is a mechanism of generating profits and creating employment and income.	Price increases may generate profits without expansion (though consumers may reduce consumption).[43] Employment can also be created in the public service sector, and in entrepreneurialism. Unemployment and underemployment may increase.[44]
5. For any given level of production, the lower the labor costs, the less employment is generated per unit produced/consumed.	As production increases, labor costs may rise faster than other factors of production.[45]
6. Over time, monopoly capitalism uses profits to increase the uses of capital in high technology, and decreases the labor input to production: This increases the "productivity of labor."[46]	Total labor income may rise, while employment falls: A "labor aristocracy" emerges. This concentrates worker income, but does not counter unemployment. Direct employment in production is often reduced, while corporate employment increases in white-collar and related work.[47] State incentives could also provide some stimulus to employ more labor with less capital per worker.[48]

7. Because of the increasing ratio of capital to workers, production must expand in order to provide employment for growing labor forces (from population growth) and for workers displaced by labor-reducing technologies.

The state may absorb surplus workers, but it needs tax increases to do so. This may induce the state to stimulate production expansion. Alternatively, the state may pressure producers to increase the ratio of labor to capital instead of expanding production. Finally, unemployment and underemployment may be allowed to rise.[49]

8. This production expansion increases the volume of corporate profits.

Production may go unsold; costs may be higher than anticipated; taxation may be increased to absorb profits.[50]

9. Increased volumes of profits are allocated to technological change aimed at increasing capitalization of production, and decreasing labor participation.

Profits may be consumed rather than invested, or may offset higher costs (e.g., oil price increases.) They could be allocated to high-labor types of production (as in some Third World investment), or to expanding "unproductive" white-collar work in marketing, etc.[51]

10. This expanded production must be absorbed by consumers. Either more consumers must be brought in, and/or higher incomes paid to workers.

A variety of domestic and international strategies may be followed. Higher wage settlements and credit may be permitted in both private and public sectors. New markets may be sought abroad, in industrial and Third World countries. Public sector consumption may be encouraged. Tax relief for consumers may be lobbied for.[52]

11. Such expanded consumption merely continues the process of #5 through #10 above, and frequently accelerates it. This is the essence of the treadmill, since consumption must increase at ever faster rates to offset the substitution of capital for labor in the production process.

By increasing taxation and expanding the provision of services, the state can slow the treadmill considerably. Production may be shifted abroad with more docile labor forces, in a more labor-intensive effort. Consumption may be shifted abroad as well, keeping domestic wages lower and unemployment higher.[53]

While production expansion has occurred in socialist as well as capitalist societies, the particular form of the treadmill is more evident in the latter. The basic social force driving the treadmill is the inherent nature of competition and concentration of capital:

> Because of the possibility that capital will be lost, and because of the pressures of competition, there is compulsion for profits to keep on growing. Capitalists have to make more and more profits to protect their investment, to expand the capital base, and thereby even more profits. . . . These . . . are the natural and necessary results of social relations which dictate that the material components of capital be used to maximize profits and minimize risks. (Magdoff, 1976:3)

In the modern industrial world, moreover, the scale of outside financial control of major capital-intensive industries has intensified the risks for even large-scale capital owners:

> Any corporation whose technostructure or management fails to operate it in a sufficiently profitable manner runs the grave risk of attempted takeover by the billions of dollars that are always available in or through Wall Street for a potentially highly profitable investment. The threat of the corporate raider—whether a super-rich individual, a temporary combine of financial institutions with huge resources, or another major corporation—outflanking entrenched management by buying out a company's stockholders has always been an ever present threat to any corporate management paying inadequate attention to profits. (Tanzer, 1971:18)

Competition and the quest for profitability constitute the main construction materials for the production treadmill, though the designs for the latter vary.

In general, increasing the speed of this treadmill involves increased environmental withdrawals and additions. While some capital intensification of production may lead to more efficient production techniques (Ridker, 1972), these often involve substitutions of energy for older materials. The case of plastics is a prototype. Plastics are high-energy products that serve to substitute for larger volumes of wood and metals.

The treadmill appears to operate for most industrial societies (especially private capitalist ones), and even for Third World societies. But the speed of the employment-income-production treadmill does vary across societies and historical periods. So does the acceleration in this speed. A variety of factors determine the employment effects of production. The theoretical options in Table 5.1 indicate some of these. Included are surplus-capital allocative decisions by capitalists, and the role of the state in shifting these capital surpluses.

Beyond these qualitative dimensions, there are the quantitative factors at work: levels of profits, levels of investment in capital-intensive production, and concentration of profits. In addition, there is a timing or development feature. The treadmill appears to accelerate more quickly when basic subsistance needs are met, and more discretionary income is available for nonnecessities.

Some major features of the treadmill to be discussed are: (1) the role of labor force growth; (2) technological choices; and (3) capital-intensification of production. Each of these is briefly treated.

LABOR FORCE GROWTH   There is variability in the treadmill because of population growth, and concomitant growth in the labor force. The recent situation in the U.S. illustrates this. Although unemployment increased substantially after 1973, so has employment. Part of the growth in the labor force is due to population increases, and part due to increased participation rates for females.[54]

Insofar as population growth is involved in this treadmill, the indirect role of population growth may be far more serious than generally indicated in Chapter II. That is, the direct production-expansion required to employ more workers may have a much greater environmental impact than the expanded consumption of these new members of the labor force. The faster the treadmill is moving when this expansion of the labor force occurs, the greater the production and environmental impact *per worker* likely to occur. The conventional consumer model of population impact (Ch. IV) does not take this into account. A capital-labor model to take these treadmill dimensions into somewhat greater account could be generated as follows:

$$\text{Environmental degradation} = \begin{bmatrix} \text{Number of} \\ \text{producers} \end{bmatrix} \times \begin{bmatrix} \text{Average} \\ \text{work-force} \end{bmatrix} \times$$

$$\begin{bmatrix} \text{Capital} \\ \text{per worker} \end{bmatrix} \times \begin{bmatrix} \text{Production} \\ \text{per unit} \\ \text{capital} \end{bmatrix} \times \begin{bmatrix} \text{Average} \\ \text{withdrawals} \\ \text{\& additions} \\ \text{per unit product} \end{bmatrix}$$

The second-to-last term in the equation takes account of what Commoner (1977) stresses in his capital-productivity analyses. The capital/worker term incorporates a key element in the treadmill: the capital-intensification of production. If we think of all but the first term of this equation as relating to a specific firm, and the environmental effects cumulated across all producers (firms), then there is some social meaning to such a modified producer model. Conversely, if we simply aggregate all these terms across a national economy, we miss a great deal of the realities of monopoly-capital expansion. For the treadmill is most appropriate to this sector, and its indicators are muted when lumped together with the competitive capital sector.

TECHNOLOGICAL CHOICES   There is, in this model, a kind of economic entropy at work.[55] A given level of consumption expenditure tends to lose some of its employment-creation potential by the allocation of some of this money to monopoly-capital technological investments. The level of inefficiency, or dollar-loss (analogous to the loss of potential energy to randomized heat energy), varies with the extent of high-technology dominance of production. As with ecological systems, it is possible in theory to construct various mechanisms to minimize the loss of use-value associated with this "degrading" entropy. We can construct a social analogue to use more of the waste energy inherent in the accelerated treadmill. Schumacher (1973) focuses on such social reforms designed to absorb the profits of production and turn them to more socially useful employment and social utility generation. But just as there are many technical problems involved in creating more efficient heat pumps to use low-level waste energy, there are even more political and social problems inherent in our social analogue.[56]

This dynamic model is not antitechnological in and of itself. There are elements of technological innovation, including highly capital-intensive ones, that may be vital for satisfying many social needs. Some of these are necessary because of expansion of population. The obvious example of this is in the area of agricultural production, and some aspects of transportation of people and goods. However, the model above stresses that technological innovation is not determined by social needs, or even needs of individual consumers, but by producer needs for both profit expansion and profit absorption (Morris, 1974). Nor is the model irrevocably anticapitalistic, since part of the concern with profit structures relates to the socioeconomic organization by which surplus is generated, and through which it is allocated. Whether monopoly capitalist organization is capable of altering these structures remains to be seen.

CAPITAL INTENSIFICATION   What is interesting about the capital intensification of the model is that many of the basic facts underlying it are well-known. But the interpretations in conventional economic growth theory and corporate management are inverted. Representative of such interpretations is the following excerpt from a talk by Lewis W. Foy, Chairman of Bethlehem Steel Corp.:

> About a million-and-a-half people will be entering the private labor force every year between now and 1980, and we want to make sure there are jobs for them, and I mean good jobs. But the average investment to create just a single new job opportunity is rising all the time. It's about $25,000 now, and it'll be close to $35,000 by 1980. . . .
> But we won't get the economy back into gear unless and until the private sector can generate the capital funds needed for modernization and growth. (23 July 1975)

Foy refers to the "productive enterprise" as "the engines of growth and progress." The model of the treadmill not only incorporates the concept of the engine, but points to the context in which the engine is operating. The treadmill is viewed by Foy as continuing its historical acceleration, from a per-job investment of $25,000 in 1975 to $35,000 in 1980. Any long-term extrapolation of such growth of capital requirements per worker is potentially untenable. Enormous production levels would be needed to sustain such investment and generate a fair return on investment. Yet the basic justification of the capital-accumulation policies advocated in Foy's speech is ostensibly employment generation—not socially necessary production or even consumption. Most casual readers of the speech would assume that profit-maximization is the major goal of Bethlehem Steel. The treadmill model shows employment generation is indeed tied, directly or indirectly, to just such profit-and-production increases in the present concentrated industrial systems. Thus, the *de*scription presented in Foy's address may be accurate. However, the *pre*scription for more of the same entails serious ecological and social risks.[57]

In an era of supposedly unlimited resources and limited ecosystem disruption, the treadmill or "trickle-down" model of economic development could accelerate with little major risk. Increased problems of energy development and concomitant biospheric costs of energy extraction and its production usage alter the viability of such a model. Such economic organization may persist across the whole sphere of monopoly capitalism for a limited time, and within some production sectors (with lesser energy/material inputs and outputs) for a much longer time. But ecological restraints will preclude a simple extension of this model. These restraints may be held at bay for some period, by means of social immiseration of some parts of the labor force. But ultimately, a more efficient allocation of environmental resources for sustenance of the entire labor force will have to emerge, or repression increased.[58]

The variability of labor's and the state's roles in adjusting the speed and acceleration of the treadmill are treated next. Direct control over production expansion does not rest in their hands, since surplus mobilization is typically performed by capitalists. But there are a number of indirect ways, as the options segment of Table 1 indicates, in which both social segments could influence various components of the treadmill and its operations.

The Influence of Labor: By Bread Alone?

Table 1 applies especially to the so-called monopoly-capital sector of production, although it coexists with and influences the competitive sector as well. In like manner, we can distinguish between the role of monopoly capital's labor segment, and competitive capital's labor pool, in influencing production expansion. While there are serious analytic problems in distinguishing the two categories of labor—in part because many of the individual workers are interchangeable between segments—the distinction is a necessary one to simplify the discussion here. And it is congruent with much of the recent literature that refers to labor in the monopoly-capital sector as the labor aristocracy or to the existence of a dual labor market in the United States.[59] It is also a loose fit with the differentiation of "organized" and "unorganized" labor. In this context, I will lump social actions of the poor in with that of competitive capital labor. This classification is historically and theoretically meaningful because of the sizable flow of competitive capital workers into and out of poverty.[60]

Organized or monopoly-capital labor in the United States has been supportive of the expansion of production throughout the last fifty years. While this glosses over important labor conflicts, the dominant emphasis of researchers today is that organized labor has been relatively quiescent, particularly in the post-1945 period. After the vicious social, political, and economic conflicts in the earlier period of unionization, the major emphasis for most of the period was on improved wages, what some term "economism." Few labor disputes centered on either labor's desire for control of surplus mobilization, or, until recently, improvement in working conditions. Western European experience in the postwar period is considerably different, with more sustained efforts at labor control over some aspects of surplus mobilization, whether in codetermination of productive organization or in national economic planning. Whether as cause or as effect, the labor movements in western Europe have exhibited far more sustained political activity and consciousness-raising, leading to a more social democratic form of productive control in many periods and societies.

In contrast, U.S. labor has fought primarily over the *share* of surplus going to labor, and the *size* of such a surplus (in terms of wages and fringe benefits). Closely following on this concern has been a sustained pressure for reduced working hours, primarily for improving the life of workers, and secondarily providing for some increased employment opportunities in the large corporation, under some circumstances.

Generally, though, employment has not increased very dramatically in the monopoly-capital sector, though there are pockets of high employment growth in more technologically innovative areas such as electronics.[61] Moreover, labor's share of national income has not risen much in the period of organized labor.[62] What has risen has been the size of this surplus, and the increased consumption power per worker. Thus, labor has successfully pushed its very limited agenda of economism. It has done so by supporting production expansion and economic growth coalitions of business and the state.

Indeed, there is growing evidence that labor's influence has been substantially greater in state organization than in the monopoly-capital sector. Unionization of public employees has proceeded rapidly—particularly among teachers. Conversely, unionization rates have declined in many labor categories and industrial organizations, though the causes of such declines and stagnation are not at all clear. They vary from the notion that labor in the technostructural sector benefits from the "free rider" of past negotiations from organized labor, to the notion that workers are alienated from uncaring and ineffectual unions. Workers in state organizations, though, have benefited from an activist union movement, with strong organizing efforts in the last two decades especially, and leadership concern for work conditions and total compensation. In the 1960s especially, the government was pushed by a variety of factors to become a model employer, setting wages at levels corresponding to the equivalents in organized private sector employment—i.e., in the labor aristocracy within the monopoly capital sector.[63] From the combination of such forces, it now seems clear that labor has been a most enthusiastic supporter in expansion of monopoly capital production, and in the mobilization of surplus to further expand such production:

> The wealth of a society is ultimately derived from industrial production, and it is the surplus wealth that is not reinvested in industry, together with wages and taxes, which support the existence of the service sector. The greater the productivity of workers in the industrial sector, the greater will be the available surplus wealth over and above production required to reproduce these workers. (C. Anderson, 1976:63)

While Anderson refers to the entire service sector, O'Connor makes the linkage between monopoly capital and state organized labor more specifically:

> Monopoly sector money wages are pegged to productivity and cost of living. . . . There is a general tendency for state sector wages to be driven up to the level prevailing in the monopoly sector . . . [because] workers employed by state contractors . . . and state agencies . . . receive union pay scales . . . [and] many state and local government employee associations exert considerable political clout and the bargaining power of many state worker unions is growing . . . to enforce wage and salary scales commensurate with those in the monopoly sector. (O'Connor, 1973:30–31)

Such power of state labor unions can be overstated, as state response to the fiscal crisis of recent years has indicated (Johnston, 1978). Employment security has decreased, and even wage settlements rolled back, under concerted pressures from capital and squeezed worker-taxpayers. New York City's situation is merely the most dramatic of such urban phenomena in the U.S., and California's recent Proposition 13 control over state taxes is the next level up in the organization of government. Strong pressures to reduce taxes and government services now exist at all levels in the U.S. and elsewhere, in part because of this past influence of public unions. What impact this will have on production expansion is unclear, since the expansion of worker buying-power by reduced taxes will be partly offset by reduced demand from retrenched state workers. Politically, there is already increased political demand for production stimulation, with labor at the forefront. But whether sufficient capital can be squeezed from labor and the state remains to be seen, particularly in the face of indebtedness of consumers, government, and the corporate sector (Sweezy, 1978).

This recent fiscal crisis, though, also results from an unusual period of organized labor activism in the 1960s. Pushed by a variety of social movements arising among competitive sector workers and the unemployed and poor, organized labor led a successful drive to expand government services and payments to minorities and the poor. Civil unrest, the civil rights movement, and the later concern over the cost and legitimacy of the Vietnam war all led to an unusual coalition of social forces to expand the state's distributional role.[64] Monopoly capital representatives did not resist this too strenuously, because of their own expanded profits during much of the period, and because of their fears of the political and economic costs of social disorders. That is, they could afford to share the surplus, because it was so large that the problem for managers was how to find outlets for surplus capital (Baran & Sweezy, 1966). In less than a decade, though, the sociocultural production system has shifted from liquid capital surplus to a serious crisis of liquidity shortages. And the public unions have become convenient scapegoats for the growth of the state sector in the earlier period, because of their enhanced visibility and wage structure (O'Connor, 1973).

What happened in this period was that a larger part of the surplus was absorbed by the state to support its political legitimacy with the poor, minorities, and competitive sector workers. This entailed no lessening of the forces of growth, or weakening of the growth coalition of capital, labor, and the state. But it permitted greater attention to distributional issues, with only minor adjustments to the organization of production. Affirmative action employment did not change the structure or scale of production, it merely altered who filled lower-level production roles.[65] The one potential exception to this was increased government services associated with environmental protection. Pollution abatement altered, to a relatively small but absolutely large extent, the allocation of surplus capital in the productive system. In this, there was little cooperation by capitalists and managers, and extensive conflicts ensued and still continue. This conflict was intensified with the increased government role in monitoring and controlling petroleum and other energy supplies and prices following 1973–74. Such intensification arose from the simultaneous demands on surplus of increased oil and other energy prices, increased debt-servicing costs for industry, increased foreign competition for domestic and overseas markets, and no reduction in taxes.[66]

Thus, the recent fiscal crisis of the state is in fact a symptom of and arena for an underlying conflict over production expansion form and scale, a scramble for altering allocation of shares of the present surplus for public goods and services versus private sector expansion. In general, organized labor has reversed itself, and sided once more with monopoly-capital owners/managers in calling for increased production to generate jobs and wages. Some potential for altering the treadmill by increased public employment in labor-intensive activities existed in earlier versions of the Humphrey-Hawkins "full employment" bill. But organized labor has neither fought hard enough nor won very many victories in either obtaining more of the economic surplus to consume, or in having greater influence over how to use the surplus. On the other hand, public and some private sector unions have avoided some socially regressive withdrawals of public services sought by organized capital interests and "taxpayers' movements."

In fact, the New York City example indicates that public unions, by investing their pension funds in city bonds, can and do occasionally influence *some* surplus allocation decisions and can indirectly alter the shares going to public and private sectors. For if union funds are withdrawn from alternative private sector investments, the shift weakens private capital accumulation and strengthens public provisions simultaneously. Whether this is a serious impediment to future private surplus accumulation and mobilization, though, depends on how the state uses this revenue. It is entirely possible that state provision of goods and services derived from this labor source can disproportionately aid capital and not labor. In this, they may not slow the treadmill, but accelerate it after some lag.[67]

With this brief exception, then, organized labor has had relatively little influence on surplus mobilization, and only slightly greater influence on surplus allocation to various social segments. If this affluent and politically potent sector demonstrates such weakness, it is small wonder that low-paid and insecure competitive sector workers have little influence in production expansion.[68] Though they derive some benefits from monopoly sector expansion, these are highly variable across companies and industries. And union wage structures may have little influence in altering labor's shares in the competitive sector production surplus—though these too have risen. Perhaps the most politically potent force within the competitive labor segment of society in recent periods in the U.S. has been the bottom of the working class, which incorporates the unemployed and underemployed, the near-poor, the poor, and minorities. The visibility and scale of the 1960s surplus in the U.S. helped sustain both organizers and the previously unorganized members of the lower working class in this period. Public civil unrest proved a sufficient embarassment or threat that both organized labor and monopoly capital were coerced to improve the conditions of this group.[69]

However, as noted above, the movement did not seek to substantially alter the forms of surplus mobilization in the private sector. Aside from some ill-fated job training programs, little direct control over production decision-making was sought or achieved. Rather, the National Welfare Rights Organization and civil rights groups sought two types of state intervention: (1) improving the employment competition chances for the poor and minority workers, and (2) redistributing some of the increased surplus to these workers and families, through state transfer payments and services.[70] Struggles were over control of the fruits and not the means of production, in general. And, because of this political decision, pressures for production expansion increased because of these movements. For example, labor and poor people's movements often attacked environmentalist proposals as being too costly. Nor did they generally seek to support the emergent movement for an alternative technology—an alternative form of surplus mobilization. Some small coalitions have emerged in recent years, as in neighborhood production of garden produce and in solar heating.[71]

Overall, then, both organized and unorganized labor have been bound into the growth coalition. Though a number of theoretical congruencies between environmental reforms and labor's needs exist, there has been only limited integration of labor, the poor, and environmental reform movements in the U.S. In western Europe and Australia, some unprecedented coalitions—albeit fragile ones—have taken an alternative path and considered slowing the treadmill by increasing labor intensity and decreasing capital intensity of production. Until recently, though, there was neither the intellectual nor the political basis for such an alliance in the U.S. Tentative local and national discussions and organizational linkages now exist, but they are ephemeral compared to the overall forces favoring expanded production as usual. Nowhere is this clearer than in energy conflicts: Proposition 15 (the antinuclear proposal) was defeated in California in 1976 in part because of the opposition of the AFL-CIO federation. Bottle bills have been similarly defeated by such capital-labor coalitions, despite the fact that net employment might rise. In part, as Hannon (1975) has noted, the organized labor opposition is rational in its self-interest. New jobs will require less skill and will be in competitive industries. Retail store employment is not as attractive as container-manufacturing, at least on economistic and job security grounds.

Conversely, though, there has been somewhat greater enthusiasm for state and private support for solar energy. The peculiar alliance exists because of diverse self-interests. For the poor and lower working-class, solar energy promises some reduced energy budgets and perhaps employment in installation of solar heaters. For organized labor, increased solar use would likely involve greater production jobs in solar eqipment manufacturing and distribution. It would also free other energy sources to cover more of the needs for future expansion of production. Thus, not all solar supporters are wedded to Amory Lovins's (1977) "soft energy path" and the social and environmental transformation it entails (Morrison, 1978).

Nonetheless, potential contradictions exist within labor movements. Environmental degradation frequently affects them more directly than it does managers and capital owners. Unfortunately, this is truer for the less-organized segment of labor, which has fallen into a period of consolidation after the street scenes of a decade ago. Suburbanized monopoly-capital labor can avoid some of the immediate ravages of air and water pollution, and does not suffer as much from increased energy costs. Yet their recreational activity, at least, is dependent on improved environmental protection, and increasingly there are hints that both health and economic security are in jeopardy because of conventional models of production expansion.[72] This leads to conflicting demands on the state, as I will note in the next sections.

The Role of the State: Giving and Taking

It is remarkable how disparately various theorists view the state, in its relation to production expansion. As with Lindblom's (1977) polar theorists, Adam Smith and Karl Marx, contemporary observers seem to be polarized along the same dimensions: markets versus politics.

One initial way of characterizing these differences is to distinguish the "taking" from the "giving" state. The former emphasizes the withdrawal of capital from the market by the state: "Because the Treasury's claim on the nation's stock of capital is so strong, it is supposed to borrow heavily only to revive a flagging economy—stepping aside when others want money" (*Business Week*, 1978:82). While there are other nuances, the primacy of the market and the concept of the state as a drag on the market are the dominant worldviews of this business medium. Essentially, this model argues that the state preempts the organization of surplus by private capital, that it takes away degrees of freedom.

In sharp contrast is the model of neo-Marxists, who see the state as bound in many ways by the dictates of monopoly capital. Such a view emphasizes the giving of capital, in one form or another, to monopoly capital. Rather than being a drag, this is primarily a spur to capital accumulation, and a greater mobilization of surplus by the monopoly capital sector:

> Like a leaking tire, the economy must be unflaggingly pumped if it is not to go flat and come to a full stop. . . . The three most important pumping mechanisms [are] . . . (1) the credit system, (2) government finances, and (3) the central bank (Federal Reserve System). . . . In principle, government finances can operate either to inflate or deflate the economy. In practice, they almost always operate as an inflator. (Sweezy & Magdoff, 1974:2–3)

> The blockages to capital formation, which are inherent in monopoly capitalism, were removed . . . by an enormous increase in government . . . debt . . . which opened up all valves for surplus value creation. (Morris, 1974:7)

In this world-view, the state is seen as not only pumping up the economy, but as focusing its efforts in ways that primarily—or at least disproportionately—facilitate greater surplus accumulation by monopoly capital (Shabecoff, 1978).

Neither perspective captures the reality of state involvement. For, just as the state has the dual roles of supporting economic growth and maintaining political legitimacy, it has both a giving and taking role, not exclusively tied to either mission (Kolko, 1976: Ch. 9). This becomes apparent when we consider four real-world factors: (1) the state has various *sources of revenue;* (2) the state has various *patterns of expenditure;* (3) the state has control over the operations of the *credit system;* and (4) the state has *legislative sanctions.*

THE FISCAL ROLE   The first two factors relate to the *fiscal* role of the state, and most directly touch on giving and taking. In modern industrial societies, the state is given enormous powers to reallocate surplus. Corporate taxation and capital gains taxes represent a direct taking of surplus capital. Likewise, consumer-worker income taxes remove consumption potential, and thereby indirectly some surplus capital potential from foregone consumption of goods and services. On the other hand, the state keeps little for itself, particularly in the United States where nationalized industries other than railroads are virtually nonexistent (Gintis, 1972). So the state is also involved in giving. First, the state employs workers to provide services to capital and labor. In one sense, this is a keeping of revenues. But the wages thereby generated flow out of the state and into markets. Second, the state contracts with private industry to build capital projects, such as dams and highways, again releasing funds from the state into markets. Moreover, such physical capital enables private sector investments to be made, since profits are possible when large-scale infrastructure has been provided. Third, the state redistributes its revenues as transfer payments, generally to various categories of labor: Social Security, unemployment insurance, medicare, general welfare payments, recreational subsidies, and the like. These transfer payments in turn are used to purchase market goods and services, representing another return of capital to the market.

Most of the apparent exceptions to this recycling of capital from the market to the state and back to the market prove the rule. Military equipment, for example, is part of the physical capital of the state. But it is primarily purchased on the market. Though it is not directly productive, it does serve to protect private capital domestically and abroad, as well as to soak up surplus low-skill labor (Kolko, 1976: Ch. 9). Likewise, the many structures occupied by government were built by the private sector, especially in the U.S. (with the exception of the Depression period, when Works Progress Administration did some of this). Although they, like the military plant, are not directly productive, this is true of much of the private sector expenditure as well.

From the above perspective, it would appear that the defenders of business are wrong in their notion of the taking state, and the neo-Marxists correct in their view of the giving state. However, this is only a half-truth. For insofar as the state recycles capital back into the market, it tends to retain the existing division of surplus in the market. In terms of the fiscal activities of the state, though, there are also a variety of possibilities for funneling or redistribution—both upward and downward. A given volume of state revenue may be used to purchase either a given set of military equipment, say, or to provide a number of service jobs in the public sector for a given period. In general, the former expenditure will accelerate the treadmill more, because it reinforces the capital-intensive form of production. Revenues withdrawn from the market have been used for higher-than-average capital intensity of goods (which are also typically more energy-intensive). On the other hand, labor-intensive public service usages involve lower-than-average capital intensity, and tend to slow the treadmill.[73] This assumes workers of the state have typical consumption patterns—a reasonable assumption.

THE CREDIT ROLE   A state with fairly heavy indebtedness can have either accelerative or decelerative effects on the treadmill. For the patterns of taxation (withdrawal of surplus) and expenditures (recycling of surplus) influence the shares of capital and labor in this surplus. State indebtedness typically leads to inflation, and inflation to higher profit margins of large enterprises.[74] But a pattern of careful taxation of corporate gains and public service expenditures could still provide a reasonable share to labor, without as much acceleration of the treadmill as alternative state fiscal patterns.[75] Table 1, of course, indicates a number of these options for various components of the treadmill. On the other hand, when this state indebtedness is accompanied by state banking controls that permit higher levels of consumer and corporate indebtedness, the treadmill invariably accelerates.

As indicated earlier, this is a use of *future* surplus to generate present production. From the neo-classical and Keynesian economists' views, such indebtedness is short-lived, ideally, to be amortized gradually as production and wages expand. In theory, this means that the surplus available in some future period will be less, and production expansion decreased in that future. To some extent, this is the situation in recent years, where corporations have used production expansion and the resulting profit increase to pay off short-term debt (Sweezy & Magdoff, 1977a). As a result, they are in a less indebted position than they were some years ago, but their profits have not gone to spur production investments (*Business Week*, 1978). Employment lags, therefore, and more pressure remains on the state to "revive a flagging economy"—or more accurately, an excessively productive economy.

THE LEGISLATIVE ROLE   One of the best mechanisms for decelerating the treadmill would appear to be the prohibitionary powers of the state. Regulation of negative externalities—from unemployment to resource depletion—is theoretically in its power. And it appears that the exercise of such powers has vastly increased in the twentieth century industrial state. More accurately, the expenses of regulation have increased (O'Connor, 1973). Among political historians, there is a growing acknowledgement that much of the regulation of the treadmill has in fact been regulation by the treadmill. That is, policies ostensibly to correct the abuses of monopoly capital have been turned toward the suppression of competition and the enhancement of monopoly capital.

The general process is: (1) capture of regulatory agencies by the monopoly-capital sectors they purport to regulate, and/or (2) elimination of competitive capital by the high costs of conforming to regulation. This is especially true of the reforms of the early twentieth century in the U.S. Under such situations, monopoly-capital interests can at the same time rebuke state agencies publicly and yet still derive private gains, all the while decrying fiscal irresponsibility of the state.[76]

Environmental costs of the treadmill and its acceleration have also been treated by state regulation, in the last decade especially. As with military expenditures, these "nonproductive" programs, primarily pollution abatement, have recycled capital. Only this time, when corporations are spending their own revenues, it is a mixture of corporations recycling to other corporations (e.g., pollution abatement equipment manufacturers), and the state recycling its lost revenues to these as well. As I will note in Chapter VII, there are especially acute conflicts in many of these programs. Specific corporations are actually losing control of some of their capital. Yet environmental melioration has been the political focus of a strong public interest movement in this period. Control over conventional natural resources, such as fossil fuels, is another potent state control.[77] But, although it has led to some new forms of land and energy control outside the direct control of monopoly capital, there is no dramatic move to remove the material base from the monopoly capital treadmill. Indeed, Hays (1969) and Kolko (1963) have argued that earlier twentieth century conservation legislation served to increase the efficiency of big business in utilizing public lands and resources, and drove out smaller competitive users. How much new environmental regulations are doing the same thing is unclear, but there is some evidence for it.[78] Costly record-keeping requirements for businesses mean advantages for large corporations in two ways. First, they can amortize the costs more readily over a larger revenue base. Second, they can often obscure their records in ways that are difficult for enforcement agencies to unravel.

With sufficient political pressures, the state can enhance its regulation of monopoly capital in specific negative externalities, such as pollution. Success in the one domain, however, often leads to little slowing of the treadmill and to future acceleration. Thus, corporations have been privately and publicly lobbying for tax relief and selected deregulation in the U.S. because of the ostensible (and real) burdens of environmental protection and other state controls.[79] They point to increased corporate costs, increased state taxes and expenditures, and argue that there is insufficient capital left for economic growth via new investment. The state is then faced with the incompatibility of (1) the reality of the treadmill, (2) the joint capital and labor demands for slower inflation, and (3) labor's demands for more employment opportunity. So the pump is primed in ways that accelerate the treadmill again. In some periods, this can be avoided by increased public service jobs. But in the U.S., the demeaning of public service as make-work has led to strong pressures against this socially effective route of supplying needed services and resolving unemployment. Government services are, by this process, relegated to less prestigious and vital enterprises, while private goods dominate. This creates a self-fulfilling prophecy, since government is defined as unable to produce efficiently, while profit-making monopoly capital is treated as the quintessence of efficiency (e.g., NYT, 1977b). That the two should be subject to different definitions of efficiency is rarely made clear. Nor is the heavy influence of the technostructure in *producing* government inefficiency made apparent to most observers. When corporations overcharge agencies for goods and services, it is the agencies that are made the scapegoats, thus reinforcing the negative expectations about many state services.

While the state can thus deal with pieces of the social and environmental problems generated by the treadmill, it has rarely been able to reverse it. Depressions and recessions are the major exceptions to this.

THEORY AND PRACTICE OF THE STATE   The theoretical freedom of the state is great because of the relatively large volumes of surplus it collects. Such liquid surplus or capital could be allocated directly to public services, as the most direct way of stimulating employment. Or it could be allocated to public goods, which involves some leakage away from labor and to capital interests. Or it can be used to stimulate labor-intensive competitive capital business, as the Small Business Administration was created to do. Or, it may be given as subsidies to monopoly capital to expand employment opportunity. These follow roughly from most to least efficient in generating employment in some socially productive way. The range is from community health centers to tax write-offs of oil exploration costs.

Such freedom is restricted in a number of ways. First, as the magnitude of negative externalities of production and the treadmill increases, the demands on the state increase. Thus, high unemployment, uncompensated occupational diseases, blighted cities, decaying transportation systems, and ecosystem threats all compete for these revenues. Second, the demands are weighted by the political power of the interests involved. The economic centrality of businessmen—and particularly monopoly capitalists—makes them potent claimants on the public trough, and potent influences on the list of public expenditures. Labor and poor people's movements have their influences as well, especially during periods of social strife, as in the 1960s in the U.S. But these movements often settle for broad-brush expansionary efforts at stimulating business expansion, regardless of the social efficiency of such a state path. Rare is the voice that calls for government productive organizations to be set up in the U.S. Public services do have their own strong interest groups—of deliverers and of clients. Public employee unions find little problem in being liberal and advocating expanded social service programs, for it is in their interest to do so. Private-sector unions may not show such general enthusiasm, though.

The combination of a large public service union, the environmental challenge to business as usual, and the cumulation of unresolved unemployment and poverty problems represents some potential for change (Johnston, 1978). Models from alternative technology proponents, and linkages between the disaffected elements of society, are vital for any such change to occur. But they do not ensure such change will either occur or endure. That will be the focus of the final section of this chapter.

REVERSING THE TREADMILL: PREREQUISITES FOR CHANGE

Consciousness, Coordination, and Conflict

Though it is true everywhere in the modern industrial world that the treadmill has accelerated somewhat, there are substantial differences in its velocity within this spectrum. These are loosely correlated with indices like energy consumption per capita, since both the volume and source of a treadmill production is high-energy monopoly-capital industry (Mazur & Rosa, 1974). Such differences are associated with varying political and social strengths of capital, labor, and state parties. In addition, they reflect differences in national positions in the modern world-system, on trade and geopolitical dimensions.

For the United States, state intervention to restructure the treadmill is in no sense imminent. Yet, because of its geopolitical position, the theoretical possibilities of an extensive restructuring are greater:

> The experience of other countries in which state capitalism is more developed than in the United States would perhaps lead to the conclusion that something can be achieved in the way of propping up investment and employment, but not very much as long as they are dependent, as most of them are, on international developments beyond their control. But it would be very wrong to transfer this conclusion directly to the United States, if only because [it] . . . is by far the largest member of the world capitalist system and hence

plays a disproportionately large part in determining the international developments which bear so heavily on others. It may be argued that *if state capitalism in the United States could decisively improve the performance of this largest unit in the system, it would at the same time enable the others to reap the full potential benefits of state capitalism for themselves.* (Sweezy & Magdoff, 1975b:10; my italics)

Having once raised this near-utopian vision, though, these two observers immediately dash our hopes of ever eliminating the irrationalities of the treadmill:

These incredibly wasteful and absurd irrationalities . . . each and every one of them is the fortress or hiding place of vested interests which wield enormous political power and have absolutely no intention of making the least sacrifice for the common good, even if that somewhat elusive concept is defined wholly in capitalist terms. (Sweezy & Magdoff, 1975b:11)

The paradox is made complete by observing that these vested interests are the U.S. multinationals, with the global reach (Barnet & Müller, 1974) that makes the U.S. the core society in the modern world-system (Wallerstein, 1974). International freedom achieved at the cost of domestic entrapment?

Such domestic entrapment is a function not only of the treadmill, but of the structures and processes associated with it. First, the longer the treadmill operates, the more of the economy that is brought under the influence of concentrated or monopoly-capital production. The volumes of production, profits, physical plant investment, and perhaps of employment associated with monopoly capital rise as the treadmill operates or accelerates. Conversely, the forces opposing it shrink in relative economic influence. Second, while the treadmill speeds up or even operates at a level speed, the fewer are the options to the treadmill which are perceived by significant groups within society.

Conversely, though, the treadmill's operations create conditions for its vulnerability as well:

Gradually the underlying contradiction between the tendencies to unlimited expansion of production and restricted consumption exerts itself . . . the capital-goods sectors are discovered to have grown to a size that cannot be sustained and their collapse follows, with dire consequences for the functioning of the entire system. (Sweezy, 1978:11)

This contradiction or dilemma for treadmill proponents is stated most forcefully elsewhere by Sweezy:

> Capitalism's utopia in a sense is a situation in which workers live on air, allowing their entire product to take the form of surplus value; and in which capitalists accumulate all their surplus value. (Sweezy, 1974a:54)

If the treadmill is to be slowed and reversed, the central social agency that will have to bring this about is the state, acting to rechannel production surplus in non-treadmill directions. But the state can only do so when there is both a sufficient crisis of faith in the treadmill, and sufficient political support for production apart from the treadmill. To date, this combination does not exist in advanced industrial societies like the United States.

There does exist some consciousness of the failures of the treadmill to achieve sustained social welfare. And the environmental and energy problems, culminating in the loose appropriate technology movement, have reinforced both the sense of vulnerability to environmental threats and the logic of an alternative production system. The problem is that labor and environmental movements have neither sufficiently coordinated their efforts, nor shared their consciousness of the limits of the treadmill. Not until social equity movements merge forces with appropriate technology groups is there any hope for sufficient political mobilization to alter state behavior. The political struggle for change will only begin in earnest at that point. Until then, it will remain at the level of intellectual debate, and not enter into genuine organized political conflict.

Such intellectual debate is itself at an early state, for the dominance of the economic growth coalition is pervasive throughout advanced industrial societies. The logic of the treadmill is treated as virtually a natural law of economic development via production expansion (speeding up the treadmill). This is clearest in the writings of Edward Denison (1974, 1977), whose empirical description of the path of economic growth in the western world simultaneously serves as a blueprint for the future. The disparity between this model of growth and the "soft path" of E. F. Schumacher (1973), Amory Lovins (1977), and other appropriate technology advocates is indicated by two features of his work. Among the mechanisms that improve the efficiency—i.e., increase the rate of growth—of national economies, Denison (1974:117) lists (1) the removal of people from self-employment, and (2) the removal of workers from agriculture. For most appropriate technologists, these are two touchstones of production reorganization: increased self-reliance in production and increased use of labor in agriculture. At the most fundamental level, then, there is an intrinsic conflict between the conventional treadmill view of economic growth and the views of appropriate technologists.

The growth/no-growth debate is not simply about growth, then, but about the social and environmental relationships of production. Until a social movement can dissociate the natural desires of the bulk of labor for a comfortable life from the treadmill model for providing such a life, little change in the treadmill will occur. High on the agenda are the following items: (1) educating labor to the discomforts—the environmental hazards—of the treadmill; (2) educating labor to the socially inefficient role of the state in its allocation of surplus to the treadmill; and (3) educating labor as to the alternatives to the present state-supported treadmill system. Each of these problems in consciousness formation and sociopolitical mobilization will be treated in turn in the next three chapters. Completing these agenda items will not be easy, straightforward, or rapid. But they will have to be accomplished, if the treadmill is to be slowed and reversed.

NOTES

1. Works that come close to this position include Baran & Sweezy (1966), Galbraith (1971), and C. Anderson (1976).

2. Lindblom (1977) stands as perhaps the best single example of such a position, though Heilbroner (1976, 1978) parallels some of this reasoning.

3. In terms of major "economizing" roles, this view of the modern corporation is contained in Daniel Bell's (1973) work, although he recognizes the tensions between this economizing role and the "socializing" role of the state.

4. For a critical discussion of mobilization of labor time in capitalist societies, see Gordon (1976). Succinct treatments of mobilization of capital are included in Morris (1974) and Braverman (1975), which indicate the variability in the factors driving such mobilization, as well as in the allocation of the surplus generated by such mobilization.

5. See Brooks & Andrews (1974) for an extreme version of this surplus stock model, relying on extraction of minerals from the earth's crust.

6. Such decision making exists at a global as well as a domestic level in the modern world-system of capitalist relationships. Global decisions are discussed in Frieden (1977), who treats the Trilateral Commission as a centralized conflict resolution body (cf. critique of Sweezy & Magdoff, 1977c, of the conflicts in surplus mobilization policies that Frieden discusses). The problematic nature of

decisions, especially on the part of major capital owners, is emphasized in Sweezy (1975) and Sweezy & Magdoff (1975b).

7. This perspective reflects an uneasy position among critics of the growth-oriented capitalist industrial society regarding the nature of capital. While some favor a *reallocation* of existing capital for social welfare purposes (e.g., Schumacher, 1973), others suggest a *disaccumulation and reduction* of total capital to reduce total production and production potential (e.g., C. Anderson, 1976; Stretton, 1976). Most solve the dilemma of dealing with capital by ignoring the issue (e.g., H. Brooks, 1973).

8. Though much has been made of the supposed separation of ownership and management of capital (e.g., Galbraith, 1971), there is little evidence for any major loss of control over capital by its owners, or for any departure from profitability as a managerial criterion of behavior (Kolko, 1976:334–36; Tanzer, 1971:15–24; Zeitlin, 1974).

9. For a neo-Marxist position on the necessity for the expansion of capital through any available means, see Sweezy (1974a, 1978). Among non-Marxist economists, essentially the same dynamic is relabeled as a need for *national* economic growth (e.g., Denison, 1977).

10. For an overview of the constraints on state action in freely allocating surplus, see O'Connor (1973), Morris (1974), and Sweezy & Magdoff (1975b). A less one-sided view of state and labor actions is in Gurley (1977), Boddy & Crotty (1974, 1976), and Bell (1973: Ch. 4; 1976: Ch. 6). These last pieces treat the state as in somewhat greater control over corporations, on the one hand, and as supporting somewhat greater power of labor, on the other, through the improved social welfare system for workers. Unfortunately, there are strong opposing views to such a freer role of the state and labor (e.g., Sherman, 1976; Kolko, 1976: Ch. 5, 9).

11. Two collections (Olson & Landsberg, 1973: Daly, 1973) of position papers illustrate both the commitments to growth and the potential for reorganizing constituencies away from conventional growth models. While it is true that the nation-level debate about growth versus no-growth is ultimately a sterile one, the danger of retreating to a less abstract discussion of specific growth constituencies is that many of the social-system dynamics at the national and international level are lost in the more concrete discussions of more localized groupings. In particular, national and international capital competition and accumulation is often ignored (e.g., Sweezy, 1973), thereby ignoring some of the factors that inhibit corporate cooperation with state actions designed to meliorate the negative externalities of production expansion (McKean, 1973; Boulding, 1973; Olson, 1973).

12. One of the richest treatments of the growth coalition is that of Molotch (1976a,b), who fleshes out the analytic structure of Harvey (1973). Both refer to the city level of social organization, though, and this often obscures other national and international dimensions of growth support (e.g., see the critiques of Logan, 1976, and Alonso, 1973, of a community-based analytic stance). On the other hand, the city has historically been the locus for major forms of production expansion and capital accumulation, even where production occurs in more remote ecosystems, so that an analysis of cities' coalitions, perhaps coupled with the national and international organizational perspective (e.g., Kolko, 1963, 1976) is most useful.

13. Anderson (1976:61–65) has an excellent discussion of the enduring relation-

ships of these social sectors in the so-called postindustrial society. His critique of the latter concept parallels my earlier treatment of this in chapter IV.

14. Among the most frequently cited false predictions are the declining rates of profit and increased impoverishment of the working class (e.g., Bell, 1973:40–42). In contrast, Sweezy & Magdoff (1975a,b) indicate that this is an oversimplification of Marx's theories, and that the basic social relationships he posited have endured. Although profits have not fallen nor impoverishment increased in industrial societies, the tendencies of overproduction Marx posited remain, rooted today in persistent economic policy dilemmas in the post-Keynesian period (e.g., Sweezy & Magdoff, 1974).

15. This "new class" has been noted in many treatments in the last decades (e.g., Galbraith, 1958, 1971; Bell, 1962: Ch. 10; 1973, Ch. 3; 1976, Ch. 1). A parallel argument about the "new class" within the state sector—what Bell (1973) would term the "sociologizing" rather than the "economizing" class—has been posited by Kristol (1977). This, he claims, has led to the controls over the corporation that Bell (1973: Ch. 4) refers to. A strong repudiation of the views is presented by Kolko (1976: Ch. 9), who sees both the persistence of ownership dominating industry, and ownership dominating many state decisions. A parallel critique is that of Sweezy (1973). To some extent, Giddens (1973) takes an intermediate position, documenting new bases of differentiation of labor in advanced industrial societies, but not arguing as forcefully as Galbraith or Bell how far this leads to distinctive new groupings and behavior.

16. This analysis is consistent with the descriptions in O'Connor (1973), and Sweezy & Magdoff (1975a,b), among others.

17. See Kolko (1976: Ch. 9), Morris (1974), Sweezy & Magdoff (1977a) and Sweezy (1975) for discussions of these problems and the state and corporate response through indebtedness.

18. Sweezy (1974b) notes that his late colleague Paul Baran was one of the earliest observers who indicated the threats of inflation to the credit structure and the orderly mobilization of present surplus for future surplus generation. A much more belated business response is indicated in *Business Week* (1974, 1978) special editions dealing with indebtedness. Despite the fact that indebtedness has especially favored profits, the standard business response has been to attack government profligacy. This view has been repeated so often as to have swayed public opinion along these lines (American Institute of Public Opinion, 1978). About half of all Americans surveyed believe government is both responsible for inflation and is the biggest threat to the future of the country. A more accurate diagnosis appears in Heilbroner (1978).

19. The political repercussions of stagnation are expressed as clearly by representatives of business (e.g., *Business Week*, 1975) and of neoclassical economics (e.g., Olson et al., 1973; McKean, 1973; Roberts, 1973; Barkley & Seckler, 1972), as by neo-Marxists (Morris, 1974; Sweezy & Magdoff, 1977a; Sweezy, 1978).

20. On this growth period, see Kolko (1976: Ch. 5, 9) and Sweezy & Magdoff (1975a,b).

21. Commoner (1977) and Heilbroner (1975, 1976, 1978) both see increased energy dependency and decreased capitalist efficiency as part of a singular process of unsustainable development in the twentieth century.

22. On the left, the challenges arising from stagflation have been well articulated in the following: Morris (1974), Sweezy & Magdoff (1974, 1975a, b), O'Connor (1973), and Johnson (1973). Reactions to such views include frontal attacks on the antigrowth advocates (e.g., Klein, 1972; Olson, 1973; Zeckhauser, 1973), on the one hand, and mild reformist suggestions for altered state policies on the other (e.g., Roberts, 1973; Barkley & Seckler, 1972) to deal directly with negative externalities of production. Despite the extensive critiques of the social productivity of capital expansion (e.g., Mazur & Rosa, 1974; Mishan, 1967, 1973), the standard economist's response has been to prescribe more state aid for investment and development (e.g., Bernstein, 1977; Sullivan, 1978; *New York Times*, 1977a). Even Denison, whose empirical work (e.g., 1974) has called into question the *economic* efficiency of increased capital-investment without technological change, indicates the standard refrain:

> In the short run we might want special aids to investment in order to support economic recovery. Even in the long run it is possible that we might want more investment than a well functioning economy . . . would provide. But the purpose would be to raise future living standards, including protection of the environment, and perhaps to enhance energy independence. (1977:75)

23. For the energy issues, see Wilford (1977), Energy Policy Project (1974), and especially Lovins (1977). On a broader economic-environmental critique, see Heilbroner (1975, 1976, 1978), and Kolko (1976) for a nonenvironmental critique.

24. An articulate early view of this is in O'Connor (1973).

25. For a discussion of this role of labor, see Kolko (1976: Ch. 5) and Wiley (1967).

26. See Tanzer (1971), Morris (1974), and Kolko (1976: Ch. 9) on this view.

27. This is the essence of the ideological underpinning of "political capitalism" eloquently treated in Kolko (1963, 1976): the increased identification of the state with the fate of large-scale industry.

28. In general, this period exemplifies not only Kolko's (1963) political capitalism, but a more fundamental view of the state as a primary sociopolitical mechanism for protecting and expanding capital interests (e.g., Gintis, 1972). Critics of the modern state, whether "constitutionalists" or "insurrectionists" (Miliband, 1977:155), tend to see the state as separating political debates from fundamental questions about economic structure. Thus, social and political reforms (e.g., Kolko, 1976: Ch. 5) benefiting labor are done within the context of conventional production organization and expansion. In Okun's (1975) terms, equality issues can be treated politically, but only within the overall context of striving for maximal economic efficiency (growth). That *social* policy is set within the context of *economic* policy advice from the Council of Economic Advisors in the U.S. is a testimonial to the dominance of efficiency concerns, and to the fact that "economists are the gurus of growth" (Zeckhauser, 1973:115).

29. One of the major lines of criticism prior to the present period has been of the military-industrial complex, or the warfare state (e.g., Melman, 1971). The central theme of such analyses is that the state has propped up the capitalist sectors by direct military consumption of unprecedented magnitudes (e.g., Kolko, 1976: Ch. 6, 9)

following World War II. This stimulated domestic production, and in the application of U.S. military power abroad, helped protect growing U.S. investments in Europe and the underdeveloped nations (e.g., Magdoff, 1969). The latter investments, in turn, raised the profitability of U.S. multinational corporations and enhanced their control over U.S. foreign and domestic policies (Barnet & Müller, 1974). One of the first departures from this warfare state critique was Mishan's (1967) critique of social welfare efficiency of the industrial system. It stands somewhere between the constitutionalist and insurrectionary views of the state, arguing for possible state rearrangements to alter this system, but simultaneously raising doubts about the political feasibility of this (e.g., Mishan, 1973).

30. See the critiques of economic theories in Morris (1974) and Sweezy & Magdoff (1974; 1975a,b).

31. For example, there has been renewed criticism of data on unemployment measures in the modern economy (DuBoff, 1977; Sweezy & Magdoff, 1975c). Ironically, despite this analytic weakness, many of the leading economists of the postwar period have built their economic programs around employment creation, in view of the political desirability of this goal. Despite the long overdue humility of the Committee on Economic Development noted above (DeChazeau et al., 1946), just two years earlier the Committee had issued a plea (Groves, 1944) for federal tax aid to generate new production, taxes, and *jobs*. This despite the uncertainties of employment multipliers for any federal tax policy! Some thirty years later, the Committee (1978) issued yet another report on unemployment, which called for improved federal subsidization for the "hard-to-employ" workers. Unsurprisingly, this report coincided with strong business pressures for additional investment incentives, through removal or reduction of corporate taxes (e.g., Regan, 1978; *New York Times*, 1977b). What is slightly novel is a quest for state support of a variety of *specific* programs (Freund, 1977) rather than broad monetary or fiscal ones. This may reflect the desirability for less broad-brush programs, which are subject to more open political debate than some of the narrower "technical" programs of support. Throughout these discussions, there is concern with the climate for investment, affirming the key role that Lindblom (1977:176) attributes to businessmen, and reinforcing Sweezy's (1975) thesis that investment is far more uncertain than savings in modern capitalist economies. Perhaps the quintessence of Kolko's (1963) political capitalism is this: The state has become the major social agency that can be blamed for the failures of capitalists to invest.

It is a bitter irony, as Hymer (1978) has noted, that Keynes is the key figure that facilitated this increased burden of the state: Keynes advocated the substitution of state for private production, not the protection of capitalists by the state. On the other hand, Thorstein Veblen was writing about similar problems in the period immediately following World War I (Veblen, 1947). He saw both government and businessmen "sabotaging" production for the sake of profits and enhanced "free income" (later known as "capital gains"). Even then, he argued that businessmen could "hold fast by an undiminished free income for the vested interests at the possible cost of any popular discontent... and then, *with the help of the courts and the military arm*, presently make terms with any popular discontent that may arise" Veblen, 1947:16; (my italics). The change in the post-World War II period was in the direct state fiscal role in private sector growth, not in state congruence with capital interests.

32. See Galbraith (1971), Baran & Sweezy (1966), Bell (1973), Tanzer (1971), O'Connor (1973), and Barnet & Müller (1974) for similar definitions of this sector.

33. Oligopolies are groups of corporations that dominate a given industry, with few effective competitors. Monopolies, in contrast, are single-corporations which dominate industrial sectors. In recent years, the technically-accurate term oligopoly has become less socially definitive, as earlier oligopolies have increased in (1) scale, (2) dominance of an industry, and (3) sociopolitical power. Moreover, most of the monopoly capital enterprises are also multinational in operation, thus extending their scope from national to global (Barnet & Müller, 1974). Tanzer (1971:19) has noted that among 80 oligopolies in the Fortune 500 in 1962, there had been a disappearance by 1968 through incorporation in other corporations in one form or another. This again suggests some quantitative disparities between earlier oligopolies and larger-scale "monopoly capital" enterprises formed in the conglomerate merger period (J. Brooks, 1973).

34. In line with the analysis of Kolko (1976: Ch. 9), Sweezy & Magdoff (1975a) attribute the post-1945 growth in the U.S. economy to (1) new technologies, (2) imperialist expansion and wars, (3) war preparations and reconstruction. DuBoff (1977) analyzes the failure of the growth period to generate low unemployment, and Rosenberg (1976:67) discusses the need for corporate predictability and control of its market and production environment as a precondition for investment in capital-intensive technology. The latter implies a diminished degree of freedom for the corporation, once this fixed capital is in place, since it cannot be laid off, as workers may be. This is especially true, as Veblen (1947) noted some 60 years ago, when finance capital is involved in this capitalization, and thus commands a need for profits on its loans. On the other hand, he was one of the first to note that corporate "sabotage" of production existed, to keep prices up by keeping volume down, i.e., another form of excess capacity. In the modern period, where competition is often replaced by quasi-controlled or administered prices in oligopolistic industries, production capacity is reduced because profits do not require such high production, nor can markets often absorb high production.

35. There is striking agreement on the quantitative dimensions of the liquidity crisis between the business media (*Business Week*, 1975) and neo-Marxist critics (Sweezy & Magdoff, 1975a,b). On the other hand, prescriptions for appropriate behavior differ, with business demanding reduced taxes and critics asking for increased state capitalism to achieve more effective social welfare gains. Both see the politically and socially costly recession/depression threats, though, as one possible outcome. One of the best treatments of Wall Street liquidity crises, including that of F.I. DuPont brokerage house, is in J. Brooks (1973, especially 334–46).

36. See the discussion on this in Kolko (1976: Ch. 9, 10).

37. The differences in corporate liquidity between 1974 and 1978 are documented in two issues of *Business Week* (1974, 1978). Profitability increases in the period have partly gone to pay off short-term debts incurred earlier (Sweezy & Magdoff, 1977a). Much of the current trend was anticipated by Veblen (1947), who

saw increased control of industries by financiers. What he could not anticipate was the enlarged fiscal role of the state in the 1940s and beyond.

38. Avineri (1968:172–74) stresses that Marx was perfectly aware of the posibilities for improvement in conditions for industrial workers, although he expected that this would be achieved at the expense of lower-level workers. But Marx emphasized that the gap would grow between stable workers and capital owners, as it has for monopoly-capital owners. On Marx's anticipation of the separation of ownership, management, and financing of modern corporations, see Avineri (1968:174–80), which treats views that strikingly anticipate Veblen's (1947) later observations, as well as more recent views. On the increasing concentration of monopoly-capital power, Avineri (1968:174–75) indicates that Marx linked this to improved financing and markets. On the state, Marx indicated its central role in legitimizing the expansion of capitalism (Avineri, 1968:19–27, 202–20), in part through its responsiveness to increased worker pressures for social and economic reform, as well as through increased suffrage.

39. On agricultural expansion, see Lappé & Collins (1977). The process of increased concentration in industrial sectors in treated in Kolko (1976: Ch. 9), and of expanded service sector control in Braverman (1974) and Mandel (1975: Ch. 12). The extension of this domestic control to the world-system is treated in Barnet & Müller (1974). While the emphasis in this chapter is on the increase in such monopoly-capital production, it should be noted that this varies considerably across sectors and societies. For example, public ownership has increased in some sectors (Cutler, 1975), including energy supplies in some Third World countries. In addition, smaller-scale competitive enterprises coexist with monopoly-capital enterprises where technology is not so capital-intensive, as in electronics and semiconductor fields, where employment has grown (Braverman, 1975). Finally, balance of payments problems and domestic unemployment have led to renewed concerns with overseas investments of multinational corporations (Robock, 1978; Musgrave, 1975). None of these negates the general trend, though they may slow the increases in monopoly-capital expansion.

40. The standard neoclassical assessment of self-employment is that it is of lower efficiency (GNP growth production):

> Actual and potential national income differ in any year . . . because . . . [of] two broad components. One is the change in the proportion of labor potentially available . . . that is actually in use . . . together with related effects on overallocation to farming and self-employment. . . . (Denison, 1974:117)

41. Gintis (1972) discusses the limited role of U.S. state policies in provision of services and goods, while Sweezy & Magdoff (1975b) indicate a broader range of state capitalist efforts in European and other societies.

42. See Boddy & Crotty (1974, 1976) for variability of profits within the business cycle, and Tanzer (1971: Ch. 1) on varying competition for capital.

43. On the price-volume relations in production, the typical historical process of monopoly-capital expansion is two-fold. Initially, markets are expanded and production increased through changes in technology, keeping unit prices lower. Once the market reaches a given scale, and products taken as normal consumption goods, the oligopolistic structure of many of these markets permits forms of price administra-

tion (Baran & Sweezy, 1966). This presupposes the existence of cooperative pricing mechanisms among the corporations involved, and relative price inelasticity of demand, i.e., consumers who are committed to the product enough to purchase it despite somewhat higher prices. If both (or either, in some cases) of these conditions are met, then profitability can be maintained at lower-than-capacity levels of production, despite the fixed capital costs of the corporation. Generally, firms do not *seek* this overcapacity. Rather, they accept overcapacity when it appears that demand has reached a peak at a given price level, rather than attempting to cut prices and thereby increase the number of consumers. That is, they profit more intensively from a smaller number of consumers than might be possible. This implies a lower price elasticity of demand from "committed" consumers than from "uncommitted" consumers, or at least a difference in demand curves between the two groups (perhaps based on income, or taste).

44. Denison's (1974:165) analysis indicates that during 1929–69 in the U.S., government employment had increased by over 11 million workers, while nonfarm wage and salary workers increased by about 26 million. Farm employment in the period dropped by about 6.5 million, while unpaid family work and self-employment grew by under two million. Thus, government employment growth absorbed almost ⅓ of the labor force expansion in the period. This growth has slowed considerably, and even reversed itself in the case of the federal government in the subsequent period (*Information Please*, 1978), with less than 2 million public workers added. This is also the period in which unemployment has risen substantially, reflecting the importance of the earlier public employment (DuBoff, 1977; Braverman, 1975). While total employment has risen somewhat, there are also changes in underemployment and discouraged workers (Sweezy & Magdoff, 1975c).

45. Braverman (1975) traces the far lower growth in employment than in volume of production in recent years in many sectors. He also notes that employment has grown most quickly in the occupational categories that have wages below the subsistence level of living for a family of four—e.g., service and retail workers.

46. The standard economic indicators report on labor productivity, while Commoner's (1977) critique is of decreasing capital productivity. In general, increased capital-intensification is a result of anticipated increases in profitability by reducing per-unit labor inputs that are recurrent expenses (though depreciation and maintenance are functionally equivalent expenses for machines). Among the many explanations of historical increases of capitalization of production, Rosenberg (1976:64) concurs with Marx's notions of increased predictability and control as both a facilitation of such increased investment, and of the pressures towards selective growth of this investment sector (p.67). He also notes the importance of the growing capital-goods (machine manufacturing) sector, a point which Sweezy (1978) stresses as a key part of recent stagnation. Over time, the actual profitability of monopoly-capital enterprises varies considerably, although less than the liquidity does. For example, the Baran and Sweezy (1966) analysis was done in a period of high liquidity and profitability, while the 1970s have brought extreme liquidity squeezes and somewhat lower profitability (Sweezy & Magdoff, 1975a,b). However, the fact remains that corporate management exercises considerable discretion in investment patterns (Sweezy, 1975) regardless of the liquidity or profitability levels. In periods of higher liquidity, investment in plant expansion may still not occur (Sweezy &

Magdoff, 1977a). And heavy borrowing may occur during periods of low liquidity to finance expansion (Sweezy & Magdoff, 1975a,b). Moreover, beyond some initial levels, corporations may seek ways to save capital as well as labor costs, in order to enhance profitability (Sweezy, 1974:45).

47. Although the term labor aristocracy was first used to describe the African economy (Arrighi & Saul, 1973), it has equal bearing for the U.S. and industrial economies in general. In the U.S., it generally refers to organized labor, which is disproportionately involved in capital-intensive and energy-intensive production. While wages have risen substantially in this sector, organized labor has shown little inclination to expand employment or, in many cases, to protect current employment. Thus, the post-World War II labor peace has involved labor contracts that improve benefits for this stratum, but do not expand the number of such jobs (Kolko, 1976: Ch. 5; Braverman, 1974, 1975). These disparities have intensified the work on "dual" or "split" labor markets in the U.S. (Burawoy, 1976; Bonacich, 1972, 1975), which follows the earlier concepts of "dualism" in the economies of the Third World.

48. While the state is entreated by capital and labor alike to increase employment opportunities, the typical form of response and encouragement is by a broad fiscal or tax stimulus to encourage investment (e.g., Committee for Economic Development, 1976). In countries with low levels of state capitalism like the U.S. (Gintis, 1972), there is a kind of schizoid quality to state obligations. Though the state is expected to counter the employment failures of the private sector, it is not assigned any legitimacy in deciding *how* surplus is to be mobilized to further this end.

49. Unless profitability decreases, corporations can only absorb more labor if their production technologies become more efficient. Some of this increased efficiency has certainly taken place in the post-1945 period, allowing for increased employment in large corporations, largely outside the direct production operations (Braverman, 1974, 1975). But productivity gains have also gone into profitability gains, thereby reducing employment increases. Whereas there has been some protection for smaller labor-intensive enterprises in some Western European countries, in the U.S. there has been steady growth of the concentration of employment in larger corporations, and decline in the proportion of self-employment (Denison, 1974:165; Kolko, 1976: Ch. 5).

One measure of the rise in capital levels per worker can be computed from Denison's (1974:165, 265) decomposition of economic growth factors. Using straight-line depreciation and net value at current prices, we can conservatively trace the increase: In 1929, there was approximately $2800 of "structures and equipment" in the nonfarm corporate sector for each wage/salary worker in the nonfarm business sector. The latter group includes self-employed and other noncorporate workers, so this initial figure is an underestimate for the corporate sector (for which we have no separate employment figure). By 1969, this figure had risen to just under $10,000 per such worker. Since the proportion of noncorporate workers declined in the 40-year period, this comparison somewhat overstates the increase. Likewise, inflation also overstates it. Nonetheless, it seems clear that there has been a real increase in total capital requirements per worker in 1929–69. With a crude correction for inflation, capital grew from $5400 to $7800, in 1958 prices. If we add in the noncorporate, nonfarm structures and equipment, $3200 to $11,600 per worker in current prices, or from $6100 to $9100 in 1958 prices. These figures exclude land and inventories, which would raise all these figures somewhat, but leave the *increases* basically the same. These increases understate what has happened in the monopoly sector, overall, especially in industries such as energy.

Such capital requirements help to explain why, in periods of recent liquidity problems, the state and monopoly-capital interests have permitted unemployment to increase rather than to attempt to maintain such investments (Sweezy & Magdoff, 1975b,c). Extant programs of income security, inadequate as they are (Kolko, 1976:324–27; Raskin, 1974) have nonetheless permitted such unemployment increases without high political costs (Gurley, 1977).

50. The general mechanisms supporting higher profit rates are described in Sweezy (1974a), and he deals as well with factors that reduce profit rates. Liquidity problems are treated in *Business Week* (1974, 1975, 1978) and Sweezy & Magdoff (1976). Increased debt financing of monopoly capital does lead to higher costs of production, because debt servicing is more expensive than other forms of equity increase (e.g., stock market, depreciation allowances [Baran & Sweezy, 1966]). During recessions, inventories rise and production goes unsold, as has happened during the post-1973 period. Moreover, excess capacity has risen, as productive capacity exceeds consumptive potential by a greater margin than in the past (Sweezy, 1974a, 1978). Taxation of individual capital gains has risen with inflation (Regan, 1978), but this is true of all income. And income security taxes have risen even faster (Kolko, 1976:325–27) for workers.

51. See Denison (1974) for an analysis of capital increases and technological change. Unfortunately, his measures of the latter are indirect, casting doubt on the assessment of capital growth versus technological change in stimulating growth in national income. There have been evaluations of some U.S. tax bills in earlier years that suggest pressures for consumption versus investment (Dale, 1976). A contrary view is suggested by Brown (1977) and Eisner (1978). Profitability trends and their interpretation are not always clear (Magnuson, 1977), unfortunately. However, it is clear that service employment, typically at lower wages than the labor aristocracy, has increased total corporate costs (Braverman, 1974, 1975) for labor. Equally clear is an increase in investment by multinationals in the Third World (Magdoff, 1969, 1974, 1976; Barnet & Müller, 1974; Tanzer, 1971: Ch. 3).

52. On wage structures, see Boddy & Crotty (1974, 1976) and the response by Sherman (1976). The recent expansion of credit is well-documented (*Business Week*, 1974, 1978), as is the push for both public sector consumption and tax relief (Sweezy & Magdoff, 1975a,b). Contradictions in the demands of monopoly capital (e.g., Committee for Economic Development, 1976, 1978) include the simultaneous quest for increased government consumption, tax relief, and reduction of debt and borrowing by the state! The international investment patterns—including the use of U.S. capital to draw in capital from the Third World (Baran, 1968; Barnet & Müller, 1974) are clear, but there is substantial dispute about the actual levels of profits from such ventures, in part because of accounting practices of multinationals (Magdoff, 1969, 1974; J. Brooks, 1973).

53. Arguments about the treadmill structure and speed paralleling Table 1 can be found in Sweezy (1974a) and Sweezy & Magdoff (1977a). The most succinct

linkage of this to overseas investment patterns is in Magdoff (1976, 1977). It should be noted that growing capital flight (overseas investment) appears to have worsened the opportunity structure for labor in the U.S. (Musgrave, 1975), despite the potential for repatriation of profits and investment domestically. On the one hand, then, this lack of domestic investment slows the U.S. treadmill. On the other, though, it suggests that the treadmill will have to be accelerated at a faster rate in the future to generate employment opportunities in the monopoly capital sector, since even high rates of domestic and foreign production produce less of an employment multiplier than we would expect.

54. From 1955 to 1976, female labor force participation rates in the U.S. rose from 46% to 59% for single women, and from 29% to 46% for married women. The most striking increases among married women (with husbands present) were for the younger (20–24 years old) women, whose rates rose from 32% to 57% (U.S. Bureau of the Census, 1977:391). Part of this increase reflects decreased fertility and older ages of childbearing (Schnaiberg, 1978). But the latter may reflect the need for increased income as much as any movement for female liberation. It is important to note that producers have developed policies to adjust to considerable variations in the labor force pool (Easterlin et al., 1978), so that the demographic predictions are often quite muted in production practice.

55. Georgescu-Roegen (1973) discusses the concept of economic entropy in a usage parallel to mine here.

56. Models of labor-intensification of production (Dickson, 1975; Morrison, 1978), which will be treated in Ch. IX below, are frequently dismissed by neoclassical economists (e.g., Barkley & Seckler, 1972:189).

57. See note 49 for some overall estimates of capital per worker, which are far below Foy's figures. Presumably, Foy has included a variety of other capital figures, such as land holdings, as well as restricted his analysis to steel corporations or equivalents in other sectors. The motivation for Foy's position is clear (Sweezy & Magdoff, 1977b): the U.S. steel industry has suffered from a decreasing demand for domestic steel, and profits are being squeezed. Another equally striking example of the treadmill appears in a recent advertisement (American Electric Power, 1978). With the high energy input this firm provides, it notes a capital investment by "coal, chemical, oil, steel, automotive, aluminum" and other industries of $1.04 billion, including 218 new plants and 295 expansions. That "translates into 21,700 new jobs," according to their estimates. This leads to an average of $47,926 capital required per new job, a figure that is even higher than Foy's! Though the advertisement is clearly designed to show the social growth potential arising from energy production, then, what we have instead is another indicator of the inefficiency of the treadmill for rapid employment generation.

58. Discussions of this trickle-down model include England & Bluestone (1973) and Schnaiberg (1975). Skepticism about the future of the treadmill is most ripe in Heilbroner (1975, 1976, 1978) and Sweezy (1978). Both of them note the potential for serious social repression in the clash between the treadmill and ecosystem realities. So does Stretton (1976: Ch. 1), who provides the most detailed descriptions of possible repressive and progressive options.

59. See Bonacich (1972, 1975) on two-track labor markets, as well as Reich et al. (1973).

60. On links between poverty and employment, see Cloward & Piven (1974) and Piven & Cloward (1977).

61. Kolko (1976: Ch. 5) summarizes many of these trends, though he notes that the social context of U.S. labor differs from many western European ones, and helps to explain low levels of labor politicization (cf. Wiley, 1967). One of the few instances of socially visible opposition to mechanization is by the United Farm Workers, a new union (Lindsey, 1977). In contrast, European workers have often been more militant regarding job losses (e.g., Kessler, 1978). Braverman (1974, 1975) has indicated differences in employment growth by sector.

62. In the period from 1929 to 1969, total employee compensation has risen in the farm and nonfarm sectors from 61% to 72% of national income. This includes a period of high growth in the labor force, of course, in the 1960s. During the same period, corporate nonfarm income has stayed virtually constant, though, as a share of national income (ranging from 13% to 16%, from 14% in 1929 to 13% in 1969). These data are drawn from Denison (1974:263).

63. On public employee unionization, see O'Connor (1973) and DiTomaso (1978), and the critique and hopes expressed in Johnston (1978). For a critical view of earlier labor organization and the bureaucratization of its leadership, see Kotz (1977).

64. For two perspectives on the mobilization of the poor, see Kotz & Kotz (1977) on the National Welfare Rights Organization, and Piven & Cloward (1977) on civil disobedience actions and potential influence.

65. See O'Connor (1973) and Friedland et al. (1977) on the cumulation of state programs of income security and social services. But Kolko (1976:325-27) argues that the bottom strata have more than paid for these gains through various social security and other tax programs, so that their *net* gains are small or nonexistent. A sharply contrasting view of such transfer payments is M. Anderson's (1978), which claims that the economic security of the poor is much enhanced (see also Gurley, 1977, for a similar argument). Conversely, Kolko (1976:339-45) emphasizes the underreporting of income and wealth by the upper end of the income distribution, renewing a thesis of relative if not absolute losses of income by the lower end. Both Okun (1975) and Stretton (1976) raise doubts about the precision of data on wealth inequalities, though neither doubt that inequality has coexisted with economic growth.

66. Observers are split on the degree to which there has been collaboration and manipulation by monopoly-capital interests in the environmental movement. Barkley & Weissman's (1970) analysis was typical of one position, that the movement was stimulated and created by big business. Their assessment is reaffirmed by the behavior of Laurance Rockefeller (Collier & Horowitz, 1976: 304-9, 384-404). In addition, the argument of Gellen (1970) about the profitability of the pollution-abatement equipment sector has been confirmed by later experience (Rattner, 1977). On the other hand, the dominant evidence is one of conflicts, arising from increased costs of pollution abatement and the drain on markets from such cost and price increases (e.g., *Business Week*, 1974, 1975, 1978). It is still true that there are sectoral differences in responses to energy problems, because of technological differences. For example, aluminum manufacturers have clearly benefited (Ibrahim, 1977).

67. The conditions of black and youth unemployment have been graphically stated in a number of places (e.g., Gilder, 1977; Raskin, 1976). Despite the intense labor lobbying for the Humphrey-Hawkins bill in a strong form (Raskin, 1977), neither it nor job tax credits have wound up as very significant at the time of final passage and implementation (NYT, 1977a; Keyserling, 1977; Browne, 1977). One critical view of the union position in New York City is in Sweezy & Magdoff (1975a).

68. See Kotz & Kotz (1977) and Piven & Cloward (1977) on the 1960s movements. The latter argue that the movement failed because it became over-organized, and abandoned civil disobedience too early. The abandonment was, of course, strongly urged by organized labor and management alike, in an effort to stabilize both the society and the economy.

69. This interpretation is consistent with both the neo-Marxist analysis of O'Connor (1973) and the conservative one of M. Anderson (1978).

70. A summary of the ineffectuality of U.S. job training programs is in Dembart (1977). On the NWRO movement, see Kotz & Kotz (1977) and Piven & Cloward (1977).

71. The Center for Science in the Public Interest has, for example, attempted to stimulate such mergers of traditional poverty concerns with appropriate technology (e.g., Center for Science in the Public Interest, 1976), and Congress has established a National Center for Appropriate Technology. The latter grew out of the Community Services Administration, one of the surviving agencies from the Office of Economic Opportunity, the major federal institution produced by the poor people's movements of the 1960s. It is a neighborhood, rather than a national, program, though.

72. On the geographic distribution of pollution, see Council on Environmental Quality (1971: Ch. 6) reports on urban areas; on occupational health, see Brodeur (1974) and Scott (1974). Recent state responses to the latter have improved (Shabecoff, 1978) after an initial ineffectuality. Finally, the risks of economic contraction following earlier growth periods are forcefully stated by both radical critics (e.g., Sweezy, 1978) and business analysts (e.g., *Business Week*, 1975, 1978).

73. Despite the generally harsh evaluations by Kolko (1976: Ch. 4) of the inadequacies of the New Deal and other U.S. programs of the 1930s, it is striking how the institutional structure of the state in this period remains a model for contemporary policy debates. Duscha (1974), for example, cites the Works Progress Administration program for employment generation. Felix Rohatyn's program for government support of cities (Sweezy & Magdoff, 1975b) draws heavily on the Reconstruction Finance Corporation, which lasted from 1932 to 1953, for government financing of capital expansion.

74. On the profitability of inflation, see Sweezy (1974), Sweezy & Magdoff (1977a), and Levinson (1971).

75. A recent study by the International Brotherhood of Teamsters (NYT, 1976) indicates the crucial role of public employment in the 1973–75 recessionary period.

76. The strongest presentation of such a perspective is Kolko's (1963, 1976) work on the development of political capitalism in the U.S.

77. For a discussion of political mobilization by energy corporations, see Naughton (1977).

78. One of the interesting case studies is Tucker's (1978) account of problems of a small company, Zoecon, in registering biological controls for insects (pheromones). Environmental Protection Agency obstacles have effectively precluded any development of such products for the market, despite the fact that these pheromones are environmentally safer than current insecticides. Similar problems are reported for Conrel, although this small firm eventually achieved registration of a pheromone for a cotton pest. Although part of Tucker's argument is that such regulation is very difficult for small companies, it is somewhat ironic to note that both these firms were set up as subsidiaries of larger enterprises: e.g., Zoecon was established by Syntex Corporation, which clearly falls into the monopoly capital sector, with 1978 assets of $483 million (*Business Week*, 1978:122).

79. In addition to large-scale advertising in all media regarding the effects of government control and the need for investment spurs to induce employment gains, organizations such as the Committee for Economic Development (1976, 1978) have been communicating with educators and other opinion influencers as to social needs and contributions by business. Typical of such efforts is the competition for teachers sponsored by the International Paper Company Foundation (Joint Council on Economic Education, 1978). To stimulate teachers, in addition to the awards, "Many award winners now serve as consultants, and a significant number have been approached by publishing companies" (iv). Those persons whose "formal preparation in economics is minimal should consult an economist regarding the accuracy and appropriateness of the economics contained in the report" (vii). A typical report (e.g., Gray, 1978) indicates teacher familiarity with much of the neoclassical economics prepared by business and advertising groups, and distributed through the U.S. Department of Commerce. Following the analysis of Tanzer (1971:23–24), this particular project attempts to educate fifth-graders to the need for admission charges in a public zoo. This is a trivial example of the mechanism by which the private sector efficiency criterion is applied to the public sector (see Ch. VII for an extended analysis of this model). Not surprisingly, one finds few criticisms of the "free market system" in such prize-winning reports. In the zoo example (Gray, 1978:33), the students eventually voted 6 to 1 in favor of the fee, thus choosing efficiency over equality.

An equally sophisticated and expensive approach is the recent publication of an account of "Coca-Cola's project" on migrant orange grove workers in Florida (Harris & Allen, 1978). In an effort to publicize the corporate contributions to the workers' development (aided by substantial grants from the U.S. Department of Health, Education and Welfare), the resulting paean of praise for Coca-Cola's social responsibility nowhere lists the corporate costs of this program, but does indicate some corporate benefits. Moreover, the fact that the book was published through and copyrighted by Rawson Associates Publishers, Inc., and distributed free to academics like myself through this same company (rather than through the official publisher, New American Library) strongly suggests subsidization by Coca-Cola company. My own skimming of the book, incidentally, indicates to me little financial commitment to the worker program by Coca-Cola.

264   THE SEARCH FOR CAUSES AND SOLUTIONS

REFERENCES

ALONSO, WILLIAM
1973   "Urban zero population growth." Pp. 191–206 in M. Olson and H. H. Landsberg (eds.), The No-Growth Society. New York: W. W. Norton.

AMERICAN ELECTRIC POWER
1978   "We spent zero promoting our area, yet it grew by $1,040,000,000." Advertisement. Newsweek, 18 Sept.: 55.

AMERICAN INSTITUTE OF PUBLIC OPINION
1978   "U.S. blamed for inflation." Chicago Sun-Times, 15 Oct.

ANDERSON, CHARLES H.
1976   The Sociology of Survival: Social Problems of Growth. Homewood, Ill.: Dorsey Press.

ANDERSON, MARTIN
1978   Welfare: The Political Economy of Welfare Reform in the United States. Stanford, Cal.: Hoover Institute Press.

ARRIGHI, GIOVANNI AND J.S. SAUL (EDS.)
1973   Essays in the Political Economy of Africa. New York: Monthly Review Press.

AVINERI, SHLOMO
1968   The Social and Political Thought of Karl Marx. Cambridge: Cambridge University Press.

BARAN, PAUL A.
1968   The Political Economy of Growth. New York: Modern Reader Paperbacks.

BARAN, PAUL AND P.M. SWEEZY
1966   Monopoly Capital: An Essay on the American Economic and Social Order. New York: Modern Reader Paperbacks.

BARKLEY, KATHERINE AND S. WEISSMAN
1970   "The eco-establishment." Pp. 15–24 by the editors of Ramparts, Eco-Catastrophe. San Francisco: Canfield Press.

BARKLEY, PAUL W. AND D.W. SECKLER
1972   Economic Growth and Environmental Decay: The Solution Becomes the Problem. New York: Harcourt, Brace, Jovanovich.

BARNET, RICHARD J. AND R.E. MÜLLER
1974   Global Reach: The Power of the Multinational Corporations. New York: Simon and Schuster.

BELL, DANIEL
1962   The End of Ideology: On the Exhaustion of Political Ideas in the Fifties. Revised edition. New York: Free Press.
1973   The Coming of Post-Industrial Society: A Venture in Social Forecasting. New York: Basic Books.

1976   The Cultural Contradictions of Capitalism. New York: Basic Books.

BENNETT, ROBERT A.
1978   "Oil and the price/productivity gap." New York Times, 2 July.

BERNSTEIN, PETER L.
1977   "Productivity: rewards needed for taking risks." New York Times, 24 Apr.

BODDY, RAFORD AND J. CROTTY
1974   "Class conflict, Keynesian policies, and the business cycle." Monthly Review 26 (5):1-17.
1976   "Wage-push and working class power: A reply to Howard Sherman." Monthly Review 27 (10):35-43.

BONACICH, EDNA
1972   "A theory of ethnic antagonism: the split labor market." American Sociological Review 37 (Oct.):547-559.
1975   "Abolition, the extension of slavery, and the position of free blacks: A study of the split labor markets in the United States." American Journal of Sociology 81 (Nov.):601-628.

BOULDING, KENNETH E.
1973   "The shadow of the stationary state." Pp. 89-101 in M. Olson and H. H. Landsberg (eds.), The No-Growth Society. New York: W.W. Norton,

BRAVERMAN, HARRY
1974   Labor and Monopoly Capital: The Degradation of Work in the Twentieth Century. New York: Monthly Review Press.
1975   "Work and unemployment." Monthly Review 27 (2):18-31

BRODEUR, PAUL
1974   Expendable Americans. New York: Viking.

BROOKS, DAVID B. AND P.W. ANDREWS
1974   "Mineral resources, economic growth, and world population." Science 185 (5 July):13-19.

BROOKS, HARVEY
1973   "The technology of zero growth." Pp. 139-152 in M. Olson and H.H. Landsberg (eds.), The No-Growth society. New York: W.W. Norton.

BROOKS, JOHN
1973   The Go-Go Years. New York: Weybright and Talley.

BROWN, WILLIAM J.
1977   "The myth of capital gain taxes." New York Times, 14 Aug.

BROWNE, ROBERT S.
1977   "Blacks and jobs." New York Times, 2 Oct.

BURAWOY, MICHAEL
1976   "The functions and reproduction of migrant labor: Comparative material from Southern Africa and the United States." American Journal of Sociology 81 (5):1050-1087.

BUSINESS WEEK
1974   "The debt economy." Special issue. 12 Oct.

1975   "Capital crisis: The $4.5 trillion America needs to grow." Special issue. 22 Sept.

1978   "The new debt economy." Special issue. 16 Oct.

CENTER FOR SCIENCE IN THE PUBLIC INTEREST
1976   "Pioneering appropriate technology." People and Energy. II (3):1–3.

CLOWARD, RICHARD A. AND F. FOX PIVEN
1974   The Politics of Turmoil: Essays on Poverty, Race and the Urban Crisis. New York: Vintage.

COLLIER, PETER AND D. HOROWITZ
1976   The Rockefellers: An American Dynasty. New York: Holt, Rinehart, and Winston.

COMMITTEE FOR ECONOMIC DEVELOPMENT
1976   "The Economy in 1977–78: Strategy for an Enduring Expansion." Statement: Dec. New York.

1978   Jobs for the Hard-to-Employ: New Directions for a Public-Private Partnership. Statement: Jan. New York.

COMMONER, BARRY
1977   The Poverty of Power: Energy and the Economic Crisis. New York: Bantam Books.

COUNCIL ON ENVIRONMENTAL QUALITY
1971   "The inner city environment." Pp. 189–207 in Council on Environmental Quality, Environmental Quality—1971. Washington, D.C.: Government Printing Office.

CRENSON, MATTHEW A.
1971   The Un-Politics of Air Pollution: A Study of Non-Decision Making in the Cities. Baltimore: Johns Hopkins University Press.

CRITTENDEN, ANN
1977   "A new index on the quality of life." New York Times, 13 Mar.

CUTLER, LLOYD N.
1975   "Adjusting to growth of public ownership." New York Times, 5 Jan.

DALE, EDWIN L., JR.
1976   "Capital formation and tax revision." Washington Report. New York Times, 19 Sept.

DALY, HERMAN E. (ED.)
1973   Toward a Steady-State Economy. San Francisco: W.H. Freeman.

DECHAZEAU, MELVIN G., A.G. HART, G.C. MEANS, H.B. MYERS, H. STEIN, AND T.O. YNTEMA
1946   Jobs and Markets: How to Prevent Inflation and Depression in the Transition. New York: McGraw-Hill.

DEMBART, LEE
1977   "Federal job training, the project nearly impossible to evaluate." New York Times, 10 Apr.

DENISON, EDWARD F.
1974   Accounting for United States Economic Growth, 1929–1969. Washington, D.C.: The Brookings Institution.
1977   The Contribution of Capital to the Postwar Growth of Industrial Countries. General Series Reprint no. 324. Washington, D.C.: The Brookings Institution.

DICKSON, DAVID
1975   The Politics of Alternative Technology. New York: Universe Books.

DITOMASO, NANCY
1978   "Public employee unions and the urban fiscal crisis." Paper presented at meetings of Society for the Study of Social Problems, San Francisco, Sept.

DUBOFF, RICHARD B.
1977   "Unemployment in the United States: An historical summary." Monthly Review 29 (6):10–24.

DUSCHA, JULIUS
1974   "Jobs in the Great Depression: W.P.A. still a model for today's planning." New York Times, 22 Dec.

EASTERLIN, RICHARD A., M.L. WACHTER, AND S.M. WACHTER
1978   "Demographic influences on economic stability: the United States experience." Population and Development Review (1):1–22.

EISNER, ROBERT
1978   "Tax credits: the poor investment incentive." Letter to the editor. New York Times, 28 May.

ENERGY POLICY PROJECT
1974   A Time to Choose: America's Energy Future. Cambridge, Mass.: Ballinger.

ENGLAND, RICHARD AND B. BLUESTONE
1973   "Ecology and social conflict." Pp. 190–214 in H.E. Daly (ed.), Toward A Steady-State Economy. San Francisco: W.H. Freeman.

FOY, LEWIS W.
1975   "A progressive program for 'a backward nation.'" Address to Downtown Rotary Club, Washington, D.C.: 23 July (reprinted).

FREUND, WILLIAM C.
1977   "High price of prodding the economy." New York Times, 23 Oct.

FRIEDEN, JEFF
1977   "The Trilateral Commission: economics and politics in the 1970s." Monthly Review 29 (7):1–18.

FRIEDLAND, ROGER, F.F. PIVEN, AND R.R. ALFORD
1977   "Political conflict, urban structure, and the fiscal crisis." International Journal of Urban and Regional Research 1 (3):447–71.

GALBRAITH, JOHN K.
1958   The Affluent Society. New York: New American Library.
1971   The New Industrial State. Second Edition. New York: New American Library.

GELLEN, MARTIN
1970   "The making of a pollution-industrial complex." Pp. 73–83 by the editors of Ramparts, Eco-Catastrophe. San Francisco: Canfield Press.

GEORGESCU-ROEGEN, NICHOLAS
1973   "The entropy law and the economic problem," Pp. 37–49 in H.E. Daly (ed.), Toward A Steady-State Economy. San Francisco: W.H. Freeman.

GIDDENS, ANTHONY
1973   The Class Structure of Advanced Societies. New York: Harper & Row.

GILDER, GEORGE
1977   "To be young, black and out of work." New York Times Magazine, 23 Oct.:39–61.

GINTIS, HERBERT
1972   "Consumer behavior and the concept of sovereignty: explanations of social decay." The American Economic Review 62 (2):267–78.

GORDON, DAVID M.
1976   "Capitalist efficiency and socialist efficiency." Monthly Review 28 (3):19–39.

GRAY, POLLY
1978   "Monkey business is money business." Pp. 28–34 in Economic Education Experiences of Enterprising Teachers. New York: Joint Council on Economic Education.

GROVES, HAROLD M.
1944   Production, Jobs and Taxes: Postwar Revision of the Federal Tax System to Help Achieve Higher Production and More Jobs. New York: McGraw-Hill.

GURLEY, JOHN G.
1977   "Unemployment and inflation." Monthly Review 29 (7):23–28.

HANNON, BRUCE
1975   "Energy conservation and the consumer," Science 189 (11 July):95–102.

HARRINGTON, MICHAEL
1962   The Other America. New York: Macmillan.

HARRIS, SARA AND R.F. ALLEN
1978   The Quiet Revolution: The Story of a Small Miracle in American Life. New York: New American Library.

HARVEY, DAVID
1973   Social Justice and the City. Baltimore: Johns Hopkins University Press.

HAYS, SAMUEL P.
1969   Conservation and the Gospel of Efficiency: The Progressive Conservation Movement, 1890–1920. New York: Atheneum Books.

HEILBRONER, ROBERT L.
1975   An Inquiry Into the Human Prospect. New York: W.W. Norton.
1976   Business Civilization in Decline. New York: W.W. Norton.
1978   "Boom and crash." New Yorker, 28 Aug.:52–73.

HYMER, STEPHAN
1978   "International politics and international economics: A radical approach."
        Monthly Review 29 (10):15–35.

IBRAHIM, YOUSEF M.
1977   "For aluminum, the energy crunch was a blessing." New York Times,
        11 Dec.

INFORMATION PLEASE
1978   Information Please Almanac. New York: Information Please Publishing.

JOHNSON, WILLARD R.
1973   "Should the poor buy no-growth?" Pp. 165–189 in M. Olson and H.H.
        Landsberg (eds.), The No-Growth Society. New York: W.W. Norton.

JOHNSTON, PAUL
1978   "The promise of public-service unionism." Monthly Review 30 (4):1–
        17.

JOINT COUNCIL ON ECONOMIC EDUCATION
1978   Economic Education Experiences on Enterprising Teachers. Volume 15.
        New York.

KESSLER, FELIX
1978   "French workers stage sit-ins at failing firms, citing 'right to work.'"
        Wall Street Journal, 30 Oct.

KEYSERLING, LEON H.
1977   "Humphrey-Hawkins." Letter to Business Editor. New York Times, 20
        Feb.

KLEIN, RUDOLF
1972   "Growth and its enemies." Commentary, June:37–44.

KOLKO, GABRIEL
1963   The Triumph of Conservatism: A Reinterpretation of American History,
        1900–1916. New York: The Free Press.
1976   Main Currents in Modern American History. New York: Harper & Row.

KOTZ, NICK
1977   "Can labor's tired leaders deal with a troubled movement?" New York
        Times Magazine, 4 Sept.:8ff.

KOTZ, NICK AND M.L. KOTZ
1977   A Passion for Equality: George A. Wiley and the Movement. New York:
        W.W. Norton.

KRISTOL, IRVING
1977   Two Cheers for Capitalism. New York: Basic Books.

LAPPÉ, FRANCIS M. AND J. COLLINS
1977   Food First: Beyond the Myth of Scarcity. Boston: Houghton Mifflin.

LEVINSON, CHARLES
1971   Capital, Inflation and the Multinationals. New York: Macmillan.

LINDBLOM, CHARLES E.
1977   Politics and Markets: The World's Political-Economic Systems. New York: Basic Books.

LINDSEY, ROBERT
1977   "Coast farm workers begin fight on machine harvesting." New York Times, 18 Sept.

LOGAN, JOHN R.
1976   "Notes on the growth machine—toward a comparative political economy of place." American Journal of Sociology 82 (2): 349–52.

LOVINS, AMORY
1977   Soft Energy Paths. Cambridge, Mass.: Ballinger.

MAGDOFF, HARRY
1969   The Age of Imperialism: The Economics of U.S. Foreign Policy. New York: Modern Reader Paperbacks.
1974   "Imperial expansion: Accident and design." Monthly Review 25 (8):15–30.
1976   "Capital, technology, and development." Monthly Review 27 (8):1–11.
1977   "How to make a molehill out of a mountain." Monthly Review 28 (10):1–18.

MAGNUSON, ROBERT
1977   "Debate on profits: A clash of titans." New York Times, 8 May.

MANDEL, ERNEST
1975   Late Capitalism. Translated by J. DeBres. London: New Left Books.

MAZUR, ALLAN AND E. ROSA
1974   "Energy and life-style." Science 186 (15 Nov.):607–610.

MCKEAN, ROLAND N.
1973   "Growth vs. no-growth: An evaluation." Pp. 207–27 in M. Olson and H.H. Landsberg (eds.), The No-Growth Society. New York: W.W. Norton.

MELMAN, SEYMOUR (ED.)
1971   The War Economy of the United States: Readings on Military Industry and Economy. New York: St. Martin's Press.

MILIBAND, RALPH
1977   Marxism and Politics. London: Oxford University Press.

MISHAN, EZRA J.
1967   The Costs of Economic Growth. New York: Frederick A. Praeger.
1973   "Ills, bads, and disamenities: The wages of growth." Pp. 63–87 in M. Olson and H.H. Landsberg (eds.), the No-Growth Society. New York: W.W. Norton.

MOLOTCH, HARVEY
1976a   "The city as a growth machine: Toward a political economy of place." American Journal of Sociology 82 (2):309–332.

1976b "Varieties of growth strategy: Some comments on Logan." American Journal of Sociology 82 (2):352–55.

MOORE, WILBERT
1965 The Impact of Industry. Englewood Cliffs, N.J.: Prentice-Hall.

MORRIS, JACOB
1974 "Stagflation." Monthly Review 26 (7):1–10.

MORRISON, DENTON E.
1978 "Energy, appropriate technology, and international interdependence." Paper presented at meetings of Society for the Study of Social Problems, San Francisco, August.

MUSGRAVE, PEGGY B.
1975 "Direct investment abroad and the multinationals: Effects on the United States economy." Report to Subcommittee on Multinational Corporations, Senate Committee on Foreign Relations. Washington, D.C.: U.S. Government Printing Office, Aug.

NAUGHTON, JAMES N.
1977 "Petropolitics at work on Capitol Hill." New York Times, 3 Apr.

NEW YORK TIMES (NYT)
1976 "Increase in public jobs called aid to economy." New York Times, 10 Oct.
1977a "The job tax credit's hollow promise." Editorial. New York Times, 13 Feb.
1976b "Abolish the corporate income tax." Editorial. New York Times, 11 Sept.

O'CONNOR, JAMES
1973 The Fiscal Crisis of the State. New York: St. Martin's Press.

OKUN, ARTHUR
1975 Equality and Efficiency: The Big Tradeoff. Washington, D.C.: The Brookings Institution.

OLSON, MANCUR
1973 "Introduction." Pp. 1–13 in M. Olson and H.H. Landsberg (eds.), The No-Growth Society. New York: W.W. Norton.

OLSON, MANCUR AND H.H. LANDSBERG (EDS.)
1973 The No-Growth Society. New York: W.W. Norton.

PIVEN, FRANCES FOX AND R.A. CLOWARD
1977 Poor People's Movements: Why They Succeed, How They Fail. New York: Pantheon.

RASKIN, A.H.
1974 "The unemployed have better crutches now, but still limp." New York Times, 15 Dec.
1976 "The system keeps the young waiting." New York Times, 5 Dec.
1977 "A tougher approach to jobs." New York Times, 20 Nov.

RATTNER, STEVEN
1977 "Pollution control has become a large American business." New York Times, 17 Apr.

REGAN, DONALD T.
1978 "Inflation's toll on capital gains." New York Times, 21 May.

REICH, MICHAEL, D. GORDON, AND R. EDWARDS
1973 "The theory of labor market segmentation." American Economic Review
63 (2):359–65.

RIDKER, RONALD G.
1972 "Population and pollution in the United States." Science 176 (9
June):1085–90.

ROBERTS, MARC J.
1973 "On reforming economic growth." Pp. 119–137 in M. Olson and H.H.
Landsberg (eds.), The No-Growth Society. New York: W.W. Norton.

ROBOCK, STEFAN H.
1978 "Multinationals vs. the trade gap." New York Times, 21 May.

ROSENBERG, NATHAN
1976 "Marx as a student of technology." Monthly Review 28 (3):56–77.

SAMUELSON, PAUL A.
1967 Economics: An Introductory Analysis. Seventh edition. New York:
McGraw-Hill.

SCHNAIBERG, ALLAN
1975 "Social syntheses of the societal-environmental dialectic: The role of
distributional impacts." Social Science Quarterly 56 (June):5–20.
1978 "Social policy and family myths: ZPG and other mystiques." Paper presented at meetings of Illinois Sociological Association, Chicago, Oct.

SCHUMACHER, E.F.
1973 Small is Beautiful: Economics as if People Mattered. New York: Harper
& Row.

SCOTT, RACHEL
1974 Muscle and Blood. New York: E.P. Dutton.

SERVICE, ELMAN R.
1958 A Profile of Primitive Culture. New York: Harper and Brothers.

SHABECOFF, PHILIP
1978 "The woman who turned OSHA around." New York Times, 19 Feb.

SHERMAN, HOWARD
1976 "Inflation, unemployment, and monopoly capital." Monthly Review 27
(10):25–35.

STRETTON, HUGH
1976 Capitalism, Socialism, and the Environment. Cambridge: Cambridge
University Press.

SULLIVAN, WALTER
1978 "A call for industrial research as a key to growth." New York Times, 19
Feb.

SWEEZY, PAUL M.
1973 "Utopian reformism." Monthly Review 25 (6):1–11.

1974a "Some problems in the theory of capital accumulation." Monthly Review 26 (1):38–55.

1974b "Baran and the danger of inflation." Monthly Review 26 (7):11–14.

1975 "Savings, consumption, and investment." Monthly Review 27 (7):1–7.

1978 "The present stage of the global crisis of capitalism." Monthly Review 29 (11):1–12.

SWEEZY, PAUL M. AND H. MAGDOFF

1974 "Keynesian chickens come home to roost." Monthly Review 25 (11):1–12.

1975a "The economic crisis in historical perspective." Monthly Review 26 (10):1–8.

1975b "The economic crisis in historical perspective—part II." Monthly Review 26 (11):1–13.

1975c "Capitalism and unemployment." Monthly Review 27 (2):1–14.

1976 "Capital shortage: Fact and fancy." Monthly Review 27 (11):1–19.

1977a "Creeping stagnation." Monthly Review 28 (8):1–14.

1977b "Steel and stagnation." Monthly Review 29 (6):1–9.

1977c "Comment by the editors." Monthly Review 29 (7):19–22.

TANZER, MICHAEL

1971 The Sick Society: An Economic Examination. Chicago: Holt, Rinehart, & Winston.

TUCKER, WILLIAM

1978 "Of mites and men." Harper's, Aug.:43–58.

U.S. BUREAU OF THE CENSUS

1977 Statistical Abstract of the United States–1977. Washington, D.C.: Government Printing Office.

VEBLEN, THORSTEIN

1947 The Engineers and the Price System. New York: Viking Press.

WALLERSTEIN, IMMANUEL

1974 The Modern World-System: Capitalist Agriculture and the Origins of the European World-Economy in the Sixteenth Century. New York: Academic Press.

WILEY, NORBERT

1967 "America's unique class politics: The interplay of the labor, credit and commodity markets." American Sociological Review 32 (Aug.):525–541.

WILFORD, JOHN N.

1977 "The 'good life' has found a limit." New York Times, 17 July.

ZECKHAUSER, RICHARD

1973 "The risks of growth." Pp. 103–118 in M. Olson and H.H. Landsberg (eds.), The No-Growth Society. New York: W.W. Norton.

ZEITLIN, MAURICE

1974 "Corporate ownership and control: The large corporation and the capitalist class." American Journal of Sociology 79 (5):1073–1119.

3 SOCIAL RESPONSES TO ENVIRONMENTAL CHANGE

VI ENVIRONMENTAL INTELLIGENCE
Constraints on Scientists and
Technologists

OBSTACLES TO ENVIRONMENTAL RESEARCH BY SCIENTISTS

The Roles of Science and Technology

Scientific and technology activity have a special place in the creation and the resolution of environmental problems: (1) The major technological changes noted in chapter III have been made possible in large part through organized scientific and technological research; (2) through these production-oriented achievements, the expansion of production noted in Chapters IV and V has been made both possible and necessary by the treadmill; and (3) the negative environmental externalities (Chapter I) of such production changes have also been noted by scientists.

The central argument in this chapter will be that (a) the production roles of scientists and technologists have far outweighed their environmental contributions, and (b) the reasons for this lie in the social and economic context within which science and technology are carried out in advanced industrial societies. Science and technology are viewed here as social institutions, engaged in social, economic, and political relationships with those who control the major means of production.

Much of the material in this chapter appeared in an article by the author in *Social Problems*, June 1977.

Emphasis is placed not on *individual* creative acts of scientists and technologists, but on *collective* products of these two social institutions, and the social forces marshalled by powerful groups—particularly monopoly capitalists—that heavily influence such outcomes.[1] Science, following Schooler (1971:27) is "the social creation of knowledge," and technology is "the application of knowledge in the processes of social production." While the two institutions are distinctive in important ways (Brooks, 1971), they are subject to some common forms of social control. But technologists, because of their closer involvement with productive technology, operate under a broader array of such controls.[2]

In essence, this chapter seeks to answer the question: Why have we been able to mobilize our social intelligence to expand high-technology production, but not to understand the environmental effects of this production? In what ways have scientific and technological research been organized so heavily toward expansionism, and so little toward assessing and meliorating the by-products of this material expansion?

There are some grounds for optimism with the growth of ecological consciousness in the past decade. Consciousness of scientists and technologists has been raised by the environmental movement. Conversely, consciousness of the movement's potential constituencies has been raised *by* scientists and technologists, through the development of a "critical science."[3] But it is far more uncertain just how much this has offset existing intelligence within the scientific-technological and broader communities. The barriers to biospheric research noted in this chapter are only slightly reduced at the present time. Moreover, this history of unawareness of ecosystem impacts of sociocultural production imposes severe restrictions on contemporary impact research, as noted in Chapter VII. And the failure of current impact research and the environmental movement to overcome the pressures of the treadmill of production leaves environmental researchers vulnerable to a reestablishment of all barriers analyzed here.[4] Indeed, there is some suggestion that impact research in the U.S. under the National Environmental Policy Act distracts researchers and impedes the development of environmental knowledge. This, in turn, hampers the creation of social welfare consciousness based on new insights into environmental limits. The social impact assessment process analysed in Chapter VII clearly reflects this.[5]

Impediments to environmental consciousness described here, and related impediments to social welfare consciousness regarding bio-spheric uses in production, can only undermine future reforms of the treadmill of production, for consciousness is a necessary condition for reform.[6] Past development of awareness of environmental disorganiza-tion permitted the rise of the modern environmental movement, lead-ing to some technological reforms and greater support for some types of environmental research. Failure to overcome the pressures to re-main at this plateau of research and reform enhances the legitimacy of the treadmill and increases the risks of more serious ecological and concomitant social problems in the future.[7]

The major themes discussed below include: (1) the division of scientific labor and power; (2) the control of scientific missions; (3) the control of publication/communication access; and (4) direct eco-nomic and social coercion of scientists. All of these act to obscure the negative externalities of high-technology production.

The Division of Scientific Labor and Power

If the study of ecology stresses the unity of biosphere processes, the social organization of scientific study has historically progressed in the opposite direction—toward fragmentation. Scientific disciplines, whether practiced in universities, industry, or government, have in-creasingly carved out narrower ranges of problems for themselves, in part, it is claimed, because of the increased complexity of any single ciscipline.[8]

While many of these trends are inherent in modern conceptions of "science," it is nonetheless true that such trends have been supported and accelerated by a variety of interest groups, including those of high-technology industries. The tendency to specialize has been histor-ically reinforced by the allocation of material support, both research funding and the funding of industrial consultation. Both tend to flow to disciplinary specialists, especially those whose research has indus-trial applications. Indirect products of such disciplinary reinforcement include specialized curriculum development in universities, insuring a reproduction of scientists whose orientations are generally directed toward similar research.[9]

Such historical capital-state forces have ensured, then, that a dispro-portionate share of scientific support is geared towards the *internalities* of high-technology production. Chemistry and high-energy physics are examples. Conversely, far lower levels of funding have been available to disciplines with potential for managing the environmental externalities of production, disciplines such as biological sciences in general and bioecology in particular. And most of their funding has come through public, not industrial sources. Moreover, until recently, scientific teams were rarely assembled to evaluate both internal and external effects of given scientific innovations—even after, let alone before their introduction into technological production. Finally, even though any evaluations of environmental problems are inextricably tied to social and economic evaluations of technological impact, cooperative research between physical and biological scientists and social scientists has been minimal.[10]

There are fundamental differences in interests and skills between the "technological-production" and the "environmental-social impact" sciences. Conventional social models of "science" relate to the former type: the laboratory, precision of measurement, proof, and ready replicability—a model of greater certainty. Impact sciences are generally, and by definition, quite deviant: field research, tentative projections, qualitative measurement, and difficult replicability.[11] High-technology organizations persistently reinforce our identification of "real science" with the former, by their funding and advertising of the superiority of the "hard" sciences, the "precise" sciences, the "practical" sciences. Industrial fellowships for study typically are allocated to such fields, and formal industrial-academic interaction primarily occurs there.[12]

Moreover, there is an additional fundamental but rarely acknowledged difference between the two sets of sciences. For the technological-production group, there is a far more elaborated social division of labor, with scientists themselves required to conduct only the laboratory/bench top experimental stages of research. On rare occasions, their work extends to pilot system projects (as in nuclear reactors). The benefitting industrial organizations carry through all of the later stages of technological and economic evaluation, primarily with their own personnel and at their own expense. Thus a chemist synthesizing a new pesticide may have little responsibility beyond pilot testing on the particular target species.

But contrast this line of responsibility with those of impact scientists. Bioecologists, evaluating the impact of a new pesticide, have no such industrial organization for support. They must be, almost by definition, simultaneously scientists, applied scientists, and technologists. Similarly, economists evaluating economic losses from an introduction of such technology, through health threats or negative impacts on local marine resources, have no such organizational resource.[13] Such lack of routinized institutional support reinforces the general process of *externalizing* environmental (and social) problems arising from high-technology production. It is because the "nonproductive" portions of the environment are "nonproductive" (in the views of large-scale capital interests) that such institutional support is lacking. In short, such environmental evaluation remains exceedingly difficult for many of the same reasons that environmental problems have become so acute—domination of the economy by high-technology groups.

Thus, the issue of the division of labor extends not only within the scientific community, but between it and major social and economic institutions. Production sciences are given highest priority and funding, while impact sciences are lowest. Similarly, production researchers (even those from impact sciences) tend to maintain greater status than do impact researchers (even if trained in production sciences). This inequality in large part results from the dominance of high-technology producers. Team efforts in science addressing environmental impacts of technology are likely to be unbalanced, without heavy weighting of impact sciences to negate this historical inequality. In contrast, many reports of such study groups indicate that what emerges is the continuity of traditional scientific-production biases, rather than a more novel balance.[14]

The Control of Scientific "Missions"

Mission determination processes may stem from two sources: supply factors and demand factors. Supply factors involve the preexisting structure of scientific organization, creating a scientific establishment, with a set of largely disciplinary interest groups (including their professional associations). Demand factors emerge from contemporary definitions of social problems. Problems are defined by legislatures, the media, executive branches of governments (agencies), and various levels of both private and public "advisory groups." Inasmuch as owners and managers of high-technology capital influence these two sets of factors, they have influence over the direction of scientific research—or at least research requiring significant amounts of public or private sector funding. The previous subsection reviewed how the preexisting "stock" of scientists has been partly structured by the influence of such high-technology controllers, and it follows that this influence becomes translated here into supply factors partly shaping the direction of missions. These factors are reflected in the composition of advisory groups, such as those of the National Academy of Sciences. These groups frequently are asked to review and revise the programs of governmental agencies such as the National Science Foundation and the Environmental Protection Agency, which fund both production and impact research.[15] Social scientists in general (and sociologists in particular) are underrepresented within the NAS; but production scientists such as chemists and physicists are overrepresented. Such overrepresentation leads to obvious biases in determining missions by underconcern for impacts, or by pejorative ratings of the feasibility of impact research. Moreover, naivete regarding impact research sets impractical missions for the given funding levels— thereby perpetuating the model of production sciences as more "scientific" and "productive."[16]

Parallel patterns appear in demand factors that reflect high-technology producer controls. Congress, for example, must rely on the testimony of "experts" in assessing the importance of various technology-related problems, and in assessing how to manage such problems through scientific research. Experts are often the most prestigious scientists within the production sciences, since the "objectivity" of members of such scientific establishments as NAS is presumed helpful in this consultation process. This legislative acceptance of the importance, legitimacy, and objectivity of the production sciences is coupled with concomitant suspicion of and even hostility toward many of the impact sciences (especially the social sciences). Consider, for example, the recent and protracted hearings on energy policy in general, and nuclear power in particular, with the bulk of the experts drawn from production sciences. Attention has been focused on the more "logical" route of expanding energy supplies rather than the more environmentally sane one of the systematic reorganization of production and consumption to reduce energy consumption. The results are predictable: the programs of the major energy agencies are oriented toward production and hardware, not conservation. Treadmill biases persist despite the unprecedented volume of testimony by both production and impact scientific opponents of this imbalance. This testimony appeared largely through organizational pressures from environmental interest groups outside the established scientific hierarchy, e.g., Sierra Club and National Union of Concerned Scientists.[17]

These Congressional hearings are the most open, or socially visible, elements of the mission determining process in the public sector. Of the less visible elements of this decision making, the largest is the executive branch of the federal government, operating at levels from the Presidency, through the cabinet, and down to multiple levels of agencies. Many of the abstract and general "mandates" from Congress are implemented at these levels, and pressure from high-technology industries to influence the process rises accordingly. Since many of the agencies have insufficient in-house manpower to decide on mission priorities, they are frequently forced to turn to advisory groups from outside the government.[18] Such advisory groups are either constituted of unpaid participants, or of participants whose direct expenses are covered, but not their salaries. In other cases participants receive a nominal per diem fee plus expenses. These advisory groups often meet in closed sessions for protracted periods, requiring prolonged absences of scientific advisors from their normal employment. When this is coupled with minimal remuneration, only certain classes of scientists can afford the time and expense of participation. A typical university faculty member cannot arrange prolonged absences from teaching. But scientists on various large-scale research grants can often get away. The most secure form of time and expense reimbursement frequently comes from industrial high-technology enterprises, who can freely release *their* scientists for such "public interest" and "blue-ribbon" committee tasks.[19] Indeed, this pattern is even facilitated by corporate tax regulations, allowing the companies to recapture some salary allocation as tax-exemptions or tax credits. Organizations may be altruistic in releasing their senior scientists, but self-interest motives are also inherent in the process. Business influence over missions often leads to (a) reduced scientific scrutiny of production externalities and/or (b) increased public revenues for production internalities.[20] Thus, for example, an oil company releasing a top petroleum scientist or engineer anticipates that energy-research policies arising from participation will diminish environmentalist pressures and provide incentives for energy production.[21]

Finally, if we examine the nature of mission determination in the private sector—especially the largest foundations—we find similar overrepresentation of scientists and managers from high-technology enterprises. As one illustration, the Advisory Board for the Ford Foundation "Energy Policy Project" listed eight members from the high-technology (high-energy) production sector, out of a total of twenty-one, slightly under forty percent of the Board.[22] Conversely, two or at most three of the remaining thirteen were environmental activists (those from the Sierra Club and Lake Michigan Federation; and the lawyer, Joseph Sax). Among the regular project staff list, no biologist or sociologist appears (although several are included among the consultants). In the final report of this project, the discussion most involved with conservation (the "zero growth" model) represents only a modest form of energy conservation, and little industrial restructuring. As one apologia for the lack of more attention to energy-reduction strategies, the Advisory Board noted that:

> There can be no doubt that more emphasis should be given at the national level to conservation while work continues on development of energy supplies. However, much remains to be learned in planning for such activities. Experience in influencing energy use is very limited; until recently the emphasis has been almost wholly on growth, and basic studies of methods and implications are lacking. (Energy Policy Project, 1974:351)

One cynical interpretation of this message is that although the Board called for commitment to production action, it only went as far as research into conservation options.

The separate discussions of legislature, executive, and private sector evaluations of scientific missions may understate the interrelationships among such apparently disparate elements of decision making. Citations from hearings and reports are freely borrowed, as are some of the personnel themselves.[23] For energy missions, the emerging priority appears to be: (1) continued research on existing methods of energy production; (2) expanded research on alternative methods of energy production; and (3) research on social and economic means of stimulating some conservation action.[24]

The Controls of Publication/ Communication Access

Assume for a moment that a diligent production scientist has avoided the enticements and constraints of ready funding, avoided the blandishments of public agencies regarding the priorities for research, and chosen to engage his or her talents in detailing impact research. Further assume that his/her findings point to extreme environmental hazards of some particular chemical, and he/she must now communicate these findings. First, he/she must find a medium (a scientific journal) that will agree to review the article; second, he/she must face the peer review process; and third, he/she must find some means of rapid dissemination of the published information to a broad scientific and policy audience, beyond the journal's subscription list.

Scientific journals reflect the division of labor and power within the scientific community. Thus, a scientist whose work mixes skills of the production sciences with concerns of the impact sciences has been faced (especially in the past) with the absence of "acceptable" publication media. Such media have a status recognized by others in the same field, so that articles published there offer appropriate criteria for promotion and salary increases. Unfortunately, an inverse relationship often exists between such acceptability and the breadth of readership of journals—the most acceptable having the most narrow audience. And, the review process for acceptable journals often reaffirms the division of labor, so that reviewers reject manuscripts as "unimportant," "inappropriate," or "not scientific enough" by standards of the production sciences for a mixture of production/impact science.[25] Scientists are then faced with either revising their work or seeking an alternative publication source that may prove less acceptable. Still another dilemma may appear. Production scientists whose works contain impact findings of sufficient importance may jeopardize their credibility and that of their department as well, through the publication of their work. While many scientists may be willing to engage temporarily in impact studies, therefore, few are willing to risk their careers with prolonged involvement.

This kind of professional hazard is subtle, persistent, and paradoxical: The norms of production sciences for "scientifically" valid work eliminate the possibility of covering a wider range of impact studies. Conversely, heavy focus on impact studies exposes one to the repudiation by conventional science. And this case, the impact researcher must be one step ahead, by having the skills and knowledge of the production scientists to prevent their rejection of him. The dilemma has been poignantly illustrated by one of the scientific precursors of the contemporary environmental movement, Rachel Carson:

> The research, she discovered, was of highly sophisticated nature, dealing with much of the most recent work in biology and chemistry.... The material required all of skills of a trained scientist to evaluate, for little of it had as yet been interpreted for the public.... It was clear now in Rachel Carson's mind what her book would be. Using science as its base, it must nonetheless transcend those limited confines of the average scientist's mind which had pulled the world into its current morass.... She knew that her book must *persuade* as well as inform; it must synthesize scientific fact with the most profound sort of propaganda. She knew that she must be able to sway the professional scientist who often is afraid to stick his neck out unless it is for the simplest one-to-one relationship. (Graham, 1970:21–22)

This passage refers to *Silent Spring*, one of those rare examples of scientific work covering production and impact sciences, *and* attempting to reach a large lay audience. The difficulties that an established marine biologist like Carson faced, both in gathering information and piecing together the framework that emerged in the final book, are well documented by Graham. The economic, professional, and personal risks Carson faced in producing *Silent Spring* attest to the difficulties confronting a scientist who steps out of her narrow field of expertise to document negative environmental impacts and to ensure that this statement reaches many interest groups and a large lay public. The harsh treatment accorded the work, and the personal attacks on Carson's credibility can deter many impact-sensitive scientists from imitation. While many of these attacks were by scientists directly employed by the agricultural-chemicals industry, many more were from "objective" production scientists in universities, fearful of the economic consequences should such agrichemical industries and their research be undercut, and jealous of *their* predominance in the study of agricultural chemicals. Even those scientists offering some assistance to Carson, by giving her U.S. Department of Agriculture information about environmental hazards of agrichemicals, withdrew from overt support.[26]

Carson's work illustrates much of the preceeding analysis. First, note that Carson undertook no *new* empirical impact research, but relied on preexisting studies, drawn from a broad array of impact science journals. Second, the sensitizing effects of her work consisted precisely in the power of this synthesis. The original works had found their way into print over the decade prior to her project (1950–60), but their effectiveness in mobilizing public support was nullified by the lack of exposure of production scientists, of public sector decision-makers, and of interested individuals and groups within the U.S. The effectiveness of impact research was minimized, even when published in scientific media. Whatever the obstacles are to publication, it is but the first stage of communicating findings.

Carson and other impact scientists faced a far more formidable task in the period up until 1962 in communicating such findings, in what Frank Graham called "The McCarthy Era of the Conservation Movement" (1970:20), than has been true since. Among many other consequences of the so-called environmental movement, there has been a liberation of some constraints on the impact sciences—a movement to establish new journals, to have access to public sector decision-makers, to incorporate more production scientists in impact work. But as Graham documents, this opening is only a partial liberation. The resources to publish and disseminate information still rest mainly with the high-technology production sector, its managers, and its share of the scientific community.[27]

Consider two aspects of this difference. The costs of reprints of scientific reports have risen sharply, making their widespread circulation costly to scientists with little funding. Add to this the mailing costs, and a trivial expenditure becomes a major obstacle to disseminating information across a broad spectrum of scientists and agency decision-makers. If this is the ridiculous, then let us turn to the sublime. Few scientists have the resources to engage in a round of speeches to a variety of public and private sector decision-makers, nor do they tend to be invited to many such meetings. Yet production scientists, particularly those with direct sponsorship of major high-technology corporations, are often heavily funded for just such speech making, to disseminate the production rather than the impact aspect of a given technology. The variety of uses of the mass media by the agrichemical industries and their cooperative agents within the federal and state governments was made possible by the economic and political influence of high-technology producers.[28] In contrast, only a variety of serendipitous and circuitous routes drew Carson and other impact scientists to media attention.

The essential difference between the dissemination of information from production and from impact science is that the former has large and continuous support from industry, which in turn has the continuous attention of decision makers. Environmental reform groups rarely have impact science members who circulate between such groups and governmental or industrial enterprises; production scientists constantly engage in such circulation, ensuring a continuous openness to their research in those sectors. Resources for "public interest" advertising are limited in the extreme among impact scientists, even those in large-scale environmental reform groups as the Sierra Club or the national Union of Concerned Scientists.[29] In contrast, the high-technology industries spread the message of production sciences in advertisements in mass readership publications, scientific journals, and a variety of special interest magaaines. In addition, they help underwrite and disseminate an enormous range of production science "reports," often subject to no peer review. Generally, impact scientists at universities have fewer opportunities for preparing such well-funded reports through consultative relationships; they must survive economically through maintenance of professional status—requiring the more conservative peer review process.

If all of these imbalances in favor of dissemination of production science information fail, then more direct methods may be required. Graham cites two such approaches; in the first case, the general counsel of a major chemical firm threatened the publisher of *Silent Spring*, Houghton Mifflin, with a lawsuit if the book were published as written (1970:48–49). The second case was less overtly pressuring: chemical manufacturers allegedly threatened to withdraw advertising from magazines and journals that included favorable *reviews* of Carson's book (Graham, 1970:57–58). Evidently, both of these tactics failed—in the short run, at least. But if such corporate approaches are always latent threats, then monopoly capital can always exert pressure on a variety of journals (including medical journals) that rely heavily on advertising revenues from this same group of high-technology producer organizations.[30]

These illustrations come from the case of Carson's inquiry into the agrichemical industry and its environmental effects, but many others exist. The most prominent are the nuclear industry's efforts to contain impact scientific studies showing the hazards of radiation—in particular the *cause célèbre* of Gofman and Tamplin of the Lawrence Radiation Laboratory and the history of suppression and repudiation of air pollution and health hazard findings about automobile exhausts. We can only assume that such suppression is commonplace, since coverage has been limited.[31]

Direct Social and Economic Coercion of Scientists

We may speculate whether Rachel Carson could have written *Silent Spring* as she did, had she occupied some other role in the scientific labor market. When she did most of her work, Carson was partly self-supported by royalties from *The Sea Around Us* and *The Edge of the Sea*, books that combined scientific research findings with a fine literary style. During the almost five years preceeding the publication of *Silent Spring*, Carson lived on these resources, supplemented by part-time teaching in a local college. Moreover, her social network then included scientists in universities and government service, with friendships and professional associations acquired by her earlier employment in the U.S. Fish and Wildlife Service. This network was based on her reputation both as a competent marine biologist and as a popular writer.

This dual economic and social support is rare for most contemporary scientists, however. Even those production and impact scientists in the universities, supposedly more removed from mundane constraints, are in fact hampered by such limitations. Carson was able to withstand both the blandishments and threats of the agricultural chemicals industry and its governmental and university supporters precisely because she had this rare support. But most scientists today are scientific laborers, and the expansion of this labor pool means vulnerability to a variety of direct and indirect economic threats.[32]

Thus scientists need employment for survival and a "good reputation" for employment, whether they are researchers in universities, or in industrial and governmental posts. Constraints are greatest for industrial scientists, whose professional interests are necessarily tightly intertwined with the economic interests of their employers. Public statements about the negative production externalities of their employers' product are grounds for instant dismissal, and possible blackballing for future employment, at least in the same industrial sectors (and since capital owners may operate over a variety of sectors, in many others as well). Even surreptitious impact research is difficult, since it frequently involves using corporate equipment and is difficult to disguise. While the hardy few may become "whistle-blowers" and provide minor contributions to activist organizations like Ralph Nader's, their efforts are less effective than well-documented and publicized impact research. Unfortunately, even the rarity of such deviance allows corporate representatives to question the motives and hence the credibility of the scientists. This was a major strategy in General Electric's handling of the resignations of three of its nuclear engineers.[33]

Graham's account of the secret communications between Carson and her colleagues in government posts indicate how risky it is for such scientists even to communicate findings of other scientists, information which is often buried in internal governmental reports. John Hightower and the Pound Committee (Wade, 1973), for example, documented the historical failure of Agricultural Research Service scientists to systematically analyze the social and environment impact of the industrialization of agriculture in the United States. Although in theory this analysis fell within their mission, the combined efforts of agribusiness and its governmental supporters (many of them engaged in a rotation of posts from industry to government) precluded such ongoing ARS research. Dismissal, demotion, and sustained attacks on "scientific integrity" help maintain such structured ignorance. The dismissal and harassment of Arthur Tamplin and John Gofman for their critiques of Atomic Energy Commission estimates of radiation hazards (Boffey, 1970) is one clear example of the risks that discourage other dissenters in the impact sciences. Ironically, some of these cases even enhance the controls of the industrial sector, since such scientists often move to a public, nonscientific forum, opening them the charge of being "nonscientific."[34]

The final group of scientists are those engaged in university research, or in research for private agencies accepting contracts and grants for research. A variety of social and economic forces act even on this structurally liberated group. First, most of these scientists are constantly concerned with their professional reputations, and this concern acts as a brake on "unfavorable" interpretations of ambiguous data. It also inhibits their willingness to seek out research areas where such ambiguities are likely outcomes of the research—thus diminishing their participation in a wide variety of impact studies.

Such concerns for professional reputations arise from the social and economic matrix in which research scientists operate. The flow of grants, consultantships, and the like are in part contingent on the reputation of the individuals (and/or their work groups). In turn, such grants and outside professional activities reinforce the professional status of a scientist, particularly a production scientist. For a scientist who errs on the side of helping implement a technology with large negative externalitites, the resulting risk to reputation may be offset by direct and indirect material and status rewards from the production sector. But the scientist who errs (or is labelled as erring) in anticipating too large a negative impact of technology has no such back-up, except perhaps from some of the environmental action organizations, with only modest budgets and status-conferring powers. He or she may fall back on earlier work as a foundation for rebuilding a reputation, but his or her ability to garner large research grants, positions on scientific committees evaluating research missions, or governmental consultantships may be irreparably crippled. While alternative economic support may be found in teaching or academic administration, his or her role as a *research* scientist is injured by the reputation of "irresponsibility." Moreover, corporations with substantial contributions to particular academic institutions (both institutional grants and research block grants) sometimes threaten to withdraw support if such scientists are allowed to continue as principle investigators on major projects.

Thus, as Rachel Carson noted, scientists are generally unwilling to "stick their neck out." The system is self-enforcing, in that reputations are established more on the basis of the classical norms of "hard science," and these reputations allow production scientist to dominate the scientific hierarchy. However limited the direct role of the monopoly capital sector is in acting upon the individual scientist, the perception of such risks lead most to avoid ambiguous impact work. Moreover, while events over the last decade may have increased the legitimacy and support of impact research, even by production sciences, it has often led to the application of classical "scientific" evidentiary models for such impact work. This means that impacts considered are often more narrowly defined, thus constraining the range of impact research.[35]

OBSTACLES TO ENVIRONMENTAL RESEARCH BY TECHNOLOGISTS

Differences between Technologists and Scientists

The prototypical "technologist" is an engineer, employed at a university, a government agency, or (especially) an industrial organization. Layton's work (1971) on the engineering profession documents one of its most important characteristics: its lack of independence from owner-managers of production. While it is true that many engineers are employed in the publc sector (in public works), it is the *political* control in that sector that dominates engineering decision-making. Moreover, while the newer label that some academic engineers have sought—applied science—is in part an attempt to raise the status of the profession by affiliating it more closely with the supposedly autonomous enterprise of "science," the other portion of even this freely-chosen label—applied—belies autonomy.[36] If the economic and political control over scientists discussed above do exist, then it follows that all of the constraints on scientific autonomy and effectiveness in impact evaluation apply even more directly to engineers.

Consider for a moment the inherent logic of an "applied" science. If the symbol of production sciences is the laboratory, the corresponding symbol for engineers is the pilot plant. While the term *pilot* suggests relatively low levels of capital requirements, the term *plant* ties engineering research far more closely to the operations of production. Indeed, the whole history of the engineering profession is geared to a practical, operational approach to issues, an approach virtually inseparable from the logic of production enterprises themselves. While scientists may operate in substantial ignorance of the details of existing technological-production organizations, it is virtually inconceivable for engineers to do so. For engineers, the goal of their professional activities is the application of technology in production; their knowledge base is intimately tied to the history of such applications, and their counsel is sought largely for extension of such applications. This is a double-edged sword, of course, in that engineers have greater influence over decision making in the production sector, but are also in turn far more dependent on this sector for their daily professional activities. While engineers stress the former attribute, for our purposes it is more important to acknowledge the latter one, to appreciate the obstacles to technologists' influence. In addition to the four factors controlling the actions of scientists, then, this section considers the peculiar features of monopoly-capital controls over technological research.

First let us distinguish between "production engineering" and "impact engineering." Production engineering dominates the engineering profession even more than does production science, but there do exist some impact engineering disciplines as well. Historically, the most significant of these is sanitary engineering, the branch most concerned with the disposal of and treatment of social wastes. It is no accident that this area is one of the bases of the newer branch of environmental engineering. Nor is it sheer coincidence that sanitary engineers have been almost exclusively employed in the public sector and in universities, since by definition this branch has dealt with the externalities of production (and consumption). While the sanitary engineer historically dealt with water systems primarily, the modern environmental engineer also deals with air and land systems, and principally with the problem of pollution of these systems. For other environmental problems, there is no distinctive branch of engineering that has been established, and research on these problems falls within the province of production engineers: chemical, civil, electrical, mechanical, and the newer hybrid branches, nuclear and petroleum. While environmental engineers are frequently well-trained in the impact sciences, especially the biological ones, relatively few of the production branches are so trained (with the possible exception of some nuclear engineering programs). Conversely, virtually all branches of engineering include substantial preparation in the production sciences (especially physics and chemistry). Thus, production engineering and production science backgrounds are predominant in the engineering field, producing biases against socioenvironmental analysis that are even larger than those of the sciences (Cousteau, 1976).

Such predispositions are reinforced by a number of social and economic controls exerted directly or indirectly by high-technology production organizations. These include: (1) control over access to data, (2) control over consultantships, (3) the ideology of "feasibility," and (4) the nontransferability of skills across industrial sectors. Each of these will be briefly discussed as factors that control "technological reform" through the inactivity of technologists, over and above the four types of controls noted in the previous section for scientists.

Control Over Access to Data

For technological impact research, production details must be much more elaborated than for scientific impact projects. Consider the case of automobile emissions. Biochemists, medical researchers, biologists, and the like require little information about the nature of the production and operation of the internal combustion engine. They must be able to obtain data on *emissions* from vehicles, but these are accessible through such means as field-testing autos. For an engineer to do research linking the alternative modes of engine design, fuel mixtures, and vehicle construction to issues of emission control, an intimate knowledge of the problems of manufacturing and vehicle operation is imperative.[37] The crucial nature of this link stems from the mission of engineers as innovators in "feasible" technologies, requiring a knowledge of current and prospective production alternatives. Engineers in such research would have to know the theoretical estimates and models used by producer organizations to estimate emissions, the production problems that might inhibit the achievement of these theoretical levels of emissions, the range of alternatives that have been considered by producer organizations, and the reasons for their rejection. All of this would be essential to a project that would aim at technological reforms of the automobile. For transportation engineers, other projects might stress alternatives to the automobile for reasons of energy conservation and/or air pollution control—and these might require less information on the production aspects of automobiles. But such transportation research would require equal depth of information about mass transit systems, including data on the engineering parameters of equipment manufacturing, as well as systems operation parameters. An even more striking example of such production information requirement is the case of environmental engineers seeking technological reforms in power plant operations, where the detailed engineering features of specific types of equipment—both theoretical and operational features—would be essential to controlling air pollution, water pollution, thermal emissions, and radioactive emissions from normal operations and waste generation (in the case of nuclear power plants).[38]

It is precisely in cases like these that inside information is crucial for "responsible" engineering researchers who seek workable reforms of technology. But the production sector has enormous potential for denying precisely this level of access to "privileged" or "proprietary" corporate information. Note that this is not a case of structured ignorance internal to the production organization, but rather a denial of access to outsiders.

This denial may operate on two levels: individual and categorical. In the first case, the organization involved denies the "competence" of the researcher and the "adequacy" of the research project, because of the "biased" aspects of both. Researchers with a history of work critical of high-technology production organizations are locked out, precisely because of this past research. Arguments are made about the technical competence of such researchers, based on the prior "biased," "sloppy," "imprecise," and "hasty" judgments inherent in the earlier research. Such arguments frequently conclude with testimonials that "we are doing our own work in this area, and have no need of outside help," citing the technical qualifications of their own staff. The electrical industries are typical of such responses, citing their own research through the Edison Electric Institute, and noting the millions of dollars expended in past and current projects aimed at air or thermal pollution.

Typically, such arguments cannot be readily refuted by outsider researchers since they are not privy to the internal accounts of such organizations, nor to the internal research reports. Moreover, even when such reports are produced, it becomes difficult for the outsider to judge the quality of the internal research itself. Such judgment requires prior knowledge of the plant operations in order to make such judgments.

While individual external researchers may protest about the quantity and quality of such internal research, target corporations/industries can usually minimize such pressures. This pattern provides structural dilemmas for research engineers seeking production data for impact research: any given piece of work that leads to conclusions critical of the organization/industry becomes the basis for denial of future access from at least these organizations. Thus continuity of technological research is inhibited, at least within a given sphere of production operations. Researchers can make two responses in the face of these risks: (1) they can either remove themselves from serious impact research and/or (2) they may write up findings from a given piece of impact research in the most benign and obscure form possible, giving little cause for corporate repudiation.

The second form of denial of access is categorical, rather than individual. Here a whole class of researchers is denied access, for many of the same proprietary arguments. The class may include researchers who have been funded under a given environmental research program (governmental or foundation), or who are defined as having "no experience in production problems"—i.e., those without formal affiliations to the industry involved. Many of these responses have existed for some period in the nuclear power industry, perpetuating a system where those with the strongest stakes in benign impact evaluations are permitted to do much of the evaluation research.[39] The process was best exemplified by the structure of the Atomic Energy Commission itself, which served both as advocate of nuclear power and as evaluator of nuclear plant safety. While outside researchers were funded for some types of laboratory research, the detailed evaluation of the complex reactor systems rested within the utilities and equipment suppliers. None of this necessarily proves the poor quality of internal engineering research; but it does raise difficulties for external researchers in evaluating the quality. Recent restructuring of the Commission (now the Nuclear Regulatory Commission), to remove the safety evaluation apparatus entirely from it, has validated the conflict of interest charge that many impact researchers had made for many years.[40]

Access to operational data is also often categorically denied. Reinemer (1970) has noted that despite federal legislation in the late 1960s requiring industrial reporting of waste discharges in considerable detail, no such data were gathered for at least five years. This omission was achieved by the simple mechanism of having advisory committees to the Bureau of the Budget (now the Office of Management and the Budget) primarily composed of industrial representatives. They consistently advised the Bureau that such data-gathering violated proprietary rights. Since even such advisory meetings were usually held in secret, concerned scientists and engineers had no means of recognizing where the delays in reporting were caused. Successful efforts at making such advisory committee meetings open to "the public" have at least pinpointed the difficulties. Unfortunately, they have not necessarily provided access to information, because of the disproportionate influence of high-technology producers in the executive branch of the U.S. Government. Even researchers carrying out research mandated by law can be effectively restrained. And ultimately governmental agencies are restrained by their own lack of inside information to evaluate the validity of producer organization claims of risk. The long history of information denial about air pollution by automobile emission attests to the power of such organizations (Esposito, 1970).

The value of this form of data control by producer organizations is twofold: (1) it permits them to defer external pressures for reform by citing internal research, and (2) it induces outside researchers to be excessively cautious in their interpretations of research, when they have been given access to data. Both of these clearly inhibit strong pressures for reform of technology in these organizations.

The Control of Consultantships

The conceptualization of an applied science entails some organizational linkages between university professionals and industrial appliers of technology. It likewise incorporates the circulation of engineers between government and industrial positions. In both cases, there are benefits for both sending and receiving agencies: universities seek out such contacts to provide opportunities to place their graduates and to receive research funding. And government agencies are very willing to hire engineers with industrial experience because of the practical knowledge they bring to government service, as well as some of the technical (and other) contacts they may have in industries— particularly those the agency is regulating. While both of these are important in the control of engineering research, I will discuss primarily the university flow in this section, since this is where the bulk of nonindustrial engineering research is conducted in the United States.

For schools and departments of applied science, the interaction with producer organizations is deemed a necessity. Knowledge of the state of the art can frequently be gathered only in producer settings, faculty and student research often requires cooperative industrial efforts, and much funding for ongoing research and student aid flows from these organizations. Moreover, unlike the case in many other university departments, faculty are often drawn, on a part-time basis especially, from the ranks of industrial engineers. In a very real sense, the industrial setting is both an extension of the classroom and a research site. Indeed, the lines between university and industry are often blurred when applied university research laboratories are established with industrial funding, sometimes on industrial sites, and with both industrial and university personnel engaged in research and development (Graham, 1970:58–59).

While historically this structure has produced very rapid advancement of the state of technological development, and an equally rapid dissemination of technology to students, it carries a risk with it. One recent example is the case of the Massachusetts Institute of Technology Energy Laboratory, where research on methanol additives to gasoline to power internal combustion engines appears to have been cut short by the intervention of industrial (automobile and oil) representatives to the laboratory. Similar instances have emerged in many other areas of environmental research, including nuclear power and automobile emissions, and for many of the same reasons: conflicting perspectives of industrial and academic researchers.[41]

In addition to data control and the reduction or elimination of industrial funding of such enterprises, industrial representatives may also strongly object to the participation of particular engineering personnel. Such objections generally are phrased in terms of incompetence or bias in the offending researchers—but the truth is often that these researchers merely seek to document some discomforting technological effects. The effects of such objections are threefold: (1) they neutralize particular engineering researchers and the lines of research they are following; (2) they inhibit other colleagues from pursuing such lines of inquiry, for fear of funding cut-offs or damage to reputations; and (3) they increase academic institutional pressures on engineering "dissidents" to alter their research, lower their professional voices, and discourage their students from embarking on certain lines of research. Since academic institutions training engineers are often dependent on both industrial aid and industrial lobbying for particular lines of research support from governmental agencies (Gillette, 1973c), the threat of industrial opposition entails institutional as well as individual risks. This is particularly true where there are several schools of engineering in a small region, allowing for competition between these schools for research, consultations and other support. As we will note later, the more specialized the training in engineering subdisciplines, the more dependent these departments may be on continued support from industries in the area. The regional constraints arise because faculty often consult and teach in the same periods of the academic year, and prefer consultations close by. Moreover, students are often even more constrained to gain practical experience and/or to carry out cooperative research near where they live.

Thus a repudiation of a particular scientist may jeopardize his/her colleagues in research, and even the financial stability of the university's training program. All of these pressures serve to inhibit researchers or research groups from emphasizing negative impacts and from beginning impact research. Since the complexity of modern technology has increased so substantially, this pressure places serious limits on impact research requiring access to production data.[42]

The Ideology of "Feasibility"

In the previous discussion of the constraints on impact engineering studies, the issue of the practicality of technological reform has emerged several times. Engineers, unlike scientists, are presumed (and trained) to be practical—to deal with the *feasible*, not the ideal. This is part of their essence as applied scientists. But "feasibility" is in large measure a social construction, not a scientific fact. Thus engineering studies of technology that propose reforms must address issues often well beyond their professional scope. For example, an engineer who argues that power plants should require stack scrubbers to reduce air pollution must be able to document (a) that such scrubbers exist, (b) that their on-production-line performance is reliable, and (c) that they are not "excessively costly." It is not sufficient to argue that current power generation processes create substantial particulate emissions— but that alternative processes are feasible according to these three criteria. Feasibility is itself defined by the production organization whose processes are studied—and the limits of feasibility are subject to considerable flux. Ten years ago it was rather more difficult for a "responsible" engineer to argue that stack gas scrubbers were feasible, since the utility industries had failed to invest much capital in this type of control equipment. This neglect allowed corporate technologists nad managers to argue that reform was "infeasibile"—and ignore the self-fulfilling aspect of their argument. What was infeasible in 1965 turned out, for a variety of reasons (including legislative and litigative ones) to be more feasible by 1970 and quite feasible by 1975. While some might argue that the changes arose from altered technological possibilities, this merely raises the question of how such possibilities became altered (Dickson, 1975). And any serious analysis of this transition would indicate the role of external pressures (from organized environmental groups, government agencies, legislatures, etc.), and a concomitant flow of capital to produce more reliable emission control equipment. The history of automobile emission controls documents this extratechnological dimension quite well (Esposito, 1970).

In one sense, the challenge of feasibility requires impact engineers to double as production engineers, also doubling (at least) their burden. Because of the difficulties of access, funding, and continuity of good relationships with production industries, engineers are often driven away from impact research. And even when they are not, the challenge of feasibility imposes a need to make suggestions for minimal technological reforms, dealing only with the narrowest impact-control solution at hand. Thus the "revolutionary" catalytic converter to control automobile emissions ignores many other air pollution (and energy depletion) problems intrinsic to the internal combustion engine, problems engineers have known about for some time (Salpukas, 1975). And it took many years to induce even this change in automobile design, because of the supposed "infeasibility" of introducing the converter (Esposito, 1970). Such minimalist approaches to "solutions" of technological problems arise precisely because the impact researcher generally lacks resources for both impact and production research, and thus scales down the latter (and often the former, to make the reform appear to fit the problematic impact even better). Conversely, such minimalist research fits the material interests of producers, since it requires minimal investment of capital to alter production processes. The case of automobile emission controls is an interesting example. Emission controls were the central focus for many years, yielding in turn (and in part) to concerns of energy conservation. Yet is is generally true that engines and auto designs that produce better mileage (lower energy consumption per mile) also produce lower emissions per mile travelled, since such emissions are directly related to the volume of combustion per mile. While it might appear that manufacturers in fact wasted considerable capital in single-mindedly pursuing a limited emission control strategy, they also *saved* substantial amounts by delaying research and development on more efficient engines and smaller vehicles (reliant on very old technologies), avoiding capital expenditures as long as politically and economically possible.

The strategic use, by owners and managers of the high-technology production, of the label of infeasibility, has serious implications for the volume and content of impact research: It restricts (1) the numbers of engineering researchers, (2) the range of impacts they address, and (3) the production reforms they seek. Ironically, the resulting forms of research often represent hidden subsidies for producers, since external *impact* researchers (often with governmental funding) create *production* research and development for the affected industries. This is another way capitalists are able to externalize the costs of production problems, to the society at large and taxpayers in particular. At minimum, the ideology of feasibility seriously retards comprehensive engineering evaluations of technological impacts.

The Nontransferability of Specialized Engineering Skills

Consider for a moment the professional differences between an organic chemist and a petroleum engineer. The former may choose to work on production issues, including development of a range of chemicals from petroleum/oil. But many of the technical skills developed are equally applicable to a diverse range of other production research, as well as impact research. And so, the dependence of such a scientist on any particular industrial sector may be quite limited—although he or she may still be dependent on the good will, funding, and consultation with the high-technology production sector in general. In contrast, the highly trained petroleum engineer is restricted, by virtue of training and experience, to a single, large, and important industrial sector: the oil industry. While he or she may move between corporations, his/her orbit is primarily within the one technological sphere. Thus, given the close contacts between corporations in the one sphere of production, he/she is highly vulnerable to accusations of disloyalty or incompetence, by any single employer or consultant. The extreme specialization that permits the "fine tuning" of professional engineers makes them extremely valuable to the single industrial sector, but also makes them equally vulnerable to pressures from sector representatives. And this is true of similarly specialized university and government departments, too. Ill-will generated by one of their members makes the whole department vulnerable to funding and access constraints (Gillette, 1975d).

Insofar as university schools of engineering offer greater specialization of training, therefore, they are increasingly vulnerable to industrial control of research agendas. Thus, as recently illustrated by the difficulty experienced by the U.S. Geological Survey in obtaining "independent" (and presumably objective) estimates of oil reserves of various types, it is virtually impossible to carry out research by recruiting petroleum engineers with *no* ties to the oil industry.[43] Indeed, such a search points out the inherent paradox, inasmuch as petroleum engineers must by definition have some training or experience with the oil industries throughout the world. A similar situation prevails for nuclear engineers, but with some important differences. Experience and training may occur in either the private sector (with nuclear equipment manufacturers and/or power companies), or with government agencies that themselves operate a limited range of nuclear reactors. While there is convergence in many societies (like the United States) between public and private sector operations of nuclear reactors, there are at least some empirical and potential differences between the social and economic restraints in the public and private sectors. And this means greater independence for some nuclear engineers than for petroleum engineers. An interesting consequence is the much livelier conflict over the future of nuclear power than over the nature of oil reserves and the oil-based U.S. production system. While the latter has drawn many nonexperts into debate, it is noteworthy how few engineers and petroleum geologists have appeared on the "public interest" side of the debate over oil reserves and oil utilization induced by the "energy-crisis".[44]

While even these engineering professionals could find *some* forms of employment in other areas because of their generalized engineering training/experience, the move would probably involve substantial status and income losses. And specialized departments have even fewer degrees of freedom, inasmuch as their *raison d'être* is intimately intertwined with the corresponding industry. Ironically, it may be only the very young or the very old within these professional orbits that have somewhat greater autonomy: the young because they may be freer of commitments immediately after their training, and the old because their livelihoods no longer depend on such cooperative activity. But these represent a tiny minority of the professional engineers, and one that lacks credibility (in the case of the young), or one that may be dismissed as senile or "outmoded" (in the case of the old).

The paradox here, as in the other types of controls, is that those who may be most knowledgeable about the state of the art and prospects for change are the most entrapped in the industrial sphere they can observe. Extensive distinctions in training and work of modern hybrid engineers has maximized not only their productivity, but also their dependency and society's vulnerability. In one sense, this is parallel to the ecological maxim that production maximization is often achieved at the cost of ecosystem vulnerability. While such risks exist in the scientific as well as the technological enterprise, the latter represents the last buffer between a lay society and the managers or owners of production; when it fails, the potential for orderly technological change disappears.[45]

FROM PRODUCTION TO IMPACT RESEARCH?

Future Balances and Imbalances

The four engineering constraints, when added to the four discussed in the scientific arena, help to explain why such a small proportion of technological research has focused on melioration of environmental impacts of production. Industrial apologists point to the massive sums expended on research and development (R & D) along these lines, but these remain trivial compared to R & D aimed at expanding the hegemony of producers, regardless of the environmental (or social) impact. Boulding (1965) and Barnet and Müller (1974) have argued that the growth of knowledge is the most important dimension of the later industrial revolution. Such knowledge has reinforced the existing controls by high-technology producers, and has led to little melioration of environmental externalities of such production. The combination of incentives for narrower production-oriented research, and the disincentives for straying toward serious impact analysis are subtle, but crucial.[46]

Exhortations from environmental activists will achieve relatively little until the treadmill's incentives and disincentives have been altered. The role of the state is increasing in this regard, partly in response to calls from critical scientists.[47] New agencies within the state, such as the Congressional Office of Technology Assessment and the White House Office of Science and Technology Policy, help legitimate some of this criticism (e.g., Metz, 1978). On the other hand, recent doubts about the effectiveness of both environmental legislation and the associated agencies force a more cautious reading of these changes.[48]

To these doubts we must add some reservations about the professional and scholarly conflicts in scientific and technological communities (Nelkin, 1977b). Natural scientists and technologists have been called upon to make, or to legitimate, social and economic policy for the utilization of natural resources. Implicit in this role has been a "social impact assessment" of such resource use in the sociocultural production systems. Chapter VII explores the underlying biases of such assessment, whether performed by untrained natural scientists or by technical economists. Conflicts about both environmental and social welfare impacts of production are likely to intensify, as more assessment is done under existing legislation. Nelkin (1975:54) points to one likely consciousness-raising effect of such conflict:

> The influence of experts is based on public trust in the infallibility of expertise. Ironically, the increasing participation of scientists in political life may reduce their effectiveness, for the conflict among scientists . . . in controversial policies highlights their fallibility, demystifies their special expertise and calls attention to non-technical and political assumptions that influence technical advice.

This aura of infallibility, of the technical nature of production decisions, reinforces the existing treadmill of production. While the scientific community may lose prestige, social gains from an increasing awareness of other social and political choices may far outweigh these losses, for the fallibility of environmental science is matched by the fallibility of the social benefit-cost models that undergird the treadmill. That fallibility is documented in the next chapter.

NOTES

1. In the abstract, this is treated in Boulding (1965). Broad but more concrete analyses are in Dickson (1975), Landes (1969), and Barnet & Müller (1974).

2. LaPorte & Methay (1975) report findings of a large California survey, where "science" is far more highly evaluated than "technology," both among mass publics and the better-educated "potential public." This differential evaluation is consistent with the analysis here. I argue that "technologists" are far more subject to constraints by monopoly capitalists, whose profit-maximization is not directly tied to direct surplus extraction from labor but from capital investments. In the California survey, in contrast, respondents felt that "technology" ought to have as its primary goal employment expansion. Their judgment points to the social and economic externalities of technology (Schnaiberg, 1975), while this chapter focuses on environmental externalities.

3. The concept of "critical science" is taken from Ravetz (1971), in contrast to what he calls "industrialized science." In this chapter, the former is called *impact science*, the latter, *production science*. Nelkin (1977b) indicates the increased social consciousness of impact scientists (professional ecologists) as a result of the environmental movement and the passage of the National Environmental Policy Act (NEPA).

4. The attempt to evaluate all government regulation, including environmental regulation, on a benefit-cost basis (Walsh, 1978:598), is affirmation of the principles of treadmill organization and the ascendance of the technical and efficiency models over broader political views of environmental issues. To date, the mobilization of agencies and movement constituencies has offset some of this pressure (Carter, 1978), but the threats remain. The relationship between regulators and

environmental scientists produces a double bind, according to James Pitts, Jr., an air pollution researcher: "If you don't have an air quality standard defined for a pollutant, there's no money to go out and really make the measurements you have to make to get the standard. . . . If you don't have a standard, you can't measure it; and you can't measure it until you have a regulation" (Marshall, 1978:950).

5. See Fairfax (1978) on the charge against NEPA, also partly echoed in Nelkin's (1977b) assessment of the disillusionment of scholarly ecologists with the quick-and-dirty approach to environmental impact research under NEPA. The Environmental Protection Agency is attempting to learn from the organizational and political problems of administering NEPA in administering the new Toxic Substances Control Act of 1976. But the lack of definitive research and the multiplicity of interpretations of research in carcinogenicity and toxicity of chemicals make for an uncertain procedure (e.g., Epstein, 1978; Maugh, 1978a,b; Smith, 1978a,b). McBride et al. (1978) and Metz (1978) indicate the substantial environmental impact uncertainties of energy policies, given the lack of past research, as does the fundamental research of McLean (1978) on effects of carbon dioxide on climate and on food chains.

6. Uncertainty about biospheric impacts of sociocultural production, arising from the constraints noted in this chapter, make it feasible for treadmill proponents to draw on their own array of scientific and technological expertise to confound policy makers and the public (Mazur, 1973; Nelkin, 1977b). Such adversarial models, while they are often necessary, leave impact scientists especially vulnerable, since the discreditation of "science" (Mazur, 1973) affects basic impact scientists more than production scientists. For, as I argue later, the latter group have a firmer base under monopoly capital pressure for technological innovation based in part on scientific research.

7. A useful treatment of the obscuring of air pollution consciousness is in Crenson (1971).

8. On the broad shifts in science, see Mumford (1970:123–27, 181 ff.) and Leo Marx (1970).

9. Treatment of some of these issues is in Gershinowitz (1972) and Pitzer (1971).

10. On the timing issue of research, see Eipper (1970). Discussion of the paucity of cooperative research is indicated in Hammond (1975a), Baram (1971, 1973), and Metz (1978). Under NEPA and the Toxic Substances Control Act, social and economic research is mandatory, since a balancing of benefits and costs is required (Carter, 1978; Walsh, 1978). Chapter VII treats this issue at length.

11. This difference is noted in Carpenter (1976) and Nelkin (1977b).

12. See Roy (1972) for a plea for greater interaction, one that exemplifies much of the ideology of the treadmill.

13. The social scientific interest in "social indicators" has similar problems. Many of the *available* indicators do not tap important "negative externalities" of production, since both the externalities and the systematic scientific recording of them are subject to monopoly-capital control (e.g., Reinemer, 1970; Wade, 1973, 1975). This becomes clear when researchers attempt to quantify environmental hazards (e.g., Lave & Seskin, 1970).

14. Examples of this continuity include Gillette (1971, 1972f), Carter (1975,

1978), Shapley (1973a), Wade (1971, 1973, 1975), Epstein (1978) and Metz (1978).

15. Boffey (1975a) and Carter (1974a) indicate this condition for these agencies, and Metz (1978) reports on similar situations in the new Department of Energy, which draws more heavily on industries and its own production-oriented sites for research than do other federal agencies.

16. Gillette (1974a,c) discusses these contrasts for nuclear energy analyses. Duncan (1978) indicates that earlier social science critiques of nuclear energy policy were disregarded in the 1950s and 1960s.

17. On the hardware-orientation, see summaries in Boffey (1975c), and later ERDA revisions in Metz (1975). Participation in hearings is described in Gillette (1975a). Problems of energy policy persist in the ERDA successor: the Department of Energy (Metz, 1978).

18. Reinemer (1970) notes the closed-meeting period in the Bureau of the Budget (now the Office of Management and Budget). In recent years, there has been a trend to open meetings, as in EPA regulation of toxic substances. However, one result of this, as seen by a representative of the Environmental Defense Fund, is that "EPA seems to be taking a head-count of the industry and environmental representatives to resolve the issue, and the tally was usually 50 to 3" (Walsh, 1978:601). Environmentalists complain about EPA's "role of neutral arbitrator," while industry representatives saw it as an "advocate" (Walsh, 1978:601).

19. Discussions of this are in Reinemer (1970) and Gillette (1975c,g).

20. Instances of these phenomena are reported in Shapley (1973a,b) and Gillette (1973c).

21. Examples of this flexibility are Shapley (1975), Gillette (1973c; 1975a,c,g) and Hammond (1974a).

22. This is reported in Energy Policy Project (1974:347–48).

23. On this interchange between industrial and state views, see Carter (1974c), Hammond (1974b), and Gillette (1973c, 1975a).

24. There have been some recent shifts towards greater support of conservation research and some action (e.g., Metz, 1975, 1978) for energy missions. These arise, in part, from increased adversarial scientific activities within the federal government, particularly the Congressional Office of Technology Assessment (Boffey, 1975c) and the Environmental Protection Agency (Gillette 1974e). An interesting parallel exists in the area of research into cancer, where the production science model of viral influences has been at least partly replaced by the impact science model of environmental causation (Carter, 1974a; Gillette, 1974d; Epstein, 1978). This latter model poses a much greater potential threat to monopoly capital manufacturing industries, whose products and processes are increasingly emerging as causal agents (Epstein, 1978).

25. A strong attack is made in Stokinger (1971), which reflects some of the reactions of scholarly ecologists (Nelkin, 1977b) to policy research sloppiness. Wade (1972b) traces the case of diethylstilbesterone (DES), where delays in regulation were caused by the lack of "highly definitive" studies.

26. Graham (1970: Ch. 3, 4) discusses these scientists' reactions.

27. The treatment of publishing problems of Carson versus the agrichemical industry is in Graham (1970: Ch. 4,5).

28. For example, the Manufacturing Chemists Association mailed out *100,000* "fact kits," many to medical personnel (Graham, 1970:58–59). Monsanto distributed some 5000 parodies of Carson's work (entitled "The Desolate Year") to media representatives (Graham, 1970:64–65). Legitimation of many of these "facts" was provided by The Nutrition Foundation, an organization heavily dominated by consultants to the agribusiness industry (Graham, 1970:58–59).

29. Holden (1975) discusses some of these fiscal limitations; see also Ch. VIII.

30. The *AMA News*, a journal heavily subsidized by revenues from chemical industry advertising, suggested to its readers that they contact the MCA (Manufacturing Chemists Association) and other *trade associations* for "the facts" to reassure their patients. That this is standard practice for pharmaceutical information only reinforces our sense of the capture of such "impact sciences" by monopoly capital.

31. On the Gofman-Tamplin charges and rebuttals, see Boffey (1970) and Gillette (1971a,b,c,d,e). Some positive responses to their charges are reported in Gillette (1972g). Esposito (1970) traces the air pollution regulation history. Among the few reports of suppression are Boffey (1975b) and Rosenbaum (n.d.).

32. Consider the recent statement by the distinguished physicist Weiskopf: "Specialization has made of the rational method a profession, and not an avocation" (Hammond, 1975a). Ravetz (1971) makes similar observations.

33. Recent years have seen a spate of analyses of governmental whistle-blowers: see Holden (1971), Lublin (1976), and Committee on Governmental Affairs (1978). On the General Electric case, see Wilford (1976).

34. The general pattern of regulatory agencies becoming "captured" or co-opted by the monopoly-capital industries that they seek to regulate has been very well-documented (e.g., Frome, 1971; Gillette, 1975d). Difficulties of internal critics within these agencies are less adequately studied, although Gillette's reports (1972a,b,c,d,e) should provide valuable raw material for sociologists interested in the nuclear power sector. There has been only a little study on the successful critic— the public whistle-blower (Committee on Governmental Affairs, 1978; Graham, 1970, Ch. 4,5). An interesting deviant case is that of M. King Hubbert, a petroleum geologist originally employed by Shell Oil. He criticized Shell's methodology of computing oil reserves (in 1956), and the parallel method of the U.S. Geological Survey. Both of these, it appears, may have overstated reserves (Gillette, 1975b,f). The USGS recruited him from Shell despite his repudiation of the USGS methodology, which they have continued to use until recently. Hubbert has remained a highly visible professional critic within the USGS, and has influenced the National Academy of Science study of the USGS methods (Gillette, 1974b, 1975b). As a result, the USGS finally accepted much of his own 1956 analysis (Gillette, 1975f). But Hubbert's case seems highly unusual.

35. Perl (1971) notes the limitations on scientific advice to the government, which underscore those reported by Schooler (1971) and Nelkin (1975). The quest for a broader role for a White House science adviser (Skolnikoff and Brooks, 1975) has yielded a White House Science Adviser in the Carter administration, and an Office of Science and Technology Policy.

36. This is the position in Perucci (1970).

37. On air pollution control issues, see Esposito (1970: Ch. 2,3).

38. Some discussion of nuclear dissenters' problems is given in Gillette (1972a).

The range of technical data needed for evaluations is illustrated in recent analyses of McBride et al. (1978). These researchers are employed at Oak Ridge National Laboratory, a former AEC and ERDA facility now under the Department of Energy (cf. Metz, 1978, on such research and its limitations).

39. Illustrations for the nuclear power case are in Gillette (1972b,c,d,e; 1974a). Ravetz (1971) makes the argument more generally regarding the impotence of critical science relative to industrial science.

40. Critiques of the AEC inlude Gillette (1973b), Gofman and Tamplin (1971), with changes noted in Gillette (1975e). Recent analyses by the Office of Science and Technology Policy (Metz, 1978) indicate a continuing bias in research, which focuses on short-term problems.

41. The MIT case is described in Hammond (1975b); the charges of harassment have been denied by university and corporate officials. Gofman and Tamplin (1971) make the case for nuclear power, and Esposito (1970) for auto emissions.

42. Unfortunately, documentation of the preceeding constraints is difficult. This has been a "non-issue" (Crenson, 1971) in engineering schools, subject to "un-politics" and an "un-literature"! Many of the above observations are based on almost a decade of personal interaction with "applied scientists" at major midwestern schools. They ground the abstractions of Mumford's (1967, 1970) sweeping and insightful observations on the social control of technology. My views are reinforced by a number of influential scientific-technological "establishment" figures (e.g., Brooks, 1971; Skolnikoff & Brooks, 1975; Perl, 1971) and a few scholars (e.g., Perucci, 1970; Schooler, 1971; Landes, 1969; Dickson, 1975; Nelkin, 1975).

While it is true that sociologists have shown interest in "science," little interest has extended to "applied science" or engineering. This suggests that "outsiders" have insufficiently penetrated this area. "Insiders," in contrast, have had little incentive to write on these issues (and much disincentive), particularly with the declining status of technology (LaPorte & Methay, 1975). One of the rare examples of an insider's power to reveal the structure of decision making is the late Arthur Morgan's (1971) work. He systematically documents the capture of the Army Corps of Engineers earlier in its history by monopoly-capital interests (and others). But Morgan wrote this "exposé" long after he had become an outsider, as head of Antioch.

43. Gillette (1974b; 1975b,f) notes some of these problems. For the exception that proves the rule, see note 34 on M. King Hubbert.

44. The difficulty of making estimates is documented in Gilette (1974b; 1975a,b,d,f).

45. See Carroll (1971) on participatory technology, and Ravetz (1971) on critical science.

46. This mixture is treated in Landes (1969:24–26) and Dickson (1975).

47. Early pleas include those of von Hippel and Primack (1972), Revelle (1975), and the more recent quest for a "science court" (Boffey, 1976). Nelkin (1977a) criticizes this latter proposal, for its creation of a false dichotomy between "technical" and "social" issues. The distinction is explored in Ch. VII, reaffirming Nelkin's argument.

48. Fairfax (1978) makes a strong argument for the diversionary influence of NEPA's environmental impact assessment process. Part of her argument is that little

enhancement of impact science has occurred as a result of NEPA; I agree with this assessment. But the question of consciousness-raising among the public and among movement participants is much more open to other interpretations, such as those made in Ch. VII.

REFERENCES

BARAM, MICHAEL S.
1971 "Social control of science and technology." Science 172 (7 May):535–539.
1973 "Technology assessment and social control." Science 180 (4 May):465–473.

BARAN, PAUL A. AND P.M. SWEEZY
1966 Monopoly Capital: An Essay on the American Economic and Social Order. New York: Modern Reader Paperbacks.

BARNET, RICHARD J. AND R.E. MÜLLER
1974 Global Reach: The Power of the Multinational Corporations. New York: Simon and Schuster.

BOFFEY, PHILLIP M.
1970 "Gofman and Tamplin: Harrassment charges against AEC, Livermore." Science 169 (28 Aug.):838–843.
1975a The Brain Bank of America: An Inquiry into the Politics of Science. New York: McGraw Hill.
1975b "NSF grantee does slow burn as coal study ignites flap." Science 190 (31 Oct.):446.
1975c "Energy research: A harsh critique says federal effort may backfire." Science 190 (7 Nov.):535–537.
1976 "Science court: High officials back test of controversial concept." Science 194 (8 Oct.):167–169.

BOULDING, KENNETH E.
1965 The Meaning of the 20th Century: The Great Transition. New York: Harper Colophon.

BROOKS, HARVEY
1971 "Can science survive in the modern age?" Science 174 (1 Oct.)21–30.

CARPENTER, RICHARD A.
1976 "Tensions between materials and environmental quality." Science 191 (20 Feb.):665–668.

CARROLL, JAMES D.
1971 "Participatory technology." Science 171 (19 Feb.):647–653.

CARTER, LUTHER J.
1974a "EPA study: National Academy set to serve two masters." Science 185 (23 Aug.):678, 680.

1974b "Cancer and the environment (I): A creaky system grinds on." Science 186 (18 Oct.):239–242.

1974c "A 'White Paper' for energy conservation." Science 186 (1 Nov.):427.

1975 "Energy: Nuclear critics say Academy names a 'stacked' study pannel." Science 190 (5 Dec.):961–964.

1978 "Regulators defend their turf." Science 202 (10 Nov.):603.

COMMITTEE ON GOVERNMENT AFFAIRS.
1978 The Whistleblowers: A Report on Federal Employees who Disclose Acts of Governmental Waste, Abuse, and Corruption. United States Senate. Washington, D.C.: Government Printing Office. February.

COUSTEAU, JACQUES Y.
1976 "The peaceful and warlike atoms—living without both." New York Times (Aug. 8).

CRENSON, MATTHEW A.
1971 The Un-Politics of Air Pollution: A Study of Non-Decisionmaking in the Cities. Baltimore: The Johns Hopkins Press.

DICKSON, DAVID
1975 The Politics of Alternative Technology. New York: Universe Books.

DUNCAN, OTIS D.
1978 "Sociologists should reconsider nuclear energy." Social Forces 57 (1):1–22.

EIPPER, ALFRED W.
1970 "Pollution problems, resource policy, and the scientist." Science 169 (3 July):11–15.

EPSTEIN, SAMUEL S.
1978 The Politics of Cancer. San Francisco: Sierra Club Books.

ENERGY POLICY PROJECT (EPP)
1974 A Time to Choose: America's Energy Future. Cambridge, Mass.: Ballinger.

ESPOSITO, JOHN C.
1970 Vanishing Air. New York: Grossmann.

FAIRFAX, SALLY K.
1978 "A disaster in the environmental movement." Science 199 (17 Feb.):743–748.

FROME, MICHAEL
1971 The Forest Service. New York: Praeger.

GERSHINOWITZ, HAROLD
1972 "Applied research for the public good: A suggestion." Science 176 (28 Apr.):380–386.

GILLETTE, ROBERT
1971 "Lead in the air: Industry weight on Academy panel challenged." Science 174 (19 Nov.):800–802.

1972a "Nuclear reactor safety: At the AEC the way of the dissenter is hard." Science 176 (5 May):492–498.

1972b "Nuclear safety (I): The roots of dissent." Science 177 (1 Sept.):771–776.

1972c "Nuclear safety (II): The years of delay." Science 177 (8 Sept.):867–971.

1972d "Nuclear safety (III): Critics charge conflicts of interest." Science 177 (15 Sept.):970–975.

1972e "Nuclear safety (IV): Barriers to communications." Science 177 (22 Sept.):1080–1082.

1972f "Academy food committees: New criticism of industry bias." Science 177 (29 Sept.):1172–1175.

1972g "Radiation standards: the last word or at least a definitive one." Science 178 (1 Dec.):966–967, 1012.

1973a "Nuclear safety: AEC report makes the best of it." Science 179 (26 Jan.):360–362.

1973b "Radiation spill at Hanford: The anatomy of an accident." Science 181 (24 Aug.):728–730.

1973c "Energy R & D: Slicing the pie." Science 181 (24 Aug.):728–730.

1974a "Low marks for AEC's breeder reactor study." Science 184 (24 May):877.

1974b "Oil and gas resources: Did USGS gush too high?" Science 185 (12 July):127–130.

1974c "Nuclear safety: Calculating the odds of disaster." Science 185 (6 Sept.):838–839.

1974d "Cancer and the environment (II): Groping for new remedies." Science 186 (18 Oct.):242–245.

1974e "EPA cites errors in AEC's reactor risk study." Science 186 (13 Dec.):1008.

1975a "In energy impasse, conservation keeps popping up." Science 187 (10 Jan.):42–45.

1975b "Oil and gas resources: Academy calls USGS math 'misleading.'" Science 187 (28 Feb.):723–727.

1975c "Nuclear power: Hard times and a questioning public." Science 187 (21 Mar.):1059–1062.

1975d "Geological survey faulted." Science 187 (28 Mar.):1174.

1975e "William Anders: A new regulator enters a critical situation." Science 187 (28 Mar.):1173–1175.

1975f "Geological Survey lowers its sights." Science 189 (18 July):200.

1975g "Nuclear critics escalate war of numbers." Science 189 (25 Aug.):621.

GOFMAN, JOHN W. AND A.R. RAMPLIN

1971 Poisoned Power: The Case against Nuclear Power Plants. Emmaus, Penn.: Rodale Press.

GRAHAM, FRANK, JR.

1970 Since Silent Spring. Boston, Mass.: Houghton Mifflin.

HAMMOND, ALLEN L.

1974a "Academy says energy self-sufficiency unlikely." Science 184 (31 May):964.

1974b "Energy: Ford Foundation study urges action on conservation." Science 186 (1 Nov.): 426, 428.

1975a "Weisskopf on the frontiers and limits of science." Science 188 (16 May):723.

1975b "Methanol at M.I.T.: Industry influence charged in project cancellation." Science 190 (21 Nov.):761–764.

HAYS, SAMUEL P.

1969   Conservation and the Gospel of Efficiency: The Progressive Conservation Movement, 1890–1920. New York: Atheneum.

HOLDEN, CONSTANCE

1971   "Public interest: New group seeks redefinition of scientists' role." Science 173 (9 July):131–132.

1972   "Environmental action organizations are suffering from money shortages, slump in public commitment." Science 175 (28 Jan.):394–395.

LANDES, DAVID S.

1969   The Unbound Prometheus: Technological Change and Industrial Development in Western Europe from 1750 to the Present. Cambridge: Cambridge University Press.

LAPORTE, TODD R. AND D. METHAY

1975   "Technology observed: Attitudes of a wary public." Science 188 (11 Apr.):121–127.

LAVE, LESTER B. AND E.P. SESKIN

1970   "Air pollution and human health." Science 169 (21 Aug.): 723–733.

LAYTON, EDWARD T., JR.

1971   The Revolt of the Engineers: Social Responsibility and the American Engineering Profession. Cleveland: Case Western Reserve University Press.

LUBLIN, JOHN S.

1976   "Spilling the beans: Disclosing misdeeds of corporations can backfire on tattlers." Wall Street Journal (21 May).

MARSHALL, ELIOT

1978   "EPA smog standard attacked by industry, science advisers." Science 202 (1 Dec.):949–950.

MARX, LEO

1970   "American institutions and ecological ideals." Science 170 (27 Nov.):945–952.

MAUGH, THOMAS H., II

1978a "Chemical carcinogens: How dangerous are low doses?" Science 202 (6 Oct.):37–41.

1978b "Industry council challenges HEW on cancer in the workplace." Science 202 (10 Nov.):602–604.

MAZUR, ALLAN
1973   "Disputes between experts." Minerva 11 (Apr.):243–262.

MCBRIDE, J.P., R.E. MOORE, J.P. WITHERSPOON, AND R.E. BLANCO
1978   "Radiological impact of airborne effluents of coal and nuclear plants."
Science 202 (8 Dec.):1045–1050.

MCLEAN, DEWEY M.
1978   "A terminal mesozoic 'greenhouse': Lessons from the past." Science 201
(4 Aug.):401–406.

METZ, WILLIAM D.
1975   "Energy: ERDA stresses multiple sources and conservation." Science 189
(1 Aug.):369–370.
1978   "OSTP faults energy research quality: Fossil and solar found wanting."
Science 202 (20 Oct.):293–294.

MORGAN, ARTHUR E.
1971   Dams and Other Disasters: A Century of the Army Corps of Engineers in
Civil Works. Boston: Porter Sargent.

MORRISON, DENTON E., K.E. HORNBACK, AND W.K. WARNER
1972   "The environmental movement: Some preliminary observations and predictions." Pp. 259–279 in W.R. Burch, Jr., N.H. Cheek, Jr., and L.
Taylor (eds.), Social Behavior, Natural Resources, and the Environment.
New York: Harper and Row.

MUMFORD, LEWIS
1963   Technics and Civilization. New York: Harcourt, Brace, and World.
1967   The Myth of the Machine: Technics and Human Development. New
York: Harcourt, Brace, Jovanovich.
1970   The Myth of the Machine: The Pentagon of Power. New York: Harcourt, Brace, Jovanovich.

NELKIN, DOROTHY
1975   "The political impact of technical expertise." Social Studies of Science 5
(1):35–54.
1977a   "Thoughts on the proposed science court." Harvard University Newsletter
on Science, Technology and Human Values. Jan.:20–31.
1977b   "Scientists and professional responsibility: The experience of American
ecologists." Social Studies of Science 7 (1):75–95.

O'CONNOR, JAMES
1973   The Fiscal Crisis of the State. New York: St. Martin's Press.

PERL, MARTIN L.
1971   "The scientific advisory system: Some observations." Science 173 (24
Sept.):1211–1215.

PERUCCI, ROBERT
1970   "Engineering: Professional servant of power." American Behavioral Scientist, 41(Mar.–Apr.):492–506.

PITZER, KENNETH S.
1971   "Science and society: Some policy changes are needed." Science 172 (16
Apr.):223–226.

RAVETZ, JEROME R.
1971   Scientific Knowledge and Its Social Problems. Oxford: Clarendon Press.

REINEMER, VIC
1970   "Budget Bureau: Do advisory panels have an industry bias?" Science 169 (3 July):36–39.

REVELLE, ROGER
1975   "The scientist and the politician." Science 187 (21 Mar.):1100–1105.

ROSENBAUM, WALTER A.
n.d.   "The burning of the farm population estimates." Inter-University Case Program #83. Indianapolis, Ind.: Bobbs-Merrill.

ROY, RUSTUM
1972   "University-industry interaction patterns." Science 178 (1 Dec.):955–960.

SALPUKAS, AGIS
1975   "Detroit has always known small cars were coming." New York Times (2 Feb.).

SCHNAIBERG, ALLAN
1975   "Social syntheses of the societal-environmental dialectic: The role of distributional impacts." Social Science Quarterly 56 (June):5–20.

SCHOOLER, DEAN, JR.
1971   Science, Scientists, and Public Policy. New York: Free Press.

SHAPLEY, DEBORAH
1973a   "Auto pollution: Research group charged with conflict of interest." Science 181 (24 Aug.):733–735.
1973b   "The NOAA budget: Agency's role in ocean research threatened." Science 181 (31 Aug.): 830–832.
1975   "Americans for Energy Independence: Independence from whom?" Science 190 (3 Oct.):31–32.

SKOLNIKOFF, EUGENE B. AND H. BROOKS
1975   "Scientific advice in the White House? Continuation of a debate." Science 187 (10 Jan.):35–41.

SMITH, R. JEFFREY
1978a   "NAS saccharin report sweetens FDA position, but not by much." Science 202 (24 Nov.):852–853.
1978b   "Dioxins have been present since the advent of fire, says Dow." Science 202 (15 Dec.):1166–1167.

STOKINGER, H.E.
1971   "Sanity in research and evaluation of environmental health." Science 174 (12 Nov.):662–665.

VON HIPPEL, FRANK AND J. PRIMACK
1972   "Public interest science." Science 177 (29 Sept.):1166–1171.

WADE, NICHOLAS
1971 "Decision on 2,4,5-T:leaked reports compel regulatory responsibility." Science 173 (13 Aug.):610–615.
1972a "Freedom of Information: officials thwart public right to know." Science 175 (4 Feb.): 498–502.
1972b "DES: A case study of regulatory abdication." Science 177 (28 July):335–337.
1973 "Agriculture: Social sciences oppressed and poverty stricken." Science 180 (18 May):719–722.
1975 "Agriculture: Academy group suggests major shakeup to President Ford." Science 190 (5 Dec.):959–961.

WALSH, JOHN
1978 "EPA and toxic substances law: Dealing with uncertainty." Science 202 (10 Nov.):598–602.

WILFORD, JOHN N.
1976 "Scientists discuss dual loyalty on the job." New York Times (22 Feb.).

VII SOCIAL WELFARE INTELLIGENCE
Social Impact Assessment Biases

THE UTILITARIAN MODEL
OF POLICY EVALUATION
Formal and Informal Impact Assessment

The dismal history of environmental evaluation of production noted in Chapter VI was deemed by some environmentalists to have ended with the passage of the National Environmental Policy Act of 1969 (NEPA). With unprecedented breadth, NEPA called for an environmental impact statement (EIS) to be filed by every federal agency whenever an action was expected to have a "significant" effect on the "human environment." These effects to be assessed included direct and indirect effects, and eventually their range included:

> ecological (such as the effects on natural resources and on the components, structures, and functioning of affected ecosystems), economic, social or health, whether direct, indirect, or cumulative. Effects may also include those resulting from actions which may have both beneficial and detrimental effects, even if on balance the agency believes that the effect will be beneficial. (Council on Environmental Quality, 1978:25244)

NEPA was to usher in a new era of state action regarding environmental assessment. It apparently also inaugurated a new social welfare accounting of state actions. Following the arguments of Chapter V,

An earlier version of this chapter was presented in Schnaiberg and Meidinger (1978).

the EIS process would create a new consciousness of both the environmental and social welfare negative externalities of the treadmill of production. While this would apply only to projects at the federal level under NEPA, a variety of similar legislation mandated parallel requirements at the state government level. And similar requirements also were created for specific federal agencies, such as the Federal Power Commission. Although this chapter focuses on the outcome of NEPA itself, then, many of its implications extend to other state actions on social welfare assessment of production. Some research (e.g., W. Friedland et al., 1978) lives up to the lofty expectations implied above, but much of this is outside the formal impact assessment processes.

Euphoria about NEPA's potential role in reshaping state support for the treadmill of production was short-lived. While EISs multiplied, it seemed that agencies followed the form rather than the substance of the proprosed environmental and social welfare assessment (Fairfax, 1978). Such obfuscation paralleled the long history of impact distortion by the U.S. Army Corps of Engineers (noted by its former head, Arthur Morgan, 1971) and continuing to the present (King, 1978). It also exemplified problems of social welfare assessment in public projects that had been noted by economists (Haveman & Margolis, 1970).

In terms of consciousness-raising regarding the welfare effects of the treadmill, NEPA and similar processes have undoubtedly increased the breadth of participation in assessment. But the social and political effectiveness of such participation is far more questionable (Alford & Friedland, 1975). In part, this uncertainty comes from the contradictions within NEPA, reflecting contradictions within the contemporary state.[1] As noted in Chapter V, the state operates to enhance economic development, on the one hand, and social peace, on the other. In practice, this typically involves support for expansions of monopoly capital, and policies aimed at distributing enough social surplus to labor and the poor to avoid social turbulence and political conflict.

The general argument in this chapter is that this duality of government functions is reflected in a comparable duality of the EIS process. Recent commentary suggests that the EISs produced since NEPA have both a scientific and a political dimension, providing technical information and a base for political and litigative activity. These reflect the qualities of EISs themselves as: (1) scientific observation and (2) political and economic advocacy.[2]

What makes the NEPA process especially interesting is that it incorporates in a single process activities that typically have been dissociated in modern democratic governments. R. Friedland et al. (1977) note that, especially at the urban level, governments are typically divided into two types of agencies—those that deal with economic growth, and those that relate to political legitimation. The former tend to engage in technical planning, the latter in political controversy:

> Freed . . . from partisan and popular constraints . . . [the economic development] agencies develop external constituencies among those economic groups that have a keen interest in public policies that influence the parameters of economic growth. . . . The ideology of technical planning and professionalism with which these agencies cloak themselves not only legitimates their insulation, but it also discourages any attempts at popular intervention, for it argues that what is being done is not political but technical. . . . (p. 458)

In contrast, though,

> agencies which attract the political participation of groups who are excluded from the benefits of economic growth or who may even be its victims, are far less autonomous, their policies are far more visible. . . . The agencies need constantly to mobilize allies from a diverse . . . constituency to ensure renewal of their legislative mandate and funding. (pp. 458–59)

Typically, these two types of agencies follow procedures designed to lower or raise social consciousness about government actions. The unprecedented quality of the EIS process follows, then, from the contradictory nature of the NEPA-mandated process. On the one hand, all mission agencies, whose activities complement and reinforce in varying degrees economic activities of the private investment sector, were obligated to raise the consciousness of interested environmental groups regarding possible environmental hazards of their new programs. On the other hand, though, this was to be done in the most scientific manner possible, and with some limitations on the range of public involvement in evaluation and decision making.[3]

The actual EIS mandate from NEPA was a procedural one, obligating all federal agencies to evaluate and then report publically upon environmental dimensions of their projects before they were ever begun. The newly created Council on Environmental Quality was to monitor the formal submissions of draft EISs, and other federal agencies and public groups were to comment substantively on these drafts. In terms of political and legal actions, this process permitted formal and substantive protests. That is, EISs could be found inadequate in not treating technically enough environmental consequences of a project. Or, from the details reported, the agency might reveal substantive violations of existing federal regulations on air or water pollution, endangered species, or other laws. With respect to these last violations, the primary agency charged with reviewing and bringing action to counter such projects was the Environmental Protection Agency (EPA), a master agency designed to administer the cumulative federal laws on environmental quality.

Assessments of the actual consequences of the EIS procedure in the past eight years vary widely, with attacks by both industrialists and environmentalists. Both the Council on Environmental Quality and the Environmental Protection Agency have been charged with falling short of expectations that many groups derived from the logic of NEPA. While some projects have been altered, others cancelled, and still others delayed through the EIS process, there is a good deal of evidence that the overwhelming majority of projects go through the process unscathed. Many agencies have perfected a routine for EIS report writing (Fairfax, 1978). EISs are written to justify past project decisions, rather than to seek advice for improving projects. Typically, few other federal agencies comment on most EISs, and even the EPA does a rather poor job of review.[4] Finally, the "public" confrontation over EISs typically does not materialize in most projects (Alford & Friedland, 1975). Environmental interest groups may, though, challenge the EIS, and mobilize membership, staff, and community participants to present systematic critiques (Nelkin & Fallows, 1977).

If NEPA is viewed solely as an environmental reform piece of legislation, these results would be surprising. However, it seems more accurate to view NEPA as a political response to the social problem claims raised by environmental movement organizations in the 1960s—an attempt to deal with these groups as political claimants.[5] Undoubtedly, the support for NEPA drew genuine environmental concern among legislators and their constituents, but it was also an overtly political response to environmentalists. It was drafted, though, with a recognition that conventional public projects providing infrastructure for private investment and economic growth were threatened by "excessive" environmental reforms. Moreover, traditional mission agencies were threatened by demands for a new environmental accountability. Overt political debate in legislatures rose, in contrast to typical insulation of such agencies and to their frequent capture and co-optation by private economic interests they purported to regulate and influence.[6]

Thus, NEPA was an uneasy balancing between two sets of claimants—economic interests, and environmentalists. Overall, the assessment in this chapter is that the NEPA has favored economic interests over environmentalists. The logic-in-use of the EIS will be examined in some detail to explain how this biasing has occurred. Next, an extended discussion of means of redressing some of this bias follows, with a view to both the technical and political dimensions of EISs, particularly with regard to their social impact assessments. In both aspects, the emphasis here is on the ways in which EISs have reduced social consciousness of environmental problems and many socioeconomic effects, and on means of increasing this consciousness.[7] Finally, drawing upon illustrations from research done outside the formal EIS procedure, particularly in energy development, some potential scientific and political paths for the future balancing of NEPA are explored.

Benefit-Cost Analysis: Science or Politics?

Beyond its formal ecological accounting mandate, NEPA also integrated broader scientific and policy concerns. Not only were ecological impacts to be assessed, but so were social impacts of environmental policies. Over the years since its enactment, NEPA has given rise to an EIS that typically incorporates a "Social Impact Statement (SIS)." Although this was permitted and encouraged in NEPA itself, these SISs became the subject of litigation. Culhane (1974) noted that *Calvert Cliffs v. AEC* (449.F.2d 1109 [1971]) formalized the weighing of economic benefits against potential environmental costs. EISs were to include a social impact statement (SIS) to permit this balancing of socioeconomic and ecological considerations. Since many agencies act as advocates rather than scientific observers within the EIS context, many EISs already contained the elements of some social impact evaluation. Advocacy, after all, implies that drafters emphasize the socioeconomic gains of a project and minimize the ecological losses. And NEPA stressed that environmental concerns were to be merged into the regular agency's mission by "all practical means, consistent with other essential considerations of national policy."[8]

In one sense, the need for such social accounting is obvious. Group interests in ecological disruptions reflect social concerns about the viability of our societies. Production expansion and environmental protection, insofar as they both allocate scarce environmental resources to social entities, must thereby have various forms of social impact. On these grounds, one would welcome a joint EIS-SIS as a first approximation to a genuine socioenvironmental accounting system.

This initial enthusiasm, however, must give way before several realities. The first is the rather poor ecological accounting presented in many EISs, in part reflecting past obstacles to environmental research (Schnaiberg, 1977). If this is true in the more limited ecological sphere, can the EIS really be much improved when this new burden of SIS is added to its already biased base? A second perspective is offered by Friesema and Culhane (1976:340–41), who note the long and rather dismal tradition of scientific management in public administration that underlies this elaborate form of evaluation:

> The expectation that NEPA will cause federal agencies to produce scientific, holistic, optimizing, evaluating, mitigating, and coordinating policy seems to be the latest manifestation of the rational decision-making perspective on bureaucratic behavior. . . . [But] public administration behavior is not scientific management; it is politics.

The technique most associated with this tradition of scientific public management is benefit-cost analysis, and the essential logic of this approach has been carried forward into state environmental policies. This logic is simple in the abstract: The state ought to support those projects whose social benefits exceed their social costs. This implies that alternative forms of public expenditures be considered and evaluated against the proposed project. But this is rarely done seriously, outside of recent energy projects.[9] Nonetheless, the *ideology* is one of utilitarian evaluation: seeking projects with the greatest good for the greatest number. It is, of course, the ideology rationalizing the treadmill as well (Ch. V).

Table 7.1 provides a basic schematic outline of a typical assessment. In this case, project X is to be evaluated. Its negative ecological effects are **A,** and its socioeconomic benefits are **B.** In turn, the

Table 7.1   Benefit-Cost Model of Project X Evaluation
(Environmental-Social Impact Statement)

	Project X	Alternative to Project X
Ecological costs	A	——
Socioeconomic		
Benefits	B	D(=C)
Costs	C	E(=B)

socioeconomic costs of **A** are designated as **C.** These components of project or program X are then contrasted with some hypothetical alternative, generally *not* doing X. Although in principle and in law a wide variety of alternative public sector actions could and should be compared with X, this is typically not the case. Among other reasons, agency representatives frequently argue that they have no expertise in government actions outside their narrow policy area, and thus cannot provide any "objective" evaluation of the socioenvironmental impacts of these hypothetical alternatives. While this is often valid for any single agency, this fragmentation between and within agencies undercuts the general social utility of impact analysis.[10] As Friesema and Culhane (1976:340) note, this is precisely the fragmentation that has historically existed in public administration in the United States.

Let us now examine the biases underlying thses components. First, following the historical barriers to environmental research, it is invariably the case that **A** underestimates the true range of environmental withdrawals/additions. Underdevelopment of impact sciences and impact research findings provides far less documentable ecological impacts than are likely to exist.[11] Since the EIS and the benefit-cost model both emphasize quantifiable impacts, this weakness of the social intelligence base in turn lowers the estimates of **A.** In effect, this biases the evaluation in favor of the treadmill of production, and against environmental impact aspects.

The socioeconomic benefits and costs can be of two types: direct and indirect. Direct costs are expenditures, which many agencies have long underestimated (Morgan, 1971; King, 1978) in order to improve the attractiveness of projects. Indirect costs include opportunity costs—the loss of potential gains from equivalent expenditures in other projects. Typically, the agency has little information on this, and even theoretical economists acknowledge that "Economic analysis and research rather naturally gravitated to the areas where information and data is readily available" (Haveman, 1970a:2). Other indirect costs include the socioeconomic effects of ecological impacts. These are understated, since (1) **A** is an underestimate and (2) we have had little social scientific data on the socioeconomic dimensions of **A**. Taking all these factors together, **C** is generally underestimated.[12]

When we turn to the socioeconomic benefits of the project, though, we find no such biases in **B**. Economic research has been historically oriented to just such tasks, with a variety of theoretical and emprircal approaches to economic multipliers deriving from employment and income generation from the project. Moreover, the base data from the project on such dimensions are invariably given (indeed, often in inflated terms) by agencies and production organizations involved. In the most neutral sense, then, we can state with assurance that few project benefits will go undocumented.[13]

In the second column of Table 7.1, we generally find no entry for ecological costs, since this typically involves no production action. What we find is some crude estimate of socioeconomic costs, **E**, which is usually the obverse of **B**: so many jobs lost, so much GNP foregone. In terms of benefits, **D**, we can generally only count on the obverse of **C**, i.e., the socioeconomic benefits derived from preservation of the environment.

With these biases in mind, there is generally no contest between the benefits and costs of any project proposed. For project X, we find that underestimated costs **C** rarely will reach accurate or inflated benefits **B** levels. On this socioenvironmental basis, then, there is a net surplus of stated benefits over costs. Moreover, in terms of alternatives to X the depressed benefits of avoiding the project, **D**, are far less than the socioeconomic costs, **E**, of engaging in this avoidance. There are no surprises, then, and project X is seen to be in the national interest, on balance. It may be rejected on conventional economic efficiency grounds, of *direct* costs versus benefits, though. This view is congruent with Ophuls's recent assessment:

> Sponsoring agencies have turned it into a *pro forma,* paperwork compliance with the requirements of Section 102. . . . Reviewing agencies . . . [give] perfunctory review, thus saving themselves the money and the staff time that would have had to go to a genuine study . . . [With] overworked and underfinanced public-interest groups, the vast majority of impact statements receive pitifully inadequate reviews. (1977:177–78)

There is certainly widespread agreement that to date, the EIS process has been bad science, in terms of ecological and socioeconomic dimensions. Economic interests see "scientific Philistines" impeding the progress of technology. Progressive social scientists bemoan the lack of "full disclosure of the kind of information needed to internalize the costs of production and make intelligent decisions on future development."[14] Explanations for the failure to create this good science likewise vary, from a lack of sufficient public expenditure research, to the self-perpetuation desires of bureaucratic public agencies. An extreme view is that good science would be "deeply threatening to the industrial order and to a political and economic system that has thrived on the invisibility of the invisible hand."[15]

The range of such views is understandable, again, when we observe that the EIS process has the technical-political duality noted earlier. Confusion is magnified when either dimension is stressed, to the exclusion of the other. Those who see impact assessment as a science are frustrated by the political dimensions and the lack of science. Conversely, those who see the EIS process as a purely political arena are disheartened by the cumbersome rules of the game that are imposed by a facade of science. Confusion and frustration are enhanced by the false promises that benefit-cost logic has always had. Both the theory and practice of benefit-cost analysis reflect an ultimately political component, regardless of whether one takes a pro- or antienvironmental position. This reality is attested to by professional public expenditure and welfare economists:

> [Whether] conclusions... are to be accepted or rejected is... a matter of judgement and opinion. There is no question of proof.... rigour and refinement are probably worse than useless... (I.M.D. Little, 1957:277, 279)

> Distributive weights must... be made on non-economic grounds, say, by political decision-makers. The economist may... present the alternative evaluations to the politician for ultimate choice. (Boadway, 1974:938)

> The cases where investigators have succeeded in providing some quantification of external costs and benefits are extremely rare. Many types of externality (that is, the impairment of health) that is caused by pollutants simply are not readily translated into financial terms. (Baumol, 1970:283)

Measurement of goal attainment is often reduced to gross rules of thumb, smearing and confusing the original legislative intent. (Bonnen, 1970:253)

These [real-life] complexities . . . necessitate a good deal of simplification of the full richness of reality. (Dorfman & Jacoby, 1970:228)

I would rather measure only what I have confidence in measuring with some accuracy and leave "incommensurables" to be decided by explicit choice . . . it may be better to be vaguely right than precisely wrong. (Steiner, 1970:53)

Benefit-cost analysis cannot answer the most important policy questions associated with . . . fusion-based economy . . . these questions are of a deep ethical character. Benefit-cost analysis . . . may well obscure them. (Kneese, 1973:1)

That is, the economists most familiar with traditional public welfare analysis recognize the "transeconomic" quality of socioeconomic impact assessment: "They involve political, social, and ethical issues, not the issue of efficient resource allocation that neo-classical, marginalist, economics was designed to handle" (Ophuls, 1977:173). Yet the confusion as to the science involved in impact assessment is also enhanced by the self-serving and often self-delusory qualities of economic impact professionals. Wildavsky evaluates the new conservation-minded economists as follows:

In cases of doubt and undeterminancy, the new economists want the values they favor included rather than excluded. But they are inhibited by a nostalgia for the credibility accorded to the old economists they once were. (1967:1121)

And:

How does the "old economics" of natural resources differ from the "new economics"? The old economics was mostly economics. The new economics is mostly politics. (1967:1115)

From this range of theoretical observations, it is clear that politics emerges at multiple stages of any *application* of benefit-cost modeling within the EIS process. Agencies have their own political agendas in drafting an EIS. Professional economists have a stake in presenting a facade of science even where it is unjustified. Review agencies may benefit from a mutual hands-off policy with respect to other agencies' EISs. Finally, environmental and community groups have their own values and interests at risk in intervening in the review process.

On the other hand, it would be insensitive to argue that there is *no* scientific input to the EIS process. A good deal of both valid information and potentially valid data is presented at various stages in the EIS creation and review. There is overwhelming evidence that this is inadequate to achieve perfect predictability of project impacts. But there is also some suggestion that no amount of improvement will ever achieve this ideal scientific goal. For in theory each EIS is addressing the question: What would the world be like with versus without this project? As will be noted later, we have rarely been able to achieve such answers for any past project, and the EIS essentially asks this same question for an even more uncertain future (Meidinger, 1979).

What is argued for here is an extension of the science portion of the hybrid EIS process, to enable more effective political intervention by social groups, both conventional environmental interest groups and others. The suggestions that follow later are intended to make more socially visible the dimensions of project impacts. By this route, social and political consciousness may be raised and mobilization of affected interests increased.[16]

Some general assumptions are required here. First, it is assumed that many capital-owning groups already appreciate the potential benefits of such projects, so that their consciousness has already been raised. Second, from a series of interactions between these groups and organized labor, there has gradually emerged in the United States an organized labor support for many of the projects supported by large-scale capital, especially energy development projects. Bruce Hannon's work has indicated why, at least in the short run, both of these groups are acting in their self-interest, particularly with regard to expanding energy supplies and total consumption.[17] Therefore, these two major groups, in the typical EIS process, are currently disposed to a subversion of any dramatic ecologically-induced change in production. They support the current NEPA process (or ask for its contraction) in order to get on with business, to accelerate the treadmill.

Revisions of social impact statements along the lines suggested below will, then, have some limited but foreseeable effects. They will likely strengthen the case of environmental interest groups, both on environmental and socioeconomic grounds. If the outcome of revisions in the EIS-SIS process indicates a broader array of environmental damage and more socially regressive socioeconomic impacts, environmentalists should be able to expand their social constituencies within unorganized and organized labor. In the process, the movement will become even less elitist than it is at present, and potentially a force for more egalitarian reorganization of the economy. In the language of economists, this would reinforce equity movements and offset the efficiency emphasis that generally undergirds the typical EIS process today.[18]

Environmentalists appear to share this evaluation since they "deplore the ineffectiveness of NEPA, but... react vigorously against any attempt to weaken or restrict its applicability" (Friesema & Culhane, 1976:356). From a social structural perspective, attempts to broaden the science of the EIS in the directions suggested here will be resisted by large-scale capital interests and their supporters in government and the labor movement. As Ophuls (1977:176) has noted with particular regard to nuclear energy:

> Capitalism is thus an economic system founded on hidden social costs, in which development (at least as we have experienced it) would not have occurred if all the costs had been counted in advance. . . . In brief, honesty and "progress" may not be compatible.

For those interested in changing the social system to a more sustainable and less unequal one, the potential benefits from an extension and modification of the current benefit-cost modesl of EISs and social impact components outweigh the risks. It is likely foolhardy to view this as a tool for attacking the bedrock of capitalist organization, but not at all insensible as an approach to reformation of some of the more pernicious inequality dimensions.[19]

QUANTIFICATION AND DISTRIBUTION: BIASES AND REMEDIES

Projective versus Retrospective Accounting

In the next three sections, some of the political and social costs of the premature quantification entailed in many EISs are outlined and alternative qualitative strategies suggested. The model of impact assessment as equivalent to natural science is challenged, and a more qualitative model of social and environmental research at least added as a valid component. Three dimensions are treated here: (1) the prospective nature of benefit-cost modeling in impact assessment, (2) the creation of a qualitative list of impacts, and (3) the quantification of impacts. Later sections deal with more substantive problems of equity that are underassessed in current EISs.

Viewing impact assessment as ecological and socioeconomic accounting leads to false expectations. Accounting typically has an after-the-fact quality. One "does the books" at some point after the events have occurred. But the logic of EIS-SIS benefit-cost models is that they operate for prospective projects or programs before the events occur. In principle, these models can be used for existing projects, but there are few such EIS applications. Benefit-cost modeling has been used, however, for broader environmental policy research on existing production.[20] Prospective EIS-SIS modeling, like its precursor, technology assessment, has been lauded as part of a rational planning approach to avoid disasters. The notion of planning reinforces again the technical dimension of economic growth. Unfortunately, there is insufficient social recognition of the difficulties of such prospective analysis. We might classify this as the difference between a technical "doing the books" and a more political "making the books."

The problems with making the books are staggering. The withdrawals and benefits entailed in any given project cover a vastly variegated set of phenomena and academic specialities: from water quality to cultural composition. Typically the projections within each and the interactions between the various dimensions are rarely integrated. Moreover, the models employed in any given dimension contain major components of uncertainty. Meidinger (1978a) has examined the models currently used to project socioeconomic impacts in some detail. Sizable error components and biases due to flawed model assumptions and inadequate data appear, together with profound theoretical limitations. Shifting social and economic parameters encountered are responded to with guesswork at best, and are as often simply ignored.

These conditions contribute to the lopsided accounting that emerges. Much more effort is usually devoted to assessing the probable benefits in planning any given project. Potential investors and backers ensure that their risks are likely to be justified. Thus when a developed plan emerges as a proposal, its benefits (e.g., profits and jobs) are likely to be well (if perhaps over) estimated and characterized. Costs, on the other hand, given the incomplete and largely invalid models in use, are far less likely to be either enumerated or enumerable. As with the EIS's predecessor, technology assessment, we find that:

> There is never any lack of articulation of the benefits of a technology. Every technology has powerful vested interests—private and frequently governmental and political. . . . [But] the negative factors are never fully or even adequately articulated . . . [and the] risks totally unappreciated until a later date. (H. Green, 1972:51)

In all these projections of future impacts, the assessment can only be made in terms of (1) the linkage of proposed projects to similar ones of the past, (2) evaluation of the historical impacts of these other projects, and (3) incorporation of these past effects in some model of future effects of the proposed EIS project. Historically the environmental impact sciences were underdeveloped. A lack of sustained attention to the specific and synergistic effects of much of the past public and private infrastructure was clear. Therefore, we can have little closure for cumulating past impacts, and hence little can exist for future impacts. What scientific data we do have may be used, but it can only be a small portion of the total range of likely and possible effects of an EIS project.[21] Hence the range of impacts to be included is always an underestimate. Underestimation will remain as long as strict evidentiary rules for inclusion of potential ecological effects are standing. At this point, the political dimension looms larger, in that it must be a "transscientific" question of *what* environmental effects are to be considered, and how to consider them.

In regard to socioeconomic impacts, a parallel situation occurs. A broad range of socioeconomic effects of past public projects has simply not been utilized in past research. For example, it has been noted that many of the socioeconomic effects of massive public infrastructure for agricultural development has not been documented, though the growth in agricultural output was. A similar situation exists for energy development, though this has changed rather dramatically in the years since the 1973–74 "oil crisis." We have seen a substantial increase in community-impact studies of energy development, on the one hand, and of the consumption effects of the changing oil situation, on the other. For most projects, the only apparent certainties are some private and public sector employment and wage impacts. And even these may be called into question as models for future impacts.[22]

When the realities of the socioeconomic system are taken into account, the simple economic balancing models for benefits versus costs are increasingly unclear. As Robert Havemen indicates, in the presence of factors such as monopoly, unemployment, incomplete knowledge, or spillovers of effects into private sectors, "market observations must be appropriately adjusted to compensate for the imperfection" (1970a:18, footnote 8). That is, as the real world is considered, we can rely less and less on the crude indicators of economic and social bookkeeping from past developments: we need new data. Among other things, data will be needed on new socioeconomic goals "decided on by the political process and consistently applied in evaluating public expenditures" (Haveman, 1970a:12).

In sharp contrast is the typical EIS impact model. To provide for its scientific qualities, drafters typically fix on "whatever 'statistical' relationships could be picked up among the odds and ends of available data" (Meidinger, 1978:7). This arrangement, where the supply of data leads to delineation of impacts, is in contrast to the *theory* of public expenditures, The latter argues for political specification of goals and for the collection of data addressing the degree to which the project achieves the goals, and with what costs. In fact, the *practice* of public expenditure benefit-cost has rarely been any more scientific than the EIS impact assessment model now in place. Its only virtue has been the open recognition of political choices.[23]

The social reality of prospective impact assessment is that it cannot claim to achieve a high level of scientific modeling. Choices must be made among approaches to such impact modelings to guide and coordinate data-gathering efforts. Following Levins (1966), these impact models may be general, realistic, or precise. Typically, there are unavoidable conflicts between creating models that have all three characteristics, so that we must again choose, both politically and technically, which impact models to use for any project. On grounds of raising political consciousness, the first objective should be for models that are realistic in their projections. A second goal should be for models that are general. This would permit interest groups to more effectively confront repeated instances of victimization or increased inequality that characterize many projects and programs. Environmental and social action groups have inadequate resources to learn the intricate, minute differences among impacts of a large class of similar projects (highways, for example). But if highways were typically assessed using a realistic and general model, such interest groups would have more political efficacy in the EIS review process, and potentially in the decisions about projects approved.[24]

In face of the above social and environmental science limitations and their political implications, the following two programmatic suggestions seem desirable.

Listing of Qualitative Impacts

Following the limits noted above there is a continuum of a priori procedural decisions that agencies and analysis can make. At one extreme, only the most obvious, direct, and "significant" impacts or effects will be listed: the model of primary effects. At the other extreme, every conceivable outcome will be listed: the model of full effects. Generally, the former is the operant model for most benefit-cost analyses, including many recent ecological ones. While this may be the least controversial and most honest approach given the state of ecological and socioeconomic theory and research, it tends to be the most socially conservative approach as well. It breaks no new ground, challenges no existing deficiencies in the literatures of impact and production sciences. Ultimately, it maximizes the likelihood that past decision-making criteria will be upheld in the name of "social progress." In short, it is maximally congruent with the production treadmill and minimally congruent with major socioenvironmental change.

Why is this so? The focus is likely to be on only those ecological and socioeconomic impacts that have reached a more advanced stage of public consciousness within the society. Many issues that analysts may be aware of are less likely to be incorporated in the list, since it is far less likely that past research has been adequate in these areas to document highly probable impacts. Conversely, the materials of production sciences, emphasizing the immediate socioeconomic gains from a project, are far more likely to find their way onto the listing of impacts: "Analysis must insure that these secondary impacts are treated uniformly on both the benefit and cost sides of the ledger. . . . [Bias occurs] because of the visibility and concentration of secondary benefits relative to secondary costs" (Haveman, 1970a:10).

In general, the shorter the list presented, the more EISs are biased in favor of past production practices, for the least documentable ecological and social externalities of production are likely to be dropped from review. Past political pressures thus get reproduced: When data on past externalities cannot be found in the literature, they are excluded from concern. Historical "non-issueness" becomes translated into present and future "non-issueness."

For reasons of redressing environmental and socioeconomic grievances, then, efforts should be directed to a broader range of impacts.[25]

Quantification of Impacts

For analysts who have opted for a minimal list, the quantification stage is made easier by having both fewer items to evaluate and items whose calculus is somewhat more straightforward. This precision is frequently done at the expense of social validity. Public expenditure analysis stresses quantification in monetary terms, though at this time there have been many other schemes proposed. Since the ultimate aim of a benefit-cost analysis is to provide some measure of *net social utility* of a project, there is some justification for this, though many of Schumacher's (1973) criticisms of "economism" are well-taken. In theory, a set of creative analysts could provide shadow prices for virtually any kind of impact, regardless of whether any of the ecological, social, or economic impacts have ever been priced in the market. From an abstract level, this is so because an analyst in theory could spin out a reasonable set of meliorative actions, with their costs, i.e., "the amount which would have to be paid to all of the people adversely affected by the decision, just to compensate them for the dissatisfaction which they incurred" (Haveman, 1970a:8).

In fact, what is the more typical practical outcome of public expenditure analysis is a minimal compensation for a minimal list of socioeconomic harms. Displacement of the poor by highway construction has only small relocation costs per capita, a gross underestimation of true disruptions in people's lives. Moreover, even at a theoretical level, the monetization of compensation has been criticized because it assumes universal equivalencies of groups' structures of needs and preferences.[26]

At a more basic level, quantification pressures ignore a variety of other socially realistic concerns. In particular, (1) the probabilities of future impacts occurring and (2) the conditions that would produce the occurrence or nonoccurence of any ecological or especially socioeconomic impact, are important issues. The critique of the Rasmussen report on nuclear power plant safety revolves around issues of uncertainty and risk. In particular, critics have argued that Rasmussen ignored human factors in safety estimates. Realistically, though, it seems clear that precise probability estimates are never going to be scientifically grounded. Moreover, many of the impact social sciences are not especially well-developed with regard to the probabilistic analysis required here. Many of the elements of this probability estimation reflect multiple causation. The simultaneous influence of many factors may only operate with particular combinations of levels of each factor: e.g., unemployment may be a result of age structure of a population, in combination with education and skill levels, ethnicity, and the like. All of these may occur, say, when strip mining operations disrupt some particular types of agriculture.[27]

Following from this complexity of risk-uncertainty analysis, a number of *political* choices are possible. From the point of prospective victims, their political preference should be for maximal listing of impacts. For each, there should be some crude (high/medium/low) assessment of their likelihood. Where impacts can be easily assessed quantitatively, they should be given a summary assessment only after probability and estimation assumptions have been reported separately. As much as possible, impacts should be decomposed into separate segments so that social reviewers can respond to meaningful pieces of action consequences. That is, the aggregation should be done by reviewers, not agency analysts, so that reviewers get to see the separate costs and benefits, and not simply the "net benefits" in any area (employment, etc.).

Where impacts are listed without any quantification, it should be made clear whether (1) empirical research has been minimal on similar projects that have been enacted in the past, and/or (2) the projects are sufficiently different from past projects such that little such empirical basis could possibly exist. Proponents of a given program/project typically argue that the latter is the usual condition, and hence absolve themselves of responsibility to carry out more detailed analyses of proposed actions. More often, it is the case that research *could* have been done on similar potential effects from past policies, but has not been. Reasons for the lack of such past impact research have been spelled out elsewhere (Schnaiberg, 1977). Where there is a type 2 rather than a type 1 response to critics, proponents simply are able to legitimately say, "We cannot possibly assess this impact," and ignore it. To slowly correct this dual bias, even if past research is nonexistent, every approved project that has been subject to benefit-cost analysis should have a monitoring component built in as part of policy approval. Then, in the future, similar projects will have no such social excuses.[28]

In practice, a politically useful EIS would have the following types of information about benefits and costs:

1. specification of each potential impact
2. estimation of the probability of its occurrence (e.g., high/medium/low)
3. conditions under which impact is more/less likely to occur
4. quantitative dimensions of the impact
5. basis for this quantification
6. qualitative impacts, and reasons for lack of quantifiability
7. plans for improving quantifiability of impact
8. what remedial costs will be for negative impacts, and how these costs are to be organized.

Actually, we could determine a range of information for EISs that could go on and on, without ever achieving scientific closure. For social contituencies, the objective should be an enlarged and more technically accessible document. All the omissions of any document will be interpreted quite differently by proponents and opponents of projects. Proponents will argue that there is *only* so much definable risk (excluding the range of uncertainty). Opponents will claim *fully* so much definable risk (including the residual uncertainty in this judgment). Translating as much uncertainty as possible into some roughly calculable risk will reduce, but never eliminate, such discrepancies of interpretation (Hirshleifer & Shapiro, 1970).

Distribution of Costs and Benefits

The typical unit for which public project assessment is computed is the nation-state. NEPA itself made provisions for assessments of environmental impact, in the context of *national* objectives. But the reality of all public projects, those with or without an EIS, is that they may have:

> Built-in biases, since interest groups surrounding proposals to undertake certain types of natural resource development projects often systematically favor such decisions... [because of] the disassociation of the incidence of benefits from that of the costs of the projects... the gain to those individuals favoring the project is

large relative to the magnitude of the loss falling on individual taxpayers. (Knetsch, 1970:565)

Knetsch was referring only to direct (tax dollar) costs of such projects, and not the full range of socioeconomic and environmental impacts of such projects. But his point is applicable to the latter as well. For the costs and benefits of any project are distributed unequally in physical and social space. Moreover, ignoring this reality typically permits socially regressive projects to survive review.

This section treats project distribution of costs and benefits. The two sections following examine social efficiency of projects and the discounting of the future.

While economists have focused especially on direct costs of projects, the concern here is on the distribution of project impacts. In the political realities of the EIS system, capital and other economic interests are concerned with *minimizing* perceived social and environmental costs of projects. The true social costs may be quite high to other social groups and classes within the society. Conversely, they seek to *maximize* the social perception of benefits to social groups and classes, while minimizing the publicly anticipated returns on private-sector investment. Thus, for example, a typical EIS would stress employment gains, but not profit accumulation from a public project. It might even include new investment stimulated by the project, but it is unlikely to focus on the returns.

Despite the fact that investment, profit making, and employment may occur in different social groups, the typical EIS focuses its assessment either on the national or local level. That is, it has a geographical rather than a social frame of reference. Highways typically are evaluated on their local impact, while energy developments have a local and a national level of aggregation. But it is rare in official EISs to get a specification of concrete social groups and their potential gains and losses: "Despite our society's equity commitments, many public programs are administered with little attention to their distributional impact... we almost always fail to collect information on distributional aspects of programs" (Bonnen, 1970:246).

This comment by a public expenditure economist, while it predates the EIS process, has two implications: (1) there is little past data to be relied on for distributional estimates for EIS-reviewed projects, and (2) this can be used for justifying still further ignoring of such issues. Again, while there are technical problems in projecting distributional outcomes, the more overriding concern in evading such a calculus is typically political and allows for perpetuation of socially regressive programs: "The focus in many resource programs may be prejudiced in favor of those projects which are more quantifiable at the expense of those which may be as meaningful but less easily measured" (Knetsch, 1970:572).

Knetsch emphasizes that the past failure to consider dimensions of improved life quality as part of project planning is widespread, and leads to a lack of pressure to resist. "Projections . . . [are] made to legitimatize increases in the current means of providing a resource service. . . . [D]emand data show that more of the program in question is needed" (Knetsch, 1970:568). Put more bluntly, economic interests that disproportionately benefit from public projects stimulating economic growth derive considerable political gains from ignoring distributional features of government programs.

Ironically, the one type of distributional feature in an EIS is the *local* impact assessment, on a community, corridor, or region (as in highway segments). What is ironic is that this is a fallacious distributional analysis. Such projects include benefits from increased local investments as a secondary impact, but

> profits created . . . will be offset by decreased profits experienced elsewhere because of decreased spending of those who bear the cost of the [project]. . . . [The] positive secondary effects in the region in which it is located . . . [are] matched by negative secondary effects elsewhere in the economy. [An] analysis must insure that these secondary impacts are treated uniformly on both the benefit and cost sides of the ledger. (Haveman, 1970a:10)

Similar biases exist in justifying energy developments, since local economic bases are built up—while employment and income typically decline in some unspecified alternative locus of investment. The latter effect is rarely taken into account. Thus local community support can be mobilized to support energy projects, at least before local costs are experienced, while no organized opposition arises from potential losers.[29]

In the United States, the most striking examples of such erroneous logic are metropolitan areas. Large (and old) central cities have steadily lost economic opportunities as residents and commercial enterprises relocate to suburban areas. Suburban freeways have made suburban growth possible, while central cities have become the destination of poorer migrants. Influx of the poor was often induced by the "miraculous" transformation of American agriculture from labor to capital intensity, steadily driving rural farmers and farm-workers off the land, with the aid from the Department of Agriculture. In a social class rather than a regional analysis, this situation is one in which state programs have heavily subsidized the material progress of middle- and upper-income suburbanites. This has been at the expense of working- and poverty-class urban dwellers, whose tax burdens grow and whose social services decline. New York City's fiscal crisis results from its welfare burden and its net of suburban freeways and highways, illustrating this economic redistribution.[30]

The typical effect of public projects using natural resources has disproportionately favored the economically and politically powerful elements of the society. "Societal progress" through material affluence has involved large benefits in favor of those who have least felt the sting of local and regional ecological disruption—especially large-scale capital owners. Conversely, the relatively immobile local and regional working and poverty classes have historically have paid the costs of such ecological disruption. As with preindustrial history, industrial history since the "First Industrial Revolution" shows these sharp differences in the case of mining—as illustrated by the coal mining areas of both Appalachia and Wales. Recent dam and other disasters are merely part of a continuous chain of ecosystem disorganization and the harmful (and often fatal) consequences for local residents.[31] A true concern for justice in ecological exploitation would take such inequities into account when contemplating future project distribution of benefits and costs. Local mining communities should be allocated far more revenue from mining activity to partly offset these inequities. Ironically, up to the present, such inequalities enter into most benefit-cost analyses in the opposite way. Those who have suffered the most (both economically and ecologically) are most vulnerable to being saddled with future costs and minimal benefits. This is precisely because of their low levels of material accumulation, and thus their relative powerlessness to alter the course of public and private investment.

In the past years, there has been more concern with distributional features of public policies. From a distance, we can see (1) increased research outside of EISs on local costs of energy development in smaller communities, (2) distributional studies of the effect of OPEC oil price increases on consumption and production, and (3) some "quality of life" reviews of the programs of environmental protection of the EPA.[32] Although these are all important sources of social knowledge, none of them represent distributional analysis of *public infrastructure investment within EISs*. That is, official concern with the socioeconomic effects of alternative production plans does not yet appear in these official social impact assessments.

That some such research has been done indicates its technical feasibility and political importance. Recent literature has pointed to the possibilities of linking innovative input-output analysis measures to conventional benefit-cost schemes to provide at least crude distributional estimates.[33] There is the obvious, increasing political demand of constituent groups—ranging from organized labor unions to poverty groups—for such information and for more equitable distributions of benefits and costs in the future. Moreover, in the absence of such formal studies, considerable misinformation about distributional features is likely to be disseminated by economic and other interest groups. This may lead to political demands that may be grounded in false perceptions of socioenvironmental reality. For example, the rejection of the antinuclear Proposition 15 in California's referendum was based in part on a false evaluation of the true costs to labor and consumers of a nuclear shutdown in that state. Inflated statements of the *costs* to residents of shutdowns (which would produce ecological benefits in many areas), coupled with systematically deflated costs of expansion of nuclear power, led many voters to vote against what might have been in their best long-term interest. Among the deflated costs of continuing nuclear power, the two most prominent were the growing federal tax investment in nuclear energy, and the likely future costs of both uranium and enriched fuels through fuel rod reprocessing. What amount of solar energy installations, for example, could have been purchased with the annual ERDA or Department of Energy budget for nuclear energy alone? Questions like this are raised publicly only following nuclear accidents such as the recent one in Pennsylvania (Lewis, 1979).

If distributional analysis is extended to EISs along with better lists, the likely effect is increased consciousness among many social constituencies as to how badly they have fared in past government (and private sector) decision making, where such project costs have not been systematically included. Moreover, once the cost dimensions have been included, the potential for such constituencies to politically demand their fair share likewise increases, with official legitimation of their grievances through the benefit-cost analysis. This assumes, of course, that such analysis is made public (cf. Alford & Friedland, 1975). Risks entailed in the public access to EISs have created a consciousness among many political and economic elites as to the political dangers inherent in such "freedom of information" (cf. Friesema & Culhane, 1976). Conversely, though, there are risks for progressive activists that social groups will discover new benefits as well as new costs in projects and mobilize to oppose environmentalists and others. This is a lesser danger, though, inasmuch as economic and political interests already distribute such information as widely as possible.[34]

At present, then, in neither the national nor the community level benefit-cost analysis do we get a realistic model for the true distribution of positive and negative impacts on society. The virtue of the former is that, theoretically, it includes all such benefits and costs. The strength of the latter is that it refers to some real social groupings, but ignores many of the benefits and especially some of the costs. As a basis for politicoeconomic judgment of programs and projects, we need both kinds of strengths. This requires the *extensity* of national lists of impacts and the *intensity* of focus that community studies give to particular groups. We as yet have little data on the importance of impacts on groups differing in economic, social, and political power. It is this common social disproof of current models that reinforces a need for a more participatory and adversarial process of impact assessment. Both the formulation and use of benefit-cost models must include varying social interest groups.

We will next briefly discuss two aspects of altering and evaluating distributional features of public projects.

Social Rates of Return

In public expenditure analysis, projects are viewed as "economic" if benefits exceed costs, or if the ratio of benefits to costs is greater than one. In addition, some projects may be deemed more cost-effective as their benefit-to-cost ratios increase beyond one. Given the mandate of NEPA and its litigative history, mission agencies should, then, be responsible for comparing alternative projects to best utilize a given set of natural resources, and/or to achieve some economic growth goals. With some exceptions in the Forest Service and the Department of Energy, though, the typical EIS merely compares a proposed project with no project at all.

Typically, the rationale for such procedure is that the particular agency does not have jurisdiction over many innovative alternative projects, or that information is lacking for such projects:

> Alternative means of obtaining objectives and goals are often over-looked, and alternative uses of resources are seldom realistically examined and compared. . . . All too often single-purpose pro-jections are made to legitimize increases in the current means of providing a resource service. . . . This outcome tends to become locked into the planning procedure as a result of the constraints on the demand studies which are undertaken. (Knetsch, 1970:568)

So long as mission agencies were primarily responsive to economic interest groups whose concerns were with such single purposes, political conflicts were mitigated. However, with the public political focus of EISs, the short-sightedness of projects with narrow goals of providing economic infrastructure and little concern with systematic effects on the biosphere or the socioeconomic system, opposition has arisen from a variety of public interest groups.

Such opposition often raises one of two questions: (1) Is the goal of the project a desirable one, and/or (2) are there more socially acceptable means of accomplishing these goals? By socially acceptable, they may mean as minor a modification as increasing the revenues to rural western communities affected by massive energy projects on leased government land. Or, far more fundamental questions may be raised about the social costs of nuclear energy, in terms of the political and social controls necessary to protect against future radiation leakages.

At a broader level, the entire thrust of the appropriate technology or "soft energy path" movements is a sustained critique of the ecological costs and social inefficiency of current modes of production. Their critiques of EISs require far more revision in the planning and EIS writing processes than a simple melioration of "boom-town" disloca-tions. In effect, what such groups are calling for is a calculation of a true *social* rate of return on public projects—a detailed evaluation of the progressive distributive outcomes of projects and programs.[35] That is, it applies the benefit-cost ratio to specific social groups or classes to examine the equity of projects, and not simply their economic efficiency. And all this is done in the context of minimizing ecological disorganization.

Outside the formal EIS process, there have been a number of attempts to scientifically confront such questions, particularly in the energy field. These typically point to the nonredistributive aspects of most public projects—i.e., they tend to favor more affluent investors and highly-skilled workers. A simple political solution is a reformation of the tax system to compensate for such inequities. But political opposition to such direct approaches is formidable, as the recent history of the U.S. negative income tax suggests.[36] Moreover, such an approach again typifies the bias of a single-purpose model: public projects would be aimed at economic efficiency, and tax programs at social equality. This model is favored by liberal economists like Arthur Okun, whose critique of socialist collectivized systems he might extend to project alternatives proposed here:

> The collectivized system would... achieve only a small improvement in equality at the expense of a significant worsening of efficiency.... [We need] private enterprise... for... experimentation and innovation [and] where flexibility matters more than accountability. (Okun, 1975:61)

The alternative that might be offered is a genuine internalization of equity concerns in public projects, accountable within the EIS's social impact assessment. This is a clear political choice, rather than a scientific decision. Equity analysis would focus on a system at the point in which the law provides some leverage for disadvantaged groups to criticize alternative public (and, indirectly, private) investment decisions. Okun's concern about public versus private investment would be partly offset by the fact that most public expenditure is channeled to private contractors today, following the decline he notes (1975:101–2) in direct public goods and increase in transfer payments by governments. In other words, equity increases could be generated by federal funds redirecting private economic interests.

To meet the goal of a social rate of return, then, pressures would be required by political interest groups to have a specification of likely distributions of costs and benefits of alternative projects. The choice of alternative projects would be politically determined, through political debate and pressures to force broader cooperation among federal agencies. In this context, the use of the Office of Technology Assessment to consider broad technological alternatives might be helpful, despite the limitations on this office.[37]

Proponents of the science of impact assessment will object to the formidability of such tasks. But the social reality is that impact assessment is as much politics as science. The redirection would force more parity between the currently overt science and covert politics. Given the volume of recent work on energy alternatives, and the fact that alteration of the energy usage in society will affect all production organization, we are moving to a position in which such considerations are not at all utopian. Imperfect consideration of options appears more socially progressive, finally, than detailed documentation for prior regressive modes of public investment.

Discounting the Future

A standard technique in benefit-cost analysis is to discount future benefits and costs by an appropriate rate. Each future estimate is divided by a discount rate, compounded for as many years as the period before which it will appear. In practice, this means that projects with distant benefits and more immediate costs will be discouraged, in favor of those with more imminent benefits. Typically, this means that projects with construction jobs, for example, will be economically favored, since employment and wages will flow at the early stages of projects. On the other hand, those with some long-term environmental gains will appear less "economic." These require a long period before the environmental improvements generate sufficient stimulation of related recreational or other activity.

Economists have debated the discount rate issue largely in terms of how large the rate should be. In an effort to debate their fellow economists on their home ground, the "new" conservation-minded economists like Krutilla have questioned the logic of discounting itself.[38] Though the debate is complex, it centers around the notion that, should money not be spent on a project, it could go into the private sector and generate economic growth with a given rate of return. The standard debate is around *which* sectors the funds might go to, and *what* the appropriate rate of return should be, to judge public investments. It has been argued (Krutilla, 1967b, 1973) that wilderness areas in fact appreciate in value over time because of their increased scarcity. Hence preservation actions should have a positive or appreciation rate. Thse arguments, though apparently scientific, are in fact political (Wildavsky, 1967).

The essence of the standard debate assumes (1) the desirability of economic growth as the basic goal of society, and (2) the evaluation of government investment for just this goal. In light of the discussion above, the issue can be widened in several ways. First, we can accept the first premise, but include distributional concerns on a parity with national economic growth, or even as the primary objective, depending on a group's political agenda. In addition, the flow of benefits and costs over time may be perceived in a variety of different ways by political groups. Therefore, a schedule of such impacts should be presented, rather than just a congealed summary of these in any kind of a discounted single net value.

The discount rate concept presupposes that some fictive social entity (the society) would in fact obtain the same rate of return if tax funds were released into various sectors of the *private* market. Such is indeed the treadmill argument underlying most general tax cuts—to stimulate demand, and hence increase production and the universal benefits of growth. One essential failing of this conventional argument is that there may be more political control by a variety of disadvantaged groups in the public investment side than in the private marketplace. Thus, the equality rates or "social" rates of return may be far different than the aggregative national growth return.[39]

A second approach to this issue is to argue for a broader utilitarian approach to public investment. A variety of individual and social group needs that are not priced in the market can be met better by public investments. Thus, while various aspects of health costs due to increased pollution may be quantified, many other psychic and physical risks of pollution cannot be, and should not be dismissed from a political goal of public projects.[40] This can be stated within the EIS and exempted from the kinds of discounting logic. At an abstract level, the conceptual foundation of grants economics offered in Boulding (1973) stresses the possibilities that parents defer consumption for the sake of their children, and implicitly weakens a notion that the future is always discounted.

These two approaches reflect two different senses of how the discounting approach has been used in past public expenditure. Apparently, a low discount rate has often allowed massive ecological disruption and unequal social benefits from projects, especially water projects done by the Army Corps of Engineers (Morgan, 1971). Therefore, raising the rate to the level of opportunity costs (alternative returns in the private sector) would discourage such ecologically and socially harmful projects. In this sense, political interest groups should welcome some such discounting. On the other hand, concern with creating more opportunities for a steady-state system of production, rather than maximizing production in the short-run, argues against raising such discount rates.

The issue falls into the category of intergenerational welfare politics, a subject with little solid material to sustain arguments. Generally, provision for children suggests a lower discounting of the future. Conversely, economists argue that with economic growth, the future generations will be able to afford projects better than present generations, so that there is intergenerational inequality impinging on present generations. But the essence of the environmentalist critique is precisely that diminishing availability of future resources will make for a *decline* in the conditions of future generations, negating such an argument. Likewise, the commitments of workers to forego present consumption in favor of insurance schemes of all types indicates that social systems do not operate on a single future discounting model.[41]

From these contradictions, it is clear that discounting is another political and not a technical issue. Its mechanical application should be restrained in this light.

NEW CONTEXTS FOR IMPACT ASSESSMENT

Social Impact Assessment: Some Political Futures

Recent years have brought some interesting developments in social impact assessment, but largely outside the formal EIS process. The single area in which this has occurred has been in energy issues, and primarily since the 1973–74 "oil crisis."[42] It would appear that the reasons for this are more political than scientific, and give some hope that revisions in the EIS are both possible and likely under assumptions of future political climates.

Energy analyses have included a large number of distributional studies, unfortunately dealing too heavily with short-term consumption issues following the oil crisis and rise in costs. But there have been broader studies of employment and long-term consumption effects of changing energy price and availability. Many of the methods used to do research in this area could have some limited value in improving the science in impact assessment, but this should not be overstated.

Energy issues reflect a duality that is not shared by other socio-environmental amenities, such as pollution. Energy is a factor of production. It is an element that is consumed virtually directly by consumers. And it is thus routinely observed and accounted for in the public and private sectors, and among individuals to a lesser extent. Wilderness, air, water and even land do not have these same qualities, at least to the extent that packaged energy does. In terms of both consciousness and calculability, then, energy stands apart from other environmental issues. Indeed, it has become common to talk of energy *and* environmental problems, as if they were distinct and not part of a general ecological-social interaction.

Energy impact assessment techniques will confront far less data in terms of other environmental and social connections resulting from public projects. While Leontief (1972) has, for example, indicated an input-output approach for pollution that parallels some energy analyses, there are grave data problems in the former. Some quasi-scientific information can certainly result from the attempt to incorporate such techniques and political concerns into the deficient EIS.

Moreover, there are two other features of the energy situation that perhaps bode well for future impact politics. The first is that the political (especially distributive) concerns of energy policies and projects raise the level of political consciousness in all public project impact reviews, for it is the same intervening public-interest groups that engage in both energy and other project evaluations. And energy distributive concerns clearly spill over into other impact areas.

Second, as noted earlier, energy issues are the tails that can indeed wag the production dogs. Changes in conservation policy can have a material bearing on the reorganization of production, along soft versus hard energy paths—labor versus capital intensity.[43] While it by no means follows that all environmental and social threats will diminish because of altered energy forms and levels, the potential changes are greater than those from any other reform of production.

Even the much-touted case in which the Tellico dam was "stopped" by the provisions of the Endangered Species Act and the presence of the snail darter hardly speaks for the typical power of impact assessment. The dam was threatened only because a specific piece of legislation was in place, and a determination of a threatened specie was relatively straightforward. The dam was finally *not* stopped, but its course simply rerouted to avoid disturbing the snail darter habitat. And, at the height of the controversy, legislative response leaned toward revising the Act rather than stopping the dam.[44] Similar backlashes are continuously threatened over other impact controls, such as cancer-inducing chemicals in foods, in the workplace, or in the community, despite the enactment of the Toxic Substances Control Act of 1976. Many of these areas show even less refinement of benefit-cost models than recent EISs, and the political battle to counter narrow economic and technical ideologies will not be easy.[45]

Recognizing that impact assessment is an inherently political activity is important. It assures us that political conflict is likely to surround all future impact assessments. But it by no means predicts the outcomes of the conflict. They will ultimately reflect the relative power and influence of the parties to the conflict.[46] Chapter VIII traces the most important party in recent environmental conflicts—the environmental movement. Its rise and transformation influences not only public *consciousness*, our concern in the past two chapters, but the form and level of political *conflict*.

NOTES

1. A review of this position is in Wolfe (1974), and an explicit discussion of the recent U.S. government conflicts around these issues in O'Connor (1973).

2. The most interesting view of this is in Friesema & Culhane (1976) and Fairfax (1978), who stress the political dimensions (see also Schindler, 1976). In contrast, Alston (1974) notes the political dimensions but offers a more formalized "resolution" of them, urging social scientists to "structure clientele conflict," a position that former EPA Director Russell Train underscores: "Polarization of conflict is unproductive." He prefers "reaching actual accomodation on some issues . . . and developing a more rational approach . . . before . . . a situation is deadlocked" (1978:324). The acknowledgement of some conflict in EISs is widespread, but various observers lean toward politicization as they follow a conflict approach versus an order approach to environmental problems (see Buttel & Flinn, 1975, on the outlines of these two positions).

3. For a comparison of this mandate with earlier federal agency decision-making, see Culhane (1974), who was cautiously optimistic about the changes to be brought

about. A skeptical view of citizen involvement in energy and other areas is given by Nelkin & Fallows (1977); they note the more effective involvement of citizen groups in some western European settings (e.g., Lewis, 1979).

4. The Council on Environmental Quality does not have the staff to do much beyond circulate impact statements and coordinate comments by agencies and other reviewers. And EPA itself appears to do a weaker job, when it contracts out reviews of EISs in agency branches that lack a strong internal technical staff, as reported in Butz & Senew (1974). Hill (1976), in a positive view of EISs, assumes that problems originate because agencies cannot verify that their consultants are providing accurate data in the EIS draft. There are grounds for suspicion that agencies consciously *make* a non-issue of this, in order to discourage public consciousness of some problems and yet maintain a stance of agency neutrality (see Crenson, 1971, for application of the non-issueness model). Extensive critiques of EPA inadequacy in NEPA review are contained in National Research Council (1977a,b) reports.

5. Following Spector & Kitsuse (1977), we can focus on environmental groups claiming the existence of a serious social problem in the 1960s, and various political and social agencies creating policies to deal with the claimants as much or more than their claims (Meidinger & Schnaiberg, 1978).

6. Culhane (1974:40) argues that NEPA was increasingly viewed as a balancing of new environmentalist concerns with older agency missions; there are doubts expressed here as to how much the balancing has swung back with more economic arguments *against* environmental melioration.

7. The focus here is on typical impact assessment within the environmental impact statement procedure under NEPA. Two other areas of impact assessment exist, though they are only touched upon here: (1) technology assessment (e.g., Kasper, 1972), in which future courses of large government-supported programs are evaluated well before final project commitment is made (or so the theory goes); and (2) studies of social impact of projects outside the agencies, by universities or social action groups (e.g., Crowfoot & Bryant, 1977; Peelle, 1977, particularly for energy projects).

8. On advocacy of agencies and their capture by economic interests, see the review in Culhane (1974) and Friesema & Culhane (1976). F. Anderson (1973) discusses the legal dimensions of balancing under NEPA.

9. The theory of benefit-cost analysis is well elaborated, as in Haveman & Margolis (1970). But wherever one turns in such discussions, there is a paucity of concrete data to undergird the theory. While this may suggest that adequate data are "just around the corner," it is equally likely that there are institutional barriers to obtaining such data that are formidable, as in the case of ecological data (e.g., Schnaiberg, 1977). Hence, while adoption of the benefit-cost *logic* of "balancing" in EISs is understandable, there is little indication that agency representatives acknowledge the serious technical and political problems of benefit-cost analysis and its foundation in welfare economics (e.g., I.M.D. Little, 1957). The theory indicates that techniques be used not only to discuss whether a project is economic, but which projects are *more* efficient. This ignores the reality that agencies seek to perpetuate their missions (Culhane, 1974; Knetsch, 1970) and seek to *justify* their expenditures, not to find the theoretically best solution for a public problem.

10. This decision was in *Natural Resources Defense Council v. Morton*,

D.C.C.A., F. 2d, 827, 1972, reprinted in the *102 Monitor* (Council on Environmental Quality, 1972). It required the Department of the Interior to consider alternatives to outer continential shelf oil and gas leasing to companies, "including those which depend for implementation on legislative or executive action outside of the direct control of the agency" (CEQ, 1972:2).

11. See Schnaiberg (1977) on problems in generating environmental analysis.

12. As noted earlier, public expenditure economists are rich in theory and impoverished in data (Goddard, 1972). In part, this results from economists drawing upon data collected by public agencies, rather than generating their own. Political forces that reduce the propensity to collect information on economic "bads," the ecological and social by-products of production, thereby get reinforced into "nonissueness" by this pattern of economic research (see Crenson, 1971; Samuels, 1972). A typical response of public welfare economists to the absence of data is to impute "shadow prices" to goods without market prices, without a clear acknowledgement of the multiplicity of social and economic assumptions involved in any such "data" (e.g., Margolis, 1970). A more honest position is that of Steiner (1970), who restricts such extensive quantification.

13. One of the few attempts to *empirically* test economic projection models, in the case of employment modeling of energy developments, is by Meidinger (1977, 1978, 1979). In testing projective models with data from past public projects, the errors in local employment predictions are quite substantial, and typically though not universally in the direction of overestimating secondary jobs. Even this sophisticated critique must assume that (1) the estimates of primary employment given in most projects are accurate, and (2) that we cannot assess job *losses* outside the impacted community that offset these secondary gains (see below).

14. The position of economic interests is forcefully stated in L. Green (1972:198). The progressive position is from Ophuls (1977:178).

15. The position for more research is in Haveman (1970a), Bonnen (1970) and Hill (1976), for example; Knetsch (1970) and Friesema & Culhane (1976) are more oriented toward a recognition of bureaucratic self-protection as a failing of EISs; the dramatic quotation is from Ophuls (1977:178).

16. From the perspective of Marxists (e.g., Poulantzas, 1973), such actions achieve a reduction of the ideological "hegemony" that has encouraged commitment to conventional economic growth in the belief that it brings social betterment, and is the only route to do so.

17. Hannon (1975) projects that energy conservation would increase opportunities for low-skill workers, but diminish them for high-skill workers (see also Bezdek & Hannon, 1974, for a specific transportation example). An excellent overview of such issues is in Morrison's (1976, 1977) synthesis of the recent literature. In contrast, the benign or positive economic benefits of pollution control reviewed by the government (CEQ, 1977:332) do not distinguish between such categories of labor.

18. Efficiency simply means getting more economic growth for less input; equity refers to the distribution of national income among different income groups (e.g., Okun, 1975).

19. Equity issues have become increasingly incorporated in discussions of en-

vironmental and especially energy policy (e.g., Morrison, 1977; Schnaiberg, 1975), in part because earlier environmental movements ignored these concerns and the resulting regressive effects of environmental protection policies (e.g., Dorfman, 1977; Schnaiberg, 1973), and were subject to the charge of "elitism." How much such concerns permeate the nonacademic establishment is a matter of speculation, though such academic debate can only increase the potential mobilization around such issues.

20. Programs of environmental quality have drawn special attention in the annual *Environmental Quality* reports of the Council on Environmental Quality. While initial reviews (e.g., CEQ, 1975: Ch. 4) tended to look at macrostructural effects on inflation and on industry-specific effects, recent efforts (e.g., CEQ, 1976:152–54) include more concentration on employment factors and anticipated benefit-cost ratios (e.g., CEQ, 1977:323). Ironically, there has been far more attention to the equity issue with respect to environmental protection activity than for most public expenditures that *stimulate economic growth* (e.g., Weisbrod, 1970; Haveman, 1970b; Bonnen, 1970). Indeed, the continuing review of EPA programs, now with respect to their inflationary impacts, has drawn the fire of environmental action groups (NRDC, 1978) who object to the unusual attention.

21. Schnaiberg (1977) treats some of the general problems of impact sciences and Meidinger (1977, 1978) points to the empirical and theoretical difficulties of creating and testing models of future impact, using past data, as do Meidinger & Schnaiberg (1978).

22. Wade (1973, 1975) reviews some of the inattention that the Agricultural Research Service gave to the distributive effects of U.S. agency policies in mechanization of agriculture. Morrison (1977) summarizes the general empirical literature on inequality of impacts of energy price and quantity shifts following the 1973–74 OPEC crisis, which again indicates socially regressive impacts (see also Schnaiberg, 1975). Most of the studies focus on consumption patterns, except for Meidinger (1977, 1978). Early (1974) and A. Carter (1974) focus on employment issues as well. Peelle (1977) reviews the general effects of recent energy developments on "boom towns," and efforts to remedy local social and economic disorganization. Interestingly, the Little & Lovejoy (1976) and R. Little (1976) studies raise some of the same questions as does Meidinger's (1977, 1978, 1979) work, with regard to the actual employment gains for local populations from capital-intensive energy projects (a point that further illustrates the Hannon, 1975, concern).

23. There is a real danger in the attempt to systematize social impact assessment, where agencies seek to "develop and implement standarized matrices" (Friesema & Culhane, 1976:342, footnote 21), since these will typically rely heavily on the inadequate public data collected in the past by agencies. Insofar as social scientists concur in this "systematic" approach to impact assessment (e.g., Olsen et al., 1977; Finsterbusch & Wolf, 1977), they tend to sublimate the underlying political conflicts inherent in selective availability of public data, and falsely reinforce the technical over the political dimensions of the EIS review (e.g., Cicchetti et al., 1973; Meidinger & Schnaiberg, 1978).

24. Where, as Culhane (1974) notes, there are *programs* for review rather than projects, public effectiveness in providing political input may be higher (for the

Forest Service program, see Alston, 1974). In the case of highways, a piecemeal approach still dominates (Leavitt, 1970; Caro, 1975; Lupo et al., 1971) leading to substantial local efforts and little national mobilization of interest groups. One example of many of the equity and other analytic problems noted above is the model of Stenehjem (1975), which is a precise, general model for impact forecasting.

25. Buttel (1976) stresses that analysts involved more closely with reformist efforts of government agencies may tend to retreat to a less politicized or "social order" view of environmental issues, unlike more socially and politically distant analysts, with a "social conflict" view. The problem is that agencies tend to recruit and resocialize the former, and thereby undercut efforts to systematically broaden equity concerns associated with the latter group. Equity activists, therefore, might continue to do better as outsiders, making issues out of non-issues (Crenson, 1971) as Friesema & Culhane (1976) advise, rather than guiding impact analysis from inside agencies.

26. Robert Caro (1975: Ch. 37, 38) provides the most graphic description of how transportation agencies manipulate displaced residents. Despite some improvements in the period since Robert Moses's activities, it is nonetheless true that State Departments of Transportation often have a conflict of interest. They want to minimize road costs (in benefit-cost analysis). But they also have to pay for dislocation costs. The result is pitifully inadequate settlements, especially for the powerless. Moreover, Boadway (1974) questions the usual economic simplification that equal monetary settlements to affected groups provides perfect compensation.

27. Slovic (1977) has treated with some skepticism the possibility of rational public discourse under conditions of risk and uncertainty, with various media and other distortions of technical information (e.g., see Nelkin, 1974 on the politicization of technical hearings). While there are some studies indicating severe cognitive problems in handling uncertainty (e.g., Tversky & Kahneman, 1974), it is not clear that experts are far superior in their judgment, particularly when operating in an insulated position, in agencies. Open adversarial *and* cooperative problem-solving approaches (e.g., Train, 1978) may be better.

28. This approach is recommended in Olsen et al. (1977).

29. For example, most of the detailed impact studies cited in Peelle (1977; cf. Shields, 1975) typically focus on the local community, rather than (a) specific groups within the community, and (b) indirectly affected groups outside the community/region (who suffer opportunities foregone because of local investment patterns). Nonetheless, local groups can respond to negative effects, if these are noted early enough (Gilmore, 1976).

30. See Leavitt (1970) on the impact of the Interstate Highway system on communities, O'Connor (1973) for a discussion of the fiscal crisis pressures, and Friedland et al. (1977) for the specific dimensions of this at the local urban level.

31. Mumford (1963:65–81) graphically traces the joint ecological and social consequences of mining through the centuries. The recent collapse of the Teton Dam (Gallagher, 1976) is but one example of the disasters pointed to by Morgan (1971), reviewing the work of the U.S. Army Corps of Engineers. It is not without some irony that one notes the crucial gatekeeping role of the Corps in enforcing water quality in the 1970s.

32. On community effects, see the review in Peelle (1977); for a review of energy impacts, see Morrison (1977) and Frankena et al. (1976). A brief recounting of the economic reviews of EPA is in NRDC (1978), and of the broader agency mission in L. Carter (1974) and Webster (1976).

33. See work of A. Carter (1974), Bezdek & Hannon (1974), and Hannon (1975).

34. Prior to Proposition 15's vote on 8 June 1976, the *California Energy Bulletin* (No on 15 Committee, 1976:1) headlined "U.S. Report Warns of Proposition 15 Nuclear Shutdown: $40 Billion Cost, $7,500 per Family, Seen for California," based on some rather questionable assumptions of an ERDA report. The widespread dissemination of similar messages is typical of the capacity of organized capital (often along with organized labor) to argue for the benefits of economic development as usual.

35. Schumacher's (1973) critique was first a social equity concern, and second an environmental critique. In contrast, Lovins (1976) was first an ecological or re-source critique, and second a social distributive one. Thus, while Lovins anticipates and calculates employment possibilities, Schumacher is more concerned with the human satisfactions from the nature of work, a theme that Stretton (1976) and C. Anderson (1976) return to repeatedly. Part of the reason for the wider reception policymakers have accorded Lovins, is, perhaps, the narrower set of claims and demands his "soft path" entails than from these broader social critics.

36. Okun (1975:114–17) argues that a taxation system that would subsidize private employment and aid the working poor is politically more feasible than either outright unconditional federal grants to the poor, or massive federal projects to employ the unemployed. Weisbrod (1970) is more supportive of federal programs to achieve redistribution, but stresses the need to monitor their actual effects closely, while Arrow (1970) reviews some criteria that might lead to choice of public versus private provision of goods and services. Haveman (1970b) indicates that the true social costs for government projects are substantially lower when they employ pre-viously unemployed workers, though the monetary project costs don't show this (again, an agency fragmentation problem, since typically another agency is paying the costs of unemployment insurance).

37. The political troubles of the Office of Technology Assessment since 1972 (Lyons, 1978) seem to reflect the views of H. Green: "I do not agree that there is any viable distinction between political assessment and technology assessment" (1972:50).

38. See Baumol (1970) for a strong statement on using market rates of discount, and Krutilla (1967a,b; 1973) on the concept of an estate and its conservation implications.

39. Okun (1975:99) approvingly notes that "collective decision-making—not the marketplace—controls the whole area of public capital formation." He stresses that the poor have more control through their votes than through their economic power, a pluralist assumption (1975:100).

40. An early attempt to quantify health risks is Lave & Seskin (1970). More recently, Wilson (1978) has argued for a stricter benefit-cost approach to dealing with such health risks. His approach exemplifies some of the quantification biases

noted earlier. Stretton critiques such marginalist approaches (1976: footnote 24). A broad overview of meliorative policies is in Davis & Kamien (1970).

41. While Heilbroner (1975) has raised the issue of social commitments to future generations, no simple answers have yet emerged. Boulding (1971, 1973) has toyed with the notion of parental commitments to future estates, especially for their children. Simon (1977) has, conversely, stressed the regressive aspect of current generations paying for future, richer generations' infrastructure. Zeckhauser (1970) has examined some hypothetical models of community response to future risks and uncertainties and concludes we need even higher discount rates. Haveman (1976) notes the problems are compounded in measuring family versus societal welfare.

42. See, for example, Morrison (1977) and Frankena et al. (1976) for reviews of various equity concerns in energy research.

43. In addition to the lofty abstractions of Lovins (1976), a practical political plea revolving around Montana's energy production is in Christiansen & Clack (1976).

44. For a general discussion of the dam conflict, see Shabecoff (1978). The litigative conflicts are described in Mohr (1978) and the successful defense of the bill in Smith (1978).

45. Wilson's (1978) plea for a benefit-cost approach to cancer is but one approach of the opposition to prohibition. Commoner (1977) indicates fears that such balancing in the Toxic Substances Control Act of 1976 will hamper control of carcinogenic petrochemicals, a fear that seems borne out by agency problems (Vinocur, 1977). It may not be a coincidence, therefore, that "the chemical industry, which fought the more stringent requirements of earlier versions . . . now seems prepared to live with the consequences of the law that passed" (Brody, 1977).

46. While this interaction is labelled as "political" here, others see these interactions more neutrally as "cooperative" (Train, 1978) or "participatory" (Meadows, 1977).

REFERENCES

ALFORD, ROBERT R. AND R. FRIEDLAND
   1975   "Political participation and public policy." Pp. 429–479 in A. Inkeles, J. Coleman, and N. Smelser (eds.), Annual Review of Sociology. Volume I. Palo Alto, Cal.: Annual Reviews, Inc.

ALSTON, ROBERT M.
   1974   "Socio-economic considerations in environmental decision-making." Humboldt Journal of Social Relations 2(1):58–66.

ANDERSON, CHARLES A.
   1976   The Sociology of Survival: Social Problems of Growth. Homewood, Illinois: Dorsey Press.

ANDERSON, FREDERICK
   1973   NEPA in the Courts: A Legal Analysis of the National Environmental Policy Act. Baltimore: Johns Hopkins University Press.

ARROW, KENNETH J.
1970   "The organization of economic activity: Issues pertinent to the choice of market versus nonmarket allocation." Pp. 59–73 in R.H. Haveman and J. Margolis (eds.), Public Expenditures and Policy Analysis. Chicago: Markham-Rand McNally.

BAUMOL, WILLIAM J.
1970   "On the discount rate for public projects." Pp. 273–290 in R.H. Haveman and J. Margolis (eds.), Public Expenditures and Policy Analysis. Chicago: Markham-Rand McNally.

BEZDEK, ROGER AND B. HANNON
1974   "Energy, manpower, and the Highway Trust Fund." Science 185 (23 Aug.):669–675.

BOADWAY, ROBIN W.
1974   "The welfare foundations of cost-benefit analysis." The Economic Journal 84 (336):926–939.

BONNEN, JAMES T.
1970   "The absence of knowledge of distributional impacts: An obstacle to effective policy analysis and decisions." Pp. 246–270 in R.H. Haveman and J. Margolis (eds.), Public Expenditures and Policy Analysis. Chicago: Markham-Rand McNally.

BOULDING, KENNETH E.
1971   "The economics of the coming spaceship earth." Pp. 180–187 in J. P. Holdren and P.R. Ehrlich (eds.), Global Ecology: Readings Toward a Rational Strategy for Man. New York: Harcourt, Brace, Jovanovich.
1973   The Economy of Love and Fear: A Preface to Grants Economics. Belmont, California: Wadsworth.

BRODY, JANE E.
1977   "Chemicals: Health is the new priority." New York Times, 9 Jan.

BUTTEL, FREDERICK H.
1976   "Social science and the environment: Competing theories." Social Science Quarterly 57 (2):307–323.

BUTTEL, FREDERICK H. AND W.L. FLINN
1975   "Methodological issues in the sociology of natural resources." Humboldt Journal of Social Relations 3 (1):63–72.

BUTZ, BRIAN P. AND M.J. SENEW
1974   A Methodology to Measure the Performance of the EPA Regional EIS Review Process. Report ANL/ES-41. Argonne, Ill.: Argonne National Laboratory.

CARO, ROBERT A.
1975   The Power Broker: Robert Moses and the Fall of New York. New York: Vintage Books.

CARTER, ANNE P.
1974   "Applications of input-output analysis to energy problems." Science 184 (19 Apr.):325–329.

CARTER, LUTHER J.
1974   "EPA study: National Academy set to serve two masters." Science 185 (23 Aug.):678–680.

CHRISTIANSEN, BILL AND T.H. CLACK, JR.
1976   "A western perspective on energy: A plea for rational energy planning." Science 194 (5 Nov.):578–584.

CICCHETTI, CHARLES J. ET AL.
1973   "Evaluating federal water projects: A critique of proposed standards." Science 181 (24 Aug.):723–728.

COMMONER, BARRY
1977   "The promise and perils of petrochemicals." New York Times Magazine, 25 Sept.:38ff.

COUNCIL ON ENVIRONMENTAL QUALITY (CEQ)
1972   "NRDC v. Morton: Significant new appellate decision on Section 102 of NEPA." Council on Environmental Quality, 102 Monitor 2 (1):1–20.
1975   Environmental Quality-1975. Washington, D.C.: Council on Environmental Quality.
1976   Environmental Quality-1976. Washington, D.C.: Council on Environmental Quality.
1977   Environmental Quality-1977. Washington, D.C.: Council on Environmental Quality.

CRENSON, MATTHEW A.
1971   The Un-Politics of Air Pollution: A Study of Non-Decision-making in the Cities. Baltimore: Johns Hopkins University Press.

CROWFOOT, JAMES E. AND B.I. BRYANT, JR.
1977   "Environmental advocacy: An action strategy for dealing with environmental problems." Paper presented at meetings of Society for Study of Social Problems, Chicago, September.

CULHANE, PAUL J.
1974   "Federal agency organizational change in response to environmentalism." Humboldt Journal of Social Relations 2 (1):31–44.

DAVIS, OTTO A. AND M.I. KAMIEN
1970   "Externalities, information and alternative collective action." Pp. 74–95 in R. H. Haveman and J. Margolis (eds.), Public Expenditures and Policy Analysis. Chicago: Markham-Rand McNally.

DORFMAN, ROBERT
1977   "Benefits and costs of environmental programs." Society, Mar.–Apr.:63–66.

DORFMAN, ROBERT AND H.D. JACOBY
1970   "A model of public decisions illustrated by a water pollution policy problem." Pp. 173–231 in R.H. Haveman and J. Margolis (eds.), Public Expenditures and Policy Analysis. Chicago: Markham-Rand McNally.

EARLY, JOHN F.
1974 "Effect of the energy crisis on employment." Monthly Labor Review 97 (8):8-16.

FAIRFAX, SALLY K.
1978 "A disaster in the environmental movement." Science 199 (17 Feb.):743-748.

FINSTERBUSCH, KURT AND C.P. WOLF (EDS.)
1977 Methodology of Social Impact Assessment. Strondsberg, Pennsylvania: Dowden, Hutchinson, and Ross.

FRANKENA, FREDERICK L., F.H. BUTTEL, AND D.E. MORRISON
1976 "Energy/Society Annotations." East Lansing, Michigan: Michigan State University, Department of Sociology, Nov.

FRIEDLAND, ROGER, F.F. PIVEN, AND R.R. ALFORD
1977 "Political conflict, urban structure, and the fiscal crisis." International Journal of Urban and Regional Research 1 (3):447-471.

FRIEDLAND, WILLIAM H., A.E. BARTON, AND R.J. THOMAS
1978 Manufacturing Green Gold: The Conditions and Social Consequences of Lettuce Harvest Mechanization: A Social Impact Analysis. Davis, Cal.: Department of Applied Behavioral Science, College of Agriculture and Environmental Studies, University of California, Davis.

FRIESEMA, H. PAUL AND P.J. CULHANE
1976 "Social impacts, politics, and the environmental impact statement process." Natural Resources Journal 16(Apr.):339-356.

GALLAGHER, DOROTHY
1976 "The collapse of the great Teton dam." New York Times Magazine, 19 Sept.:16ff.

GILMORE, JOHN
1976 "Boom towns may hinder energy resource development." Science 191 (13 Feb.):535-540.

GODDARD, HAYNES G.
1972 "Environmental policy as economic policy." Environmental Affairs 2 (3): 630-637.

GREEN, HAROLD P.
1972 "The adversary process in technology assessment." Pp. 49-62 in R.G. Kasper (ed.), Technology Assessment: Understanding the Social Consequences of Technological Applications. New York: Praeger Books.

GREEN, LEON G., JR.
1972 "Technology assessment or technology harassment: The attacks on science and technology." Pp. 195-221 in R.G. Kasper, (ed.), Technology Assessment: Understanding the Social Consequences of Technological Applications. New York: Praeger Books.

HANNON, BRUCE
1975 "Energy conservation and the consumer." Science 189 (11 July):95-102.

HAVEMAN, ROBERT H.
1970a "Public expenditures and policy analysis: An overview." Pp. 1–18 in
       R.H. Haveman and J. Margolis (eds.), Public Expenditures and Policy
       Analysis. Chicago: Markham-Rand McNally.
1970b "Evaluating public expenditures under conditions of unemployment."
       Pp. 330–346 in R.H. Haveman and J. Margolis (eds.), Public Expendi-
       tures and Policy Analysis. Chicago: Markham-Rand McNally.
1976   "Benefit-cost analysis and family planning programs." Population and
       Development Review 2(1):37–64.

HAVEMAN, ROBERT H. AND J. MARGOLIS (EDS.)
1970   Public Expenditures and Policy Analysis. Chicago: Markham-Rand Mc-
       Nally.

HEILBRONER, ROBERT L.
1975   An Inquiry Into the Human Prospect. New York: W.W. Norton.

HILL, GLADWIN
1976   "Environmental impact statements, practically a revolution." New York
       Times, 5 Dec.

HIRSHLEIFER, JACK AND D.L. SHAPIRO
1970   "The treatment of risk and uncertainty." Pp. 291–313 in R.H. Haveman
       and J. Margolis (eds.), Public Expenditures and Policy Analysis.
       Chicago: Markham-Rand McNally.

KASPER, RAPHAEL G. (ED.)
1972   Technology Assessment: Understanding the Social Consequences of
       Technological Applications. New York: Praeger Books.

KING, WAYNE
1978   "Documents indicate Corps misled Congress on major southern canal."
       New York Times, 26 Nov.

KNEESE, ALLEN V.
1973   "The Faustian bargain: Benefit-cost analysis and unscheduled events in
       the nuclear fuel cycle." Resources 44:1–5.

KNETSCH, JACK L.
1970   "Economic analysis in natural resource programs." Pp. 562–579 in R.
       H. Haveman and J. Margolis (eds.), Public Expenditures and Policy
       Analysis. Chicago: Markham-Rand McNally.

KRUTILLA, JOHN V.
1967a "Some environmental effects of economic development." Daedalus,
       Fall:1058–1070.
1967b "Conservation reconsidered." American Economic Review 57 (4):777–
       786.

KRUTILLA, JOHN V. (ED.)
1973   Natural Environments: Studies in Theoretical and Applied Analysis. Bal-
       timore: Johns Hopkins University Press.

LAVE, LESTER B. AND E.P. SESKIN
1970   "Air pollution and human health." Science 169 (21 Aug.):723–733.

LEAVITT, HELEN
1970   Superhighway-Superhoax. New York: Ballantine Books.

LEONTIEF, WASSILY
1972   "Environmental repercussions and the economic structure: An input-output approach." Pp. 403–422 in R. Dorfman and N.S. Dorfman (eds.), Economics of the Environment: Selected Readings. New York: W.W. Norton.

LEVINS, RICHARD
1966   "The strategy of model building in population biology." American Scientist 54 (4):421–431.

LEWIS, FLORA
1979   "In Europe, the nuclear debate looms even larger." New York Times, 8 Apr.

LITTLE, I.M.D.
1957   A Critique of Welfare Economics. Second Edition. London: Oxford University Press.

LITTLE, RONALD L.
1976   "Some social consequences of boom towns." Unpublished paper, Department of Sociology, Utah State University, Logan, Utah.

LITTLE, RONALD L. AND S.B. LOVEJOY
1976   "Employment benefits from rural industrialization." Logan, Utah: Department of Sociology, Utah State University.

LOVINS, AMORY
1976   "Energy strategy: The road not taken?" Foreign Affairs 55(1):65–96.

LUPO, ALAN, F. COLCORD, AND E.P. FOWLER
1971   Rites of Way: The Politics of Transportation in Boston and the U.S. City. Boston: Little, Brown.

LYONS, RICHARD D.
1978   "Congress' expert help in scientific matters ran afoul of politics." New York Times, 12 Mar.

MARGOLIS, JULIUS
1970   "Shadow prices for incorrect or nonexistent market prices." Pp. 314–329 in R.H. Haveman and J. Margolis (eds.), Public Expenditures and Policy Analysis. Chicago: Markham-Rand McNally.

MEADOWS, PAUL
1977   "Technology assessment and impact analysis: A sociological perspective." Paper presented at meetings of Society for Study of Social Problems, Chicago, Aug.

MEIDINGER, ERROL E.
1977   "Projecting secondary jobs: an empirical examination and epistemological critique." Paper presented at meetings of American Sociological Association, Chicago, September.
1978   "Modeling the local impacts of energy development: a case study and

epistemological critique." Paper presented to International Symposium on Modeling, Simulation and Decision in Energy Systems, Montreal, June.

1979   "Multi-variate Modeling" in R. McCleary, R.A. Hay, E.E. Meidinger, and D. McDowall, Applied Time Series Analysis for the Social Sciences: An Introduction to the Box-Jenkins Approach to Impact Assessment and Forecasting. Beverly Hills, Cal.: Sage (forthcoming).

MEIDINGER, ERROL E. AND A. SCHNAIBERG
1978   "Social impact assessment as evaluation research: Claimants and claims." Paper presented at meetings of Society for the Study of Social Problems, San Francisco, Sept.

MOHR, CHARLES
1978   "Some little fish and a mighty law at risk." New York Times, 23 Apr.

MORGAN, ARTHUR E.
1971   Dams and Other Disasters: A Century of the Army Corps of Engineers in Civil Works. Boston: Porter Sargent.

MORRISON, DENTON E.
1976   "Growth, environment, equity and scarcity." Social Science Quarterly 57 (2):292–306.

1977   "Equity impacts of some major energy alternatives." Draft Report to Risk/Impact Panel, Sociopolitical Resource Group, Committee on Nuclear and Alternative Energy Systems, National Research Council, National Academy of Sciences.

MUMFORD, LEWIS
1963   Technics and Civilization. New York: Harcourt, Brace, and World.

NATIONAL RESEARCH COUNCIL (NAS-NRC)
1977a   Decision Making in the Environmental Protection Agency. Report of the Environmental Studies Board, Commission on Natural Resources. Washington, D.C.: National Academy of Sciences.

1977b   Research and Development in the Environmental Protection Agency. Report of the Research Assessment Committee, Commission on Natural Resources. Washington, D.C.: National Academy of Sciences.

NATURAL RESOURCES DEFENSE COUNCIL (NRDC)
1978   "Inflation review of environmental regulations: new quality of life review?" Natural Resources Defense Council, NRDC newsletter 7 (2/3):11.

NELKIN, DOROTHY
1974   "The role of experts in a nuclear siting controversy." Bulletin of the Atomic Scientists 30 (9):29–36.

NELKIN, DOROTHY AND S. FALLOWS
1977   "The politics of participation in energy policy." Draft Report to Risk/Impact Panel, Sociopolitical Resource Group, Committee on Nuclear and Alternative Energy Systems, National Research Council, National Academy of Sciences.

NO ON 15 COMMITTEE
1976 California Energy Bulletin. Glendale, California: No on 15 Committee/Californians Against the Nuclear Shutdown.

O'CONNOR, JAMES
1973 The Fiscal Crisis of the State. New York: St. Martin's Press.

OKUN, ARTHUR M.
1975 Equality and Efficiency: The Big Tradeoff. Washington, D.C.: The Brookings Institution.

OLSEN, MARVIN E., M.G. CURRY, M.R. GREEN, B.D. MELBER, AND D.J. MERWIN
1977 A Social Impact Assessment and Management Methodology Using Social Indicators and Planning Strategies. Draft Report. Seattle, Washington: Battelle Human Affairs Research Centers.

OPHULS, WILLIAM
1977 Ecology and the Politics of Scarcity: Prologue to a Political Theory of the Steady State. San Francisco: W.H. Freeman.

PEELLE, ELIZABETH
1977 "Community and regional impact and response to energy production and use." Draft Report to Risk/Impact Panel, Sociopolitical Resource Group, Committee on Nuclear and Alternative Energy Systems, National Research Council, National Academy of Sciences.

POULANTZAS, NICOS
1973 Political Power and Social Classes. London: New Left Books and Sheed and Ward.

SAMUELS, WARREN J.
1972 "Ecosystem policy and the problem of power." Environmental Affairs 2 (3):580–596.

SCHINDLER, D.W.
1976 "The impact statement boondoggle." Science 192 (7 May):509.

SCHNAIBERG, ALLAN
1973 "Politics, participation, and pollution: The 'environmental movement.'" Pp. 605–627 in J. Walton and D.E. Carns (eds.), Cities in Change: Studies on the Urban Condition. Boston: Allyn and Bacon.
1975 "Social syntheses of the societal-environmental dialectic: The role of distributional impacts." Social Science Quarterly 56 (1):5–20.
1977 "Obstacles to environmental research by scientists and technologists: A social structural analysis." Social Problems 24 (5):500–520.

SCHNAIBERG, ALLAN AND E. MEIDINGER
1978 "Social reality versus analytic mythology: Social impact assessment of natural resource utilization." Paper presented at American Sociological Association meetings, San Francisco, September.

SCHUMACHER, E.F.
1973 Small Is Beautiful: Economics as if People Mattered. New York: Harper and Row.

SHABECOFF, PHILIP
1978   "New battles over endangered species." New York Times Magazine, 4 June:38–44.

SHIELDS, MARK A.
1975   "Social impact studies: An exploratory analysis." Environment and Behavior 7 (3):265–284.

SIMON, JULIAN L.
1977   The Economics of Population Growth. Princeton, N.J.: Princeton University Press.

SLOVIC, PAUL
1977   "Perception and acceptability of risk from nuclear and alternative energy sources." Draft Report to Risk/Impact Panel, Sociopolitical Resource Group, Committee on Nuclear and Alternative Energy Systems, National Research Council, National Academy of Sciences.

SMITH, R. JEFFREY
1978   "Endangered Species Act survives Senate hunters." Science 201 (4 Aug.):426–428.

SPECTOR, MALCOLM AND J.I. KITSUSE
1977   Constructing Social Problems. Menlo Park, Cal.: Cummings Publishing Company.

STEINER, PETER O.
1970   "The public sector and the public interest." Pp. 21–58 in R.H. Haveman and J. Margolis (eds.), Public Expenditures and Policy Analysis. Chicago: Markham-Rand McNally.

STENEHJEM, ERIK J.
1975   Forecasting the Local Economic Impacts of Energy Resource Development: A Methodological Approach. Report ANL/AA-3. Argonne, Ill.: Argonne National Laboratory.

STRETTON, HUGH
1976   Capitalism, Socialism and the Environment. Cambridge: Cambridge University Press.

TRAIN, RUSSELL E.
1978   "The environment today." Science 201 (28 July):320–324.

TVERSKY, AMOS AND D. KAHNEMAN
1974   "Judgement under uncertainty: Heuristics and biases." Science 185 (27 Sept.):1124–1131.

VINOCUR, JOHN
1977   "Major enforcement gaps hobble law to control toxic substances." New York Times, 30 Oct.

WADE, NICHOLAS
1973   "Agriculture: Social sciences oppressed and poverty stricken." Science 180 (18 May):719–722.

1975 "Agriculture: Academy group suggests major shakeup to President Ford." Science 190 (5 Dec.):959–961.

WEBSTER, BAYARD
1976 "EPA's 5-year plan is criticized for focus on short-term issues." New York Times, 19 Sept.

WEISBROD, BURTON A.
1970 "Collective action and the distribution of income: A conceptual approach." Pp. 117–141 in R.H. Haveman and J. Margolis (eds.), Public Expenditures and Policy Analysis. Chicago: Markham-Rand McNally.

WILDAVSKY, AARON
1967 "Aesthetic power or the triumph of the sensitive minority over the vulgar mass: A political analysis of the new economics." Daedalus, Fall:1115–1128.

WILSON, RICHARD
1978 "A rational approach to reducing cancer risk." New York Times, 9 July.

WOLFE, ALAN
1974 "New directions in the Marxist theory of politics." Politics and Society, Winter:131–159.

ZECKHAUSER, RICHARD
1970 "Uncertainty and the need for collective action." Pp. 96–116 in R.H. Haveman and J. Margolis (eds.), Public Expenditures and Policy Analysis. Chicago: Markham-Rand McNally.

VIII THE ENVIRONMENTAL MOVEMENT
Roots and Transformations

THE CONTEMPORARY MOVEMENT
The Movement in Analytic Perspective

The two preceding chapters indicate a set of historical barriers to achieving social consciousness of ecological and socioeconomic problems relating to sociocultural production and its use of the biosphere. Such barriers are now more clearly perceived than they were a decade ago. In part this is due to the increased awareness of ecological structure, the organized social efforts to destroy some of these barriers, and the efforts to achieve changes in production. The development of such awareness and the resulting social actions are labeled in this chapter as the "environmental movement." Both the constraints of the barriers earlier noted and the actions of this movement exemplify the structural tensions in society, noted in 1852 by Karl Marx in *The Eighteenth Brumaire of Louis Bonaparte:*[1] "Men make their own history, but they do not make it just as they please; they do not make it under circumstances chosen by themselves, but under circumstances directly encountered, given, and transmitted from the past" (Feuer, 1959:320).

In this chapter, my primary emphasis will be on this making of recent history by the movement, and on its potential for future historical changes in environmental usage and social welfare. At one extreme, this will encompass the drive to restructure future social production by the appropriate technology branch of the movement. But it is almost as important to comprehend the circumstances of the past, and their influence and limiting powers. The euphoria of the 1960s has given way to forms of institutionalized conflict in the 1970s that induce social changes falling far short of the earlier expectations.[2] Unlike many casual participants in and observers of the movement, though, we should be in a good position to understand these limitations, given the materials in chapters IV through VII especially.

Perceptions and programs of various parts of the contemporary environmental movement are quite different. It has become clearer that the agenda of environmental protection organizations involves a challenge to aspects of existing sociocultural production systems. The nature of this challenge is less clear. For some movement organizations and participants, these challenges are sometimes at the level of "superstructure"—the ideological or value level of society. In others, they are at the "substructural" level, involving concrete production organization. Still others are focused on the "social structural" level, challenging existing social class and political organization.[3]

In general, though, the modern environmental movement in the United States and elsewhere constitutes a social protest or challenge movement. Although some social movement theorists have treated the environmental movement lightly, and see it as an "even less radical constituency" than the anti–Vietnam War movement in the U.S. (Ash, 1972:239), reality is more complex than this. While the movement has, in recent years, taken on a clearly reformist cast, targets of the movement have often been more radically challenged than this label suggests. From the overt ideology of some branches of the movement, it appears to be yet another modern, middle-class reformist movement engaged in largely symbolic *moral* protest, with

> ideological amorphousness and ambiguity. These movements are concerned above all with great issues. . . . Beyond these commitments to generalized aims there is no common ideological consensus within the movements, either on the means by which such aims are to be realized, or upon a general programme of social and political reforms . . . it is easier to tell what they are "against" than what they are "for." (Wilkinson, 1971:118–19)

The argument presented in this chapter is that this is an increasingly misleading evaluation of the movement. Over the past decade, there have been changes in the organization and ideology of the movement, refinements of goals and means, and a clearer sense of the political conflicts ahead.[4] While there remain many utopian elements within the present movement, even these have clearer programs of large-scale social engineering rather than simply millenarian quests for ultimate ends.[5]

Despite the often amorphous quality of this movement, I view it as a social movement and not simply an ephemeral instance of short-lived collective behavior. To treat it in the framework of the range of collective behavior is to emphasize more the social origins of its members and less the impetus for social change of the movement and its organizations.[6] Following Banks (1972:15), I see the environmental movement as "socially *constructive*," falling into a perspective of "social movements . . . as creators rather than creatures of social change." Yet, as Marx so aptly noted, this making of social history is constrained by the structure of history itself. First, the very processes of production expansion have permitted the emergence of such a protest movement. They create a level of affluence in some portions of society that affords greater social innovativeness:

> To ignore the element of deliberate constructiveness in social affairs, as *itself creating* dissatisfaction with things as they are, is to ignore the human capacity for artifice from motives of simple curiosity and the desire to make a discovery or to build something no one has succeeded in building before. (Banks, 1972:55)

This permissiveness of the expansionary system is also coupled with the increased potential for observation of ecosystem destruction and weakness induced by the selfsame production expansion. Science, however hampered as noted in Chapter VI, nonetheless gained improved powers of documenting ecosystem disorganization in recent decades. And mounting biospheric disruption made such observations both easier to make and, once made, more socially significant.[7] Such permissiveness of the growth system frequently ends, though, when the *substance* of environmental challenges to the system is considered. Thus, while there has been unusually broad acceptance or legitimacy of the environmental movement through NEPA and other legislation, each gain has increased the forces of reaction. Legislation often fails by lack of enforcement. Litigation has often succeeded, but only skirmishes have been fought. The struggle against the current production expansion cannot be fought in court, for want of fiscal and other movement resources. Mobilization of new environmental constituencies has succeeded by raising consciousness of problems. But the efforts of monopoly capital to diminish such consciousness have likewise increased.[8]

Reaction, though, is in part a measure of success. For an absence of conflict would imply that the environmental movement is not threatening various interests within the present growth coalition. Up to some level, the growth of such conflict is also cause for hope, for it indicates a spread of the movement's mission. Beyond that level, it portends collapse of a movement and repudiation of its message. No one can estimate an optimal level of conflict, as one pessimistic account indicates:

> Apathy to change . . . is possible only as long as the changes do not become real. As changes take place, the scope and character of their costs become apparent and the chain reaction of cost displacement begins. At the end of the chain are the worker and the consumer. The skepticism that was visible [in] . . . 1970 became the dominant characteristic of the movement's attentive public by 1972. (Hornback, 1974:200–201)

On the other hand, there was relatively little major reform commitment by many elements of the monopoly capital group even early in this process, though there was acquiescence to some movement demands. With the "energy crisis" of 1973–74, though, positions hardened among both reformists and reactionaries.[9] But they also changed, with new attempts at coalition in both groups. Contrary to many assertions that this movement was only a moral protest concerned with status politics, the environmental movement has encompassed reform, reaction, and reorganized reform efforts (along with new reactions).[10] In the process, many movement organizations have died and recruits have been lost, but new ones have been formed and new constituents found. The first part of this chapter emphasizes some of these shifts and some explanations for them. These are far more tentative than other sections of this book, though, because of the limited amount of careful study given to the movement itself. Too much attention has been given to the study of public opinion polls, and too little to the structure of and processes of change of movement organizations. In part this stems from the excessive emphasis on the collective behavior dimensions of environmentalism, and the under-emphasis on the major dimensions of social change and social conflict represented by some branches of the movement (Traugott, 1978). The polls, moreover, show far more inconsistency from study to study than is indicated in the social movement organizations themselves. Both are real phenomena, but difficult to integrate.[11]

After this recent movement history and a decomposition of the movement ideologies and organizations, I turn next to some comparisons with precursors to the environmental movement. In particular, some contrasts are drawn with the earlier (and continuing) conservation movement that came to fruition in the early twentieth century. On balance, the evidence suggests a clear departure of the current movement and a shift away from the political capitalism that many observers now understand to be a consequence of the Progressive Era. Moving from the past to the future, the key issue confronting environmentalism is the incorporation of both the ecological and socioeconomic policies of the appropriate technology movement. In its most elaborated form, the latter represents the most striking shift away from protest—from being "against"—to reconstruction of the sociocultural production system. But the latter also represents the strongest challenge to existing production organization and social relations, as well as ideology.[12]

In closing, this chapter points to risks and potential of the current movement mix. In this and in the final chapter, I, as a social scientist, find little firm ground for prediction—which is an art rather than a science.[13] These concluding remarks will thus be more tentative than those in the earlier parts of the book.

The Trajectory of the Contemporary Movement

The modern "environmental movement" is sufficiently diverse that a question arises as to whether it is really proper to label such diversity with a single name. Environmental organizations and their memberships differ often in their choice of concern over particular environmental withdrawals and additions, in their analysis of the social causes of such ecological changes, and in their prescriptions for appropriate social changes. These are important differences, which create strains within a so-called environmental movement, and which color social policy disputes around environmental issues. Yet what is shared by all these organizations is a concern about socioenvironmental relationships.[14] This shared concern is probably sufficient to justify treatment of these organizations as a movement. Such concerns were socially invisible to the *mass* of Americans (and those in other industrial societies) prior to the mid-1960s. Thus, the emergence and growth of environmental organizations appeared to be a genuine sociohistorical watershed. That is, the relative novelty of this concern was great enough to set it off from social protests and social movements of earlier periods. Moreover, the novelty was also sufficiently striking that outsiders and insiders alike of the movement found sufficient commonality in the diverse forms of "environmentalism" to shape a movement. By attacking all "environmentalists," opponents of the movement helped to integrate it as much as did the members themselves. This fusion was at best partial, and movement fission has continued apace in the last decade, but with important continuities.

From the mass of material that has been gathered on the contemporary American environmental movement, we may extract some general findings. First, this social movement rose in the late 1960s from a modest base to a fairly large one. Its public support base has since tapered off somewhat. Second, even at the peak of environmentalism, roughly during 1968–70, there was substantial opposition to many components of a broad environmental protection ideology of the movement, and this opposition has increased in recent years. Third, the major social group supporting the movement was the middle-to-upper-middle-class segment of the American population. In particular, the movement found its strongest support within the white, educated, white-collar stratum. Fourth, the movement has gradually changed from a "participatory" to a "power" strategy in dealing with conflicts around environmental issues. While public-education campaigns have by no means disappeared in recent years, the core of the active environmental movement today is focused on litigation, political lobbying, and technical evaluation rather than on mass mobilization for protest marches, petition-signing, and the like. Recent antinuclear coalitions like the Clamshell Alliance and its European counterparts have revived many of these earlier forms, though.[15]

These observations can lead us in many directions, but the argument I wish to make about the movement and its trajectory is as follows. As I will note later, part of the 1960s and 1970s movement grew out of an organizational matrix of voluntary associations connected with conservationism and especially preservationism in the preceeding period. There also existed a framework of distinctive state agencies concerned with various kinds of land control and, to a lesser extent, some forms of pollution.[16] Following the distinction noted in Chapter I, many of these preexisting organizations are concerned with *habitat* and to a much lesser extent with *sustenance*. Many of these organizations were pressure groups, focusing on particular local issues and negotiating with business and state agencies. But they did not constitute a coherent movement. Indeed, to some extent these associations were the remnants of early conservationist movements, which flowered in the early part of the twentieth century.

In the late 1960s, though, a new mass consciousness of environmental issues appeared. These issues were heavily weighted toward sustenance concerns, in the extreme towards "survival." This mass base formed a moral protest movement, with concerns about the status risks of environmental degradation. Resulting status politics (Gusfield, 1963) created a moral crusade against extravagant consumption and production. Middle-class predominance, and involvement of educated professional groups with a self-interest in expanding public service jobs in environmental protection, is not atypical:

> Outside the mass of trade unions... most voluntary associations or pressure groups with a movement dimension have a predominantly middle-class membership and leadership. . . . [They] are *par excellence* agencies of middle-class mobilization and influence. (Wilkinson, 1971:116–17)

During this early period, there was a stronger emphasis on participatory strategies, on building a social constituency for environmental concern. This period of *mobilization* of a citizenry previously unconscious of the environment effectively precluded the movement from becoming a serious social protest or social challenge group. There was no clearly defined antagonist out in the social world. And the bulk of efforts was devoted to changing the superstructure of the society—its ideological or value systems. Unlike social challenge groups, there were few consistent efforts at altering the production *sub*structure. There was, in general, no sense of a need to change the class and political elements of social structure.[17] While there was an increasing call for government regulation of pollution, there was no well-formed diagnosis of capitalist or market mobilization of surplus as the root of the environmental problem. Indeed, like many previous movements, much of this regulation was not as opposed by monopoly capital as might be anticipated. Perhaps the early environmental movement was "lending unintentional support to political capitalism because of their premise that government regulation of corporations was necessarily a step toward curbing the power of economic elites" (Ash, 1972:153).

This early period, then, saw growth of the mass base of the movement. Increases in membership were found in older preservationist organizations like the Sierra Club and National Audubon Society, as well as in conservation associations like the Izaak Walton League. Equally importantly, this period encompassed both the emergence of the models of participation exhibited in the antipoverty and antiwar movements of the 1960s, *and* a conspiratorial argument that the environmental movement was sponsored by political and economic elites to distract protestors from these precursors and coexisting movements. There is sufficient variety of organizations to suggest that some emerged for each of these, and other, reasons. Unquestionably, the participatory climate of the 1960s was an exemplar of permissiveness for social innovation that Banks (1972:55) refers to. Though opposition, especially from competitive and monopoly capital, existed in both organized and public attitude domains, it proved to be less intense than what the 1970s would bring.[18]

While this early movement had success in social acceptance, and in the advantages of new regulatory legislation like the Clean Air Act and the National Environmental Policy Act (1969), the volume of environmental problems did not rapidly disappear. Indeed, with some increases in environmental science support, new ecosystem disorganization was perceived almost weekly. Moreover, a growing sense of the pervasiveness of disorganization through production withdrawals and additions, and of the limited utility of some earlier reform efforts, emerged. To this was coupled an increasing hostility of capital interests and large parts of the state. Moreover, as environmental regulations took effect in many areas, there was displacement of smaller enterprises, loss of employment and revenue, and a concomitant growing opposition from labor and the local and state governments.

Two changes in the movement appeared. The first was an increasing challenge to existing economic elites. New environmental groups questioned the logic of private investment decisions and the conventional treadmill model of production expansion to generate economic growth.[19] To some extent, the implicit if not explicit message of some of the groups was the need for a displacement of these elites, in terms of control of surplus. This was the strongest challenge raised by the movement, and it was met with coordinated responses from major capital interests. Confidence in big business, which lagged mostly because of the environmentalist challenge, was to be countered by the Business Roundtable and the advertising and resocializing efforts of other producer groups. Every major medium appeared with new attacks on environmentalists, who ostensibly sought environmental purity at the expense of jobs and welfare of the poor and working classes.[20]

Actual job disruptions, the new fears raised by these media, and the economic insecurity of workers led to a series of new attacks from labor and the poor. Although this signalled the demise of some environmental associations and the retreat of others into less controversial meliorative efforts, it led to more complex class politics by the late 1970s. In contrast to early calls for lowered consumption and vague calls for production changes to diminish pollution, the new environmental coalition became more sensitive to social equity and political conflicts. Social structure and class relations were to be as much a feature of later environmental analyses as the ecosystem details.

The social impact statement was both a spur and a barrier to this social consciousness raising. For, as I indicated earlier, the standard SIS indicated the clear welfare value of production-expansion-as-usual. And environmentalists had little concrete substitution for this.[21] Eventually, and under the auspices of the growing appropriate technology movement, the notion of alternative production systems and their social welfare potential has begun to emerge in the critiques of SISs. As with the environmental movement itself, the social conflict around state investment and private sector growth has begun to force a more refined analysis by appropriate technologists. Not just production structure, but the social relationships around production and the distribution of social surplus were the added dimensions of the movement. In this, they were aided by the emergence of the energy crisis of 1973–74, and the sense of new limitations for production expansion. However, many potential constituents shied away from environmentalism as risks of energy scarcity and increased costs threatened consumers and workers. All of this tension was capitalized on by corporate managers and public relations experts. Consumer and worker experience was heightened into new threats of the "dark ages" being produced by environmentalists.[22]

One way of capturing this shift is to note that the early movement emphasized the benefits of environmental protection. Their early success, though, produced new social experiences of the costs of such protection. And the resultant increase in conflict and antagonism forced a much clearer and more complex effort at documenting both the costs and the benefits of environmental protection. Inherent in the latter, though, has been the evaluation of the costs and benefits of monopoly-capital production. This has shifted much of the movement away from status politics and moral protest to increasingly coordinated strategies for class politics and the reorganization of production, including the possible displacement of current economic elites. In this view, the movement has become more of a challenge to the existing social structure.[23]

However, it is important to note that this challenge, while it rests on somewhat durable public approval of environmental protection, lacks an active sustained constituency outside the middle class. Neither organized labor nor poor people's movements have accepted the analysis and prescription of the more politicized movement. And, while legislation has posed new problems for production growth, enforcement has proven to be difficult. Moreover, the state is under increasing pressure for inflation control (NRDC, 1978b). This has also led to decreased fiscal support for some environmental protection, as well as increased apprehension by monopoly and competitive capital and labor, once more facing a choice between inflation and recession. Conversely, though, energy policies have included new supports for alternative nonfossil energy sources, with somewhat diminished enthusiasm for nuclear power. Optimistically, this strengthens the arguments of appropriate technology enthusiasts for a "soft" energy path. Pessimistically, little social effort has been committed to studying alternative *uses* of new energy. It is as feasible that new energy will support older forms of substructure and social structure through conventional production expansion as that it will bring production reorganization. This is especially true since energy conversion to electricity is foremost on the state's agenda, this being applicable to a variety of industrial processes (NRDC, 1978a).

For a conversion to the soft energy paths of low-scale, decentralized, and social welfare-oriented production systems of the appropriate technologists, both increased social intelligence and the building of a constituency are called for. While the latter is barely underway, the former has advanced considerably in the last five years.[24] Yet without a political base within unorganized and organized labor, no movement can proceed to challenge and change the existing social structure. Changes in the substructure may be emerging in part because of rising costs of energy. These are often coupled with the increased costs of using the market—transaction costs—imposed by the environmental (and consumer) movements.[25] In terms of unorganized publics, moreover, the movement has lost some support in the 1970s. It has probably increased the sensitivity of the remaining supporters toward the socioeconomic dimension of environmental protection. Social surveys indicate a falling off of public perception of environmental issues as a critical American problem, back to levels that may have existed in the early growth period of the mass public base (1968–69). But despite considerable opposition and attempts at denigrating environmentalism as an elitist and irresponsible social value, monopoly-capital interests and organized labor have failed to make ecology "the last fad."[26] In the next section, I will indicate that the restructuring of the organizational and public base of the movement in the past five years has increased its potential durability as a challenge group, sensitive to class politics.

This failure of environmentalism to fade, though, is matched by an increase in organized opposition to it, as the costs of environmental reforms begin to mount and their often regressive distribution is made clearer. Ironically, it is often the case that monopoly-capital interests have claimed a special concern for the poor and working groups, to justify their quest for enlarged energy and other resource programs. These new-found "friends of the poor" have been effective in countering any potential enhanced mobilization of these groups. For the total sustenance concerns of these social strata are much more acute and subject to whims of the monopoly-capital interests than are those of the free professionals who form the strongest core of the movement.[27] While the latter, for example, may favor wilderness preservationist policies,

> since rural occupations are mainly based upon the exploitation of nature . . . nature is primarily significant as a utilitarian object. Because the relevant occupations are lumbering, mining, fishing, and agriculture, the most organized opposition to the conservation

movement is found in these rural-based industries which are able to exert political influence through their occupational and industrial associations. (Harry et al., 1969:248-49)

Given a model of typical short-term material interests, it is not surprising that such opposition has grown. Moreover, when this is coupled with the theoretical argument of Olson (1965) that even among those interested in environmental protection, there is a very limited potential for active mobilization because such protection is a "free rider." Hence, the concerned public will benefit from changes induced by others, even without personal participation in the movement organizations. Only specific movement organizational incentives can offset this, according to the theory. Alternatively, powerful external sponsors may help support a small but potentially effective movement, in the absence of active public support. Conversely, it has been argued that large-scale movement organizations can grow despite these constraints, *if* there is sufficient concern about private interests and sufficient overlap of these with the organizational goals.[28]

We can see diverse strains in the contemporary movement that illustrate all of these potential situations. Opposition grew in the early 1970s, as did public apathy for environmental actions on the part of the state. Yet some environmental organizations grew despite this. Old-line conservation groups like the Sierra Club (1892) and National Audubon Society (1905) grew (e.g., Sills, 1975) in part because they offered incentives to members (books, outdoor recreation advice, information on birds). Sponsorship of some groups by Laurance Rockefeller maintained their membership and activity, as in the case of the Conservation Foundation or Save-the-Redwoods League (cf. Collier & Horowitz, 1976:394-96). Zero Population Growth, Inc., grew by the coalescence of anticipated private benefits and the social gains from reduced populations (Tillock & Morrison, 1977). Both this coalescence and the perception of it are likelier to be present in groups with higher education and information and less immediate economic risks from such activities.

Future movement growth is a possibility, if a delicate balancing act occurs. Sufficient public support must be present to provide a political base for lobbying and other activities. Financial and other *active* support, from membership to leadership, can be drawn from the smaller set of free professional and other constituencies. If this base can create sufficient socially progressive production and perhaps social structural change—or at least increased sensitivity to such potential change on the part of labor groups—then the base may be substantially widened and future social change accelerated (Morrison, 1976). This involves a strategy of seeking benefits for social groupings that do not constitute the main membership—or even the most supportive public—of the movement, through the ongoing influence of the movement. The goal is to permit enhancement of future mobilization potential, to consolidate and extend socioenvironmental gains. One illustration of the potential and pitfalls of such a strategy is the use of movement organizations to pressure for retraining and other compensation for extractive workers in the new expansion of the Redwoods National Park in California (e.g., NRDC, 1977a). This occurred in the face of sustained labor-capital opposition to this encroachment on lumbering. Thus, activist environmental organizations were placating their "enemies" among labor groups. Recent proposals to dismantle military production systems in the U.S., though more often based on economic and geopolitical arguments, also argue for support of labor in the period of conversion of these monopoly-capital industries. This is true despite the history of joint lobbying for expanded military production by capital and organized labor interests.[29]

Such a strategy involves far more than simple consciousness-raising about environmental threats. Perception of threats must be more closely integrated into programs of reform and challenge to existing production patterns and existing controllers of surplus allocation. Although there are intermediate strategies, such as altering production to enhance worker safety and health, these points of convergence of environmentalist and labor values and interests are not numerous enough yet to substitute for the above model. They may complement it, though. If these strategies are to succeed, the nature of the environmental movement must change from a more ecological to a more *socio*-ecological concern. The next section addresses this possibility.

Composition of the Movement: A Dynamic View

This analytic history of the contemporary environmental movement must be understood in the context of the goals and means of the movement. I have divided the movement participants (and organizations) into four profiles: (1) cosmetologists, (2) meliorists, (3) reformists, and (4) radicals within the movement. The basis for such a division is the participants' evaluations of both ecological and socioeconomic reality. Such differentiation appears closely associated with the transformation of movement organization and strategies over the period noted above.

Among these four groups, there are both qualitative and quantitative distinctions. On an ecological dimension, the groups can be viewed as differing in the extensity of their perceptions of ecological withdrawals and additions associated with societal production and consumption. On a socioeconomic dimension, they differ in their views on ecological problems arising from consumption versus the organization of production. This leads to the rough delineation of the four types of participants and organizations of Table 8.1 (Schnaiberg, 1973; Albrecht & Mauss, 1975).

In this scheme, cosmetologists and meliorists suffer from limited perspectives on the ecological and socioeconomic dimensions, in contrast to reformists and radicals. The first two both emphasize primarily *consumption* issues and *voluntary* consumer action. In contrast, the last two locate the problems as stemming more from the nature of production, although both see consumer actions as flowing from producer

Table 8.1   Characteristics of Movement Members/Groups

Type	Ecological Perception	Socioeconomic Perception
Cosmetologists	Consumer waste products are the main problem (e.g., littering).	"People" are careless in their waste disposal behavior.
Meliorists	General consumer patterns are wasteful of resources (e.g., they don't recycle).	"People" need to have some new institutions to allow them to voluntarily recycle products.
Reformists	Production expansion produces ecological problems of all types.	Economic and political incentives need to be established to reduce biospheric extraction rates.
Radicals	Production in advanced industrial capitalist societies inevitably exceeds ecological limits.	Only a total socioeconomic restructuring of capitalist-industrial societies can provide social welfare and environmental protection.

decisions. Both emphasize some sociopolitical constraints that need to be imposed on producers (and consumers), rather than relying on purely voluntary consumer efforts. At one level of analysis, there is parity in ecological and socioeconomic perspectives. For both pairs, the breadth of their ecological perspectives is matched by the breadth of socioeconomic organizations involved in producing ecological problems. For cosmetologists and meliorists, their more limited list of withdrawals and additions suggests more limited changes in the socioeconomic structure of U.S. society. Reformists and radicals see the broader ecological needs as dictating broader reorganization of production and consumption. Just as meliorists have broader breadth of concern and action than do cosmetologists, so do radicals have greater breadth than reformists.[30]

Turning back to the analytic history of the movement, it appears that in the early period the base of the movement was composed mostly of cosmetologists and meliorists. This both stimulated and was reinforced by strategies that aimed at mass consumer education. During the latter part of this period, ecological perception had deepened. Meliorists and reformists formed a larger part of the movement, which shifted toward legislation and litigation. Furthermore, it is important to note that both cosmetologists and meliorists, because of their exclusive concern with narrow ecological issues and consumer behavior, were subject to manipulation by producer groups. Examples are the efforts of the Keep America Beautiful campaign (sponsored by bottling/packaging industries) to focus cosmetologists' concerns on littering. Similarly, Laurance Rockefeller effectively kept many cosmetologists and meliorists concerned with the preservation of small areas of wilderness, while he established private luxury resorts nearby. But reformists were less susceptible to such blatant monopoly-capital practices, and they provided the impetus for much of the legislative and litigative action.[31]

By the early 1970s, most cosmetologists had dropped out, some meliorists had either dropped out or become reformists or even radicals, and reformists and (to a lesser extent) radicals began to constitute the bulk of the movement. Confusion and disorganization of this period was partly due to the loss of consumer-oriented participants, and the ascendency of production-oriented groups such as the reformists. To some extent, this confusion was also between value orientations and prescriptive behavioral norm-orientations within the movement—

or between changes in "people" and institutions. Moreover, the radical component of the movement was disillusioned with the small production changes imposed by NEPA and related Acts.[32] Observing the increased opposition by capital interests to environmental reform, they saw this as a period of opportunity, of challenge, of confrontation with the forces of social inequality. In contrast, reformists had the task of dealing ever more directly with representatives of major production interests in their efforts to seek enforcement of existing legislation and new legislative mandates. The opposition to environmental policies from local, regional, and even national labor groups impinged on the consciousness of both reformists and radicals, but in different ways. For radicals, this confirmed their analysis that there was no way to achieve social justice and environmental reform in the current economic system. Conversely, reformists were confused by such opposition. This forced them to broaden their social perspective, to trace the societal impact of production changes designed to improve environmental quality. Under such cross-pressures, it is likely that some reformists dropped out of the movement. Others continued their course of action in regulating some elements of production, while still others became more radical through the combination of working class opposition and the analysis of radicals.

Most recently, cosmetologists and many meliorists have vanished from active participation in (and in some cases, support of) the movement. The core of the active movement is reformist, but with some strong radical elements remaining. The latter have been stimulated in recent years by re-organizational emphasis on appropriate technology. Opposition to environmental action has broadened and deepened, and many former participants are likely to have become passive (and perhaps even active) opponents.[33]

Apart from the participants in *ad hoc* local conflicts, many of the key participants are paid professionals (generally but not always underpaid). The various types range from lawyers to ecologists to community organizers. While participation strategies are often skillfully used in mobilizing regional or local support, the movement is much more power-oriented than it was even in its early days. Few reformists are satisfied with progress on environmental fronts, and no radicals are. But the adversarial process has generally become one of intensive and extensive negotiation rather than marches and protests. The antinuclear movement is only a partial exception to this trend.

Negotiation, of course, entails the clear and present danger of co-optation by antienvironmental opponents, whether in the state or in capitalist sectors. To some extent, this has occurred in the incremental decision-making logic tacitly agreed to by environmental reformists, exemplified by benefit-cost analyses or environmental impact statements (Ch. VII). Yet the continuing presence of radicals, including radicalized reformists and meliorists with a passion for single issues, helps offset some of this tendency toward absorption.[34]

CONSERVATIONISM, ENVIRONMENTALISM, AND APPROPRIATE TECHNOLOGY

From Conservationism to Environmentalism: Evolution or Revolution?

One argument espoused by both social and ecological radicals is that much of the contemporary environmental movement is nothing but the earlier conservation movement, with minor changes in appearance. Moreover, such interpretations see this earlier conservation movement as one that provided substantial support for political capitalism. It led to few social benefits for the mass of American citizens, and little ecological protection.[35] A counter, and equally forceful, argument is that the environmental movement represents a dramatic break with conservationist organizations and issues, with a much broader, integrated, holistic and hence more subversive orientation to production substructures and social structure. Mediating between these two polar interpretations are analyses that see both continuity and discontinuity in ecological movements.[36]

Part of the difficulty in assessing such models can be understood by reflecting on earlier sections of this chapter. *The* ecological movement was never a singular nor stable entity, but involved rather different social components. Each had its own world-view of social and ecological reality. As noted earlier, in a relatively short period from about the mid-1960s to the present time, the movement changed in size and the relative weights of these social components. Likewise, it altered its evaluations of the environmental problem and strategies for solutions. Comparisons between the two movements are made even more difficult by the reality that the conservation movement itself had similar patterns of internal heterogeneity and change over time. Recent evaluations of the Roosevelt-Pinchot era in early twentieth century America suggest it had two forms: conservation-efficiency and conservation-preservation.[37] The first dominated the Roosevelt period. In conjunction with other regulation, it helped increase the intensity of political capitalism rather than restraining monopoly capital expansion:

> The conservation movement which flourished between 1890 and
> 1910 . . . was a political movement with objectives as disparate as
> saving the forests, destroying monopolies, and maintaining
> Anglo-Saxon supremacy. *Its economic analysis was practically
> nonexistent,* though it did emphasize the importance of sustained
> yield in renewable resources. (Mason, 1978:24; my italics)

From the provocative analysis of Hays (1969), it now seems clear that the "progressive conservation" movement of 1890–1920 was in fact not economically progressive. It was not "an attempt to control private, corporate wealth for public ends," as in the conventional historical view of this movement, which emphasizes resource ownership rather than the movement's real concern, resource use (Hays, 1969:260–61). Hays indicates, moreover, that this lack of an economic analysis of ownership led not to a control of monopolies, but to its inverse: "Larger corporations could more readily afford to undertake conservation practices [and] they alone could provide the efficiency, stability of operations, and long-range planning" necessary to conservation (Hays, 1969:263). Moreover, the state ideology represented by Theodore Roosevelt and his advisers was opposed to a

> belief in the automatic beneficence of unrestricted economic com-
> petition, which, they believed, created only waste, exploitation,
> and unproductive economic rivalry. . . . The conservation move-
> ment did not involve a reaction against large-scale corporate busi-
> ness, but, in fact, shared its views in a mutual revulsion against
> unrestrained competition and undirected economic development.
> (Hays, 1969:266)

This form of conservationism, then, was concerned far more with efficiency than with equality. It is important to note that some of these themes reappear not only in the environmental movement of the 1960s, but in the appropriate technology movement in more recent years. This ideology and practice played an important role in the development of a technostructure and expanded monopoly capitalism, and in increased political capitalism that facilitated the state's role in this expansion. As I will note shortly, while the voluntary movement apparently died between 1920 and the early 1960s, its ideology and practices continued in the economic substructure and in the state. Moreover, it is clear that this branch of the movement was elitist, dominated by engineering and other specialists. It was well-integrated into the state's structure, and was eventually internalized in some large-scale primary production enterprises. It was far less a mass movement than the preservationist branch.[38]

The second form of conservationism, the preservationist movement, was very similar to the efficiency movement, though its membership overlapped only slightly. While it was the Theodore Roosevelt administration that greatly expanded wilderness and park preservation in the western United States, this preservation became a permanent concern of the state. In part, this was a result of agency self-interest in expanding the mission of the Department of the Interior, and in part a response to the pressures from the Sierra Club and Audubon Society (among other groups), both local and national. This movement was concerned with *habitat*, not sustenance, as distinct from the conservation-efficiency movement. As such, it came into less conflict with monopoly capital than did the later expanded movement of environmentalism, though local and later conflicts did occur over natural resource usage versus preservation. Indeed, this movement was often stimulated in later years by powerful sponsors such as Laurance Rockefeller.[39] These same sponsors often saw little inherent conflict between local preservationism and production expansion, and little threat from some broader environmental concerns:

> Laurance accepted without reservation the idea that growth and conservation could be familiar bedfellows.... In a 1963 address to ... the Congress of American Industry ... he tried to assure businessmen that nothing in the new concern for pure water and air threatened them. "Business can take this development in stride," he counseled, "in the same way it has, over the years, taken in its stride other steps which seemed like broad social rather than economic obligations. Like so many of the others it will turn out in the end to be just plain good business." (Collier & Horowitz, 1976:385–486)

Though some (Barkley & Weissman, 1970) have seen a conspiracy in such sponsorship, in fact there remained considerable tensions between business sponsors and the movement. A mid-1950s report to Rockefeller that predated his creation of preservationist organizations noted that as leisure and income were soon to increase drastically, conservation and the need for leadership responsive to a broad range of ideas would also increase. Groups like the Sierra Club were considered too small and their views too confined for this leadership (Collier & Horowitz, 1976:308).

From this pattern of evidence and interpretation, I would argue that the total conservation movement was not concerned with equality or social welfare, apart from the perceived congruence of social welfare with private-capital expansion and national growth. The early aim of the efficiency movement was and remained elitist, culminating in the resource analyses of the Paley Commission (on Materials Policy), whose 1952 report

> called for an opening up of U.S. resources and federal lands to private industry, inveighing against "the hairshirt concept of conservation which makes it synonymous with hoarding. A sound concept of conservation... equates it with efficient management—efficient use of manpower and materials: a positive concept compatible with growth and high consumption in place of abstinence and retrenchment." (Collier & Horowitz, 1976:304–5)

This model of conservation-efficiency was and continues to be promoted by Resources for the Future, as in the influential Barnett and Morse (1963) study. Whether this is a function of Rockefeller Foundation support for this "think-tank" is unclear, though.

Moreover, the preservationist branch of the movement continued and expanded in the 1950s and 1960s under the pressures of increased affluence and leisure, and the growth of outdoor recreation. While not pro-business, it did not constitute a major threat in the earlier years. As the Paley report and the Rockefeller excerpts indicate, though, there was an increased level of conflict over increasingly scarce public lands and their natural resources. Unlike the efficiency movement, then, the preservationist movement was not so closely tied to corporate planning. Indeed, it had frequent, local conflicts with large and small land-owners and extractive industries. In addition, this movement, while still predominantly middle-class, had support from hunting and fishing groups drawn from the working-class, as incursion of industry destroyed many of the habitats for animals and fish. Thus, the movement could coexist with corporate planners and even be captured or co-opted by monopoly capitalists like Rockefeller. But it was a more unstable alliance than that of the "progressive conservation" movement and large-scale business (Albrecht & Mauss, 1975).

From this perspective, we can see the emergence of a new environmental movement in the 1960s as integrating the habitat and sustenance concerns of the efficiency and preservation movements. But the two now subsumed a broader range of ecosystem dimensions, particularly air pollution. And especially after 1973–74, it assimilated a continuing concern with energy. The new aggregation of movement organizations also encompassed a concern for efficiency as well as preservation. Within the new movement were principles that ranged from the conservation-efficiency to the conservation-preservation movement predecessors, but which covered a broader set of ecosystem stocks and processes.[40] Small wonder that we find so much variability in ideology and programs among the new movement organizations and publics!

But in this new amalgam of concerns, we also move farther from the simpler "compatibility with growth and consumption" that the Paley Commission report anticipated. For the new movement had a concern with sustenance that frequently bordered on survival fears, and not simply on alternative paths toward economic growth. Growth became more problematic, and not simply a matter for technical adjustments. New concerns for social survival introduced broader social welfare issues, and politicized growth and production expansion decision-making.[41] In this regard at least, this was a genuinely new social movement, built on the successes and failures of efficiency and preservation precursors. We can summarize roughly these overlaps and discontinuities in Table 8.2.

The arrows indicate formative influences from earlier to later movement ideologies. While subject to exceptions, the table nonetheless expresses the main argument about the roots of modern environ-

Table 8.2   Dimensions of Environmental-Conservation Movements

	Sustenance Concern	Habitat Concern
Social Elitism	Conservation-Efficiency ↓	Conservation-Preservation ↓
Social Populism	Environmentalism (later) ←— Appropriate Technology	Environmentalism (earlier)

mentalism. A more systematic analysis of environmentalism, in comparison with conservationism, follows next.

Environmentalism and Conservationism: Analytic Comparisons

A number of dimensions have been put forth to distinguish various social movements. At the most general level, we can examine broad patterns of social participation and power activities,[42] as in Table 8.3. The environmental movement is distinguished by the breadth of its constituency, as well as the range of its power strategies. Included in the latter are litigation, lobbying, public relations use of media, electoral politicking, and especially in the case of nuclear power, civil disobedience.

Table 8.3 Participation and Power Dimensions of Conservation-Environmental Movements

	Patterns of Participation	*Patterns of Power Application*
Conservation-Efficiency	Narrowest	Technical negotiations
Conservation-Preservation	Broader	Pressure groups; Use of sponsors
Environmental	Broadest	All middle-class political devices (including civil disobedience)

A somewhat more focused comparison can be made regarding the targets of the movements: whom they sought to influence, whom to mobilize, and for whom benefits were being sought.[43] Some general distinctions along these three dimensions are summarized in Table 8.4. In examining whether these movements constituted serious protest or challenge movements, another set of dimensions has been argued as being important. This includes the scope of the demands, the nature of social surplus distribution ideologies, and the relationship to existing societal elites.[44] Table 8.5 provides a rough assessment of the several movements under these dimensions, distinguishing between two forms of environmental movement—the early and the appropriate technology one.

Table 8.4   Movement Targets: Conservation-Environmental

	Target of Influence	*Target of Mobilization*	*Target of Benefits*
Conservation-Efficiency	Corporate planners; State agencies; Political elite	Scientific-technological experts; Corporate managers	"The society": monopoly capital as de facto primary beneficiary
Conservation-Preservation	State agencies; Economic sponsors	Consumers of outdoor recreation, including wealthy sponsors	"The society": upper-middle- and some working class as de facto beneficiaries
Environmental	State agencies	Consumers and workers: de facto major appeal to middle class, especially professionalized segment	"The society": middle class and potentially working class (under appropriate technology)

These last two charts indicate the potential for social trouble-making that the contemporary environmental movement contains. The present movement, even as reduced from the levels of the 1960s, has rather disparate goals. Thus the degree to which such potential will be actualized depends, as noted earlier, on the integration of this movement with other redistributive movements in the society. There is little indication that either form of the earlier conservation movement was in fact a sustained social protest movement, with definite and persistent categories of antagonists. Conflicts between groups certainly existed, but there was far less persistence of opposing coalitions. In contrast, the alignments in the still-young environmental movement have become somewhat firmer.[45]

In general, though, all of these movements relate heavily to the organization of the state, and all have engendered intrastate conflicts. For the efficiency movement, there was continual conflict between the professional scientists and technologists within the government, and the production-oriented bureaucrats who foresaw production impediments from the new land-use policies. In the preservationist movement, the conflicts were between multiple-use and pure preservation, the former permitting greater production from land and water preserves. The environmental movement maximized these intrastate con-

Table 8.5   Nature of Social Challenges in Conservation-Environmental Movements

	Single versus Multiple Demands	*Redistributive versus Nonredistributive*	*Influence or Change Elites*
Conservation-Efficiency	Single (in each organization), multiple across organizations	Nonredistributive or socially regressive	Influence economic and political elites
Conservation-Preservation	Single (preserve habitat areas)	Nonredistributive	Influence economic and political elites
Environmental-Early form	Multiple (within and across organizations)	Nonredistributive (some socially regessive costs)	Influence political elites
Environmental-Late form (appropriate technology)	Multiple (within and across organizations)	Redistributive goals (little implementation as yet)	Change economic elites, influence political elites

flicts. It relied on scientific input to challenge the technological and production orientations of existing agencies and demand regulatory control in existing and new agencies. Finally, the appropriate technology wing of the late environmental movement extends this conflict further. It encroaches on all the technological policies of the state, as well as many of its distributive ones.[46]

Moreover, virtually all of these movements also elicited different responses and often conflicts between industrial groupings, capital interests, and organized and unorganized labor as well. The efficiency movement was often a basis of conflict between monopoly and competitive capital, and between extractive industries in the west and manufacturing and service industries in the western part of the U.S. (Hays, 1969). By the period of the environmental movement, there was somewhat more cohesion. Ironically, the extension of monopoly capitalism often integrated these industrial entities into single corporations with national and international operations. This diminished (but did not eliminate) both the regional variation in capital's responses to environmental challenges and the sectoral variation as well, especially as the costs began to become apparent.

In the case of the preservationist movement, these variations in industrial responses were perhaps greatest, for the movements often included capitalist sponsors whose interests were not threatened by localized preservation. Laurance Rockefeller is an extreme example of such a sponsor: he facilitated directly the preservation of major tracts of land surrounding the hotels that he had been building. This preservationism enhanced the recreational value of his resorts, while it precluded access to forest and other resources for extractive industries. Likewise, his fiscal support of the Save-the-Redwoods League illustrates the lack of a cohesive "monopoly-capitalist strategy" in opposition to preservationism.[47] Moreover, while there is more cohesion in opposition to environmental controls, there still remain substantial variations in part determined by costs of compliance. Even the appropriate technology movement, which from one perspective is the most serious challenge to the current decision-making regarding social surplus, finds supporters from within some of the large-scale capitalist as well as competitive capital sectors. For their concern with energy conservation and *development* of "soft paths" of energy supplies appeals to industries with rising energy costs. But there is more solid opposition by large-scale capital to the proposed *application* of energy to production through labor-intensive and limited production programs.[48]

All of these movements, regardless of these conflicts, follow middle-class political strategies. In addition, a variety of daily time and energy constraints inhibit mobilization of working class participants. Resulting actions exemplify moral protest movements, with a *"sine qua non* that deliberate physical force strategies should be rejected" (Wilkinson, 1971:118). And they reflect "the mystique of expertise . . . and belief that the middle class is more capable of judging distant events" (Ash, 1972:211).

While Ash was referring to foreign policy movements, the "distant" events in the case of the environmental movement refer to temporal distance, to future ecosystem problems, and to less visible consequences of these ecosystem disruptions. Except for the preservationist movement, the expertise dimension of the movements is enhanced by the central roles of scientists and technologists. The conservation-efficiency movement relied on technological and scientific expertise in sustained-yield forestry (silviculture), fisheries, and other agrarian and extractive industries. A key role was played by applied production scientists, whose concern was less with total ecosystem functioning than with efficiency and sustained yield in limited ecosystems. Planting and cutting strategies for trees, say, might coexist with waste management strategies that created degradation of nearby waterways, so long as the former system functioned well. For any single technical advisor there was no broadening of concern for production externalities, only a wider view of production internalities. However, the conflicts between advisors to various corporations and public agencies mounted, as in the case of competing demands for use of public lands. This competition led to increased ecological sensitivity regarding alternative productivity schedules for these uses. Coal mining and ranching could not coexist in many western lands, and there were competing models of irrigation versus channel widening for shipping in waterways. This raised some concerns about immediate production externalities, and supported some early impact sciences (see Ch. VI). But the dominant influence was exercised by applied scientists or resource technologists, whose primary concern was with production efficiency.[49]

In contrast, the environmental movement was influenced far more by impact sciences, however scattered and imperfect they were and remain. There is an attenuated role for public and private sector technologists to play in the early part of the movement, though by the 1970s such technologists were involved in a number of movement decisions. Competing technological advice, for example, is most notable in the nuclear power conflicts. Theoretical physicists, radiation health experts, and engineers with nuclear design experience appear as advisors to both sides. To some extent, these production scientists and technologists have an expanded role, as regulation affects or does not affect ongoing production systems. The questions of efficiency and effectiveness of any form of regulation—whether prohibitionary or by fiscal incentive—expands the role of both impact and production scientists, and especially technologists.[50] Given the relative scarcity of technologists available to the movement and their employment in primarily monopoly capital production, the movement is strained by such new burdens of responsibility for altering production. Part of this burden has been reduced by increased employment of impact scientists and technologists in the state, especially in the Environmental Protection Agency, the new Department of Energy, and the Department of the Interior. Additionally, older production-oriented agencies have somewhat increased their employment of impact technologists and scientists as part of the requirements of NEPA and the environmental impact reporting process.[51]

Interestingly, the preservationist movement had far lower scientific and technological requirements. Although the writings of impact-oriented ecologists, wildlife experts, fish and game administrators, and the like were influential, they were not critical for mobilizing local constituencies for preservation of land or water areas.[52] The social visibility and anticipated gains from such preservation sufficed to mobilize many localized groups. For the national organizations, there was a mixture of diffuse concerns at this level, plus more sophisticated ecological understanding. But the original tenets were enough, I believe, for many participants. It is true that education of members was based on some of the impact sciences, but this was not a device that initially created commitments of these constituencies. Thus, the membership base was drawn by extra-scientific private and public concerns. In recent years, though, there has been an increase in the scientific requirements of this branch of the modern environmental movement as preserves are studied more carefully. For example, many of the older parcels of land or stretches of waterway have proven vulnerable to ecosystem additions and withdrawals elsewhere. This has led to a new preservationist sensitivity to an ecologically based design for preserves, as opposed to an aesthetically based design, as was often the case in past preserves. On the other hand, constituencies are still mobilized by aesthetic concerns, providing a firmer base for many of these organizations.[53]

At this point all of these movements have been institutionalized to some degree. Conservation-efficiency concerns reside within corporations and state agencies, preservationist concerns in local and especially national organizations. And the mass base of the environmental movement has been transformed into a supportive public interacting with an increasingly bureaucratized movement structure. In addition to the preservationist organizational base, the last decade has brought forth highly visible national litigative and pressure groups such as the Environmental Defense Fund and the Natural Resources Defense Council. Direct political actions are mobilized through organizations such as Friends of the Earth, Environmental Action, and smaller, localized interest groups. Spanning both kinds of activities is the Ralph Nader agglomeration of national consumer-environmental groups, engaged in sophisticated interest-group action and mobilization as well as in some educational mobilization.[54]

With the partial exception of the nuclear power controversies, the social protest action now takes place in Congressional hearings, regulatory commission hearings and reports, environmental impact meetings, and in legislative lobbying and formal litigation. The fiscal base of the institutional structure is highly dependent on the concerned publics, but the actions are more centrally focused. They often occur at local levels with local branches of the movement, though.[55] Only the appropriate technology movement has the character of decentralization and partial institutionalization of the 1960s, and that appears to be changing. Both Schumacher and Lovins moved to establish research and application centers, and Lovins has been given serious attention in established state agencies.[56]

Unfortunately, though, this institutionalization occurred prior to the expansion of the social base of the movement. Without the infusion of broader labor and social equity participation, it appears that the movement is more subject to cooptation and incorporation within the structure of political capitalism.[57] If this materializes, the treadmill of production is likely to continue unabated, with only slight slowing of acceleration. What is likely to offset this tendency? That is the final issue to be addressed in this chapter.

THE FUTURE OF ENVIRONMENTALISM

Ideological Roots of Appropriate Technology: A Key Asset?

The appropriate technology movement represents the most extensive challenge to the existing treadmill of production. In many senses, it is the logical extension of environmentalism. In ideology and in proposals for changes in the substructure, it represents an agenda that incorporates the broadest sustenance and habitat concerns, going well beyond the efficiency, preservationist, and early environmental movements. Moreover, it moves towards a program that takes the movement out of a moral crusade or protest that is against something, and transforms it into one in favor of a specified alternative.

But the political efficacy of this movement also depends on its capacity to mobilize the previously unmobilized working-class constituencies. While environmentalism is no more middle class than most moral protest movements and even many class movements, the dominant emphasis in this book is that some class-consciousness and class-action is necessary to change the production treadmill.[58] The substance of decision making about social surplus allocation can only be changed by destroying the power of the economic elite to dominate this allocative process, and/or by increasing the political constraints under which this allocation occurs. To say that the growth of the state obviously implies the domination of markets by politics *or* that the welfare state has thereby arrived is to misunderstand the dual role of the state.

The state has provided direct support for monopoly-capital expansion. But the regulation produced for political legitimacy has induced only small changes in social welfare—and has increased the legitimacy of the treadmill at the same time.[59] Pollution control implies that production can expand once this corrective is made. Energy conservation measures likewise indicate that the expansion can and should be permitted once this problem is "solved." Recycling of materials, at least in the forms introduced in the U.S., pays little attention to expanded production that can only be partially recycled. Each of these measures is, of course, useful in protecting some biospheric dimensions, and perhaps producing some social welfare gains. They are not to be easily dismissed. Yet they leave largely intact the decisional structure for allocating surplus in ways that are ecologically pernicious and socially risky in the short run for at least a substantial segment of the lower working class. In the long run, of course, the ecological risks threaten a much larger segment of the society.

The considerable advantage possessed by the early appropriate technology movement was that it addressed this surplus allocation question directly. During the 1960s and early 1970s, the "intermediate technology" movement was organized around the economic development problems in Third World societies. The failures of conventional trade-and-aid policies of the industrial world to improve the conditions of the masses in these countries raised severe doubts about perpetuating such a system. Multinational corporations derived considerable profits from direct investment in these societies, and mobilized local capital to enhance this use of American capital.[60] But there was little socioeconomic improvement beyond the new middle classes and a small labor aristocracy that worked in the more capitally intense enterprises. Only China represented a major success story in the post-1945 period: the mainland because of the change in regime and reorganization of production and distribution, and Taiwan because of heavy foreign investment coupled with local entrepreneurialism and state control.

Both unconventional development economists and activists in the field came to similar conclusions. The high-technology route to socioeconomic development made little sense in countries short of capital and long on population and potential labor force. In addition, the indigenous political elites often supported—at least publicly—some new development schemes, to enhance their own legitimacy. In reality, many elites benefited from the existing maldistribution through association with foreign capital. The small "intermediate technology" movement was aided by international aid organizations in semiperipheral countries such as Canada and Sweden.[61] The goal was direct improvement in social welfare conditions for the bottom strata of Third World societies, and the enhancement of long-term economic development in such strata. New agricultural and village production techniques and low-cost equipment were developed to facilitate this. In some areas, attempts at new rural credit systems were coupled with this, though they often were more difficult to implement (Odell, 1978; Morrison, 1978).

It is from this social welfare concern and effective capital shortage, then, that the intermediate technology movement was born. Schumacher's (1973) work stemmed directly from this arena, building on his experience in India and extending the logic to industrial countries as well. For this movement, *the attempt to build a new substructure was tied to direct concerns with inequality systems in the social or class structure.* Community organization was a key element and organization was directed towards new production systems. Thus, technique and social structure reinforced each other—at least in theory. In practice, the movement has remained small and domestic, and international economic and political elites have tended to perpetuate the dominant treadmill system. But the Chinese model, which exemplified intermediate technology, served as a stimulus to the movement and a challenge to the treadmill, however limited the achievements to date. Recent efforts at Chinese modernization (Butterfield, 1978) undercut the viability of the movement. For the major alternative role model is thereby lost, and the treadmill affirmed as the appropriate model of surplus allocation.

When the movement extended to industrial societies like the U.S., the context was quite different. The greatest spur to the intermediate technology movement was the energy crisis of 1973–74, which coincided with the publication of Schumacher's (1973) "small is beautiful" theme. Decentralized energy sources and production seemed especially attractive given the new social perception of vulnerability from centralized national and international energy controllers. The dominant emphasis was on decentralization of production and energy conservation. It was far more on technique of production than on the social relationships involved in production or the control of surplus. Yet the social welfare heritage from the Third World movement was present, at least in the background of the U.S. movement. And when equity concerns about environmental protection rose with the costs of such protection, social equity regained some prominence in the movement. But it is less firmly entrenched than in the Third World branch, for capital shortages are not such a dominant feature of U.S. production. Of course the capital directly available to the lower working-class is not much greater than in the Third World. Thus the movement has an uneasy balance of ecological efficiency and social equality concerns, which can be tipped in one or another direction by social changes or changes in its mobilized constituency.[62]

In one sense, then, it is vital to have a more mobilized working-class constituency within this movement, to keep the equity issues in the forefront. For in its negotiations with state and capital elites, the movement is far more likely to be turned toward *technical* issues of resource conservation. Without a political counterweight to this, there remains the danger of incorporation of some of the techniques, without an ideology redirecting surplus toward social welfare, rather than to the treadmill's production expansion per se. This equity concern can be enhanced by the movement's critical evaluation of social impact assessments under NEPA and other state regulations, especially with regard to the distributional features and alternative production systems. Insofar as the movement takes this position, it builds some legitimacy with new constituencies, especially if these alternative investments are eventually made by the state (and private sector).

To achieve this firmer equity base, though, the movement must go beyond eager or captive constituencies. The desperate poverty of Third World villages permitted virtually any movement of hope to capture their attention for some time. Community development ventures abound, in part because of the lack of alternatives. Within the industrial societies, absolute poverty is not so overwhelming and the history of failed movements and broken state promises makes for a far more cynical and disillusioned potential constituency. The expertise in community organizing is not evident in most of the contemporary environmental movement, though it exists in other equity movements.[63] A true commitment to ecological protection and equity would draw on the techniques of appropriate technology, and the political organization of other social movements. This is no small matter, of course, since each party would have to modify their consciousness and concerns.

Environmentalists would have to take on a sharper class analysis. Equity movements would need to recognize more clearly their stake in non-treadmill production models, foregoing expectations of imitating the material life styles of their middle-class predecessors. Moreover, the interests of monopoly capital are such that every effort will be made, as it already has been, to dismiss this potential alliance and the options to the treadmill. Building on the earlier limited social analyses of the environmental and preservation movements, they will emphasize the "uneconomic" aspect of alternative technology, and the risks to all workers of attempts to deviate from traditional production goals (Parisi, 1977). That is, they will argue for changes within the treadmill, but not of the treadmill. Given the central role of private capital in making surplus allocative decisions and the pressures of competition—both domestic and international—they have little choice.

For such a joint movement to succeed, it must focus social movement efforts on the state in order to control these inherent limits in oligopolistic market systems. While the current trend is away from state control over the market, the logic of the movement can only work towards increased state control, at least in terms of market rules. One model for such change is outlined in the final chapter, though others also exist. At this point in movement history, the most crucial need is to establish firmly the dual ecological-equity goals (Morrison, 1976). Having done so, historical factors will influence the timing and form of influence over the state. It is crucial that the movement recognize that surplus allocation *choices* are possible, and necessary:

> Environmental reform can easily languish for lack of support ... it can be attempted in ways so various, from reactionary to revolutionary, as to point to grossly different directions of social change. For that last reason above all, movements for environmen-

tal reform are unlikely to get far by closing ranks and transcending party politics, as some eco-preachers recommend. They need to get into real politics rather than out of them. . . . They need to show plainly how the new costs and benefits they propose should be distributed between neighborhoods, regions, classes. (Stretton, 1976:14)

Some Left ideas of distributive justice are obsolete; some environmentalists' ideas of it are careless and some seem to have no idea of it at all. But for all their shortcomings the two still divide between them much of whatever hope and reformist talent the world has got. . . . To build better equalities into programs of environmental reform, the only imaginable equalizers and peacemakers are the political parties [and movements] of the Left. But they will need broader alliances than most of them have now . . . by diffusing egalitarian values into more and more areas of policy . . . that environmental policies must be designed to fit. (Stretton, 1976:13)

NOTES

1. In the case of social movements, this Marxist perspective on the interaction between structural-historical forces and the free will of individuals acting less predictably is shared by some contemporary theorists. Smelser's (1962) theory of structural conduciveness resembles this, as does Gusfield's (1968) synthesis of the literature. Marx's emphasis was perhaps greater on the sweep of major historical forces, in contrast to shorter-term phenomena that influence the rise and fall of particular movements.

2. By institutionalized conflict I mean the intersection of organized elements of the environmental movement with major sociopolitical institutions such as the courts, Congress, executive agencies of the state, and labor unions. This contrasts with other forms of collective behavior that are more visible and dramatic (Marx & Wood, 1975), such as mass demonstrations, which were more prevalent in the 1960s.

3. Gamson (1975:14–17) defines challenge groups involved in social protest as: (1) being able to mobilize potential constituents and (2) possessing an antagonist outside this constituency. In contrast, Ash's (1972:4–8) formulation of social movements, which involves the distinctions between substructure, social structure, and superstructure (drawing on the earlier formulations of Karl Marx), does not so sharply delineate a need for a specific antagonist. The difference is potentially important in understanding the early history of the environmental movement, when the emphasis was on participation (Morrison et al., 1972; Killian, 1964) and the ideological emphasis was "we have seen the enemy and he is us." For that period, it

may be improper to view the movement as a challenge or social protest group because the antagonist was within the constituency of the movement, namely, the entire society. Rather, this early movement typified Wilkinson's (1971:118ff) category of a moral crusade or moral protest movement.

4. This change occurred despite the increased bureaucratization and centralization of the movement. As Gusfield (1955, 1963, 1968) has stressed, such increases in the structuring of social movements do not inevitably lead to compromise and accommodation. In particular, as I will argue later in the chapter, the environmental movement changed because of the "contingencies which affect resistance, as well as those which change the character of the initial adherents" (Gusfield, 1968:449). The label of reformist designates a commitment to working within the system, rather than to changing the system. In Ash's (1972) terms, it means less attention to social structure and more to substructure, with less of a thrust towards displacing social elites than to influencing them (Gamson, 1975).

5. Millenarian movements are those exemplifying Smelser's (1962) value-orientation or Ash's (1972) superstructural focus, in a utopian religious sense. Although the term is derived from Christian theories of a thousand-year reign of Christ on earth, such movements generally have a "revolutionary promise of the advent of an age of bliss, abundance and perfect justice" (Wilkinson, 1971:70). While some aspects of the 1960s movement and the newer appropriate technology movement to be discussed later sometimes exhibit these promises, they are far more oriented towards the large-scale social engineering that Banks (1972:54) argues typifies successful utopian movements.

6. Banks (1972:8) argues that the collective behavior bias underestimates the social change potential of social movements (for a similar view, see Marx & Wood, 1975:415–16). On the other hand, he draws many of his own propositions from Smelser's (1962) work on collective behavior.

7. Morrison (1973:76), for example, notes that the environmental movement has a "top dog" mobilized constituency, whose relative comfort derives from previous economic growth (Morrison, 1976). But he also stresses that prior government agencies have provided *institutional* support for the movement, and this was also true for universities; while he is undoubtedly correct in these institutional organizations affording a social acceptance to the voluntary movement, I believe he underestimates the constraints they afforded (see Ch. VI, VII). However, I concur that the institutional movement provided the scientific inputs for the new voluntary movement, and the increased bureaucratization and centralization that accompanies this need for data collection and application (Morrison, 1973:78).

8. For examples of decline in public support for environmental reform soon after the legislative reforms of the late 1960s, see Hornback (1974), Morrison (1973, 1976), Dunlap & Van Liere (1977), Dunlap & Dillman (1976), and Buttel & Flinn (1974). Unfortunately, many of these studies use questionable indicators and samples, and are not fully comparable. Moreover, some of the decline in support is exaggerated, since a number of studies indicate that *what has declined is support for more government expenditure, rather than support increasing for less expenditure*. The response follows substantial state expenses on environmental regulation and the tendencies for movement concern to fall, especially after successful incorporation of

some of their goals (Ash, 1972:22–26, 231ff.; Zald & Ash, 1966; Mauss, 1975:61–70; Dunlap & Dillman, 1976).

9. Morrison (1973) outlined graphically the conflicts prior to the energy crisis, and his later analysis (1976) incorporated the latter elements more fully. From a comparison of the two analyses, along with other literature, it is not at all clear that there was a significant decline of support following the 1973–74 period. Data on membership and public opinion are inadequate on this (Buttel & Flinn, 1976b; Sills, 1975:27–28; Luten, 1973; Quigg, 1974), though some early studies on members exist (Zinger et al., 1973).

10. Among others, the most striking accusation against a nature-worshipping neofascist dimension of the movement is by Neuhaus (1971). Status politics refers to movement activities originating in the status losses of members (e.g., Gusfield, 1963), leading to inconsistency between dimensions of individual achievements (e.g., educational versus quality of life). In the case of the middle- or upper-middle-class membership of environmental movement organizations, the presumed status loss is in life amenities, especially aesthetic ones (loss of attractive physical environments in suburban and rural areas). Neuhaus's neofascist accusation is in part made more vivid by the long-standing assumption that Nazism's rise was built on the status politics of the German lower middle-class, whose economic position deteriorated following World War I. But recent work by Hamilton has dismissed this as the primary electoral roots of the National Socialist Party's rise in the elections of the 1930s (Hamilton, forthcoming).

11. A brief overview of these changes and uncertainties is in Sills (1975:26–29), Albrecht & Mauss (1975:567–84), and Buttel & Flinn (1976b).

12. Gale (1972) and Albrecht & Mauss (1975) trace the roots of environmentalism back to the conservationist movement, and Morrison et al. (1972) indicate the shifts in movement ideologies and goals. The challenge to incorporate equity goals is succinctly outlined in Morrison (1976). The appropriate technology movement incorporates the work of Schumacher (1973) and the emphasis of Lovins (1976, 1977) on "soft energy paths" (nonnuclear) into its view of socially useful production. Themes of the movement are summarized in Morrison (1978).

13. See Stretton (1976) for the range of future possibilities for social structural change under environmental pressures.

14. Albrecht & Mauss (1975) discuss the types of movement organizations and their varying histories, as does Rosenbaum (1973:75–88).

15. See Albrecht & Mauss (1975), Sills (1975), Buttel & Flinn (1974), Dunlap & Dillman (1976), and Dunlap & Van Liere (1977). Hornback (1974) also provides evidence of early opposition to the movement, and Sills (1975) indicates the growth in scientific opposition, as well as the uncertain trajectory of membership in recent years. The best summary of membership characteristics of the entire environmental movement is in Zinger et al. (1973), whose findings are compared by Dunlap (1975b) to other research, particularly on preservationists (e.g., Harry et al., 1969; Devall, 1970) and Zero Population Growth (L. Barnett, 1971, 1974). These latter groups are more upper middle-class than the broader range of movement volunteers. The range is still more heavily college-educated and in higher-status occupations than the overall population (Dunlap, 1975b), though this is typical of most social movements (Mauss, 1975:49–55).

But membership and support do not continue to rise into the higher income levels, in contrast to the educational differentiation, as Schnaiberg (1973) emphasizes. Buttel & Flinn (1976b) argue that environmentalism is associated with political and economic liberalism, which is more tied to education than to income beyond a given middle-class level. The discussion of shifting strategies, from participatory to power-orientations, is in Morrison et al. (1972) and Morrison (1973), among others. In all of these, Gale (1972) notes the prevalence of middle-class social action and politics, even during the "street" actions of the 1960s. This is congruent with the dominant environmental reformist or social order perspective (in contrast to a sharper class analysis or conflict perspective: e.g., see Buttel & Flinn, 1975, and Buttel, 1976). Even the recent antinuclear mass demonstrations (e.g., Ivins, 1978; Wald, 1978) are peaceful forms of civil disobedience. Moreover, they are only a small part of antinuclear tactics, which are dominated by lobbying (Tolchin, 1977; Henry, 1978; Rattner, 1977), direct electoral politics (Hill, 1978; Kandell, 1977), and even referenda actions that are occasionally successful, as in the recent Austrian elections (Hoffman, 1978). These are part of a growing American interest group structure, displacing some of the conventional two-party politics (e.g., Herbers, 1978; Buttel & Flinn, 1976b). With increasing politicization and class conflict especially there is a need, as Stretton (1976:14) has argued, for increased interaction between parties of the left and environmentalists. But the Democratic party in the U.S. is only weakly representative of the left (Judis, 1978b).

16. Morrison et al. (1972) and Morrison (1973) both emphasize the importance of these institutional parts of the movement, as opposed to the voluntary associations. The evidence is quite mixed on how enthusiastic these agencies have been, though (e.g., Culhane, 1974).

17. See Ash (1972) on social structure versus substructural movements, and Gamson (1975) on challenge or social protest movements. The latter may be oriented to either displacing or reforming the behavior of their antagonists. Gamson (1975:40–52) notes that movements with nondisplacing goals, concentrating on multiple issues, are more successful in gaining acceptance and advantages than others. This may partially explain the unusually visible success (Sills, 1975; Albrecht & Mauss, 1975) of the early part of the movement, which sought control over the excessive externalities of production with no other changes in the organization of social surplus.

18. Discussion of conflicts is most articulate in Morrison (1973) and Sills (1975). The generalized participatory climate of the 1960s and its stimulus to the environmental movement is treated in Ash (1972:234–42) and Gale (1972), with special attention to the young and college students in Hornback (1974), Dunlap & Gale (1972), and Dunlap et al. (1973). Conspiratorial models of domination of the movement by corporate elites include Barkley & Weissman (1970), which is partly documented in the case of Laurance Rockefeller by Collier & Horowitz (1976:303–9; 384–404).

19. Even in the early environmental movement period, there was tension between economic elites who served as sponsors for particular preservationist groups (such as Laurance Rockefeller and the American Conservation Association):

> His name had ceased to inspire confidence among rank-and-file conservationists, who had turned out to be far more stubborn and independent than was ever

> contemplated. The grass-roots movement... had a systemic view of the crisis... which was not quite what Laurance... and the others had in mind when they helped christen and launch the bandwagon for environmental quality. Yet... it was too late to do anything about it. The genie was out of the bottle. (Collier & Horowitz, 1976:387–88)

Thus, though these elites had influence and could partly direct the movement's attention, they did not really "capture" or repress it. These cross-pressures and the increasing opposition to the environmental movement in the 1970s are consistent with Ash's (1972:231) view that "The most successful movements have been those created by elites, sometimes but not consistently under pressure from reform and radical movements." Only part of the movement was ever under elites' control; this led to both greater movement autonomy and increased conflicts by the 1970s.

20. See Sills (1975) and Morrison (1973, 1976) on social scientific and economic elite responses to environmentalists, and a cultural interpretation of value conflicts in Dunlap (1976).

21. The lines of class conflicts are elucidated in Sills (1975) and Morrison (1976). Empirical analyses by Buttel (1978) and Buttel & Flinn (1976a) in Wisconsin indicate: (1) linkages between a desire for welfare-state policies and support for economic expansion are more prominent among the working class, and (2) there is greater articulation of the economic growth versus environmental protection tradeoff among middle-class respondents and among the educated especially. While the correlations are not that great and are subject to many problems of interpretation (see Converse, 1964), they indicate increasing conflict when economic growth is threatened and slows social welfare policies (Wilensky, 1975).

22. See, for example, the discussion in Albrecht (1973) regarding the formation of countermovements to environmentalists, as in the Four Corners power-plant controversies.

23. Morrison's (1973) discussion parallels this in terms of benefits and costs, and his later call (1976) for increased equity concerns has been partly responded to by movement organizations. While some of the early studies of Sierra Club members evidenced little interest in poverty and urban problems (Coombs, 1972; Dunlap, 1975b), changes have occurred in later years. These include coordination of efforts between environmental groups and the Oil, Chemical and Atomic Workers' Union in boycotting Shell Oil because of occupational health issues (Love, 1973). The Environmental Defense Fund, with a 1977 membership of 45,000, is sensitized to economic issues on a number of planes. Its executive director notes: "EDF's opposition to destructive or wasteful projects and policies is always combined with efforts to propose more economical, less harmful alternatives." (Schardt, 1977:1). In its analyses of bottle bills (Cooley, 1976), energy alternatives (EDF, 1978), and environmental protection (Schardt, 1978), the emphasis is on consumer benefits, jobs, and inflation. Likewise, Natural Resources Defense Council, in its activities in water conservation (NRDC, 1977b: especially 14–16) and power policies in the western United States (NRDC, 1978a:8–17), attempts to make detailed evaluations and proposals that reduce consumer costs and protect employment. In the well-publicized conflicts over the extension of the Redwood National Park (NRDC, 1977a:14–16), there is special attention paid to job protection and the state's obliga-

tions. Finally, in its asbestos regulation actions (NRDC, 1976), special attention was paid to occupational health issues as background. Other groups have sought to elect politically liberal and environmentally sensitive legislators (Hill, 1978), since political liberalism and environmentalism seem associated (Buttel & Flinn, 1976b; Dunlap, 1975a; Dunlap & Allen, 1976). As yet, there have been only limited direct interactions with organized labor (e.g., Judis, 1978a).

24. A review of both the ideas of the movement and the politics that are developing around it is the collection recently published by the Ozark Institute (1978). Funding for this issue came in part from the National Center for Appropriate Technology, which is itself a project of the Community Services Administration, the successor of the Nixon-destroyed Office of Economic Opportunity. This location in the *poverty* institutional nexus is auspicious, at least.

25. In the classical definition of Coase (1960:15), transaction costs include such things as negotiations, inspections, information collection and dispersal. With the state intervening more in production because of environmental regulation and the additional costs of direct negotiation by public interest groups, these transaction costs have risen.

26. Hornback (1974), McEvoy (1972), and Albrecht & Mauss (1975) review some of the evidence for rising and falling public support and membership of the movement and its organizations. As Dunlap & Van Liere (1977:111) note, it is not clear whether there is a widespread public backlash or simply an assumption by workers and consumers that substantial environmental protection has been achieved. Mitchell (1978), in reviewing national social surveys, finds decreased spontaneous mention of environmental issues as critical (which was Hornback's major measure of environmentalism). But he also notes that well over half the respondents were concerned about pollution issues and evidenced willingness to trade off some jobs for reduced pollution. On the other hand, coal production took precedence over strict air pollution controls for almost half of one sample. The question of whether ecology was to be a "last fad" was initially raised by Miller (1971), a committed activist.

The link between public opinion and membership is tenuous (Dunlap, 1975b), and that between either of these and political responses is even more questionable (Buttel & Flinn, 1976b). In his comparative analyses of social protest movements, for example, Gamson (1975:50–52) found that larger membership did not lead to more advantages for a movement though they did indicate greater social acceptance of it. Part of the confusion in whether the movement is rising or falling is that various observers treat public opinion of different types, membership in different movement organizations, and elite responses of different sorts as indicators.

27. Albrecht & Mauss (1975) and Sills (1975) discuss these issues.

28. Gamson (1975: Ch. 5) finds some support for Olson's theory, though he indicates that sponsorship or incentives can be effective for movements, the former more for small movements and the latter for larger ones. On the other hand, Tillock & Morrison (1977) find incentives not that important in the Zero Population Growth movement (and the domestic populationist movement does not have the powerful sponsorship that the movement oriented toward the Third World does: e.g., see McCracken, 1972).

29. Among the recent proposals, Melman's (1978) is most focused on urban

labor and employment needs. This contrasts with organized labor's past commitments to expand military production (e.g., Kolko, 1976: Ch. 5; Judis, 1978b).

30. This typology relates closely to the issue of social order versus social conflict perspectives among analysts and within the movement (Buttel & Flinn, 1975; Buttel, 1976). Cosmetologists and meliorists follow a nonconflict model of environmental problems. Radicals and many reformists see the necessity for considerable social conflict to change the workings of the social system, usually by displacing existing elites (Gamson, 1975) or at least by exercising far tighter social controls over them.

31. See Collier & Horowitz (1976:397–400) on the Rockefeller strategy. While Barkley & Weissman (1970) dismiss this reformist element as trivial, Morrison et al. (1972) take a view closer to my own.

32. Morrison (1973) discusses these conflicts and disorientations. The distinction between norm-oriented (behavioral changes) and value-oriented (ideological changes) movements is in Smelser (1962).

33. The two most powerful influences in this movement were Schumacher (1973) and Lovins (1976, 1977), with the former having more grass-roots support and the latter having more attention from economic elites (Parisi, 1977). Dickson's (1975) analysis clearly indicates the formidable opposition to such a movement, although Morrison (1976) shares my view that some constructive environmentalist ideology like this is vital (see also Schnaiberg, 1975).

34. Fairfax (1978) notes the possible goal displacement (Ash, 1972:22–26) of the movement in excessive involvement over the *analyses* rather than *policies*. All negotiation entails the risk of incorporation, becalming, routinization, or suppression of social movements (Ash, 1972:22–26); given the massive opposition to environmental protection without social negotiations (Morrison, 1973, 1976), there seem to be few options.

35. Barkley & Weissman (1970) take the strongest view of the creation of the modern movement by economic elites, intensifying the political capitalism that Kolko (1963) noted earlier by drawing the state more heavily into de facto support for large business. Gellen's (1970) analysis parallels this in the case of pollution abatement equipment manufacturers. The definitive critical view of the conservation movement is given by Hays (1969).

36. Works which emphasize the distinctive features of the environmental movement include Albrecht & Mauss (1975), Morrison et al. (1972) and Gale (1972). The concept of ecology as a "subversive" science comes from Shepard & McKinley (1969). Buttel (1976) indicates that the analytic conflict perspective would enhance this subversion of the existing capitalist social structure. He stresses that the dominant view of social analysts is of social order, and that the bulk of the movement follows this perspective, with middle-class politics as the primary action (Gale, 1972).

37. Hays (1969) reviews the 1890–1920 period, in which conservation movements and state actions were most visible (cf., Morgan, 1974). Albrecht & Mauss (1975:591) list some of the major national conservation-environmental movement organizations, with their founding dates: (1) *Early:* Sierra Club (1892), National Audubon Society (1905), National Parks Association (1919), Izaak Wal-

ton League (1922); (2) *Middle:* National Wildlife Federation (1936), Wilderness Society (1936), Conservation Foundation (1948); (3) *Late:* Environmental Defense Fund (1968), Zero Population Growth (1969), and Natural Resources Defense Council (1969).

38. Gale (1972) and Morrison et al. (1972) contrast the movement as a "utilitarian" one that stood between unrestrained corporate use of resources and perfect preservation of these resources by the preservationist movement (Smith, 1966). Following Hays (1969), though, this concept of utilitarianism in resource policy is very misleading. There was an official mandate to reconcile conflicting resource interests "from the standpoint of the greatest good for the greatest number," the John Stuart Mill–Jeremy Bentham definition of utilitarianism, in the 1900–20 period (e.g., Rosenbaum, 1973:198 on the Forest Service). But, as 19th century economists discovered, this concept does not work so simply. Progressive reforms, rather than serving "the greatest number," served disproportionately the largest corporations (Hays, 1969; Kilko, 1963). Therefore I reject this concept and prefer to label the movement as conservation-*efficiency*.

39. Morrison et al. (1972) emphasize the institutional base of the modern movement, though Culhane's (1974) analysis casts some doubt on this. The capture of many of the earlier federal and state agencies for pollution and land control by corporate interests is documented in all the Nader group's studies (e.g., Esposito, 1970; Wellford, 1972) of particular environmental problems. My use of the habitat versus sustenance concerns (Ch. I), is consistent with Morrison et al. (1972), though the language differs.

40. Albrecht & Mauss (1975) discuss the modern movement in much the same way, with the movement membership base drawn from the prior preservationist groups, and prior acceptance from the existing state agencies.

41. See Stretton (1976), Morrison (1976), and Buttel (1976) for similar indications of the politicization that is required for a *successful* environmental movement, i.e., one that will achieve environmental preservation for the broad population of society. In this sense, the modern movement is in fact utilitarian in objectives, unlike the early 20th century efficiency movement.

42. On participation and power strategies, see Morrison et al. (1972).

43. This typology of movement dimensions is taken from Gamson (1975:14–15).

44. I have taken these elements from Ash (1972) and Gamson (1975), though parallel categories exist in other social movement analyses.

45. Buttel (1976) has argued that the redistributive emphasis will be diminished, as the middle-class politics of the movement reflects its social order approach rather than a social conflict one: i.e., it seeks to work "within the system." This argument is consistent with his earlier empirical findings (Buttel & Flinn, 1976b) that environmentalism is more associated with political liberalism—state regulation of private enterprise—than with welfare-state (redistributive) liberalism.

46. See Smith (1966), Hays (1969), and Rosenbaum (1973) on the historical conflicts; Morrison (1973, 1976) has elaborated on the modern movement's conflicts within the state, as have Rosenbaum (1973) and Albrecht & Mauss (1975).

47. The discussion of his resort-preservation strategy is in Collier & Horowitz

(1976:397–400), who argue (pp. 389–90) that in fact Rockefeller was an advocate of efficiency rather than preservationism. On the Redwoods controversies, though he gave support to the League (p. 395n) his lobbying on the Redwoods National Park was motivated by the preferences of the multinational Weyerhauser Timber Company (pp. 394–96).

48. On the challenge of this movement to the technostructure, see the analyses of Bossi (1978) and Etzkowitz (1978). But others (e.g., Penner, 1978; de Moll, 1978; Bender, 1978) all indicate the degree to which the ideology and practice of the movement may be co-opted by monopoly-capital influence, and the bureaucratic momentum of the state in support of political capitalism. The state's official commitment, through the National Center for Appropriate Technology, is indicative of the dual roles of the state noted in Chapter VII. The parent agency, Community Services Administration, arises from the ashes of the distributional-political agency of the "war on poverty," the Office of Economic Opportunity. However, OEO was dismantled by Richard Nixon's administration and its tasks turned over to politicians concerned with economic growth rather than distribution.

49. This analysis is consistent with that of Morrison et al. (1972) as well as Rosenbaum (1973) and Hays (1969).

50. These concerns are especially acute within the state during the modern "fiscal crisis" (O'Connor, 1973) when the inflationary impact of environmental regulation is more and more under question (NRDC, 1978b). The problem is exacerbated when the state is forced to accept the lion's share of the blame for inflation, rather than a broader causal model in which the externalities of the treadmill (Ch. V) are seen as primary pressures for this increased role of the state and other corporate inflationary roles.

51. In addition, there is employment generated by pollution abatement industries and those focusing on new energy technologies.

52. The work of Aldo Leopold (1949) is widely cited as the bible of the preservationist movement. My suspicion is that it was far more read by leaders than members of even national groups, let alone local groups.

53. The research of Faich & Gale (1971) indicates that even traditional preservationist organizations now have broader agendas requiring more scientific input (Morrison, 1973).

54. Albrecht & Mauss (1975) review the new movement components and activities. Charlton (1978) lays out the Nader network of organizations.

55. Although earlier research on social movements indicated that centralization and bureaucratization led inevitably to decline of movement activism (Gusfield, 1968; Ash, 1972:22–26), research and theory now suggests that such institutionalization can facilitate movement success as well (e.g., Gamson, 1975: Ch. 7; Albrecht & Mauss, 1975; Mauss, 1975: Ch. 2).

56. See the Ozark Institute (1978) discussion of these ideas and state responses.

57. This is the argument of Barkley & Weissman (1970) and Buttel (1976), among others.

58. In this, I concur with Morrison (1976), Buttel (1976), and Stretton (1976).

59. This is the argument and analysis of Kolko (1963) and O'Connor (1973) with regard to the emergence of political capitalism.

60. Odell (1978) briefly indicates these roots of the appropriate technology movement, as does Dickson (1975). The context of trade-and-aid, and especially the patterns of Third World investment, are treated in Frank (1969) and Barnet & Müller (1974). Myrdal's (1968) massive work on Asian underdevelopment ended with social policy prescriptions congruent with the intermediate technology movement. Even conventional neoclassical economists had prescriptions for economic development that were not all that incongruent with intermediate technology for the Third World (e.g., Reynolds, 1963: Ch. 28), based on availability of labor as a factor in production. That these ideas did not flourish in practice indicates the nature of international as well as domestic opposition (Dickson, 1975).

61. On China's development, see Anderson (1976:242–51) on the mainland and Mueller (1977) on Taiwan. Taiwan experienced "trickle-down" development, stimulated by aid and investment from a core industrial society (Wallerstein, 1974), the U.S. Most other peripheral (Third World) countries had similar aid and investment patterns, except from some semiperipheral countries that made small investments in appropriate (intermediate) technology. Presumably such donor nations were somewhat less dependent on trade with the peripheral societies, and were more empathetic with their position of economic dependency in the modern world-system.

62. As a brief indication of these pressures to shift agendas, Bender (1978) notes that NCAT was originally to be placed under MERDI (Montana Energy and Magnetohydrodynamics Research Institute), whose board included Edward Teller (a passionate advocate of nuclear fission and fusion and of energy expansionism) and managers from Anaconda Copper and Montana Power Company. These latter groups have little interest in altering usage of energy, and much interest in preserving the existing treadmill. But their concern for alternative energy sources provides temporary alliances.

63. De Moll (1978) notes that even with use of community organizers, local poor people's groups are often not readily mobilized for appropriate technology work. The organizer attributed this to habituation to government handouts and lack of enthusiasm for hard work.

REFERENCES

ALBRECHT, STAN L.
1973 "Environmental social movements and countermovements: An overview and an illustration." Pp. 244–262 in R.R. Evans (ed.), Social Movements. Chicago: Rand McNally.

ALBRECHT, STAN L. AND A. L. MAUSS
1975 "The environment as a social problem." Pp. 556–605 in A.L. Mauss (ed.), Social Problems as Social Movements. Philadelphia: J.B. Lippincott.

ANDERSON, CHARLES H.
1976 The Sociology of Survival: Social Problems of Growth. Homewood, Ill: Dorsey Press.

ASH, ROBERTA
1972   Social Movements in America. Chicago: Markham.

BANKS, J.A.
1972   The Sociology of Social Movements. London: Macmillan.

BARKLEY, KATHERINE AND S. WEISSMAN
1970   "The eco-establishment." Pp. 15–24 by the editors of Ramparts, Eco-Catastrophe. San Francisco: Canfield Press.

BARNET, RICHARD J. AND R.G. MÜLLER
1974   Global Reach: The Power of the Multinational Corporations. New York: Simon and Schuster.

BARNETT, HAROLD J. AND C. MORSE
1963   Scarcity and Growth: The Economics of Natural Resource Availability. Baltimore: Johns Hopkins University Press.

BARNETT, LARRY D.
1971   "Zero Population Growth, Inc." Bioscience 21 (4):759–765.
1974   "Zero Population Growth, Inc.: A Second Study." Journal of Biosocial Science 6(1):1–22.

BENDER, TOM
1978   "ncat—where are you at?" Ozarka (special issue):5.

BOSSI, STEPHEN
1978   "A.T. challenges conventional wisdom." Ozarka (special issue): 11.

BUTTEL, FREDERICK H.
1976   "Social science and the environment: Competing theories." Social Science Quarterly 57 (2):307–323.
1978   "Economic growth and the welfare state: Implications for the future of environmentalism." Social Science Quarterly 58 (3):692–699.

BUTTEL, FREDERICK H. AND W.L. FLINN
1974   "The structure of support for the environmental movement, 1968–1970." Rural Sociology 39 (1):56–69.
1975   "Methodological issues in the sociology of natural resources." Humboldt Journal of Social Relations 3 (1):63–72.
1976a   "Economic growth versus the environment: Survey evidence." Social Science Quarterly 57 (2):410–420.
1976b   "Environmental politics: The structuring of partisan and ideological cleavages in mass environmental attitudes." Sociological Quarterly 17 (4):477–490.

BUTTEL, FREDERICK H. AND D.E. MORRISON
1977   The Environmental Movement: A Research Bibliography with Some State-of-the-Arts Comments. Bibliography 1308. Monticello, Ill.: Council of Planning Librarians, July.

BUTTERFIELD, FOX
1978   "Peking's poster warriors are not just paper tigers." New York Times, 26 Nov.

CHARLTON, LINDA
1978   "Ralph Nader's conglomerate is big business." New York Times, 29 Jan.

COASE, R.H.
1960   "The problem of social cost." The Journal of Law & Economics III (Oct.):1ff.

COLLIER, PETER AND D. HOROWITZ
1976   The Rockefellers: An American Dynasty. New York: Holt, Rinehart, and Winston.

CONVERSE, PHILIP E.
1964   "The nature of belief systems in mass publics." Pp. 206–261 in D. E. Apter (ed.), Ideology and Discontent. Glencoe, Ill.: Free Press.

COOLEY, ARTHUR P.
1976   "EDF action report: The bottle battle." EDF Letter, Nov./Dec.:2.

COOMBS, DON
1972   "The Club looks at itself." Sierra Club Bulletin 57 (July/Aug.):35–39.

CULHANE, PAUL J.
1974   "Federal agency organizational change in response to environmentalism." Humboldt Journal of Social Relations 2 (1):31–44.

DE MOLL, LANE
1978   "No more 'rich tech, poor tech.'" Ozarka (special issue):3.

DEVALL, WILLIAM B.
1970   "Conservation: An upper-middle class social movement: A replication." Journal of Leisure Research 2 (Spring):123–126.

DICKSON, DAVID
1975   The Politics of Alternative Technology. New York: Universe Books.

DUNLAP, RILEY E.
1975a "The impact of political orientation on environmental attitudes and action." Environment and Behavior 7 (4):428–454.
1975b "The socioeconomic basis of the environmental movement: Old data, new data, and implications for the movement's future." Paper presented at meetings of American Sociological Association, San Francisco, Aug.
1976   "Understanding opposition to the environmental movement: The importance of dominant American values." Paper presented at meetings of Society for the Study of Social Problems, New York, Aug.

DUNLAP, RILEY E. AND M.P. ALLEN
1976   "Partisan differences on environmental issues: A Congressional roll-call analysis." The Western Political Quarterly 29 (3):384–397.

DUNLAP, RILEY E. AND D.A. DILLMAN
1976   "Decline in public support for environmental protection: Evidence from a 1970–1974 panel study." Rural Sociology 41 (3):382–390.

DUNLAP, RILEY E. AND R.P. GALE
1972   "Politics and ecology: A political profile of student eco-activists." Youth and Society 3 (2):379–397.

DUNLAP, RILEY E., R.P. GALE, AND B.M. RUTHERFORD
1973   "Concern for environmental rights among college students." Journal of Economics and Sociology 32 (1):45–60.

DUNLAP, RILEY E. AND K.D. VAN LIERE
1977   "Further evidence of declining public concern with environmental problems: A research note." Western Sociological Review 8 (1):108–112.
1978   Environmental Concern: A Bibliography of Empirical Studies and Brief Appraisal of the Literature. Bibliography P-44, Public Administration Series. Monticello, Ill.: Vance Bibliographies.

ENVIRONMENTAL DEFENSE FUND (EDF)
1978   "Energy alternatives shown economically superior to coal and nuclear power." EDF Letter, May/June:1.

ESPOSITO, JOHN C.
1970   Vanishing Air. New York: Grossman Publishers.

ETZKOWITZ, HENRY
1978   "The liberation of technology." Ozarka (special issue):3–4.

FAICH, RONALD G. AND R.P. GALE
1971   "The environmental movement: From recreation to politics." Pacific Sociological Review 14 (July):270–287.

FAIRFAX, SALLY K.
1978   "A disaster in the environmental movement." Science 199 (17 Feb.):743–748.

FEUER, LEWIS S. (ED.)
1959   Basic Writings on Politics and Philosophy: Karl Marx and Friedrich Engels. Garden City, N.Y.: Anchor Books.

FRANK, ANDRÉ GUNDER
1969   Capitalism and Underdevelopment in Latin America: Historical Studies of Chile and Brazil. Revised edition. New York: Modern Reader Paperbacks.

GALE, RICHARD P.
1972   "From sit-in to hike-in: A comparison of the civil rights and environmental movements." Pp. 280–305 in W. R. Burch, N. H. Cheek, Jr., and L. Taylor (eds.), Social Behavior, Natural Resources, and the Environment. New York: Harper and Row.

GAMSON, WILLIAM A.
1975   The Strategy of Social Protest. Homewood, Ill.: Dorsey Press.

GELLEN, MARTIN
1970   "The making of a pollution-industrial complex." Pp. 73–83 by the editors of Ramparts, Eco-Catastrophe. San Francisco: Canfield Press.

GUSFIELD, JOSEPH R.
1955   "Social structure and moral reform: A study of the Women's Christian Temperance Union." American Sociological Review 61 (2):221–232.
1963   Symbolic Crusade: Status Politics and the American Temperance Movement. Urbana, Ill.: University of Illinois Press.

1968   "The study of social movements." Pp. 445–452 in D. Sills (ed), International Encyclopedia of the Social Sciences. New York: Collier-Macmillan.

HAMILTON, RICHARD F.
Forth-   The Bases of National Socialism: The Electoral Support for Hitler,
coming   1924–1932.

HARRY, JOSEPH, R. GALE, AND J. HENDEL
1969   "Conservation: An upper-middle class social movement." Journal of Leisure Research 1 (Summer):246–254.

HAYS, SAMUEL P.
1969   Conservation and the Gospel of Efficiency: The Progressive Conservation Movement, 1890–1920. New York: Atheneum.

HENRY, DIANE
1978   "Connecticut urged to restrict A-plant." New York Times, 26 Mar.

HERBERS, JOHN
1978   "Interest groups gaining influence at the expense of national parties." New York Times, 26 Mar.

HILL, GLADWIN
1978   "Environmentalists registered both gains and reverses in elections." New York Times, 12 Nov.

HOFFMAN, PAUL
1978   "Troubles mounting for Austrian chief." New York Times, 12 Nov.

HORNBACK, KENNETH E.
1974   Orbits of Opinion: The Role of Age in the Environmental Movement's Attentive Public, 1968–1972. Doctoral dissertation, Michigan State University, East Lansing, Mich.

IVINS, MOLLY
1978   "1,500 at Denver rally protest nuclear weapons plant." New York Times, 30 Apr.

JUDIS, JOHN
1978a   "UAW conference seeks new course for American left." In These Times, 25 Oct.:2ff.
1978b   "Is the party over or just beginning?" In These Times, 1 Nov.:11–13.

KANDELL, JONATHAN
1977   "Ecology is suddenly a European power." New York Times, 7 Aug.

KILLIAN, LEWIS M.
1964   "Social movements." Pp. 426–455 in R.E.L. Faris (ed.), Handbook of Modern Sociology. Chicago: Rand McNally.

KLEIN, RUDOLF
1972   "Growth and its enemies." Commentary 53 (June):37–44.

KOLKO, GABRIEL
1973   The Triumph of Conservatism: A Reinterpretation of American History, 1900–1916. New York: Free Press.

1976   Main Currents in Modern American History. New York: Harper and Row.

LEOPOLD, ALDO
1949   A Sand County Almanac. New York: Oxford University Press.

LOVE, SAM
1973   " 'To hell with Shell': Memoirs of a boycott." Environmental Action 5 (7 July):13–15.

LOVINS, AMORY
1976   "Energy strategy: The road not taken?" Foreign Affairs 55(1):65–96.
1977   Soft Energy Paths. Cambridge, Mass.: Ballinger.

LUTEN, D. B.
1973   "Fading away?" Western Outdoors Annual 40:8–12.

MARX, GARY T. AND J.W. WOOD
1975   "Strands of theory and research in collective behavior." Pp. 363–428 in A. Inkeles et al., (eds.), Annual Review of Sociology. Palo Alto, Cal.: Annual Reviews, Inc.

MASON, EDWARD S.
1978   "Resources past and future." Resources 57 (Jan.–Mar.):24.

MAUSS, ARMAND L. (WITH ASSOCIATES) (ED.)
1975   Social Problems as Social Movements. Philadelphia and New York: J.B. Lippincott.

MCCRACKEN, SAMUEL
1972   "The population controllers." Commentary 53 (May):45–52.

MCEVOY, JAMES, III
1972   "The American concern with environment." Pp. 214–236 in W.R. Burch, N.H. Cheek, Jr., and L. Taylor (eds.), Social Behavior, Natural Resources, and the Environment. New York: Harper and Row.

MELMAN, SEYMOUR
1978   "Beating 'swords' into subways." New York Times Magazine, 19 Nov.:43 ff.

MILLER, DAVID C.
1971   "Ecology—the last fad." Pp. 303–312 in F. Carvell and M. Tadlock (eds.), It's Not Too Late. Beverly Hills, Cal.: Glencoe Press.

MITCHELL, ROBERT C.
1978   "Environment: An enduring concern." Resources 57 (Jan.–Mar.):1ff.

MORGAN, H. WAYNE
1974   Industrial America: The Environment and Social Problems, 1865–1970. Chicago: Rand McNally.

MORRISON, DENTON E.
1973   "The environmental movement: Conflict dynamics." Journal of Voluntary Action Research 2 (2):74–85.
1976   "Growth, environment, equity and scarcity." Social Science Quarterly 57 (2):292–306.

1978   "Energy, appropriate technology, and international interdependence."
        Paper presented at meetings of Society for the Study of Social Problems,
        San Francisco, Aug.

MORRISON, DENTON E., K.E. HORNBACK, AND W.K. WARNER
1972   "The environmental movement: Some preliminary observations and pre-
        dictions." Pp. 259–279 in W.R. Burch, N.H. Cheek, Jr., and L.
        Taylor (eds.), Social Behavior, Natural Resources, and the Environment.
        New York: Harper and Row.

MUELLER, EVA
1977   "The impact of demographic factors on economic development in
        Taiwan." Population and Development Review 3 (1–2):1ff.

MYRDAL, GUNNAR
1968   Asian Drama: An Inquiry into the Poverty of Nations. New York:
        Pantheon.

NATURAL RESOURCES DEFENSE COUNCIL (NRDC)
1976   "NRDC petition seeks ban on cancer-causing asbestos in household patch-
        ing products." NRDC newsletter 5 (3):8–10.
1977a   "The tragedy of Redwood National Park." NRDC newsletter 6 (4):1–16.
1977b   "Waste in the west (part I): Water, California, and the Bureau of Recla-
        mation." NRDC newsletter 6 (6):1–16.
1978a   "Waste in the west (part II): The power broker." NRDC newsletter 7
        (1):1–20.
1978b   "Inflation review of environmental regulations: New 'quality of life'
        review?" NRDC newsletter, 7(2/3):11.

NEUHAUS, RICHARD J.
1971   In Defense of People: Ecology and the Seduction of Radicalism. New
        York: Macmillan.

O'CONNOR, JAMES
1973   The Fiscal Crisis of the State. New York: St. Martin's Press.

ODELL, RICE
1978   "High tech shifts into low gear." Ozarka (special issue):10.

OLSON, MANCUR, JR.
1965   The Logic of Collective Action: Public Goods and the Theory of Groups.
        New York: Schocken Books.

OZARK INSTITUTE
1978   "A special report on appropriate technology." Ozarka, Journal of the
        Ozark Institute.

PARISI, ANTHONY J.
1977   " 'Soft' energy, hard choices." New York Times, 16 Oct.

PENNER, PETER
1978   "Taking A.T. to task." Ozarka (special issue):2.

QUIGG, P. W.
1974   "Of conservationists and their critics." Saturday Review/World (1
        June):35.

RATTNER, STEVEN
1977   "The nuclear siting bill hits a snag." New York Times, 13 Nov.

REYNOLDS, LLOYD G.
1963   Economics: A General Introduction. Homewood, Ill.: Richard D. Irwin.

ROSENBAUM, WALTER A.
1973   The Politics of Environmental Concern. New York: Praeger.

SCHARDT, ARLIE W.
1977   "Executive Director's message." Pp. 1–2 in Environmental Defense
       Fund—1977 Annual Report. Washington, D.C.
1978   "A sound economy and a healthy environment: Both are possible." EDF
       Letter, May/June:2.

SCHNAIBERG, ALLAN
1973   "Politics, participation and pollution: The 'environmental movement.'"
       Pp. 605–627 in J. Walton and D.E. Carns (eds.), Cities in Change:
       Studies on the Urban Condition. Boston: Allyn and Bacon.
1975   "Social syntheses of the societal-environmental dialectic: The role of
       distributional impacts." Social Science Quarterly 56 (June):5–20.

SCHUMACHER, E. F.
1973   Small Is Beautiful: Economics as if People Mattered. New York: Harper
       and Row.

SHEPARD, PAUL AND D. MCKINLEY (EDS.)
1969   The Subversive Science: Essays Toward an Ecology of Man. Boston:
       Houghton Mifflin.

SILLS, DAVID L.
1975   "The environmental movement and its critics." Human Ecology 3
       (1):1–41.

SMELSER, NEIL T.
1962   A Theory of Collective Behavior. New York: Free Press.

SMITH, FRANK E.
1966   The Politics of Conservation. New York: Harper Colophon.

STRETTON, HUGH
1976   Capitalism, Socialism and the Environment. Cambridge: Cambridge
       University Press.

TILLOCK, HARRIET AND D.E. MORRISON
1977   "Group size and contributions to collective action: A test of Mancur
       Olson's theory in Zero Population Growth, Inc." Paper presented at
       meetings of Society for the Study of Social Problems, Chicago, Sept.

TOLCHIN, MARTIN
1977   "Lobbying in the 'public interest' is more effective." New York Times,
       20 Nov.

TRAUGOTT, MARK
1978   "Reconceiving social movements." Social Problems 26 (1):38–49.

WALD, MATTHEW L.
1978   "Connecticut is experiencing nuclear protest and bans." New York Times, 30 Apr.

WALLERSTEIN, IMMANUEL
1974   The Modern World-System: Capitalist Agriculture and the Origins of the European World-Economy in the Sixteenth Century. New York: Academic Press.

WELLFORD, HARRISON
1972   Sowing the Wind. New York: Bantam Books.

WILENSKY, HAROLD L.
1975   The Welfare State and Equality. Berkeley, Cal.: University of California Press.

WILKINSON, PAUL
1971   Social Movement. New York: Praeger.

ZALD, MAYER N. AND R. ASH
1966   "Social movement organizations: Growth, decay and change." Social Forces 44 (Mar.):327–340.

ZINGER, CLEM L., R. DALSEMER, AND H. MAGARGLE
1973   Environmental Volunteers in America. Environmental Protection Agency publication PB 214186. Government Printing Office: Washington, D.C.

IX W(H)ITHER THE ENVIRONMENT?
Summary and Suggestions

SOCIAL STRUCTURES AND SOCIAL OPTIONS

Summary of the Analysis

I will first review the essential arguments of the preceding chapters, and then outline the major social welfare choices that advanced industrial societies must make. In the last part of this concluding chapter, I delineate the political and social structural forces that need to be dealt with in any attempt at production reform.

THE ENVIRONMENT AS A SOCIAL PROBLEM   The evaluation of environmental degradation as a social problem in Chapter I was based on the models of both natural and social science. Although localized and/or temporary ecological disorganization has existed since before humankind appeared, the twentieth century has encompassed a dramatic transformation of sociocultural production. Departure from social production systems that more closely approximated biological production in other species is a defining element of advanced industrialization. While concerns for the survival of the total human species may be greatly exaggerated, it is true that advanced industrialization as a form of sociocultural production is an increasing threat to the sustenance base of societies. Because research in many of these issues is so recent and so limited, defining these threats is not easy. However, they do exist: Environmental concern is addressing more than a cosmetic or aesthetic degradation of biospheric systems. Moreover, direct and indirect social consequences flow from these elements of disorganization.

Regardless of political or social structures, the dynamics of sociocultural production expansion are diametrically opposed to models of surplus absorption in other biospheric species. Societal economies typically mobilize social surpluses to enhance the expansion of physical capital and future production. Other species generally use this surplus to expand population and biomass. Thus, while ecological principles apply to the population growth of most species through the limitation of food supplies or critical nutrients, human societies organize to avoid and overcome these ecological constraints. So far, our industrial societies have been remarkably adept in this circumvention, but with what consequences for the future, we do not yet know.

What does vary across societies is the volume and types of biospheric disruptions that industrialization has produced. All sociocultural production involves withdrawals from and additions to ecosystems. However, societies differ in the volume of withdrawals and additions, in the degree of permanence of these, in the centrality of such impacts on ecosystem organization, and in the range of ecosystems affected. All industrial societies have increased their environmental impacts on all these dimensions. But they have done so at quite different rates. These production differences reflect varying forms of control over sociocultural production. Social controls partly reflect differences in power structures and inequalities within societies created by unequal distribution of production surplus.

Moreover, the social effects of these biospheric alterations differ across and within societies. The general thesis of Chapter I is that inequality in social structures is reflected in social class differentials in (a) gains from past environmental exploitation, (b) control over the trajectory of sociocultural production, and (c) risks from both ecosystem disorganization and various environmental protection efforts. There is a far greater need for integrating social scientific and political concerns about these inequalities in environmental policies than is suggested by any simple biological extrapolation from ecological theories. Humankind *is* different from other species, despite shared biological vulnerability. That difference is the basis for the rest of the book.

THE SEARCH FOR CAUSES AND SOLUTIONS   While the past decade has seen innumerable analyses of the causes of environmental problems, I selected four major arguments for detailed evaluation in Part 2. These are, respectively, (1) growth of population, (2) changes in technology, (3) expansion of consumption, and (4) expansion of production. Each of these reflects one facet of both public and scientific opinion as to the most central issues to be addressed in environmental reforms: too many people, too rapid technological changes, too much consumer affluence, and/or too much growth in corporate size and production. While there is at least a limited validity to each of these claims, my argument is that we cannot understand the roots of environmental degradation without appreciating the structure and dynamics of the treadmill of production expansion as outlined in Chapter V.

This treadmill influences the course of population, technology, and consumption in each of the industrial countries and in the remainder of the modern world-system, including the underdeveloped or Third World countries. It does not, by any means, fully determine their paths, but it has strongly influenced many of them. And it is likely to continue to do so. Moreover, the treadmill reflects the internal and international dimensions of social inequality in income and power. Without an appreciation of this treadmill, efforts to alter environmental degradation by operating on any or all of the other three causes of such degradation must ultimately fail. This failure is likely despite the self-evidence of gains from reformation of population, technology, or consumption. My argument is a result of integrating our knowledge of social structure into the analysis of environmental protection. Many of the opposing prevailing attitudes rest on the shakiest of assumptions about the social world, assumptions that have been generated by physical scientists whose expertise lies elsewhere. These perspectives are briefly summarized in the following paragraphs.

Population Influences (Chapter II).   While it is unquestionable that a growing human population requires some minimal biological sustenance from the environment, no other simple claims can be made about "the effects" of population growth. Much of the prevailing analysis and policy direction relies on a crude population problems model. Population growth and the emergence of increased social and environmental problems are linked in questionable ways by this model. Who causes what is never clear, despite the assumptions that underly these assertions. Omitted from such analyses is the nature of the social and economic system that intervenes between population growth and ecosystem withdrawals and additions. Thus we are faced with considerable uncertainty as to the actual environmental effects of population growth.

Moreover, the path of modern demographic change has been strongly influenced by persistent internal and international social inequalities. The most rapid population growth has occurred in groups that are actual or potential *victims* of environmental degradation. In contrast, the slowest growth has been in those groups most active in creating this degradation through their control of production. And the preponderance of evidence suggests that poverty causes overpopulation, rather than the reverse assumption. Neither biological models drawn from other species nor simple interpretations of Malthusian theories are adequate to appreciate the role of inequality in perpetuating population problems. Indeed, Malthus himself was much more integrative than modern populationists acknowledge, in his concern for social welfare and his analysis of inequality. The contrasts between China and India in the last three decades indicate the differences in both social welfare and efficient use of environmental resources that can develop from initially similar population problems. Population growth is not to be dismissed as a contributory factor to some environmental degradation, then. However, its influence cannot be evaluated nor greatly altered without taking direct account of the nature of inequalities in the production and distribution systems in the modern world-system. Where social inducements are available, population growth and long-term environmental degradation may eventually decline and social welfare rise. Any other approach creates unpredictable or unjust changes in social welfare, population size and environmental withdrawals and additions.

Technological Influences (Chapter III). The qualitative and quantitative changes in twentieth century technologies of production play a key role in environmental degradation. However, there is no "technological imperative" at work. Rather, there is a set of economic and political imperatives that flow from the logic of the treadmill of production in capitalist societies. The central thrust of modern technology has been to displace human labor in goods production, and substitute physical capital and inanimate energy supplies. Such transformations of production have increased the volume of production and of profits and enhanced material welfare of some parts of the population. But they have also displaced less skilled labor and increased the capital required to create new employment.

Dynamics of technological change are subject to multiple interpretations. The source of change is often diffusely located in "the society" or in the scientific enterprise. A closer examination places a heavier responsibility on the state and the private sector, which have channeled scientific and technological research and development in these directions. This joint activity represents one dimension of political capitalism. In the case of socialist societies, the major role is played by the state, although bureaucratic influence from state industries also induces technological change.

One of the major consequences of this change in technology and labor requirements has been the increased social invisibility of modern production systems. The development of environmental concern in the recent period is a result of a small increase in research and a larger mobilization of social concern and social movements. While some of these movement organizations have the potential to modify production technology, so far the changes have been relatively small. Some increased attention has been paid to assessing some environmental and social consequences of new technologies, but little change in production has actually resulted. The reasons for this include the formidable coalitions around technological changes that promote higher production and profitability, as described in Chapter V.

Consumption Influences (Chapter IV).   One popular theme of environmental analysis in the 1960s was that rising worker-consumer affluence was the major cause of environmental withdrawals and additions. This theme was most intimately linked to a cultural explanation for environmental degradation, succinctly stated in the voice of Pogo: "We have seen the enemy and he is us." Cultural analyses ignore substantial historical and intersocietal variations in rates of withdrawals and additions, even among industrial societies. In another sense the consumer affluence thesis is tautological, since a large share of sociocultural production *is* distributed to consumers. Consumers' capacity to absorb this volume and type of production through market systems and their desire to do so is, I argue, to only a small extent a matter of free choice.

While I reject the extremes of both consumer sovereignty and perfectly determined consumption patterns, I propose a model of distorted consumption. In this, a good many features of consumer behavior and tastes are determined outside the individual by producers and the state. Contrary to recent models of the service society or postindustrialism, moreover, such distortion perpetuates past models of production and consumption that are energy- and material-intensive. Current production consists of a vast array of commodities as well as a slightly larger proportion of services. Influences on consumer preferences include advertising and social persuasion, the creation of need following earlier consumption, and the control of public-goods substitution for private consumer goods. Consumer behavior is influenced by external forces that: determine income levels, generate product features that consumers must accept, and create products to which consumers can only retrospectively respond.

Though consumers can have some influence over certain product features or production of particular brands of products, their role is far less influential than that of producers. Such impotence stems from the relatively low degree of consumer organization and the correspondingly low amount of efforts that the individual will exert in a highly organized production system.

Production Expansion Influences (Chapter V).   As noted above, the central mechanism for determining the volume and type of production is the treadmill of production. In capitalist societies, the treadmill is structured by the nature of competition between capital owners and the profitability and predictability of high-energy and capital-intense mass production. It is buttressed by the commitment of both organized labor and the state to generate employment and income through rising national production. During the post-1945 period especially, this led to a relatively stable growth coalition that promoted the expansion of production through energy-intense technology. The state has encouraged private capital expansion in this direction, through a variety of fiscal and legislative mechanisms that have created a system of political capitalism. Under this, the state allows the power of larger capital enterprises to expand, thereby shifting the forces and volume of production toward the large-scale or monopoly-capital stratum. Until recently, the net benefits of this system have been sufficient to quiet the dissent regarding this means of societal surplus mobilization and use.

The treadmill of production is a model that directs attention to the linkage of capital-intensive technology investment, profitability, and employment and income generation. It is a treadmill that has been accelerating at least since 1945, and probably for fifty years before that. The logic of the treadmill is that of an ever-growing need for capital investment in order to generate a given volume of social welfare—a trickle-down model of socioeconomic development. From the environment, it requires growing inputs of energy and material to create a given level of socioeconomic welfare. When resources are constrained, the treadmill searches for alternative sources rather than conserving and restructuring production. The treadmill operates in this way to maintain its profits and its social control over production.

In theory the state is responsible for reconciling disparities between this treadmill and the needs within the society. In practice it has often acted to accelerate the treadmill in the hope of avoiding political conflict. An extensive use of public tax funds to provide fiscal aid to the private sector, coupled with an underwriting of extensive credit systems, has permitted the state to avoid such conflict. But the recent emergence of problems of excess capacity, underinvestment, capital shortages, and resource limitations has forced the state's attention to social policy alternatives to this conventional growth response. Despite these severe perturbations, though, the growth coalition remains dominant. Only a diffusion of public consciousness of alternative production systems and of the pitfalls of the present one can undermine this coalition. Such consciousness must increase among organized labor especially, and lead to increased coordination of labor movements and the environmental movement. As well, equity movements seeking benefits for the poor and for unorganized workers need to be drawn into a coalition for restructuring production. With consciousness and coordination increased, the level of political conflict around production and surplus control must intensify for major production changes to occur. The relatively moderate conflicts to date, therefore, understate future social and political conflicts around socioenvironmental issues.

SOCIAL RESPONSES TO ENVIRONMENTAL CHANGE   Many dimensions of environmental and related social welfare problems are unknown to either the articulate and informed public or the larger mass of society. It is necessary to increase the attentive public for social policy changes in production control aimed at improved social welfare and diminished environmental exploitation. Additional educational and consciousness-raising efforts thus need to be made. Part 3 examines the social barriers that have historically operated to produce a very limited comprehension of the treadmill and its consequences, and alternatives to the treadmill. Though there has been recent growth in socioenvironmental consciousness, it has not yet been able to overcome many of these barriers.

Environmental Research Barriers (Chapter VI). With the social invisibility of many production systems in advanced industrial societies, ecological impacts of production are often poorly understood. There is a need for impact science findings, if consciousness of these is to be increased. But impact scientists have not had much social and material support in this century. Given lower funding and less prestige, their goals have been accorded lower political, social, and economic priority than production research. In addition, they have had more difficulties in publishing and disseminating to a wide public their important findings on environmental impacts. Finally, they have been subject to direct social and economic threats when their findings have threatened to call public attention to production impacts.

Impact research by engineers and other technologists has been even more constrained. The vast majority of such technical specialists have been intimately involved in the expansion of monopoly-capital production. Technologists have roles to play not only in assessing the most ecologically harmful elements of complex modern technologies, but in suggesting production reforms. Both these roles have been restricted, even for technologists employed outside the private sector in government and universities. Mechanisms of influence over these ostensibly independent professionals include controls over their access to data sources and to valued consultantships. In addition, engineering specialists are controlled by the ideology of feasibility that dismisses imprecise and uncertain findings as professionally irresponsible. Finally, the narrow technical training of many highly skilled engineers makes their careers vulnerable, if their research is threatening to a given industry.

New sources of career opportunities and rewards provide some relief from these mechanisms, but hardly enough to offset them. Expansion of environmental impact and production reform research must continue, to correct the imbalances.

Socioenvironmental Impact Assessment Barriers (Chapter VII). In recent years, one of the most hopeful gains in social intelligence has been increased attention to the social as well as the environmental effects of new projects and technologies. Past assessment efforts have urged the state to support production expansions, through direct provision of government infrastructure, facilities, or leasing arrangements. Socioenvironmental impact statements are now required for federal government projects affecting the environment under NEPA (National Environmental Policy Act).

Unfortunately, upon closer examination there is considerable distortion of NEPA and other impact evaluations. In theory, such assessments should support projects that have a utilitarian output—the greatest good for the greatest number of people. This is usually violated in practice. Such distortions replicate previous public administration attempts to make rational-scientific decisions using benefit-cost analysis. Modern impact assessment practices bear a striking resemblance to the past benefit-cost modeling and their systematic biases. Biases exist because of the prospective or predictive aspect of impact assessment and the frequent attempt to dismiss qualitative judgments in favor of quantitative ones. The lack of systematic quantitative research in social and environmental impacts thus lessens the importance of negative outcomes of projects. In addition, social impact assessment often ignores social distributional issues. This gap leaves undetermined the disparities between a social group's costs and benefits from projects, the social efficiency of such projects in generating income and employment, and the impacts on future generations.

On the other hand, given the formal mandate to perform a detailed accounting of all major socioenvironmental impacts of projects, this assessment mechanism is important for raising social consciousness. If carefully and systematically done, attacks on both projects and their impact statements can mobilize constituencies for production reform. This is especially true when alternative production suggestions are made along with the critique of proposed projects. Environmental movement organizations can then raise working-class consciousness of the social inefficiency of the growth coalition's expansion of production. This must be placed high on the agenda if environmental concern is to be broadened and made more politically potent. Only when workers and the poor understand *for whom* the environmental withdrawals and additions are being made, and *for whom* alternative patterns of environmental usage might be more effective, only then will the movement broaden.

The Environmental Movement's Influence (Chapter VIII).   The environmental movement, in both its organized and public opinion dimensions, is a product of past social intelligence *and* a contributor to current and future intelligence. It was initially hampered by the limited impact science and technology research of past decades. As it developed, it helped contribute to an improved support base for contemporary impact and ecological research.

Diversity within the movement has been considerable. Initially, it was interested in limited changes in consumer behavior and the diffusion of consumer education. Recently, it has moved toward active political challenges to existing production organization. The movement has never gone beyond the bounds of middle-class political actions. However, the reforms proposed in the 1970s pose a considerably greater challenge to existing patterns of social surplus allocation than at any point in the movement's history.

The roots of the modern movement lie partly in earlier twentieth century conservation-efficiency and conservation-preservation movements. Unlike either of these, though, the contemporary movement has a far broader ecological perspective and has become in recent years more socially sensitive to the socioeconomic impacts of environmental and resource policies. The efficiency movement was in fact tied to the rise of political capitalism, the growth of monopoly-capital aggrandizement, and the structure and acceleration of the production treadmill. In general, the preservationist movement came into little major conflict with monopoly capital except where land and water resources were in great demand by major enterprises. The early thrust of the modern movement echoed both these precedents. In fact, it has come to represent more of a social challenge movement, with concrete production reform goals rather than mere moral protest. Along with this increasing focus on production reform has come greater bureaucratization and centralization of the movement, but with increasing political activity.

The most extensive analysis of environmental problems and proposal for reform has come from the appropriate technology part of the modern movement. Although its roots lie in problems of economic development in capital-short Third World countries, many of its precepts of social development have come to be applied to advanced industrial societies in the 1970s. This phase of the movement was especially spurred by the energy problems of 1973–74 and the continuing rise in energy costs. It finds current expression in proposals for "soft" energy paths involving decentralized solar-powered production technologies. The latter involve higher human labor and decreased nuclear and fossil fuel energy and thus presumably promote social welfare expansion with more limited environmental extraction. Unfortunately, the state and monopoly capital are more concerned with technological rather than welfare reforms. The movement is thus subject to partial incorporation and disorganization. This is especially true insofar as there exists common interests between capital owners and the movement in developing cheaper alternative energy supplies. Beyond this overlap there exists so far little strong support for the rest of the appropriate technology program. With a broader worker constituency and political mobilization, the potential for production reform from this branch is greater than from any other environmental movement component. For its ideology proposes production reforms that specify for whom the biospheric systems are to be protected, and how this is to be done. This is, then, one clear agenda for the future allocation of social surplus in specific ways.

Surplus and Social Choice

Uncertainty about the social severity of resource problems arises from the inadequacy of present and past research into the relationships of sociocultural production and the biosphere. One consequence of this uncertainty is considerable dispute between experts of various sorts. Such dispute often discredits all scientific opinions on ecosystem problems. More ominously, it forces the public to confront blatantly contradictory positions on complex issues, resulting in apathy and retreat before such confusion.[1] While excesses of rhetoric have bedevilled both environmentalists and their opponents, retreat does not help build a socially reasonable approach to environmental policies.[2]

We don't know enough of the details. Perhaps many socioenvironmental policies need not be implemented now. Perhaps the environmental problem is not yet that severe, despite the recent revelations about fossil fuel shortages. Yet, following earlier debates, deferring social change until shortage is universally acknowledged is risky. Widespread recognition of the need for change will only come *after* we overshoot natural limits. At that point, it seems rather unlikely that societal responses will be reasoned enough to consider both social welfare considerations and ecological limits. It is *now*, before more extreme ecological crises arise, that we have the luxury of intense political debate over these issues. However contrived it was, the energy crisis of 1973–74 did increase the awareness of western industrial societies. First, it revealed socioeconomic vulnerability, providing some motivation for production change. Second, it showed how even small decreases in resource availability led to immobilization of policymakers under these so-called crisis conditions. It is only now in the U.S. that the government is taking serious steps to form a preliminary energy policy. Before the crisis, this was not deemed politically necessary. During the crisis, it was not feasible. After it, such a policy seemed both politically necessary and feasible.[3]

The intensity of debate over relatively modest energy proposals should forewarn us. Current legislation will have limited effects on energy demand. If future policies will have to aim at far more serious reductions, how much more intense will the debate be then? How long can we avoid confronting issues related to energy and other environmental resources? Far more holistic approaches to environmental policy need to be introduced to political debate and conflict, but without the conflict, there can be little social change.[4]

Although the particular features of this conflict will be unique to our historical period, the general outlines of this social problem have existed throughout human history. For what we will be debating is the allocation of scarcity: who gets what, and how? However, this issue is merely the obverse of the allocation of social *surplus*. Conflicts between growth tendencies and biospheric resource limitations force us to maintain dual perspectives regarding production and its distribution. Surplus and scarcity coexist in all systems, but in periods of high production expansion and economic growth the issue is predominantly one of allocating surplus. With resource threats, surplus can be generated and scarcity can nonetheless increase in some segments of society, through changing mechanisms of production organization and distribution of social rewards.

Given our uncertainties, what *do* we know? There are two basic certainties. First, we know that there is a systematic relationship between society's production system and the biosphere:

1. Production expansion in societies necessarily requires increased environmental withdrawals and additions.
2. These biospheric withdrawals and additions inevitably lead to ecological problems.

3. These ecological problems pose potential restrictions for further production expansion.

This qualitative statement can be termed the socioenvironmental dialectic. As a dialectical relationship, it states the continuing tension between a thesis (production expansion) and an antithesis (ecological limits). This tension can be reduced in various historical periods in quite different ways through syntheses of varying duration.[5]

The second thing we know is that these syntheses do not just happen. They are created by social decision-making of various types. And they have variable consequences for social groups, classes, and individuals within the affected society:

> The public control is inevitable. But its methods and purposes are wide open to choice. They may range from gentle to savage, to produce societies from very equal to very unequal . . . Conflicts about inflation, inequality and environmental management are the obvious elements of the new disorder but they mask a more important sea change in the capacities of democracy itself. *If they realize it, people have a new freedom to choose between diverse social systems and futures.* They can make their own histories, as Marx expected, though not exactly in the way or for the reasons that he had in mind. (Stretton, 1976:1; my italics)

For this choice to be made, key individuals and social groups must overcome the blinders of their social systems. They must be made aware of alternative structures of production and social organization— and these structures must respond to the social welfare demands of these constituencies. The choice situations that Stretton (1976) describes are not subject to free will but arise in hard political conflict. Decision making in the real world is a product of power, and power grows out of the current treadmill of production. The range of choice—or more accurately, the possible futures—covers a rather broad spectrum. For those with a comparative and historical breadth of vision, there is little startling within these possibilities. Two schemas demonstrate the range, those of Schnaiberg (1975) and of Stretton (1976) himself. The three syntheses to the socioenvironmental dialectic can be matched from the two perspectives, as in Table 9.1.

What is summarized in this table is a range of social welfare situations that vary from very regressive to very progressive.[6] Each of these is assumed to follow from a given change in social policy regarding the

Table 9.1   Syntheses of the Dialectic and Social Futures

Synthesis	*Core Features*	*Social Future*
Economic	Continued production expansion, with future labor vulnerability	*The Rich Rob the Poor:* future society likely to be authoritarian and unequal if environmental degradation increases quickly
Managed scarcity	Limited environmental protection: pollution control and recycling	*Business as Usual:* persistence or expansion of present inequalities, with reduced production expansion
Ecological	Appropriate technology and increased surplus share to labor	*Left Social Distribution:* increased equalities and decreased commodity consumption and production

treadmill of production, though the connections are by no means definitive. Technological changes can occur for purposes other than enhanced social welfare. Improvements in social welfare distribution can occur in any of the major categories of production stability or change. History and the complexities of modern industrial societies both indicate such degrees of variability in substructure and social structure.[7]

But the choices are not infinite either. There seems little way to achieve widespread domestic improvements in social welfare, let alone in equality of the Third World, by the economic synthesis—which would accelerate the present treadmill of production. This is true in the sense of *relative* inequality measures, and is likely to be true in the near future with respect to absolute welfare gains as well. Production expansion has a limited future and is not an especially effective mechanism for improving equality by itself.[8] While benefits can be generated for the vulnerable classes by this expansion, they are achieved only at the risk of future vulnerability of workers to economic depression because of excess capital commitments to high-energy technology. Moreover, the political efforts required to maintain and create expanded social welfare are considerable under this synthesis. Today the economic synthesis finds greatest public expression in the claims of major capitalist enterprises as to their concern with employment and income effects. But this concern is political window-dressing, to cover capital owners' needs for increased profits.[9]

The managed scarcity synthesis, which is represented by current policies in the U.S. and many other advanced capitalist societies, staves off the most serious environmental problems by altering some resource use in production. The normal politics of production reform under this synthesis rest on technical issues and do not concentrate on distributive or welfare issues. The environment is thus partly protected, but for whom is never clear. Costs of such protection are increasingly recognized as socially regressive. As political movements realize this, the synthesis becomes more unstable. Societies can have more social peace by increasing the speed of the treadmill through the economic synthesis while keeping distributional features constant. Alternatively, they must consider more serious restructuring of production to keep social peace without increasing environmental vulnerability. The latter forces a move toward an ecological synthesis and away from the politically simpler managed scarcity phase.

If the ecological synthesis could be achieved, it would be the most durable of the three. Production organization, once set around the biospheric capacities and flows, would require only small adjustments over time to maintain a sustained material production.[10] These adjustments might be necessitated by either social changes (e.g., population growth) or ecological changes (e.g., natural disasters or species declines). No eternal social peace is guaranteed by such a synthesis, though. Changes over time in the social and political structure could lead to increased pressures for production expansion. Capital accumulation could grow within certain groups, leading to constituencies favoring either managed scarcity or economic syntheses. Even slight inequalities that were permitted to grow over time could produce political shifts.[11]

Conversely, the ecological synthesis is the most difficult to anticipate because it represents a major departure from managed scarcity. But note that managed scarcity policies seem almost revolutionary from the vantage point of, say, 1950. A managed scarcity production system is barely a decade old in most western industrial societies. It represents considerable political and social intellectual change, even though it is not a fundamental restructuring of the treadmill of production. The treadmill now has at least one more regulatory mechanism —a political override, should monopoly capital and organized labor become sufficiently impatient with current economic growth accomplishments. Nonetheless, the transition from managed scarcity to ecological synthesis is likely to be a long and painful one, if it does take place.

This anticipated pain encourages the search for modifications of the three major syntheses. We seek to make them more socially and politically acceptable in order to avoid conflict. The most attractive modification is continued production expansion with improved welfare distribution. Such a system, represented by Sweden's current social democracy, is appealing.[12] But the expansionary period may be rather short, as ecological limits press on future expansion. The internal egalitarian distribution, though, is likely to permit production to shift toward appropriate technology, because it represents a social pooling of risks and benefits. Thus, if countries could shift to this egalitarian a system, this would likely facilitate production adjustments to biospheric resources. However, countries that currently lack such a political commitment to egalitarianism will struggle to achieve equal distributions. So long as the growth coalition persists, such political struggle is pacified by buying social peace through trickle-down social development. To press for redistribution within this system is to reinforce the growth coalition. This in turn reinforces the treadmill of production and sets off opposition between environmental and social welfare constituencies.[13] It achieves neither ecological protection nor social egalitarianism, partly because of this fragmentation of protest. Where the treadmill is under closer state supervision—as in state capitalist or socialist societies—the treadmill is theoretically more amenable to change. When the risks of production transformation are placed most heavily on owners and managers of monopoly capital, though, they will naturally resist with all of their considerable power.[14]

For the sake of intellectual honesty and completeness, the inverse of this system should be examined. Something like appropriate technology would be introduced, but with very unequal income distributions. This situation characterizes much of the capitalist Third World today and in the recent past. It is similar to the authoritarian response to ecological pressures (Stretton's conservative or Right environmentalism) and culminates in "the rich rob the poor" (as does the economic synthesis over the long-term). Given political inequalities and the lack of effective Left political parties in countries like the U.S., such a system is possible in currently advanced industrial societies as well. Increased consciousness of socially regressive outcomes of the managed scarcity synthesis and increased political opposition to it make this outcome less likely, though.[15]

Thus, there are choices, but only a limited number (albeit with numerous shadings and refinements). In the short-run, the range is larger. But with decreased biospheric reserves in the future, these options will be more limited, short of a lucky combination of production and technological reforms. Treadmill continuity and acceleration *could* continue with improvements in energy and material usage in every area of production, starting with agriculture. Miraculous energy discoveries of oil, natural gas, coal, and even a fusion reactor would not alone buy environmental peace. For the living ecosystems are still threatened by mineral extraction and waste dumping as well as by atmospheric heat increases through energy intensification of production. Some social groups and some societies would clearly benefit in the intermediate term by increased energy availability, of course. But the full range of industrial societies and working-class populations would not. Given the social and ecological uncertainties, no one can foretell the timing of the short, intermediate, and long term. Yet without a sense of the options open and a sense of urgency for political consideration of such options, it is unlikely that a peaceful transition to an ecological synthesis can ever occur.

In the following sections, some discussion of the possible paths toward ecological synthesis follows, along with illustrations of what this would mean for daily life. Similarities and differences in these paths between capitalist and socialist societies are noted, though much work remains to be done.

TOWARD SOCIOENVIRONMENTAL WELFARE REFORMS

Production Reorganization and Social Syntheses

The sociocultural production alternatives and the political problems associated with them can be understood in the context of Table 9.2.

Those forms of production contraction that best protect the biosphere are also the most disruptive of the treadmill of production.[16] In other words, the greater the rate of reduction of ecosystem withdrawals and additions, the more rearrangements of capital and labor in production are necessary. In one sense this is a corollary of the socioenvironmental dialectic noted earlier, since production expansion and ecosystem pressures are closely associated. We can link this to the discussion of the three major syntheses of the dialectic as follows. Economic

Table 9.2   Forms of Production Contraction

Forms of Production Contraction	Ecological Value	Transformation of Treadmill Labor-Capital Organization
Non-use of goods	Most eco-efficient	Greatest effects
Reuse of goods	Intermediate	Substantial effects
Recycling of goods	Lower level	Moderate effects
Disposal of goods	Least eco-efficient	Least effects

syntheses operate at the level of disposal. Managed scarcity syntheses, in contrast, increase the share of production that is recycled or reused. The essential difference between the two contractions is the greater production effort necessary to turn *recycled* materials into socially usable goods. To date, most managed scarcity policies have been organized around recycling, not reuse. Finally, the ecological syntheses involve far greater reuse and nonuse of goods. Both of these imply substantially reduced levels of production of many types of products.[17]

If we seek a social transition to an ecological synthesis, we must anticipate disruptions arising from treadmill disorganization, and we must deal with these as intrinsic components of environmental policy. Theory is far easier than practice, though. With detailed capital and labor input studies of production, we can estimate the results of shifting from disposal to recycling, reuse, and nonuse, for both capital and labor displacement.[18] If we had perfect socioeconomic control and unlimited time for the transition, we could move industry by industry and provide for gradual absorption of labor and partial compensation for capital displaced. But if our pace is to be greater, the simultaneous transformation of many industries leads to greater unpredictability and instability. There would also be insufficient social surplus to accomplish the transitions with social peace. Wartime destruction, of course, frequently produces just such results with coercive measures. Destruction of physical capital by bombing does work. But it is acceptable only under particular political conditions. Such repression does not seem socially acceptable for peace-time transitions, though the aim of disaccumulation of physical capital is logically similar. Essentially though, we seek a reconstruction, not a destruction of sociocultural production.

Despite the desires of some environmentalists, then, we cannot simultaneously transform the entire economy without wreaking social havoc. And this havoc is likely to be socially regressive, with large capital owners having considerable flexibility insofar as they possess liquid capital. Labor must sell its labor power under capitalist organization. If there are no buyers and the state cannot be the employer of last resort, then labor suffers. Conversely, we cannot move plant by plant either, since the time required for transition and the likelihood of reversal is too great. To alter the levels and usage of social surplus, we need other techniques and political coalitions. We require some clear targets to transform, some equally clear direction of transformation, and some sense of likely beneficiaries and benefits of the transformation.[19]

The following section illustrates one such approach to transformation and movement towards an ecological synthesis. It has considerable political weaknesses and uncertainties, but it attempts to build upon current realities of managed scarcity syntheses.

State Intervention: Taking and Giving of Surplus

We can restate the earlier thesis of Charles Lindblom (1977) on politics and markets as follows. Politics is an effective form of directional social control over production systems. But markets provide efficient allocative decisions once directions are set by the political system. In terms of social surplus, politics can dictate the *goals* of surplus allocation and mobilization, while markets may *allocate* surplus among competing users and consumers.

If our goal is merely social welfare gains, then the issue of level of surplus is, simply, the more the merrier. However, if we have to take into account the permissiveness of the biosphere, the geopolitical realities of international use of these resources, our task is more difficult.[20] We have to decide on maximal permissable surplus and its allocation and mobilization. In theory, as Westman and Gifford (1973) have argued, it is feasible to do this in terms of "natural resource units." In practice our criteria will have to be far more experimental and loose, given both ecological and geopolitical uncertainties. The recent conflicts over the international law of the sea illustrate this. Neither the total resources nor the politically most efficient allocation of these were clear. So societies set arbitrary working boundaries for exploitation of marine resources. When the ecological and social implications of these become clearer, there will be new conflicts and renegotiations.[21]

The task is a monumental technical and political one. We must first estimate a biospherically and geopolitically feasible, sustainable production level for the society. And then we must decide how to allocate the production options and the fruits of such production. Neither the state nor the market currently perform all these functions in any system—socialist or capitalist.[22] Therefore, the intervention of the state is necessary to moderate the workings of market systems, though to varying degrees. Such intervention typically involves the state taking away some share of the surplus, then reallocating it in some way within the sociocultural production system. Implicitly in most political systems, moreover, the state acts in concert with producers (either capitalist or socialist bureaucratic enterprises) to limit or increase the total production in the society and thus the total environmental demands. A more explicit ecological calculus is required to bring this into the range of environmental protection policies.

One simple state policy for ecological synthesis is outlined below. It takes account of the differences between physical (fixed) and liquid capital, and the political commitments of capitalists to each.[23] The proposed conversion policy would incorporate useful policies from the managed scarcity synthesis, but then move beyond that. It would consciously redirect social surplus towards more labor-intensive production and presumably away from higher levels of ecosystem withdrawals and additions. Consumer needs would be met in different ways: e.g., housing and transportation would gradually be altered to reduce the need to travel, and to reduce the material and energy requirements of travel. While the proposed system would generally respond to consumer desires for both stimulation and comfort, it would require persuading consumers that new products and services meet their wants.

Though all elements in this policy are amendable, it is important that any policy substituted be both taking and giving. A review of present policies indicates that the separation of taking and giving by capitalist states facilitates the segregation of economic growth and social welfare policies.[24] The major intent of the program is to maximize social welfare in economic growth, within the context of limited biospheric resources. The proposed policy is outlined below:

A Socio-Environmental Program
1. Rapid depreciation allowances for preexisting fixed capital that was highly material- and energy-intensive (to encourage conversion to liquid capital)

2. Employment tax credits, and absolute prohibition of employee "head taxes" on enterprises (a favorite of municipalities), to encourage labor intensity
3. Materials and energy taxes, to encourage conservation
4. Incentives (tax relief, credits) for material recycling
5. High effluent charges (to minimize pollution)
6. Labor training tax credits (to stimulate transfer of labor and employment of more labor)
7. Increased taxation of new fixed capital, to discourage greater capital intensity; this could be graduated to be progressively higher for higher capital-per-worker ratios

This program encourages the *disaccumulation* of physical capital that is committed today to high-energy, low-labor production. It permits the liquification of some of this capital and its allocation into alternative forms of production that are higher in labor and lower in capital. It is assumed that capital-intensification and environmental usage are at least partly correlated.[25] Additional policy measures are added to discourage production with heavier net ecosystem withdrawals and additions. Because of the political and environmental uncertainties, no quantitative measures are indicated for tax rates, incentive levels, and so forth. Social experimentation under various conditions is likely to be necessary.[26] But this experimentation must be carried out under a clear political commitment to both greater welfare equalization and environmental protection. This is vital if a socioenvironmental constituency is to be mobilized in support of this program of production conversion.

From the standpoint of political feasibility, this program has both considerable advantages and liabilities. Because most of the fiscal and legislative elements have some precedence, there is nothing startling about the proposal. It is a serious reformist, but not a revolutionary, suggestion. As such, it avoids the problems with many ecological utopian schemes, which present a set of fantasies as a program of reform. The response to such a program is predictable, as Barrington Moore has noted:

> Every "sensible" person knows they are fantasies, that he is too busy making a living, that the risk is too great. . . . Because of the stake he has in his society there is always substantial short-term rationality in being the good citizen. That short-term rationality leads to larger results that are totally absurd is obvious enough to require no elaboration. (Cited in Edel, 1973:150)

Conversely, the fact that the proposals of the above list are not fantasies leads to the risk that they will simply become incorporated into the politics of the treadmill and thereby dismissed or weakened.[27] That is indeed a political danger. But given the questionable depth of consciousness and commitment of the current environmental constituency, it is questionable whether any more extreme program is likely to succeed, short of a social revolution. And in most mature industrial societies, such revolutions hardly appear imminent.[28]

At a minimum, a serious and sustained effort at legislating such a reformist program would raise consciousness about the social and environmental costs of the treadmill, in ways that might further future social and environmental reform. The program is tangible enough to ground the debate in realistic and understandable terms. Yet it points to major concepts that call into question the benefits and irreversibility of the treadmill. It will formally end the period in which environmental degradation is seen as a technical issue, as one of a number of remediable negative externalities of industrial production, and as unrelated to social welfare issues:

> Pollution is a social and economic problem which takes on the appearance of a technical problem. . . . Capitalist society . . . was the first society to base its activities on the maxim that nothing is worth doing unless the economic benefits outweigh the costs of doing it . . . *as though the rational pursuit of private ends by separate individuals and enterprises will result in what is best for the whole society.* . . . Pollution is a particularly nasty result of such *social irrationality.* (Rothman, 1972:x; my italics)

If the program is debated long and hard enough, it should raise the consciousness of larger numbers of workers and consumers to the fact that

> the *private* economic rationality of the profit-seeking business enterprise is a *murderous providence* because it cannot guarantee the optimum use of resources [for] . . . society as a whole. It cannot avoid continually creating situations which cause the pollution of our environment. (Rothman, 1972:x)

While there is no guarantee about the political feasibility of such a program, debate might justify the presently ungrounded optimism of Rothman that more and more people are seeing current "social, economic and environmental restrictions to be *unnecessary* and avoidable" (1972:338).

This argument, of course, parallels the thesis that social impact assessment under NEPA leads to mobilization (Ch. VII). It has its share of social and political risk, to be sure.[29] But it presents a program that is both feasible and not socially regressive, a rare combination today.

From Reformism to Socialist Restructuring: Utopias, Dystopias, and Uncertainties

There was a period in the environmental movement history when a socialist alternative to the treadmill was highly regarded by radicals and many serious reformists. The theory of socialist development is an attractive alternative to the empirical reality of the treadmill and to theories of the capitalist growth coalition. A carefully constructed utopian view of a future communist society is most succinctly stated by Sherman:

> Under communism (even 80 per cent communism) an affluent, socially planned society may have less compulsion for growth, more concern for human and social costs, such as prevention of ecological destruction... [and] managers under communism are more likely to take measures to preserve the ecology as well as to produce output. (Sherman, 1972:355)

Sherman's views are far more tentative and cautious than those of many other socialist enthusiasts, in part because he appreciates the failings of contemporary socialist societies. Contrast the view above with the following:

> A socialist society, unlike a capitalist society, starts from social requirements based on the demands of the population. Members of such a society will claim as a legal and a political right a healthy environment... in which the individual can exercise choice. (Rothman, 1972:33)

What differentiates the two positions on socialist society is an awareness that the descendents of Karl Marx fall short of his ideals, as do the descendents of Adam Smith. Socialist politics have as many failings as capitalist markets, though they may offer more hope of altering the treadmill. The promise and the skepticism were present in the writings of Joseph Schumpeter three decades ago. He anticipated the future collapse of capitalism because its "success undermines the social institutions which protect it, and 'inevitably' creates conditions in which it will not be able to live and which strongly point to socialism as heir apparent" (Schumpeter, 1950:61). While his list of undermined institutions only partly overlaps with the treadmill model, there is considerable resonance between the two.[30] His evaluation of the risks of monopoly capitalism was strikingly similar to my own, though he was far more tentative about the future of this form of capitalism. But he was writing before the appearance of major environmental shortages and social movements.

In pointing to the heir apparent to capitalism—socialism—he noted that the central difference between advanced capitalism and socialism was that the latter had an "institutional pattern in which the control over means of production and over production itself is vested with a central authority . . . the economic affairs of society belong to the public and not to the private sphere" (Schumpeter, 1950:167). Stated in the concepts I have used earlier, the central differences was the state's control over surplus, both in production and in distribution: "Distribution thus becomes a distinct operation and . . . is completely severed from production. This [is a] political act or decision" (Schumpeter, 1950:173).

Beyond these key differences in structure, the processes of surplus mobilization and organization in socialist societies are indeterminate. Indeed, Schumpeter noted that socialist societies' central authorities would likely use some allocative processes akin to the rational models also used by capitalist ones, for efficiency of resource use.[31] Neither culture nor a variety of social politices could be predicted by the accession of socialist property control, though. And he noted some problems for the future socialist society, including bureaucratic management control, saving, and labor discipline.

The historical realities of the two major examples of socialist organization—the USSR and China—attest to the uncertainties that Schumpeter stressed. Utopian visions of a socialist society with perfect information, perfect responsiveness to citizen demand, and perfect control over production fly in the face of problems in internal and international social and material environments of these societies:

> It is sometimes hard to ascertain what can . . . be attributed to the communist or socialist nature of the Soviet government and what is merely due to the sociological heritage and material endowment inherited. (Goldman, 1972:218)

From a broad historical perspective, it is important to note that neither the USSR nor China moved into socialism from an advanced industrial capitalist stage. "Lessons" to be drawn from these specific histories may, therefore, be inappropriate models for future developments in the U.S. and other western societies. Neither the material productive base nor the political structure of democracy preceeded these two socialist revolutions. In like manner, though, any anticipated socioenvironmental gains from future socialist restructuring of present advanced capitalist societies must incorporate some unique elements of *present* structures. This is likely to influence especially the ways in which surplus will be mobilized and organized in these hypothetical future societies.[32]

In the Soviet Union, the political objective of increased industrialization required considerable worker-consumer sacrifice and the destruction of many ecosystems. This occurred despite the passage of many conservation laws in the Leninist period, for the major political goal was material growth. Political structures shunted aside this conservationist law whenever it threatened production expansion. Not only was environmental science kept underdeveloped, but the political structure permitted fewer social inputs:

> All too often there has been no person or group around with any power to stand up for the protection of the environment. Until the point is reached when environmental disruption causes other state interests, especially manufacturing and agriculture, to lose as much as those in favor of greater exploitation of the environment stand to gain, environmental quality in the USSR is in a very fragile condition. (Goldman, 1972:273)

Chinese history is somewhat different in this regard. Starting from an even more impoverished base in 1948, Maoist strategy involved careful husbanding of resources and intensive use of labor. Surplus was used for expanding social welfare and a smaller share was devoted to future industrialization. From some perspectives, this society thus came closer to an ecological synthesis than any other extant one. While ecosystem withdrawals and additions were often very heavy in local areas, the levels of withdrawal and addition per unit social welfare were far lower than in any recent society. On the other hand, many environmental problems existed, including air and water pollution, that threatened both workers and residents.

Recent changes in the post-Mao period, though, suggest a rather different state policy on surplus mobilization.[33] The rate of surplus creation is to be increased by using technology, and by using physical and even liquid capital from advanced capitalist societies. Some of this increased surplus will be used to enhance the material conditions of workers. Some will go toward building a greater physical production capacity in China. It is likely that both will involve increased biospheric withdrawals and additions per worker, and also increased social welfare, as modernization and capital-intensification proceed. While, as in the case of the USSR, neither of these rates of ecosystem impacts are likely to reach levels anywhere near that of the U.S., the Chinese direction is away from an ecological synthesis and toward a managed scarcity one. What distributional changes in social welfare will result is simply unclear at this point. Thus, "Socialism is no immediate and automatic panacea. Although it offers the institutional basis for coping with all problems, most political-social problems will persist, though in lessened degree" (Sherman, 1972:vii).

Socialist variability is likely to remain greater in ecological than in social welfare policies. Trends in socialist societies are toward increased democratization and worker pressures. The first pressures of workers are likely to be material: "In formal terms, the Soviet government can decide what it wishes. In realistic political terms, however, the Soviet politician must consider the increasing pressure of workers for more immediate gains in consumption" (Sherman, 1972:244). To these consumption pressures must be added the momentum of bureaucratic commitment to growth and production expansion in current socialist societies:

> Whereas in America the obstacle to... conservation has been profit-hungry corporations, in the Soviet Union it has been a bureaucracy led by a self-perpetuating leadership without much democratic control. Nevertheless, the lack of private enterprise *has* led to more conservation and less pollution. (Sherman, 1972:258)

In the analysis of socialist alternatives, then, the first realization is that equivalent levels of *industrialization* typically involve equivalent levels of ecosystem withdrawals and additions, as noted in Chapter I. However, the socialist societies have generally had lower levels of industrialization. They have achieved more equitable and higher welfare distributions within these levels than have capitalist societies. Goldman notes that worker comforts are achieved with lower levels of socialist industrialization because of state intervention in markets. In the USSR, this results in greater use of public goods, higher rates of recycling of materials, greater durability of goods, and more efficient centralized heating and power generation in cities.[34] And the power of the state offers considerable potential for future conservationist policies (Goldman, 1972:273).

Frequently socialist societies must confront the same choices in surplus generation and mobilization as capitalist societies. For the socialist societies of the near future, the choices are likely to be somewhat less politically risky, to the degree that social welfare has risen and been equitably dispersed (Moore, 1978) within their labor forces and citizenry. There is less sustained political opposition from owners of high-technology enterprise, though state bureaucrats fill some of the same oppositional roles. Labor will be less fearful of production changes, in terms of material welfare at least.

The greatest uncertainty arises from the degree of democratic participation that is likely to exist in the future in these societies, and the direction of policies arrived at by democratic choice, should democracy increase. Socialist workers are neither "demigods nor archangels," but subject to much the same tradeoffs of comforts and satisfactions as worker-consumers in capitalist societies.[35] The sudden transformations in China in 1977–78 indicate just how volatile this issue is. Balancing surplus generation and mobilization to create worker welfare and environmental protection remains as much a dialectic as in capitalist societies, and no synthesis is guaranteed to endure. On the other hand, no treadmill is forced on the societies by their sociocultural production structure, either, though they have often constructed their own modest versions of the capitalist treadmill.[36]

The potential for an ecological synthesis remains greater in socialist societies. In part this arises from their social and political structure. In part it is because they have not yet reached levels of physical capital that produce the enormous ecosystem withdrawals and additions of the U.S. and other capitalist societies. But the treadmill may be slowed or even reversed in some capitalist societies as well. Advanced social democratic industrial societies such as Sweden achieve far higher levels of social welfare for given volumes of biospheric withdrawals and additions. A higher share of surplus flows through the state, although most enterprise remains in private hands. More egalitarian total income structures exist than in countries like the U.S. Quality of life remains higher, at lower levels of energy consumption and total production.[37]

Interestingly, the Swedish example comes close to the "laborist capitalism" that Schumpeter posited as a stable intermediary between traditional capitalism and socialism. In such societies a de facto control of much of the surplus generation and mobilization exists in the state, although most of the means of production is in private hands. The state indirectly affects sociocultural production by its use of the surplus funneled through the heavy tax system, as well as by the legislative control of industry. Social welfare equalization is a prime concern of the state, though economic development policy remains high on the state's agenda as well. That this is no utopian society is indicated by the often painful experiences of European guest workers in their interaction with Swedish institutions. But Sweden is a capitalist society that remains at a high level of managed scarcity, moving towards an ecological synthesis through economic democracy as well as political and social democracy. Ironically, as this movement increases there are arguments that the Swedish Social Democratic Party is actually a core socialist party and Sweden a socialist state.[38] At minimum, we can assert that this party fulfills Stretton's call for a party of the Left—a party of egalitarianism.

Though state participation in the economy has increased in recent decades in all capitalist societies as in all socialist ones, the outcomes are quite variable. Mechanisms of pressure for production expansion vary between the capitalist treadmill and the socialist drive for industrialization in very underdeveloped countries. While dissatisfaction with the treadmill has increased, it is *not* yet true that:

> Contemporary society raises expectations. . . . When [they] are inhibited, men become uncomfortable and ready to raise their level of consciousness in order to seek out the means to smash the restrictions. This process has begun and the revolution and the environmental struggle will become one. (Rothman, 1972:338)

There are no simple mechanical predictions we can make. Neither the imminence of revolution, nor the increase of state planning herald the end of the treadmill:

> How can the environmental message be reflected in political action? We are marvellous planners here in Britain. We plan ourselves out of existence. . . . Both nationally and internationally the

pressures are too great for the kinds of solution at which we have so far excelled. (Johnson, 1973:227)

The treadmill of political capitalism was not built overnight, nor will it disappear in the short term. Sustained efforts at consciousness-raising, commitment to political conflict and the development of coordination between environmentalist and social equity movements may serve to take it apart, strut by strut. If predictions of biospheric disorganization are accurate, the joint movement *may* be spurred: "Equalitarian ideas and practices are likely to flourish in situations where supply is precarious and any given individual is liable to face an unpredictable shortage. Rationing systems in modern societies are one example" (Moore, 1978:37). If true, this would be the finest contribution of environmental limits to social welfare.

NOTES

1. Mazur (1973) notes that disputes among experts confuse both decision makers and the public, and Nelkin (1975) indicates that continued involvement of scientists in such confused debate undermines the perceived legitimacy and political effectiveness of scientists. On the other hand, prior beliefs also influence reception of scientific input (Barnes, 1972). Given the dominance of the treadmill model, rejection of environmental impact findings is certain, especially as environmental protection costs become clearer and greater.

2. Sills (1975) reviews excesses of both environmentalists and their scientific opponents, while Nelkin (1977) indicates the retreatist impulses among professional ecologists faced with the cross-pressures of practical involvement and scientific standards.

3. The "overshoot" model is described in Meadows et al. (1972): it specifies lack of societal response until major environmental problems have occurred. Energy policies have been in process of formulation in Europe and the U.S. since 1973, but have run afoul of a variety of obstacles. Increased environmental resistance to nuclear power (Lewis, 1978; NYT, 1978), criticism of lack of solar power development (e.g., Wicker, 1978), and questions about outer continental shelf oil drilling (e.g., Mohr, 1978b) have all intersected with an increased public attention to energy planning. The ambitious Carter administration programs have been severely cut back, predictable in part because of the opposition of the major industrial leaders (NYT, 1977) to many innovative social welfare provisions of the early proposals. The result of prolonged debate and limited action is a resurgence of energy consumption (though still with rates of growth lower than ever before) and increased dependency on OPEC oil imports in the U.S.

4. See Schnaiberg (1974) on dimensions of production change and resulting conflicts.

5. The dialectic and especially the detailed impacts of the social syntheses are outlined in Schnaiberg (1975), drawing upon the energy crisis of 1973–74 as an example.

6. Table 9.1 forces a fit between Stretton's (1976) and Schnaiberg's (1975) categories, since Stretton refers to social futures following *acceptance* of the need for major environmental reforms. The economic synthesis presumes an absence of such acceptance of the problem.

7. While limited in scope and quality of indicators, Mazur & Rosa's (1974) study does indicate the variability of social welfare indicators within similar levels of economic development among industrial counties.

8. Morrison (1976) indicates the dilemmas of global equity under the conditions of scarcity, but comes to a similar conclusion: this requires greater attention to equity dimensions, not an abandonment of them (cf. Moss, 1977). On the future of monopoly capital expansion, I share the pessimism of Heilbroner (1978).

9. For example, in interviews with eight major industrial leaders (NYT, 1977), not one mentioned profitability as a concern in their review of the early Carter energy proposals. They instead referred to national survival, employment, consumer costs, and other social interests.

10. Morrison (1973) comes to the conclusion that only in an equitable society are relative deprivation pressures suppressed to the point where environmental conflicts are minimized.

11. Negative evaluations of a steady-state economy (e.g., Olson & Landsberg, 1973) often make the point that societies, like ecosystems, cannot remain easily in a static state. Romantic ecological utopias ignore this reality; but opponents exaggerate the degree of fluctuation necessary to maintain an approximate steady-state as well.

12. See Lieber (1978) for a description of the Social Democratic Party policies in Sweden.

13. Okun (1975), for example, separates the issues of economic efficiency from those of distributive equality as if they derive from separable institutions rather than flowing from a single productive system of political capitalism. On the other hand, some neo-Marxists (e.g., Sweezy, 1973) go to the opposite extreme and ignore variations in welfare structures within capitalist systems.

14. Stretton (1976: Ch. 2) makes the point of the power of business, and the role of the state in allowing transfer of risks and pains from business to workers and consumers: this he terms "business as usual."

15. In his analysis of the Right scenario, Stretton (1976: Ch. 1) indicates that he thinks this the least likely future. He may be overly optimistic with regard to the U.S., where recognition of distributive inequality in environmental reforms (e.g., England & Bluestone, 1973; Schnaiberg, 1975) finds little sustained political base, as recent critiques of U.S. liberalism (e.g., Bute, 1978) make clear. Piven & Cloward (1977) indicate that in the U.S. context, the major power of the poor is through their threatening of peace in the streets. Turbulence, and neither organization nor electoral dissent, works in the interests of the poor, because it is only "when unrest among the lower classes breaks out of the confines of electoral procedures that the poor may have some influence" (p.15), while electoral dissent merely produces symbolic political responses (pp.16–18).

16. To some extent, there are important exceptions to this generalization. For example, energy conservation efforts by industry may cut their costs of production and facilitate improved profits and market share. Within a narrow band, these cuts in the use of energy may occur without reorganization of capital and labor. But in most cases, lower energy usage is associated with higher labor substitution, as in conservation of buildings versus new construction (Hannon et al., 1978). Ironically, one of the recent arguments that "supports the view of the so-called technological optimists over that of the doomsayers" (Kakela, 1978:1157) is the case of iron ore pelletization. This technological change reduced the total energy per ton of molten iron. But it "conserved labor" as well as energy, demonstrating that the major effects of the treadmill continue, even in this "exception."

17. On the changing mix of products, see Spilhaus (1972) for a consumption model of "ecolibrium." Bezdek & Hannon (1974) trace the effects of nonuse of energy for highway construction and the alternatives of railroads and mass transit, finding higher employment, especially for lower-skilled workers, in the latter. With regard to future use of leisure, see de Grazia (1964).

18. Examples of such analyses include Bezdek & Hannon (1974), Hannon (1975), Hannon et al. (1978), and Kakela (1978). On a global basis, work similar to this has been done by Leontief et al. (1977). While this latter work supports the possibilities of extending the economic synthesis into the future, the models are especially weak on environmental dimensions: "Since statistics on pollution and abatement are very scarce, estimates of coefficients in this field are necessarily rough and assumptions about abatement levels are somewhat arbitrary" (p.49).

19. Two major uncertainties exist in all appropriate technology proposals, ranging from Schumacher (1973) to Lovins (1977). The first is whether these are models of capital disaccumulation or capital redistribution. That is, will it be necessary to destroy much of the present physical capital in order to prevent high levels of productivity and environmental extraction in the future? Or will this capital be allowed to depreciate and liquid capital applied to new enterprises in different ways? Second, and related, is appropriate technology to be spread initially throughout countries and industrial sectors, or concentrated in local communities? The first approach would permit diffusion but also co-optation by established capital owners, absorbing just a small amount of appropriate technology. For example, one of the recent ironies is the planned use of solar power generating steam for improved oil recovery (Sheils et al., 1978). By concentrating efforts in a small number of localized communities, a more powerful demonstration effect of alternative sustenance and sociocultural production systems could be presented. But the degree to which this would diffuse to movements, organized labor, and political leaders is unclear. If the move to an ecological synthesis is to begin, these and other questions need clarification.

20. This is the reality that confronts socialist societies like the U.S.S.R. and China, which have had relatively low surplus and low welfare levels until fairly recently. Though their production paths have differed, both have been forced to emphasize expanded production in order to raise welfare levels, and this has led to a disregard of many environmental costs (e.g., Enloe, 1975: Ch. 6; Goldman, 1972; Anderson, 1976: Ch. 11).

21. For example, Mohr (1978a) argues that the unilateral action of coastal nations in setting 200-mile national fishing limits "will probably permit a recovery of fish populations hammered hard by overfishing." This "national selfishness" exemplifies the model of Hardin (1968). But Mohr also notes the variety of negotiations between and among these coastal nations on future rearrangements, so that selfishness and coercion do not seem likely to be the only forms of ecological control.

22. Enloe (1975:318-20) rather forcefully notes the similarities between socialist and capitalist societies in the bureaucratization and politicization of environmental protection. In socialist societies, bureaucrats act like capital owners (Gordon, 1976), and in capitalist societies, the state is increasingly drawn into technostructural planning. She notes the unusually broad planning role given the Environmental Protection Agency in the U.S., which is dissonant with the low level of political development (planning) in the U.S. Given our earlier discussions of U.S. political capitalism, she perhaps underestimates the subtler state-capital joint planning in the U.S.

23. This distinction between physical capital as commitment and the flexibility of liquid capital is stressed in Harvey (1975).

24. For example, an early Carter administration proposal on energy taxes in the U.S. included a plan to recycle these taxes to low-income consumers. This taking-and-giving model was abandoned in later legislation, leaving the welfare implications of energy policies out of the formal decisions and turning this political issue into a more technical one once more (Friedland et al., 1977).

25. On capital and energy relationships, see Commoner (1977).

26. For methods of social experimentation, see Campbell (1975) for a discussion of existing and proposed methods, as well as their political and social biases.

27. Enloe (1975: Ch. 3) notes the variety of mechanisms by which environmental issues are absorbed and dismissed by state agencies, even after environmental problems have become major public issues.

28. This assessment is diametrically opposed to those of Anderson (1976) and Rothman (1972).

29. Cooptation of the environmental movement by the paperwork of NEPA (Fairfax, 1978a,b; cf. Culhane, 1978; Liroff, 1978) has proceeded by displacing major issues with minor ones. The same can be predicted for the protected debates and studies that will be occasioned by the program suggested, although they will occur in the somewhat more open legislative arena. Legislative and executive branch studies do not necessarily preclude other social actions—including turbulence by threatened poverty groups—and frustrated legislation may in fact *induce* such turbulence (Piven & Cloward, 1977).

30. Among other factors, Schumpeter (1950) identifies price rigidity, the routinization of technological innovation, increased scale of enterprise, and increased social and political power of large-scale capital owners as factors leading to future declines of capitalism. What maintains this system, though, is increased state attention to worker security, equality of income, and regulation of industry, which he terms "laborist capitalism," a term perhaps overlapping substantively with "political capitalism" (Kolko, 1963:417-19).

31. Schumpeter (1950:182–84) notes that allocative mechanisms are similar despite disparate social goals of capitalist and socialist systems, because they both stem from rational decision-making models. McFarlane (1977:205) makes the same point more forcefully: "profit as a measure of enterprise performance and profit as a motor which drives the total economy" are quite different for him. On the other hand, Goldman (1972:268) notes that social and other costs in the USSR are misrepresented, indicating problems in assessing allocative rationality in socialist just as in capitalist societies (see Ch. VII).

32. Anderson (1976: Ch. 11) makes similar points most strongly and cogently.

33. See Anderson (1976:242–51) and Orleans & Suttmeier (1970) on the Chinese productive strategy and the role of national poverty, and Butterfield (1978) on recent changes in Chinese modernization strategies.

34. See Goldman (1972:275–83) on these Soviet advantages over U.S. productive systems.

35. This phrase was used by Schumpeter (1950:202–5) to deal with anti-socialist critics who argue that new socialist systems called for a "new socialist man," with unrealistic expectations of dramatic cultural and personality change. Schumpeter argued that institutional change would produce results without this personality and cultural transformation, an argument akin to Leo Marx's (1970) refutation of White's (1967) naive cultural explanation of the environmental problem in the U.S.

36. Goldman (1972) makes the strongest case for an almost blind bureaucratic impulse toward massive industrialization projects, regardless of their net contribution to either Soviet economic growth or social welfare. This is the closest approximation to the capitalist treadmill in which initial goals are displaced, although the capitalist model maintains an ongoing concern with profitability.

37. See Lieber (1978) and Enloe (1975:77–79) on Swedish social and environmental policy, and Schipper & Lichtenberg (1976) on energy use in Sweden.

38. This argument is presented in Lieber (1978).

REFERENCES

ANDERSON, CHARLES H.
1976　The Sociology of Survival: Social Problems of Growth. Homewood, Ill.: Dorsey Press.

BARNES, S.B.
1972　"On the reception of scientific beliefs." Pp. 269–291 in B. Barnes (ed.), Sociology of Science. Harmondsworth, England: Penguin Books.

BEZDEK, ROGER AND B.R. HANNON
1974　"Energy, manpower, and the Highway Trust Fund." Science 185 (23 Aug.):669–675.

BUTE, MONTE
1978　"Liberals must choose: Serve the corporations or serve the people." In These Times, 1 Nov.:17.

BUTTERFIELD, FOX
1978   "Settling a score with Mao." New York Times Magazine, 10 Dec.:42ff.

CAMPBELL, DONALD T.
1975   "Assessing the impact of planned social change." Pp. 3–45 in G.M. Lyons (ed.) Social Research and Public Policies. Hanover, N.H.: University Press of New England.

COMMONER, BARRY
1977   The Poverty of Power: Energy and the Economic Crisis. New York: Bantam Books.

CULHANE, PAUL J.
1978   "The effectiveness of NEPA." Science 202 (8 Dec.):1034ff.

DE GRAZIA, SEBASTIAN
1964   Of Time, Work, and Leisure. Garden City, N.Y.: Anchor Books.

EDEL, MATTHEW
1973   Economies and the Environment. Englewood Cliffs, N.J.: Prentice Hall.

ENGLAND, RICHARD AND B. BLUESTONE
1973   "Ecology and social conflict." Pp. 190–214 in H.E. Daly (ed.), Toward a Steady-State Economy. San Francisco: W. H. Freeman.

ENLOE, CYNTHIA H.
1975   The Politics of Pollution in a Comparative Perspective: Ecology and Power in Four Nations. New York: David McKay.

FAIRFAX, SALLY K.
1978a   "A disaster in the environmental movement." Science 199 (17 Feb.):743–748.
1978b   "The effectiveness of NEPA." Science 202 (8 Dec.):1038ff.

FRIEDLAND, ROGER, F.F. PIVEN, AND R.R. ALFORD
1977   "Political conflict, urban structure, and the fiscal crisis." International Journal of Urban and Regional Research 1 (3):447–471.

GOLDMAN, MARSHALL I.
1972   The Spoils of Progress: Environmental Pollution in the Soviet Union. Cambridge, Mass.: M.I.T. Press.

GORDON, DAVID M.
1976   "Capitalist efficiency and socialist efficiency." Monthly Review 28 (3):19–39.

HANNON, BRUCE
1975   "Energy conservation and the consumer." Science 189 (11 July):95–102.

HANNON, BRUCE, R.G. STEIN, B.Z. SEGAL, AND D. SERBER
1978   "Energy and labor in the construction sector." Science 202 (24 Nov):837–847.

HARDIN, GARRETT
1968   "The tragedy of the commons." Science 162 (13 Dec.):1243–1248.

HARVEY, DAVID
1975 "The geography of capitalist accumulation: A reconstruction of the Marx-ian theory." Antipode 1(2):9–21.

HEILBRONER, ROBERT L.
1978 "Boom and crash." New Yorker, 28 Aug.:52–73.

JOHNSON, STANLEY P.
1973 The Politics of Environment: The British Experience. London: Tom Stacey.

KAKELA, PETER J.
1978 "Iron ore: Energy, labor, and capital changes with technology." Science 202 (15 Dec.):1151–1157.

KOLKO, GABRIEL
1963 The Triumph of Conservatism: A Reinterpretation of American History, 1900–1916. New York: Free Press.

LEONTIEF, WASSILY ET AL.
1977 The Future of the World Economy: A United Nations Study. New York: Oxford University Press.

LEWIS, PAUL
1978 "All over Europe, the atoms are restless." New York Times, 3 Dec.

LIEBER, NANCY
1978 "Social Democrats break away from the logic of capitalism." In These Times, 25 Oct.:7ff.

LINDBLOM, CHARLES F.
1977 Politics and Markets: The World's Political-Economic Systems. New York: Basic Books.

LIROFF, RICHARD A.
1978 "The effectiveness of NEPA." Science 202 (8 Dec.):1036ff.

LOVINS, AMORY
1977 Soft Energy Paths. Cambridge, Mass.: Ballinger.

MARX, LEO
1970 "American institutions and ecological ideals." Science 170 (27 Nov.):945–952.

MAZUR, ALLAN
1973 "Disputes between experts." Minerva 11 (Apr.):243–262.

MAZUR, ALLAN AND E. ROSA
1974 "Energy and life-style." Science 186 (15 Nov.):607–610.

MCFARLANE, BRUCE
1977 "The political economy of the new right." Pp. 184–207 in A. Lindbeck (ed.), The Political Economy of the New Left: An Outsider's View. Second edition. New York: Harper and Row.

MEADOWS, DONNELLA H., D.L. MEADOWS, J. RANDERS, AND W.W. BEHRENS, III
1972 The Limits to Growth. New York: Universe Books.

MOHR, CHARLES
1978a "There are, fortunately, other fish in the sea." New York Times, 18 June.
1978b "U.S. oil-lease policy leaves questions." New York Times, 26 Nov.

MOORE, BARRINGTON, JR.
1978 Injustice: The Social Bases of Obedience and Revolt. White Plains, N.Y.: M. E. Sharpe.

MORRISON, DENTON E.
1973 "The environmental movement: Conflict dynamics." Journal of Voluntary Action Research 2 (2):74–85.
1976 "Growth, environment, equity and scarcity." Social Science Quarterly 57 (2):292–306.

MOSS, ROBERT
1977 "Let's look out for no. 1!" New York Times Magazine, 1 May:31 ff.

NELKIN, DOROTHY
1975 "The political impact of technical expertise." Social Studies of Science 5 (1):35–54.
1977 "Scientists and professional responsibility: The experience of American ecologists." Social Studies of Science 7 (1):75–95.

NEW YORK TIMES (NYT)
1977 "Industry's views on the critical choices." New York Times, 10 April.
1978 "Debacle at Seabrook." Editorial, New York Times, 9 July.

OKUN, ARTHUR
1975 Equality and Efficiency: The Big Tradeoff. Washington, D.C.: The Brookings Institution.

OLSON, MANCUR AND H.H. LANDSBERG (EDS.)
1973 The No-Growth Society. New York: W.W. Norton.

ORLEANS, LEO A. AND R.P. SUTTMEIER
1970 "The Mao ethic and environmental quality." Science 170 (11 Dec.):1173–1176.

PIVEN, FRANCES FOX AND R.A. CLOWARD
1977 Poor People's Movements: Why They Succeed, How They Fail. New York: Pantheon.

ROTHMAN, HARRY
1972 Murderous Providence: A Study of Pollution in Industrial Societies. London: Rupert Hart-Davis.

SCHIPPER, LEE AND A.J. LICHTENBERG
1976 "Efficient energy use and well-being: The Swedish example." Science 194 (3 Dec.):1001–1013.

SCHNAIBERG, ALLAN
1974 "Social conflicts in environmental decisions." Pp. 49–75 in J.E. Quon (ed.), Environmental Impact Assessment. Evanston, Ill.: Technological Institute, Northwestern University.

1975   "Social syntheses of the societal-environmental dialectic: The role of distributional impacts." Social Science Quarterly 56 (June):5–20.

SCHUMACHER, E.F.
1973   Small Is Beautiful: Economics as if People Mattered. New York: Harper and Row.

SCHUMPETER, JOSEPH A.
1950   Capitalism, Socialism, and Democracy. Third Edition. New York: Harper and Brothers.

SHEILS, MERRILL, W.J. COOK, R. HENKOFF, J.C. JONES, AND J. HUCK
1978   "Can sun power pay?" Newsweek, 18 Dec.:66ff.

SHERMAN, HOWARD
1972   Radical Political Economy: Capitalism and Socialism from a Marxist-Humanist Perspective. New York: Basic Books.

SILLS, DAVID L.
1975   "The environmental movement and its critics." Human Ecology 3 (1):1–41.

SPILHAUS, ATHELSTAN
1972   "Ecolibrium." Science 175 (18 Feb.):711–715.

STRETTON, HUGH
1976   Capitalism, Socialism and the Environment. Cambridge: Cambridge University Press.

SWEEZY, PAUL M.
1973   "Utopian reformism." Monthly Review 25 (6):1–11.

WESTMAN, WALTER E. AND R.M. GIFFORD
1973   "Environmental impact: Controlling the overall level." Science 181 (31 Aug.):819–825.

WHITE, LYNN, JR.
1967   "The historical roots of our ecologic crisis." Science 155 (10 Mar.):1203–1207.

WICKER, TOM
1978   "The future is now." New York Times, 30 Apr.
       mmmm448

AUTHOR INDEX

SUBJECT INDEX